PHILIP II *of* MACEDONIA

OTHER BOOKS BY RICHARD A. GABRIEL
- *Thutmose III: The Military Biography of Egypt's Greatest Warrior King*
- *Scipio Africanus: Rome's Greatest General*
- *The Battle Atlas of Ancient Military History*
- *The Warrior's Way: A Treatise on Military Ethics*
- *Muhammad: Islam's First Great General*
- *Soldiers' Lives Through History*
- *Jesus the Egyptian: The Origins of Christianity and the Psychology of Christ*
- *Empires at War: A Chronological Encyclopedia*
- *Subotai the Valiant: Genghis Khan's Greatest General*
- *The Military History of Ancient Israel*
- *The Great Armies of Antiquity*
- *Sebastian's Cross*
- *Gods of Our Fathers: The Memory of Egypt in Judaism and Christianity*
- *Warrior Pharaoh: A Chronicle of the Life and Deeds of Thutmose III, Great Lion of Egypt, Told in His Own Words to Thaneni the Scribe*
- *Great Captains of Antiquity*
- *The Culture of War: Invention and Early Development*
- *The Painful Field: Psychiatric Dimensions of Modern War*
- *No More Heroes: Madness and Psychiatry in War*
- *Military Incompetence: Why the U.S. Military Doesn't Win*
- *To Serve with Honor: A Treatise on Military Ethics and the Way of the Soldier (1982)*

WITH DONALD BOOSE JR.
- *Great Battles of Antiquity: A Strategic and Tactical Guide to Great Battles That Shaped the Development of War*

WITH KAREN S. METZ
- *A Short History of War: The Evolution of Warfare and Weapons*
- *History of Military Medicine, Vol. 1: From Ancient Times to the Middle Ages*
- *History of Military Medicine, Vol. 2: From the Renaissance Through Modern Times*
- *From Sumer to Rome: The Military Capabilities of Ancient Armies*

Philip II *of* Macedonia

Greater than Alexander

RICHARD A. GABRIEL

Potomac Books, Inc.
Washington, D.C.

Copyright © 2010 Potomac Books, Inc.

Published in the United States by Potomac Books, Inc. All rights reserved. No part of this book may be reproduced in any manner whatsoever without written permission from the publisher, except in the case of brief quotations embodied in critical articles and reviews.

Library of Congress Cataloging-in-Publication Data
Gabriel, Richard A.
 Philip II of Macedonia : greater than Alexander / Richard A. Gabriel.
   p. cm.
 Includes bibliographical references and index.
 ISBN 978-1-59797-519-3 (hardcover : acid-free paper)
 1. Philip II, King of Macedonia, 382-336 B.C. 2. Philip II, King of Macedonia, 382-336 B.C.—Military leadership. 3. Greece—History—Macedonian Expansion, 359-323 B.C. 4. Macedonia—History—To 168 B.C. 5. Macedonia—History, Military. 6. Greece—Kings and rulers—Biography. 7. Macedonia—Kings and rulers—Biography. I. Title.
 DF233.8.P59G33 2010
 938'.07092—dc22
 [B]
                                                    2010021519

Printed in the United States of America on acid-free paper that meets the American National Standards Institute Z39-48 Standard.

Potomac Books, Inc.
22841 Quicksilver Drive
Dulles, Virginia 20166

First Edition

10 9 8 7 6 5 4 3 2

In Memoriam

Esther D. Gabriel (1921–2010), my mother, who
died at the age of 88, keeping her promise
to outlive all her enemies

and

Anna Manning Dunn (1912–2001),
a beautiful woman who brought love, strength,
and integrity to her sons

◆

For Suzi, as always

Contents

List of Illustrations ix
Chronology xi

1. Philippos Makedonios 1
   Philip's Homeric World 5
   Wounds and Injuries. 10
   Women, Wives, and Politics 14
   Personality. 18
   A Hostage in Thebes 23
   Philip Himself. 28

2. The Strategic Environment 33
   The Land and Its People 33
   External Threats 39
   The Macedonian State 44
   Philip's Strategy. 54

3. The Macedonian War Machine 61
   The Macedonian Phalanx 62
   Cavalry. 72
   Manpower, Training, and Logistics 82
   Siegecraft. 88
   Philip's Intelligence Service 92
   The Macedonian Navy 94

4. The Unification of Macedonia 97
   The Battle at Livahdi Ridge 100

The Illyrian War 105
  The Siege of Amphipolis 110
  Expansion to the East 112

5. Thessaly and the Sacred War 117
  Thessaly 117
  The Siege of Methone 121
  The Sacred War 125
  Ambush and Defeat 127
  The Battle of the Crocus Field 132
  The Submission of Thessaly 138

6. The Road to Empire 143
  Thrace 143
  Epirus 146
  The War with Olynthos 148
  The End of the Sacred War 157

7. Warrior Diplomat 167
  The Amphictyonic Peace 168
  Athens 171
  Illyria Again 176
  Trouble in Thessaly 178
  Epirus 179
  The Thracian Campaign 181

8. The War with Athens 189
  The Chersonese 189
  The Siege of Perinthus 190
  Byzantium 194
  The Scythian Campaign 199
  The Prelude to War 204
  The Battle of Chaeronea 214

9. The End of Philip 223
  The Aftermath of Victory 223
  Who Killed Philip? 234
  Greater Than Alexander? 243

Notes 253
Selected Bibliography 283
Index 291
About the Author 303

Illustrations

FIGURES

1. Wax Bust of Philip Reconstructed from His Skull Found at Vergina — 31
2. Two Macedonian Infantry Phalanx Formations — 68
3. Philip's Attack on Bardylis's Illyrian Infantry — 107
4. Onomarchus's Ambush of Philip — 129
5. The Battle of the Crocus Field — 137
6. Parmenio's Capture of Amphissa — 213
7. The Battle of Chaeronea — 217

MAPS

1. Philip's Greece — 35
2. Logistical Range of Philip's Army — 89
3. Macedonia and Its Occupied Territories (359 BCE) — 99
4. Thessaly — 119
5. Chalcidice — 150
6. Macedonia and Its Conquests (348 BCE) — 156
7. Thermopylae — 165
8. Philip's Zone of Operations in Thrace — 184
9. The Macedonian Empire at the Time of Philip's Death (336 BCE) — 235

Chronology
Philip II of Macedonia

383/382: Philip born the youngest of three sons of Amyntas III, king of Macedonia.

368–365: Sent as a hostage to Thebes. In Thebes Philip becomes acquainted with the tactics of Epaminondas, the great Theban general.

365: Returns to Macedonia at the command of his brother Perdiccas III, who had regained the throne.

364–359: Philip is appointed a provincial governor, raises a militia force, and experiments with new weapons and tactics.

359: Perdiccas III is killed in battle against the Illyrians in Upper Macedonia. His infant son, Amyntas IV, becomes king and Philip appointed his guardian.

358–359: Philip reorganizes and trains the Macedonian army. Invents the Macedonian phalanx, equips it with new weapons, and develops new tactical doctrines for its employment.

358: Philip invades Paeonia; defeats Lyppeios. In summer, Philip attacks Illyria; defeats the Illyrian king, Bardylis; and recovers all the territory in Upper Macedonia previously taken by the Illryians. Marries Audata, Bardylis's daughter. Begins to create the new Macedonian national state. In the fall, Philip intervenes by request in Thessaly. Marries Phila of Larissa.

357: Amyntas IV is deposed by the Macedonian Assembly, and Philip is elected king. Philip attacks Amphipolis, a strategic pro-Athenian city controlling the mouth of the Strymon River, access to the sea, and the road to Thrace, which he captures by winter. Marries Olympias.

356: In the winter, Philip seizes Pydna and concludes an alliance with the Chalcidian League. Besieges the city of Crenides northeast of Mount Pangaeus in Thrace, capturing its important silver and gold mines. The wealth of the mines permits Philip to sustain his army, hire mercenaries, and bribe politicians for the next decade. Renames the city Philippi. Thracians, Illyrians, and Paeonians form a coalition against Philip, and Athens joins against Macedonia. Philip's general, Parmenio, defeats the Illyrians, and Philip captures Potidea. Apollonia, Galepsos and Oisyme also fall to Macedonian armies. Alexander is born in July.

356–355: The Phokians seize Delphi, and the Third Sacred War begins, providing Philip with opportunities for further expansion.

355: Philip lays siege to the city of Methone.

354: Captures Methone. Philip is struck by an arrow and blinded in his right eye. Captures Pagasae (?). Philip advances into Thrace, capturing Abdera, Maronea, and Neapolis.

353: That summer, Philip advances into Thessaly, gaining victories over Phayllos and the Pheraian-Phokian allies. In the fall, Philip is defeated by the Phokian general, Onomarchus, and retreats to Macedonia.

352: In the spring, Philip returns to Thessaly and defeats the Phokians under Onomarchus at the battle of the Crocus Field and captures Pherae; elected *archon* for life. Marries Nicesipolis. Threatens to move into southern Greece but does not force the pass at Thermopylae when he is opposed.

351: Philip campaigns in Thrace and falls ill. Warns Chalcidians not to break their alliance with him under penalty of war, but they move closer to Athens in defiance.

350: Philip campaigns in Epirus. Removes Arybbas as king and makes him regent for his son, Alexandros the Molossian, who is taken as a young man to Pella as a hostage.

349: Philip invades Chalcidice and destroys Stageira. Athens sends reinforcements to Olynthus. Philip intervenes again in Thessaly and suppresses a revolt in Pherae.

348: Athenians reinforce Olynthos. Philip brings the city under siege and captures it.

347: Philip takes Halus, the last city in Thessaly allied with Athens, under siege. Macedonian navy raids Athenian shipping. Philip sends peace offer to Athens, but it does not respond and attempts to form a coalition against Philip. The Sacred War continues; Philip signs an alliance with Thebes.

346: Athens undertakes diplomatic overtures to Macedonia. Philip campaigns in Thrace; defeats the Thracian king, Cersobleptes; and seizes the pass at Thermopylae. In July, the Phokians surrender to Philip, and Athens votes for peace with Philip; Philip awarded seats on the Amphictyonic League and settles affairs in Phokis.

345: In the spring, Philip defeats Pleuratos, king of the Illyrians, in a pitched battle and suffers a broken collar bone and a fractured shin.

344: Philip reenters Thessaly, puts down a revolt in some of the major cities, restructures the government, and places garrisons at key sites.

343: Philip finances and supports pro-Macedonian parties in the states of central and southern Greece in order to destabilize their governments.

342: In early spring, Philip marches on Epirus and removes Arybbas and installs Alexandros on the Molossian throne; Aristotle arrives in Macedonia to become Alexander's tutor. In July, Philip begins campaigning in Thrace.

341: Philip supports Cardia against Athens. In the spring, Athens conducts raids in the Gulf of Pagasae and against the Aegean coast of Thrace; in the summer, Philip defeats and deposes the Thracian kings Teres and Cersobleptes. Philip makes an alliance with Cothelas, king of the Getae, and marries his daughter, Meda. Founds Philippopolis, Beroe, and other Macedonian colonies in Thrace.

341–340: Over the winter, Demosthenes attempts to forge an anti-Macedonian coalition among the states of western Greece and the Peloponnese. Philip concludes an alliance with Atheas, king of the Scythians.

340: In the summer, Philip takes the city of Perinthus under siege; in September, he attacks Byzantium. Fails to capture both cities. Philip captures the Athenian grain fleet in the Bosporus. Athens declares war on Philip. In late autumn, Philip abandons the siege of Byzantium.

339: In the winter, Philip campaigns in Scythia and defeats Atheas. On the way out, his army is ambushed by the Triballi, and Philip is wounded in the leg. The Amphictyonic League declares Sacred War on Amphissa and appoints Philip as commander of the league's military forces. In the autumn, Philip occupies Elatea. Thebes and Athens form an alliance to oppose Philip.

338: Antipater attacks Amphissa and outflanks the Athenian positions. In August, Philip defeats the Theban and Athenian armies at the battle of Chaeronea. Concludes agreements with a number of city-states, imposing a new security regime for Greece.

337: Philip calls a conference at Corinth, where the League of Corinth is created. Philip is appointed *hegemon* of all Greece and commander in chief of all Macedonian and league armies. In the summer, Philip returns to Macedonia and marries Cleopatra. The league approves Philip's request to declare war on Persia.

336: In the spring, Philip sends 10,000 men under Parmenio, Amyntas, and Attalus across the sea to land at Ephesus and establish a bridgehead for the invasion to follow in the fall. Philip is assassinated in July.

1 PHILIPPOS MAKEDONIOS

A full moon hung in the night sky, casting shadows across the motionless shapes scattered on the rocky ground. The air was thick with the odor typical of late summer evenings in Greece, that mixture of lingering heat and approaching coolness. Moisture from the dampening night collected on the grass as wisps of fog drifted silently over the field. Here and there, patches of damp vapor floated above the black shapes before covering them like blankets, the way a mother covers a sleeping child to guard his slumber.

The dead who lay on that ground were the debris of battle, sprawled into grotesque shapes where they had fallen as if from some great height. Now and then the night's stillness was disturbed by the sound of suffering, as one of the dying fought his way to consciousness for a few moments before falling back into the painless dark. Five thousand men lay there; most of them were dead, others were taking far too long to die.

Against the moonlight came a solitary figure wobbling, struggling to keep his balance on his lame leg. The old soldier stumbled drunkenly over the pile of corpses that blocked his way. Somewhere near the center of the battle line, where the corpses were thickest, he stopped and drank from the wine jug he carried in the crook of his mangled arm. He wiped drops of the cool liquid from his lips with the back of his hand and looked out over the field. His face twisted into a satisfied smile. He began to sing, at first only to himself, and then his voice gradually became louder and louder until it echoed across the night. Then, Philip II of Macedonia began to dance upon the dead at Chaeronea.[1]

Philip II of Macedonia (382–336 BCE)—father of Alexander the Great, dynastic heir to the Argead kings who traced their lineage to Herakles (known as Hercules in Latin), son of the Temenid family from Argos that had ruled Macedonia since the eighth century BCE, unifier of Greece, author of Greece's first federal constitution, creator of the first national state in Europe, the first general of the Greek imperial age, founder of Europe's first great land empire, and Greece's greatest general—was one of the preeminent statesmen of the ancient world. It was Philip who saved Macedonia from disintegration, military occupation, and eventual destruction by securing it against external enemies and by bringing into existence Europe's first national territorial state, an entirely new form of political organization in the West.[2] Having made Macedonia safe, Philip developed mining, agriculture, urbanization, trade, commerce, and Greek culture and transformed a semi-feudal, tribal, pastoral society into a centralized national state governed by a powerful monarchy and protected by a modern army.

Philip achieved it all over a twenty-three-year reign marked by a program of territorial expansion and military conquest, and in the process he created a Macedonian army that revolutionized warfare in Greece and became the most effective fighting force the Western world had yet seen. Through shrewd statecraft and military force, Philip doubled the size of Macedonia and incorporated most of the Balkans into the Macedonian state. This accomplished, he overpowered the Greek city-states and, under his political leadership, united them for the first time in history in a federal constitutional order and directed them toward the greater strategic vision of conquering Persia. Philip used every means at his disposal in an effort to reach his goals—diplomacy, bribery, intimidation, deceit, subversion, sabotage, assassination, marriage, betrayal, war—and, on occasion, he even scrupulously kept his promises.[3] In short, Philip used all the same means his enemies, the political leaders of the Greek city-states, commonly employed.[4]

The first great general of the Greek imperial age, Philip was one of those rare military men who saw that the political and cultural world around him was changing and that by mastering that change he could shape his own age and the future. Had there been no Philip to bring the Macedonian national state into existence, to assemble the economic and military resources to unite Greece, to create the bold strategic vision of conquering Persia, and to invent the first modern, tactically sophisticated and strategically capable military force in Western military history as the instrument for accomplishing that vision, the exploits of Philip's son Alexander in Asia would not have been possible. Philip had provided the means, the methods, and the motives that lay behind Alexander's achievements. History may remember Alexander as a romantic international hero, but it was Philip who was the greater general and national king.⁵

Philip was born in 382 BCE, the youngest of three legitimate sons of King Amyntas III of Macedonia and his wife Eurydice, a princess of the Lyncestian royal house, one of the cantons of Upper Macedonia. Amyntas fathered three other sons and a daughter by his second wife, Gygaea. All of the king's sons were considered legitimate heirs since there was no formal requirement of primogeniture in Macedonia, a circumstance that often complicated the problem of royal succession when kings produced multiple claimants to the throne.⁶ This was a major reason why the five-century-long turbulent rule of the Temenid dynasty had been marked by civil wars, assassinations, hostage taking, incest, and other horrors following the death of a king. Foreign enemies such as Athens, Thebes, and Illyria repeatedly took advantage of these conditions to weaken Macedonia by interfering in its domestic politics and, at times, even installing their own client kings. Outside forces drove Philip's father from his throne in 393–392 and again in 388 BCE, only to have other outside powers help him regain his position.⁷ In the year that Philip was born, the Illyrians defeated Amyntas again and occupied much of Lower Macedonia, exacting hostages and tribute.⁸

Near the end of his life, Amyntas was challenged by Ptolemy of Acorus, a senior member of a branch of the royal family, who claimed the right to succeed Amyntas upon the latter's death. Amyntas had already selected his eldest son, Alexander II, as his successor. To purchase Ptolemy's ambition, Amyntas offered his daughter to Ptolemy in marriage, an arrangement that sufficed for the moment. Philip was twelve when Amyntas died of old age and Alexander II became king. Within months, Ptolemy raised a civil war against the new king, and may have been succeeding, when Thebes sent its famous general Pelopidas with an army to restore Alexander to the throne and prevent Athens, which supported Ptolemy, from increasing its influence in Macedonia. Pelopidas arranged a truce between Ptolemy and Alexander, ensuring that Alexander remained king. To guarantee the agreement, however, Pelopidas took young Philip, now fifteen, and the sons of thirty other prominent Macedonian barons to Thebes as hostages.

Little more than a year later (368–367 BCE), Alexander II was assassinated while participating in the Xandika, a traditional war dance. The assassins were probably supporters of Ptolemy, who still had designs on the Macedonian throne. His plans were frustrated, however, when the Macedonian Assembly selected Perdiccas, Alexander's brother, as king. Perdiccas was a fifteen-year-old minor, and the assembly appointed Ptolemy his guardian. A pretender, Pausanias, probably the son of Philip's half-brother Archelaus, organized an invasion of eastern Macedonia with foreign help to seize the throne. In response, Queen Mother Eurydice obtained the support of the Athenian general Iphicrates, who intervened and supported Perdiccas with easy success. It was probably concern over this Athenian intervention that forced Thebes to send Pelopidas to Macedonia again that same year to make peace between Ptolemy and Perdiccas. Ptolemy, who was still regent, was forced into an alliance with Thebes. This time Pelopidas took the sons of fifty Macedonian barons as hostages to Thebes to ensure Macedonia's observance of the agreement.

In 365 BCE Perdiccas turned eighteen, murdered Ptolemy, and assumed the Macedonian throne in his own right. During this time the great Theban general, Epaminondas, was building a fleet of a hundred triremes to counter the Athenian fleet, and Macedonia provided large quantities of timber under the terms of the treaty of alliance. Perhaps as a reward for his good faith observance of the treaty, Perdiccas secured Philip's release from Thebes and brought him back to Macedonia.[9] Eighteen years of age when he arrived in Pella, the capital, Philip was immediately appointed a provincial governor, probably in the region of Amphaxitis, an area extending from the Iron Gates of the Axius River to the head of the Thermaic Gulf. The region was of great strategic importance for defending the country and Pella itself from raids by Paeonians, Thracians, and Athenian warships landing troops on the Macedonian coast. Philip was also granted the authority to raise and train militia. The terrain in Amphaxitis lent itself more to cavalry than to infantry, and it might have been here that Philip equipped his cavalry with the longer nine- to ten-foot *xyston* (lance) to give it an advantage over the shorter six-foot spears and javelins the Greek and tribal cavalry traditionally used.[10]

During this time, Perdiccas likely arranged a marriage between Philip and Phila, the daughter of the royal house of Elimiotis and the first of Philip's seven (or possibly eight!) wives.[11] Elimiotis was the nearest and most populous of the northern Macedonian cantons and an important strategic buffer against Illyria. Perdiccas hoped to secure its support against the Illyrians through Philip's diplomatic marriage, just as Perdiccas's father had secured the support of the Lyncestis canton when he married Eurydice, the daughter of Arrhabaeus of Lyncestis.[12] The alliance seems to have been a success, given that Elimiotian cavalry later fought alongside Philip in his war with Bardylis of Illyria.

In 359 BCE the Macedonian army was destroyed in a battle with Bardylis, Macedonia's perennial enemy. Perdiccas was killed along with four thousand men. Upon hearing the news, the Macedonian Assembly met and chose a new king. According to the Greek historian Diodorus Siculus, it was then that Philip was elected king.[13] Drawing on the work of historian Theopompus, a contemporary of Philip's, the Roman historian-writer Marcus Junianus Justinus (Justin) says, conversely, that the assembly appointed Perdiccas's five-year-old son, Amyntas IV, king and named Philip, his uncle, as regent.[14] Justin says that Philip was not formally elected king until two years later (357 BCE), "at the time the more dangerous wars were impending," and "Philip assumed the kingship under compulsion from the people" when Amyntas IV was deposed.[15] Although Philip was young by modern standards to assume such responsibility, he was not so by the standards of the ancient world. At twenty-three, Philip was older than Octavian was at the death of Caesar and the start of the final Roman civil wars; older than Philip's brother Perdiccas was when he was named king; and older than his own son Alexander would be when, in his time, he ascended the throne.[16]

Philip immediately plunged into the intrigues of court politics. No fewer than five would-be usurpers challenged him for the throne. Macedonian politics was not for the weak or squeamish. The history of Philip's own family provided a sufficient example of court politics marked by murder, corruption, bribery, betrayal, adultery, incest, and torture. Philip moved immediately against his rivals by murdering his half-brother Archelaus.[17] His two other half-brothers were driven into exile, and the two additional claimants from a rival branch of the royal family were soon killed. Over the next year, Philip eliminated them all in one way or another. With his throne secure, at least for the moment, Philip turned his attention to protecting Macedonia.

PHILIP'S HOMERIC WORLD
To understand Philip's character and behavior, one must first understand the land and culture that shaped him. Culturally, the Greeks of Philip's day regarded Macedonia as a geographic backwater inhabited by untrustworthy barbarians who spoke an uncouth form of Greek; were governed by primitive

political institutions; subscribed to customs, social values, and sexual practices that bordered on the unspeakably depraved; dressed in bear pelts; drank their wine neat; and were given to regular bouts of incest, murder, and regicide. To the degree that the Greeks thought about isolated Macedonia at all, it was from the perspective of snobbish and sophisticated contempt.

Because of Macedonia's geographic location and the peculiar circumstances of its historical development, Macedonian society retained a number of practices that were Homeric in origin, form, and function.[18] Where the Greeks regarded the city-state as an expression of advanced political culture, Macedonia remained a land of clans and tribes held together by the bonds of warriorhood, dynastic bloodlines, and a powerful monarchy. In many ways the Macedonia of Philip's day was very much the society of the Mycenaean age, a male-dominated warrior society that had long since died out in Greece proper. Philip's world was one of tribal barons, one where the *Iliad* was not only an ancient heroic tale but also a reflection of how men still lived. As king, Philip was akin to Achilles—first among equals, the bravest and most able warrior, chieftain and protector of his people, the Mycenaean *wanax* (king) who maintained his authority over fierce warriors by personal example and a lineage of royal blood derived from the gods.

Philip ruled only so long as his barons respected and feared him, his position sustained by his dynastic lineage and reputation for bravery, and could be removed by the will of the assembly. He sat among his barons and wore the same clothes, purple cloak, and broad-brimmed hat of the Macedonian aristocrat; he wore no royal insignia on his person to set him apart, dressed in clothes of simple homespun fashioned by his wife,[19] and ate the same food as his men. There were no household slaves to wait on him at table, as in the households of the Greek democracies. While most Macedonians could speak proper Greek, among themselves, and especially when Philip addressed his soldiers and officers or his barons in the assembly, they spoke the more personal Macedonian dialect.[20] When hearing cases brought by common subjects or in discussions with his barons in the assembly, Philip, just as anyone else, was called only by his name, his patronymic, and his ethnic without any honorific or title. He could be called Philippos Amyntou Makedonios or simply Philippos Makedonios but not king.[21] The only requirement when addressing the king in the assembly was that the speaker had to remove his helmet as a sign of respect. Among his troops he was addressed as "fellow soldier," and he often engaged his men in public wrestling contests.²² In all his years, Philip never described himself as king in any of his official documents or public statements.²³ He was a Macedonian Achilles in every cultural sense.

A warrior culture requires values, rituals, and ceremonies to define it, and the values of Philip's Macedonia were strongly similar to those of the *Iliad*'s era, in particular those placed on the cult of the heroic personality. The highest social values were power, glory (*kydos*), and bravery (*arete*). Warriors were expected to demonstrate their bravery for the sake of honor (*time*) and reputation among fellow warriors. The noblest soldier was the warrior king fighting in defense of his people, and the appropriate arena of competition for reputation and honor was war, conquest, and performance on the field of battle.²⁴

In a very important way, however, Philip's view of war as distinct from personal bravery was decidedly un-Homeric. Unlike the *Iliad*'s heroes, this great warrior king who took the field every year of his twenty-three-year reign, save one when he was recovering from wounds; who took part in twenty-eight campaigns and eleven sieges; who captured forty-five cities (if one can trust Demosthenes); and who was seriously wounded at least five times never went to war for its own sake or only for personal glory. For Philip, war was first and foremost an instrument of state policy with which to achieve specific strategic objectives; it was always the continuation of policy by other means in the genuine Clausewitzian sense. The rhetorician Polyaenus observed that "Philip achieved no less through conversation than through battle. And, by Zeus, he prided himself more on what he acquired through words than on what he acquired through arms."²⁵ This Clausewitzian view of war led Philip to become the greatest strategist of his time.

A number of rituals and ceremonies in Philip's Macedonia lend some credence to the Greek slur of barbarism, however. War dances were a common ritual. Philip's brother Alexander II was murdered during one of these performances. Witches, too, abounded. Philip's wife Olympias was said to be a witch who worshiped snakes and to have had the quaint habit of taking the reptiles to her bed. Another of Philip's wives, Nicesipolis of Thessaly, was also reputed (by Olympias) to have been a witch. Interestingly, the two women turned out to be lifelong friends. One of the more curious and ancient Homeric practices was the Macedonian ritual of purifying the army as it set out for war. Priests cleaved a dog in two, and the army was made to walk between the severed halves to purify the soldiers.²⁶ As the Macedonians' chief priest,

Philip offered sacrifices daily for the protection of his people and must have officiated at this ritual on more than one occasion.

This all-male, violent warrior culture forced men to prove their bravery at a young age. A man who had not yet killed a wild boar single-handedly with a spear and without a net was not permitted to recline at a table and eat meat with fellow warriors; instead, he was required to sit upright for all to notice.[27] The boar hunt had its origins in Greek mythology when one of Herakles's twelve labors required him to slay the Erymanthian boar as punishment for killing his wife in a fit of rage. The Macedonians considered themselves descendants of Herakles, and the single-handed killing of a boar became a rite of passage for all young warriors. The wild northern European boar is a dangerous and aggressive animal, averaging between fifty and seventy-two inches in length and thirty-six to forty inches at the shoulder's height, and weighing from sixty to a hundred pounds. To kill a boar without a net tossed over the animal to immobilize it, and armed with only a spear, was not a task for the fainthearted.

In yet another Homeric ritual, Macedonian youths who had not yet killed a man in battle were required to wear a cord around their waists to mark them as unblooded. Only when a young man had slain his first victim was the cord removed and the young warrior permitted to join the ranks of other warriors. As a young man, Philip was required to pass all these tests. The world of Philip's youth was a loud, clamorous male world of rough soldiers who rode, drank, fought, and fornicated with rude energy and enthusiasm.

We know little of Philip's formal education, but it was probably not much different from that of his son, Alexander's. Philip was taught to read and write at an early age. A personal tutor oversaw his literary education, and "he was trained in all aspects of liberal education,"[28] including the major works of Greek literature, especially Homer. Music, too, was part of the curriculum. Philip's talent went unremarked while Alexander was known to play the lyre. Great emphasis was placed on athletics—running and wrestling in the palaestra, riding, and hunting—and on military training and proficiency with weapons. This training included building the young man's physical endurance and ability to suffer those hardships likely to be encountered on campaign. Alexander said of his tutor, Leonidas, that his idea of breakfast was a long night's march and of supper, a light breakfast. As part of his military training, Philip hunted other animals besides boars in the Macedonian forests. In a serious test of bravery, the animals Philip hunted with only a spear were lions, bears, panthers, and leopards.[29]

As a royal prince Philip attended the frequent symposia, the all-male eating and drinking bouts where drunken storytellers declaimed tales of bravery, war, killing, and exploits with women. Macedonian kings frequently entertained their friends and officers at these gatherings in much the same way a colonel entertained his officers at the mess in wartime. Here Philip heard the tales of Macedonia's history of suffering at the hands of Illyrian, Paeonian, Molossian, Thracian, Athenian, Theban, and Phokian invaders. During his own young life, Philip had witnessed Athenian and Theban armed interventions to settle Macedonian dynastic quarrels, the attempt on his father's life, the assassination of one brother, and the death of another, the latter in a war with the Illyrians who had occupied much of the country. Philip himself had been made a hostage by Macedonia's tormenters. Philip took it all in, drawing lessons that would serve him well as king when his country's fate was finally placed in his hands.

The Homeric nature of Philip's Macedonia was most evident in how Philip was interred after his death. His funeral ceremonies strongly resembled those of Patroclus and other heroes portrayed in the *Iliad*. Philip's body was cremated in a wood fire that was hot enough to destroy the flesh but not the bones.[30] His bones were retrieved from the ashes, carefully washed in wine, wrapped in purple cloth, and laid in a gold box (*larnax*) before being placed in a vault covered with a mound of earth, or tumulus. As in the funeral of Patroclus, horses were sacrificed and their remains left atop Philip's grave mound to decay. The body of Philip's assassin was hung on a cross above the king's grave for all to see before it was cut down and cast into the sea, the traditional punishment for those who had committed the sacrilege of killing a king. Two others implicated in the crime, Heromenes and Arrhabaeus, were executed at the site of the grave and their corpses allowed to rot on top of it.[31] Philip's funeral rites were those observed for the kings of the Homeric age.

To the end, Philip was strongly influenced by the martial environment to which he was exposed as a youth and in which he lived out his life. He remained a hard-drinking, womanizing, courageous soldier and general who preferred the company of his men all his life. He was also thoroughly pragmatic, no doubt the result of his experience with the murderous court politics of his youth and of his exposure to the lessons learned in the symposia. As with the heroes of the *Iliad*, Philip the warrior loved his fellow soldiers and had the greatest respect for deeds of personal courage and military valor.

WOUNDS AND INJURIES

Philip's world valued physical courage and bravery. Officers led from the front and risked their lives with their men. From all accounts Philip was a remarkably brave man who suffered at least five serious wounds in combat. Theopompus makes much of Philip's tendency to drink to excess, although he allows that Philip was always clearheaded when it came to making decisions. No Macedonian warrior needed encouragement to drink, but Philip's wounds left him in constant pain and alcohol likely reduced his suffering. He does not appear, however, to have been the alcoholic that Alexander became. While the Greeks drank their wine mixed with cold or warm water in a krater or mixing bowl, Macedonians drank their wine straight, imbibing its full 15–16 percent alcohol in the process. Thracians and Scythians also drank their wine neat, leaving the Greeks to regard the Macedonian habit as another barbarian custom.[32]

Philip suffered his first battle wound at the siege of Methone in 354 BCE. While he was inspecting sheds used to protect siege machinery, a sniper on the city wall shot an arrow into Philip's right eye.[33] Pliny the Elder tells us that Philip arrived at the field dressing station with the arrow still protruding from his eye.[34] The gods were with Philip that day, for had the arrow struck head-on, it would have penetrated his brain and killed him. Judging from the angle of the nick in the eye bone that forensic archaeologists found on Philip's skull, it is likely that he was wearing his iron helmet and had it tipped back on his head. The helmet deflected the arrow's trajectory and turned what might have been a direct hit into a glancing blow that left him alive but blind and disfigured in his right eye. Philip was probably struck with the heavier Cretan arrowhead rather than the smaller Scythian point since the arrow caused so much damage to the surrounding bone.[35]

Philip was treated by a Greek physician named Critobulus of Cos, whose reputation was made that day by successfully tending the king's wound.[36] Critobulus used an instrument called the spoon of Diokles to extract the arrowhead from Philip's eye socket.[37] Our only description of his instrument comes from Celsus.[38] Critobulus removed the arrow and extracted part of the eyeball itself, leaving the remainder in the socket to be consumed naturally by the body. The eye socket was stitched shut and, predictably, became infected. The dressing was changed each day for several weeks, and Philip was given a course of purgatives to speed his healing.[39] Philip must have been in great pain, for when Methone fell a few days later he allowed the residents to depart without further punishment so that he could return to Macedonia quickly and recover from his wound.[40] Pliny tells us that Critobulus "achieved great renown for having extracted the eye of king Philip, and for having treated the loss of the eyeball without causing disfigurement to the face."[41] To the contrary, Demetrius says that Philip was so sensitive about his disfigurement that the mere mention of it sent him into a rage.[42]

Philip was wounded again in 345 BCE during his campaign against the Illyrians, a confederation of tribes occupying the plains around modern Kosovo and south to modern Metohija. Two tribes, the Dardanians and the Ardiaei, had formed an alliance that Theopompus says was 300,000 strong, forcing Philip to move quickly and prevent such strength from assembling on his borders.[43] Philip deployed the full force of the Macedonian army and quickly defeated the Dardanians. He then marched to engage the Ardiaei, who were led by Pleuratos, the head of the royal house. The battle must have been a major engagement, and Philip himself was almost killed. A soldier named Pausanias covered Philip as he lay on the ground and shielded him from further blows, saving the king but dying himself in the process.[44] The Greek scholar Didymus Chalcenterus tells us that Philip was badly wounded along with 150 of his officers.[45] The Macedonian Companion officer corps, *asthetairoi*, comprised 800 officers. Assuming a reasonable number, say twenty, of them were killed in action, Philip's officers suffered almost 21 percent casualties in the battle. Didymus says that the Ardiaei were destroyed only after Philip's cavalry undertook a long and lethal pursuit against them.

Philip suffered two wounds that day. First a glancing blow from a cavalry lance broke his collarbone. He suffered a far more serious injury when his lower leg bones were smashed, perhaps by a club wielded by an infantryman, as Philip sat upon his horse.[46] It was probably this second wound that made Philip lame for the rest of his life.

In modern medical parlance, a "tib-fib" (referring to the tibia and fibula bones that make up the lower leg) fracture remains one of the more difficult injuries to set properly without producing atrophy and leaving the injured leg shorter. A break in the two bones results in their muscles pulling the bones in opposite directions so that the ends of the break tend to slide over one another. To set them correctly, the bones have to be pulled straight and tension maintained on them for several weeks. This treatment requires a special splint. The simple wood slat and bandage splint that Greek medicine used in Philip's day would not have sufficed. The ends of the broken bones in Philip's leg would have overlapped, retarding healing and causing a raised callous or lump to form at the break's location. These conditions would have deformed the lower leg's shape and could well have left it shorter by two inches.[47] The broken bones would have taken eight to ten months or even longer to heal and rendered Philip "lame," by which the Greeks meant that he walked with a pronounced limp.

Professor Manolis Andronikos, when excavating Philip's tomb in the late 1970s, found evidence that Philip's leg wound may be what crippled him. Andronikos found a pair of golden greaves, or metal sheathes used to protect the lower legs of Macedonian infantry and cavalrymen. The greaves in Philip's tomb were not symmetrical. The greave for the left leg was three and a half centimeters (almost two inches) shorter than the one for the right leg. In addition, the front of the left greave had an "outward bulge in the formation of the tibia,"[48] or exactly where the break in Philip's bones would have caused a lump to form. The left greave had to be deliberately manufactured to accommodate a man whose left leg was shorter than his right and whose lower leg bones were deformed.

In the winter of 339 BCE, after completing a successful campaign against the Scythians on the Danube River (the Istrus in antiquity), Philip was wounded again. Philip had taken captive some twenty thousand young men, women and children whom he intended to settle in Macedonian border towns. He had also captured twenty thousand mares, which he was going to use to supply his army and to market for cash. Returning to Macedonia, he crossed the land of the Triballi, a warrior people known for using long lances while fighting on horseback. The Triballi demanded a portion of Philip's booty as the price of safe passage through their territory. Philip refused. In the resulting battle, the Triballi made off with many of the captives and a portion of the booty and left Philip so severely wounded on the battlefield that his officers thought he was dead. Justin tells the story this way:

> But as Philip was returning from Scythia, the Triballi met him, and refused to allow him a passage unless they received a share of the spoil. Hence arose a dispute, and afterwards a battle, in which Philip received so severe a wound through his thigh that his horse was killed by it; and while it was generally supposed that he was dead, the booty was lost. Thus the Scythian spoil, as if attended with a curse, had almost proved fatal to the Macedonians.[49]

Didymus tells us that Philip was struck in the leg by a *sarissa*, by which he means the Scythian long cavalry lance and not the Macedonian infantry sarissa. Philip was not accidentally wounded by one of his own men, as has sometimes been claimed. Demosthenes says that Philip's hand was "mutilated" in the incident, most likely as a result of his horse falling on him after it was also struck by the same lance that wounded Philip. Also, Philip may have put his hand down to break his fall as the animal fell and rolled. Philip's hand and arm might have struck the ground with such force that he broke his wrist and some of the bones in his hand, leaving his hand mutilated and of limited use. The fall rendered Philip unconscious, as Plutarch implies when he tells us that Philip's troops, seeing his body lying on the battlefield, thought that he had been killed.[50]

A controversy arises over whether it was this wound inflicted by the Triballi or the earlier wound suffered at the hands of the Illyrians that caused Philip to become lame. It seems unlikely that the second wound could have caused Philip's lameness. For Philip's horse to have been killed so quickly by the same lance that struck Philip in the leg, the animal's heart must have been pierced. A horse's heart is located on the left side of its body, just above its front legs. To strike the horse's heart after piercing Philip's leg, the attack had to come from Philip's left with the lance moving at a downward trajectory. Cavalry lances typically rested on the cavalryman's shoulder prior to being thrust downward at the target. Mounted, Philip's left leg was behind the foreleg of his horse, so the lance's direction and trajectory came from behind and to Philip's left, exactly what one would expect if the attacker closed in a surprise attack from behind. Under these circumstances, there was a good chance that the lance struck Philip's thigh before continuing through the horse's body and striking the animal's heart.

The force required for the lance to penetrate Philip's thigh and the body of the horse and to pierce the animal's heart would have been insufficient if the lance had struck a bone in Philip's leg. That obstruction would have considerably reduced the weapon's momentum and likely changed its trajectory as well. In all probability, the lance that struck Philip produced a serious flesh wound to the thigh but did not strike and break a bone. A flesh wound could neither have shortened Philip's left leg nor produced the lower left leg's deformity, as indicated by the greaves found in Philip's tomb.

The severity of Philip's wounds can to some extent be assessed by the time Philip required to recover from each of them. Philip was wounded at

Methone in August 354 BCE but was back in action that winter when his army marched into Thrace. The injury suffered against the Triballi occurred in the winter of 339 BCE; however, by the following autumn, some six months later, Philip led his army into Phokis. The wound the Illyrians inflicted to Philip's shin in the spring of 345 BCE seems to have required the longest period of convalescence: Philip did not undertake a major campaign again for more than a year.[51] And while the historical record is not complete, 344 BCE seems to be the only year of Philip's reign in which he did not campaign. It seems a reasonable assumption, then, that Philip may have needed this time to recover from the broken bones that left him lame and with a deformed leg.[52] Demosthenes may not have been far off the mark when he said of Philip that "he was ready to sacrifice to the future of war every part of his body, if only the life of the shattered remnants should be a life of honor and renown."

WOMEN, WIVES, AND POLITICS

Of all the ancient Greek accounts concerning Philip, none are more distorted and propagandistic than those dealing with his wives. These accounts have accused Philip's wives of being common prostitutes, practitioners of incest, murderers of their husbands, adulteresses, and conspirators in assassination plots and of having roasted babies alive. And these outrages are all attributed remarkably to only one of Philip's wives, Olympias. While Philip's Greek enemies often wrote these tales for political purposes, undoubtedly they were widely believed in Greece at the time and were repeated as accurate in the accounts of later Roman and other historians. The disrepute in which the Greeks held Philip's wives was rooted in their cultural prejudice that the Macedonian kings' polygamy, practiced since ancient times, was little more than promiscuity and that their wives were but royal prostitutes.[53]

The nature and purpose of marriage in antiquity, in general and in Macedonia, in particular, were not for the amorous or sexual satisfaction of the bride and groom. Its primary purpose was procreation, especially so in a royal family where producing an heir of succession was of paramount importance. Beyond this necessity, Philip married for political reasons, that is, as a means of forging alliances or guaranteeing treaties.[54] Philip's father, Amyntas III, had married Philip's mother, a princess of the royal house of Lyncestis, to forge an alliance with her father against the Illyrians. It was no accident that Philip's first wife was a princess of the royal house of Elimiotis, a marriage Perdiccas arranged for him to secure a similar alliance against the Illyrians.

It was said that "Philip always married with war in mind."[55] While diplomatic marriages served as an inexpensive and effective means of conducting international diplomacy, it was obvious to the Macedonians that a king would require more than one wife.

In the royal Macedonian house, however, the most important reason for practicing polygamy was the king's need for healthy male heirs. The ancient world was a lethal place, and having enough children to ensure that at least one male survived to occupy the throne was the surest way to increase the odds that a king could pass on his realm to his son. In Philip's time, the average life span was only thirty-eight years.[56] Of a hundred children born, half died before age five. Of the fifty survivors, twenty-seven died before age twenty-five, nine died by age thirty-five, and only six lived to age fifty. Beyond that, only three of the original hundred children lived to see age sixty.[57] Under these circumstances, polygamy was almost a statistical necessity if a Macedonian king was to have a realistic chance of producing a surviving heir.

Polygamy also permitted a king to marry younger women of child-bearing age throughout his lifetime. The king increased his chances further by taking concubines and occasional lovers. Philip, an unrepentant womanizer, no doubt liked this custom. But unlike with the pharaohs, who designated one of their wives as chief wife, thus signifying that her son would be the likely heir, Macedonian royal wives enjoyed no such status. All of the king's children, whether by his wives or lovers, were regarded as legitimate heirs,[58] but only children born of royal wives were officially recorded. Justin tells us that "Philip had many sons, all recognized by royal tradition."[59] All the king's sons had an equal claim on the throne until the king himself designated an heir from among them and then the assembly had to approve that selection. The assembly usually approved the king's choice of the oldest male heir, but there was no fixed rule to this effect. In a number of instances in Macedonian history, the assembly chose another heir. Philip himself was chosen in this manner and replaced the five-year-old Amyntas IV, who had succeeded his father and Philip's brother Perdiccas III, after he was killed in battle.

Philip had at least seven—most likely, eight—wives, all acquired as a consequence of a state policy that required assurances of alliances or treaties. Besides Philip's first diplomatic marriage, before he was king, in 358 BCE Philip married Audata, the daughter (or granddaughter?) of Bardylis of Illyria, whom he had defeated in battle, to guarantee an alliance and a peace treaty. Audata died in childbirth, leaving Philip with a daughter, Cynane. In the same year he married Philinna of Larissa, Thessaly, to secure his southern border and balance the threat from Pherae by establishing an alliance with Larissa and the Thessalian League. The marriage produced Philip's first son, Arrhidaeus, who turned out to be dim-witted and unfit to rule. In 357 BCE Philip married the famous Olympias, daughter of the king of the Molossians, to shore up his northeastern border. Olympias was the mother of Alexander the Great. In 353 BCE Philip married Nicesipolis of Pherae, a niece of Jason of Pherae, to strengthen his control over Thessaly. They had a daughter whom Philip named Thessalonice (Victory in Thessaly) to commemorate his great victory at the battle of the Crocus Field.[60] Philip did not take another wife until 339 BCE when he married Meda, the daughter of Cothelas, king of the Getae, a kingdom on the Danubian plain, to seal an alliance. At about the same time Philip may have married the daughter of the Scythian king, Atheas, who had offered Philip his kingdom if he would come to his aid in a local war. After a falling out, Philip killed Atheas in battle. Marrying Atheas's daughter, however, made Philip ruler of Atheas's kingdom. In 337 BCE Philip married his final wife, Cleopatra, the ward of a powerful Macedonian baron named Attalus. She was Philip's second Macedonian wife.[61] Outside his marriages, Philip continued his rampant womanizing, and there is no estimating how many children he may have fathered.

By 340 BCE, Philip had clearly made Alexander his heir. When Alexander was only sixteen years old, Philip appointed him regent while Philip was away besieging Perinthus (modern Ereğli) and Byzantium and gave him authority to use force against the country's enemies. While regent, Alexander led an army against the Medians, a tribe on the upper Strymon River that had dared to revolt. He crushed the revolt ruthlessly and founded a "city," which he named after himself. In 338 BCE, Philip gave Alexander command of the cavalry at the battle of Chaeronea. To the day of Philip's death, no evidence exists that Philip ever changed his mind about Alexander as his prospective heir.[62] When Philip married Cleopatra, the contemporary anti-Macedonian Greeks claimed Philip was taken by his own lust and intended to produce a new heir to replace Alexander. There simply is no evidence to support this charge; however, Philip had good reasons to want to leave behind another heir before he left on his Persian campaign.

Justin notes that Philip "had many sons, all recognized by royal tradition . . . but of these some died in war and others accidentally or of natural causes."[63] Only two, Alexander and Arrhidaeus, were still alive in 337 BCE.

Surely Philip intended to take Alexander, who had already been exposed to battle in the Balkans and at Chaeronea, with him to Persia and join the greatest military adventure in Greek history. Philip's only other royal relative, his nephew, Amyntas IV, seemed content to continue his life of ease and had no royal ambitions. Philip did not therefore marry Cleopatra out of lust, as his Greek enemies charged, but for sound reasons of state: he intended to sire a royal heir in case both he and Alexander were killed in the Persian campaign. If Alexander survived, any son of Cleopatra's would be far too young to challenge Alexander's already well-established claim to succeed Philip.[64] Alexander had nothing to fear from Philip's infant son, and the Greek historians' later accusation that this fear incited the conspiracy to murder Philip is without merit.

When Alexander prepared to leave for Asia, his two oldest advisers, Parmenio and Antipater, urged him to marry and produce an heir before going off on campaign.[65] Alexander ignored the advice, putting the throne at risk should he be killed in battle. Alexander later married Roxanne of Bactria, but she was still pregnant when he died. Following Macedonian tradition, the assembly appointed Alexander's son king while he was still in utero and placed Roxanne under military guard until she delivered.[66] The boy was born in August 323 BCE and became king along with Alexander's thirty-five-year-old half-brother, Arrhidaeus, who was mentally deficient. Both Arrhidaeus and Alexander's son became pawns in an ensuing dynastic struggle that saw both of them murdered and brought the Temenid dynasty to an end after more than five hundred years.

A lingering question concerning Philip's wives is the identity of the one buried with him at Vergina. According to forensic findings, the cremated female skeletal remains, washed in wine and wrapped in purple cloth, were contained in a gold larnax similar to that containing Philip's skeleton. They are the remains of a young woman between twenty-three and twenty-seven years of age. Since all but three of Philip's wives were either dead or much older when he died, the remains can only be those of Cleopatra, Meda (the princess of the Getae), or the daughter of Atheas, the Scythian girl Philip may have married as a means of legally accepting rule over Atheas's kingdom. After Philip's death, however, Alexander's agents murdered Cleopatra's guardian, Attalus, who was then posthumously condemned by the assembly. Under Macedonian law, Attalus's entire family, including Cleopatra and her infant son, were executed, excluding her as having occupied Philip's tomb.[67]

The artifacts in the tomb also point to Philip's Scythian wife. The tomb contains a gold *gorytos*, a combination bow case and quiver containing bronze arrows, that was not suited for practical use. It may have been a symbol of Scythian royalty.[68] The bow and arrow was a basic Scythian weapon, and a similar gorytos appears on coins King Atheas minted.[69] Another gorytos, this one of silver, was found in a royal Scythian burial at Kuban and seems to have been made from the same mold as the one found in Philip's tomb.[70] The evidence points to Atheas's daughter as the wife buried with Philip.

But what stroke of misfortune caused a young woman to die when Philip was murdered so that she could be buried with him? In all probability, the girl did not die of natural causes but committed suicide. Both the Getae and Scythians practiced *suttee*: when a king died, his wife was required to take her own life so that she could be buried with him.[71] Philip had probably brought his Scythian wife to Macedonia in 339 BCE, where she lived until Philip's death, at which point she chose to observe her native custom and was buried with her husband as the true wife of a famous king.

PERSONALITY

No writer in antiquity has left an unbiased description of Philip's personality. Only Justin and Diodorus come close, with both basing their accounts on sources that were his contemporaries. Most Greek sources, by contrast, portray Philip negatively. In these accounts he is regularly portrayed as an aggressive, hard-drinking, combative, cowardly, dishonest, and cruel breaker of oaths and as a womanizer who occasionally had homosexual relationships with boys. As a reflection of their general view that Macedonians, and no less their kings, were barbarians, the Greeks' accounts of Philip's character are hardly credible. This said, it would be foolish to deny that Philip was an aggressive, hard-drinking womanizer!

The Greek statesman Aeschines, reporting to the Athenian Assembly after conducting diplomatic negotiations with Philip in Pella in 346 BCE, described a far different man: "thoroughly Greek, an oustandingly good speaker, and very great admirer of Athens."[72] Ctesiphon, another Greek diplomat, was equally impressed, saying that "he had never in all his long life seen so sweet and charming a man as Philip." He went on to comment on his powers of memory and ability as a speaker.[73] Demosthenes, a Greek diplomatic representative and Philip's greatest political enemy, criticized Philip for inviting to his court "players of mimes and composers of scurrilous songs."[74] Athenaeus says that Philip commissioned a book of jokes for the court. In truth, Philip had a love of drama and theater and sponsored dramatic contests at his court. He also had a strong interest in history, poetry, and philosophy, and some of the era's most noted intellectuals spent time in residence at Philip's court. Plato's nephew, Speusippus, who ran the Academy after Plato's death, resided for a time in Pella, and Aristotle, a boyhood friend of Philip's, became Alexander's tutor at Philip's request. Philip was hardly the barbarian that the Greeks portrayed him to be. Their prejudices led them to underestimate him and put them at great disadvantage in their dealings with him.

Philip was intelligent, educated, and experienced, and he brought these qualities to bear upon any problem he faced. He possessed an extensive knowledge of the Greek city-states, including their histories and political dynamics. He respected Athens for its history and culture while loathing the democratic system that paralyzed its will. Philip was an affable man who laughed easily and was always outwardly reasonable when dealing with the representatives of the Greek states. His regard for education is evident in the liberal education he provided for his son and the Companions' sons in the Royal Page School at Pella, a kind of military academy boarding school where the sons of important persons were educated along the Greek model and trained for military service.[75] There is evidence, too, that Philip may have established similar schools throughout Macedonia to educate officers for the militia and provide them with military training.[76]

By all accounts Philip was a superb diplomat, "charming and treacherous at the same time, the type to promise more in conversation than he would deliver, and whether the discussion was serious or light hearted, he was an artful performer."[77] He was an excellent speaker who could sway men with his words. After the Illyrians killed his brother Perdiccas III and destroyed the Macedonian army, Philip "assembled the Macedonians in successive meetings and stimulating their valor by skillful addresses, he renewed their confidence."[78] In 353 BCE, after his defeat at the hands of Onomarchus, Philip rallied his troops once again with his oratory. Justin notes that Philip "was possessed of eloquence and a remarkable oratorical talent, full of subtlety and ingenuity, so that his elegant style was not lacking fluency, nor his fluency lacking stylistic elegance."[79] Apparently the man could persuade almost anyone of almost anything.

Part of Philip's persuasiveness was his ability to conceal his true intentions and feelings, even from diplomats skilled in the art of discerning their adversaries' motives. As Justin wrote, "Philip had greater shrewdness than Alexander and was restrained in his language and discourse.... He could hide and sometimes even suppress his anger."[80] A realist, Philip understood that only the Macedonian state's interests were the ultimate basis of diplomatic agreement and that the king's personal qualities, whatever they may appear to one's adversaries at the moment, were but a means to that end or of no consequence at all. So "Philip cultivated friendships with a view toward expediency rather than genuine feelings. His usual practice was to feign warm feeling when he hated someone and to sow discord between parties that were in agreement and then try to win the favor of both."[81] Philip maintained that diplomacy was rooted in self-interest and that every man had his price. In this belief he was rarely disappointed. To confuse personal friendship or personality with national interests is a great mistake that political leaders still make but one that Philip never did. According to Justin, "his compassion and his duplicity were qualities he prized equally, and no means of gaining a victory would he consider dishonorable."[82]

Justin also says that "Philip preferred to be loved while his son, Alexander, preferred to be feared."[83] This desire led Philip to pursue victory by diplomacy over victory by war. Diplomatic agreements preserve at least the illusion of the vanquished party's voluntary acceptance of the victor's values and even the rectitude of his cause. Philip's extraordinary diplomatic skill is evident in that he achieved his most important victories in Greece by diplomatic means and not by force of arms. His election as archon of Thessaly and his appointment as a member of the Amphictyonic Council, the supreme religious authority in Greece; as president of the Pythian Games; as commander of the Amphictyonic army in the Fourth Sacred War; as hegemon (commander) of the League of Corinth; and as *strategos autokrator*, or commander in chief of the armies of all the council states after his military success at Chaeronea—all were great diplomatic achievements.

Much of Philip's diplomatic success is traceable to his well-developed political instinct and patience and his belief that war was only one of the many tools that the statesman brought to the game of politics. To be sure, Philip was a brilliant negotiator and beguiler and never one to correct his adversary's false impressions of what was promised and what was not. But statesmanship requires more than intellect and skill. A statesman must have the courage and self-confidence to undertake the bold actions that his intellectual assessment of the situation demand. And Philip was certainly brave and self-confident.[84] Philip's ultimate goal was nothing less than the transformation of the semifeudal Macedonian state into a regional superpower, a task of such magnitude that most men would have shied away from even attempting it. He succeeded admirably against all odds because he had the courage to try.

Although an excellent diplomat, Philip thought of himself first as a soldier and as much a hero as any in the *Iliad*. He felt most at home with his troops and loved being in their presence. He ate the same food, wore the same simple homespun clothes, and carried no insignia of rank, and his men addressed him by his first name. Philip, just as the commanders in the *Iliad*, was a "muddy boots" general, a commander who took the same risks as his men and suffered with them. Having survived five wounds in battle, he no doubt instilled confidence in his men. Most of all, Philip valued his men as fellow soldiers and comrades and did not consider them only as means to his ends. He protected them, paid and fed them well, promoted common soldiers to the highest ranks when their bravery deserved it, recognized the heroism of individual soldiers in military assemblies, and sent pensions to their widows when they died. Veterans were given land upon which to live and retained the right to vote in the assembly.[85] Philip knew the secret of successful military command: men cannot be managed to their deaths. They must instead be led by competent and brave officers and trust that they will not be squandered by carelessness or incompetence in marginal military adventures. Philip used his troops sparingly and always sought to reduce the danger to which they were exposed.[86] Whenever he attacked a city by storm, he sent his paid mercenaries into the streets to do the dangerous hand-to-hand fighting and kept his own Macedonian troops safely apart from the street fighting to reduce their casualties. Philip was a Homeric warrior in every sense, including the important sense that his fellow soldiers were as valuable to him almost as equals.

It is often overlooked that Philip was a conscientiously religious man and respected oaths, religious rituals, sacred shrines, and worship of the gods. Philip was not only his people's king but also their chief priest and religious leader who sacrificed daily on their behalf. He believed fervently in his special relationship with Zeus, maintained the cult of the Temenid family, and worshiped his ancestor, Herakles, the son of Zeus. The Greek historian Ephorus is insistent that Philip's reverence for the gods (*eusebeia*) was genuine and sincere.[87]

Philip's religious observance had practical implications for his politics, and he regarded those who did not keep their oaths, those who violated shrines, or those who took up arms against religion as blasphemers deserving harsh punishment. Greek treaties commonly required the parties involved to swear oaths. In numerous cases, Philip required that the oaths be sworn at a religious shrine and the written texts be deposited in the temples. Philip regarded the religious sanctions of these oaths as sacredly binding and reserved severe punishment for those who violated them. Philip often treated the populations of the cities he captured humanely and, by the standards of the day, was not a bloodthirsty general.[88] But when the city of Olynthos violated its treaty with Philip, which had been sworn in the religious manner, he destroyed the city, turned his soldiers loose on the population, and sold the survivors into slavery.

Philip also regarded the violation of a shrine as sacrilege. When the Phokians seized the temple at Delphi and stole Apollo's treasure, the Amphictyonic Council declared a Sacred War against them. When Philip met their army in the battle of the Crocus Field, his troops wore crowns of laurel to signify they were "Apollo's saviors." After the battle, he ordered three thousand of the captured enemy troops drowned and denied burial, the traditional Greek punishment for sacrilege, and their contaminated weapons were broken and thrown over the Phaedriadae cliffs at Delphi. When Philip was elected as leader of the Amphictyonic Council at the war's end, the council drafted rules regulating the proper treatment of all religious shrines in Greece and "everything else pertaining to religious practice, to common peace and to concord among the Greeks."[89] In Philip's mind, reverence for the gods mattered a great deal and affected the way one conducted oneself. This said, his adversaries were gravely mistaken if they thought they could manipulate Philip's personal devotion to influence his stronger imperatives of statecraft and national defense policy that were deeply rooted in Macedonia's strategic interests.

Perhaps it was Philip's well-known respect for the gods that led his enemies to accuse him of wanting to become a god himself. As proof, Greek sources point to the statue Philip had made of himself that was carried behind the statues of the twelve Olympic gods at his daughter's wedding and to the Philippeion, a building he had commissioned for the Olympic Games of 336 BCE that housed a statue of himself. However, the charge that Philip sought divinity is likely false on several grounds and probably resulted from writers attributing to Philip a similar practice of the later Hellenistic and Roman periods when followers made sacrifices to statues of great men and declared them divine.

Philip knew perfectly well that the Greeks considered worshiping a living man as a god as a terrible blasphemy. To do so would have alienated most Greeks just when he needed their help to invade Persia. Moreover, Diodorus describes Philip's statue as an *eikon*, a statue without any religious significance. There were hundreds of similar ones of famous men throughout Greece. If it had been a cult statue before which worshipers would render sacrifices, presumably Diodorus would have called it an agama.[90] Philip's statues were meant only to show that he was the most powerful man in Greece. Philip was too smart and practical to indulge religious vanity precisely at a time when religion could be put to such practical political uses.[91]

Together, Philip's character and training were well suited to the means and ends of the tasks he set for himself. Military historian J. F. C. Fuller describes Philip as

> a man of outstanding character; practical, long-sighted and unscrupulous. He was a master diplomatist and an astute opportunist to whom success justified everything. He was recklessly brave, yet unlike so many brave generals he would at once set force aside should he consider that bribery or liberality or feigned friendship was likely to secure his end. He possessed in marked degree the gift of divining what was in his enemy's mind, and when beaten in the field would accept defeat and prepare for victory. Throughout his life he never lost sight of his aim—to bring the whole of Greece under his dominion. As Hogarth writes of him, "Fraud before force, but force at the least was his principle of empire."[92]

A HOSTAGE IN THEBES

There is no doubt that the martial environment of his youth strongly influenced Philip throughout his life. To the end he remained a tough and courageous soldier and general who preferred the company of his men, had a soft spot for his troops, and was highly respected because of his personal courage and military valor. He was of a mostly jovial disposition but in an instant could turn serious. His pragmatism surely resulted from his experience with the murderous court politics he witnessed in his youth. Yet, none of his martial experiences and habits completely explain his great success as both a general and a statesman. The secret of Philip's greatness resides in his brilliant intellect and the excellent military education he received while a hostage at Thebes.

Philip was sent to Thebes (ca. 368 BCE) at the age of fifteen as part of a guarantee for a Theban settlement imposed on the warring factions of a dynastic dispute in Macedonia. We may correctly suppose that he arrived at the Theban court with an already developed sense of how harsh and dangerous the world could be. By now he had accepted as axiomatic that all politics—diplomacy, too—was based on self-interest and that any man could be made to do what one wanted for a price. At even this young age Philip was already a believer in realpolitik. No experience in his life ever caused him to question that belief.

The Thebans likely regarded Philip as little more than a country bumpkin, another Macedonian in need of civilizing. Diodorus records, however, that he took eagerly to his tutoring and quickly became enamored of the culture and civilization of the Hellenes, its arts and ceremonies. His tutor was Lysis of Tarentum, a Pythagorean.[93] It would be difficult to imagine a less willing convert to a creed requiring pacifism, vegetarianism, and total abstinence than young Philip! Perhaps it was in Thebes that Philip conceived of the idea of developing Macedonia along the lines of Hellenistic culture. The education he received there had a profound influence on him.

Philip lived with Pammenes, a skilled general and close friend of the great Epaminondas, who was the victor of Leuctra (371 BCE) and regarded as the best tactician in all of Greece. Philip also made the acquaintance of Pelopidas, the commander of the famous elite heavy infantry unit known as the Sacred Band and an excellent cavalry general. Philip was an eager student of war and applied himself diligently to his hosts' lessons. He had the opportunity to observe the Sacred Band's drills and observed the importance of disciplined infantry, unit cohesion, and esprit de corps. The Sacred Band later became the model for his own elite corps of infantry. From watching the Theban cavalry in its practice drills, Philip came to appreciate the need for cavalry to fight as units instead of in small tribal bands or as individuals, as was the common Macedonian method. There was, he learned, no substitute for a professional officer corps trained in common tactical drills. Only professionally skilled officers could coordinate the cavalry and infantry maneuvers characteristic of Theban tactics, and this coordination later became the hallmark of Philip's tactics. Philip learned, too, that meticulous staff planning supported by accurate intelligence lay behind tactical success.

Greek education placed a great emphasis on reading, and in Thebes Philip would have had access to Pammenes's library of the classic military treatises of the Greek world. The Persian wars and the Peloponnesian wars had led to the publication of a number of works on military training and tactics that would have been available to Philip. Of those works, only a few have survived to the present day, but it is likely that Philip read Thucydides' *History of the Peloponnesian War*, Herodotus's *The Histories* and the accounts of the Persian wars, and possibly some of the works by Xenophon, including *On Horsemanship*, *The Cavalry Commander*, and the *Anabasis*. It would be difficult to imagine where Philip might have obtained a better military education than when he was a hostage at Thebes.[94]

Epaminondas was still in active service when Philip was in Thebes. The tactics Epaminondas employed against the Spartans at the battle of Leuctra (371 BCE) marked the beginning of the end of Greek traditional methods of war. Warfare in Greece had evolved from the warrior heroes of the Mycenaean age engaging in individual combat to the citizen armies of the city-states using the infantry phalanx. Western military history begins with the Greeks, and their engagement at Leuctra marks a turning point in the development of Greek tactics. Arriving in Thebes three years after Epaminondas's great victory, Philip studied it in detail and had access to many officers and troop commanders who had fought in this engagement. Many of the structural and tactical innovations Philip introduced, and Alexander later imitated, can be traced to Philip's study of this great battle.

The victory of Thebes over the Spartans was sparked seven years before the battle when Epaminondas created the Sacred Band. Three hundred men strong, the Sacred Band was noted for its iron discipline, cohesion, tactical mobility, and bravery. The unit had originally been designed to anchor the Theban right wing in traditional fashion, but Epaminondas restructured it as an elite unit to be used at the commander's discretion.

The tactical problem for Epaminondas at Leuctra was to find a way to offset the Spartans' numerical advantage. He extended his line to the left, thinning out both the right and the center, and concentrated his forces in a single division on his extreme left. The Theban right and center were left with fewer than fifteen hundred men with a depth of no more than five ranks. The division on the left contained three thousand men arrayed in a shortened front but fifty men deep. The Theban light infantry and some cavalry were positioned on the right with the bulk of cavalry in front of the reinforced left phalanx. Farther out to the left, beyond the phalanx but close enough to move to its front, was the Sacred Band. Seen from the Spartan line, the Theban army had its greatest strength directly across from the Spartan right. The rest of the line was echeloned back on an oblique angle, or "refused" in tactical terms, with its extreme left anchored on the terrain.[95]

In deploying his forces in this manner, Epaminondas produced the first major tactical innovation in phalanx infantry that Greece had witnessed in three hundred years. Traditionally, a strong right wing engaged a weakened left. Once engaged, the armies had a tendency to rotate counterclockwise until one combatant was able to maneuver outside the opponent's flank, turn inward, and envelop it. This strategy made the left wings somewhat tentative about engaging the opponent since they always did so at a numerical disadvantage. The left wings were far more accustomed to yielding to pressure than gaining ground through advance. Aware of this tactical dynamic, Epaminondas arranged his forces to bring the greatest force concentration quickly against the enemy line's strongest point and shatter it in a single blow. He had discovered what the Germans later called the *schwerpunkt*, the point of greatest concentration of forces. Epaminondas reasoned that if he could engage the enemy's right with his stronger left wing, his own weakened center and right could hold back at the oblique and refuse battle for as long as possible. Although outnumbered in total forces, Epaminondas's deep phalanx outnumbered the Spartans across from him four to one at the schwerpunkt. Here the principle of economy of force was applied brilliantly. If the shock of battle quickly broke the Spartan right, the battle would be over before most of the Theban forces to the center and right ever engaged. As the battle developed, the Spartans attempted a countermaneuver and shuffled their units farther to the right to overlap the flank. Epaminondas countered by committing the Sacred Band, already positioned to his far left with some cavalry, and blocked the Spartans' redeployment. This move contained the battle to the area where Epaminondas had deployed his greatest concentration of force.

The battle of Leuctra taught Philip a principle of war that he applied again and again: to bring about quick and economical military decision, concentrate one's forces and strike at the enemy's strongest—not weakest—point.[96] Epaminondas's tactics were revolutionary. His use of cavalry in concert with infantry, coordinated in tempo and location with the infantry, was the first Western example of an army utilizing combined arms in battle.

Another major innovation Epaminondas contributed to Greek warfare was the strategic forced march. For centuries Greek armies terminated campaigns in single, set-piece battles. Unlike the Napoleonic (and Philippic) doctrine of the decisive battle used to achieve strategic ends, Greek armies rarely fought battles within a strategic context. Epaminondas was the first Western commander to use military means to achieve strategic ends by forcing a tactical decision in the field. After the battle of Leuctra, Epaminondas marched his army through the Peloponnese into Laconia and liberated Messenia, depriving Sparta of half its economic and manpower strength. This expedition was the first application in the West of the doctrine of strategic pursuit. Without the strategic forced march, Philip's armies would never have been able to force a strategic decision to unify Greece, and Alexander's wars against the Persians would have been unimaginable. The idea of driving an army deeply into enemy territory and daring him to give battle or watch one objective after another fall without serious military opposition was a revolutionary concept.[97] All that was required for a strategic revolution in Greek warfare was for someone to enhance the military capabilities of a Greek army and apply Epaminondas's lessons on a greater scale. That person was Philip.

But not all the instruction Philip acquired in Thebes involved military lessons. He was already a profound observer of political events, and in Thebes Philip got his first close look at the dynamics of the civic culture of the Greek city-state. And here Philip saw weakness. To Philip's eye, the democracies of Greece were dying of self-inflicted wounds. Their civic cultures were torn by constant factional and party intrigues. The annual assemblies often were unable to make timely decisions to prevent being overtaken by events. Fear of tyranny led the city-states to restrict their executive officials to a crippling degree, often granting necessary powers only when an enemy was at the gates. Annual elections made long-term planning in military affairs impossible. Greek citizen levies, even when supplemented by mercenaries, were often unreliable. The Athenian practice of selecting ten generals every year to conduct military operations struck Philip as particularly detrimental. Philip is said to have marveled at how the Athenians could find ten competent generals each year when "I have only found one in my life—Parmenio." Philip concluded that speed was a key component to military success. If he moved rapidly against his objective, he could achieve victory or surrender before the city-states' decision makers could react.[98]

The domestic politics of the Greek states were particularly vulnerable to exploitation from outside. The city-states were fiercely nationalistic and jealous guardians of their own liberties, while at the same time they were trying to destroy the liberties of others, both outside and within their polities. Much of Greece's history in the fifth and fourth centuries BCE was a history of warfare and attempts to establish hegemonies over one another, often by attempting to influence a rival state's domestic politics. Greek domestic politics were breeding grounds of subversion, factionalism, treason, expropriations of property, exile, and public executions carried out by one faction against another for political advantage. At times, the entire male population of the losing faction was put to the sword, their women and children sold into slavery, and their property confiscated. Philip became convinced that the cumulative effect of these defects was potentially fatal, and he came to believe that the political institutions of Macedonia, which the Greeks held in contempt, concentrated executive power and decision making in a way that was far better suited for war and international politics than those of the Greek states. Demosthenes seems to have grasped the essence of Philip's advantage in this regard when he said:

> In the first place, he was the despotic commander of his adherents: and in war that is the most important of all advantages. Secondly, they had their weapons constantly in their hands. Then he was well provided with money: he did whatever he chose, without giving notice by publishing decrees, or deliberating in public, without fear of prosecution by informers and indictments for illegal measures. He was responsible to nobody: he was the absolute autocrat, commander, and master of everybody and everything. And I, his chosen adversary—it is a fair inquiry—of what was I master? Of nothing at all![99]

To Philip's eye, the democracies of Greece were rotten from the inside out.

PHILIP HIMSELF

Ancient writers tell us almost nothing about Philip's physical appearance except that he wore a beard. We would have remained uninformed had Professor Andronikos not discovered Philip's tomb in 1977 at Vergina.[100] Philip's almost complete skeleton was discovered in a gold box, where it had been placed after his cremation. From this skeleton it was determined that Philip was between 1.67 and 1.72 meters tall (approximately five feet, eight inches), or somewhat taller than the average height for males of his day. He possessed all thirty-two of his teeth, a remarkable condition for a man of his age in antiquity and an indication of robust health. Philip's sound health may have been due to genetics: his father had lived beyond the age of eighty.[101] Philip suffered from a "marked degree of congenital hypoplasia (underdevelopment) of the left side of his head," which threw his jaw off midline.[102] This deformity was more noticeable when Philip was young and would have been common knowledge in Macedonian court circles. It would have become less noticeable once Philip grew his heavy beard. Macedonians traditionally wore full beards, and soldiers were trained to seize an adversary's beard when engaged in hand-to-hand fighting. Alexander's habit of going about clean shaven may have been intended as a subtle rebuke to Philip since Alexander's features were perfectly formed. As Alexander's fame spread after his death, beards fell out of style among military men throughout the Mediterranean. Hannibal went about beardless as did Scipio Africanus, who is said to have required his Roman soldiers to shave daily.[103]

Philip's life as warrior, which found him almost continually in the field on one campaign or another, suggests that he was physically strong. We hear of only one illness, during the winter campaign in Thrace. He probably had a weathered, dark-skinned complexion and the dark hair and eyes typical of many Macedonians to this day. The small ivory carvings of Philip found in the tomb show a well-formed mouth with full lips and a "very pronounced bridge to the nose, a prominent characteristic of other members of the Argead royal house."[104] His right eye was sightless, its flesh sunken in and scarred.

Philip's skull was recovered intact and sent to the University of Manchester, England, where a team of forensic archaeolgists used modern scientific techniques to reconstruct a likeness of Philip. The reconstruction team offered the following description of Philip:

> the figure of a battle-hardened warrior, a man with a square face, an obstinate chin and prominent Adam's apple, with heavy features, a distinctive nose with a remarkable bridge, prominent eyebrows with an idiosyncratic lift at the other end, a lined and slightly humorous face and furrowed brow framed by a short thick beard and moustache and thick straight hair. The face lacks symmetry, particularly in the cheeks, and the right eyebrow is scarred, the right eye sightless.[105]

A bust of Philip's likeness as reconstructed by the forensic archaeologists appears in figure 1.

It is interesting to compare Philip's likeness with the physical descriptions of Alexander that have come down to us. One of the accusations made by Alexander's and Olympias's enemies was that Philip was not Alexander's father; indeed, they maintained that Alexander was the result of Olympias's adultery. Alexander himself later denied that Philip was his father. After visiting the sacred Zeus Ammon shrine at Siwah in Egypt, Alexander came away believing that his real father was Zeus himself. Thereafter he often referred to himself as "the son of Zeus."[106]

Peter Green offers the following description of Alexander drawn from the surviving ancient accounts:

> By the time he was sixteen and made regent of Macedonia, Alexander had grown into a boy of rather below average height, but very muscular and compact of body. He was already a remarkably fast runner. His hair, blond and tousled, is traditionally said to have resembled a lion's mane, and he had that high complexion which fair-skinned people so often display. His eyes were odd, one being gray-blue and the other dark brown. His teeth were sharply pointed—"like little pegs"—says the Alexander Romance. . . . He had a somewhat high-pitched voice, which tended to harshness when he was excited. His gait was fast and nervous, a habit he picked up from old Leonidas (one of Alexander's tutors), and he carried his head to the left, whether because of some physical defect[107] or through mere affectation cannot be determined. There was something almost girlish about his earlier portraits, a hint of leashed hysteria.[108]

Philip and Olympias seemed to have worried that their son's "almost girlish" appearance and apparent lack of heterosexual interests might turn him into what Theophrastus called a *gynnis*, or "girlish introvert." Olympias went so far as to procure a Thessalian courtesan named Callixeina to "help develop his manly nature."[109] Apparently this effort was not successful. Plutarch tells us that Alexander "did not know any woman before he married other than Barsine," the daughter of Artabazus, a Persian satrap (provincial governor) and resident at Philip's court whom Alexander had met when still a young man. Captured by Parmenio at the battle of Issus (333 BCE) and sent

Figure 1. *Wax Bust of Philip Reconstructed from His Skull Found at Vergina*

to Alexander, she became his mistress and even bore him a son, Heracles. It is not difficult to see how the sheer contrast in the physical descriptions of Alexander and Philip, to say nothing of their different behavior, might have led to questions about Alexander's paternity, which Philip's enemies manipulated to diminish his and Alexander's reputations.

That Philip was disposed by his nature to the practice of war and politics is obvious enough. To those who knew him best, little Philip did would have surprised them. Even the idea of a Panhellenic alliance of Greek states united in a war against Persia was familiar, since in 380 BCE Isocrates proposed it in his long essay "Panegyricus." Later, when he was in his nineties and it was clear that Philip would unite Greece for the first time in its history, Isocrates rewrote the piece under the title of "Philippus" and commended it to Philip, who saw in it the justification for his war against the Persians.

But even simpler motives were behind Philip's wars to unite Greece after he had made Macedonia itself secure. Warrior societies fight wars because they are warrior societies and vice versa. Macedonian society strongly resembled the social order of Homeric Greece. Philip set about conquering Greece for the same reason that the warriors of the *Iliad* set out to conquer Troy: waging war is what warriors do! Without wars to fight, these men had no reason to rise from their bed or any way to achieve a reputation, wealth, and women. One might well ask, what would the warriors of the *Iliad* have done if it had not been for Troy? It is hard to imagine either Achilles or Philip turning to the plow.

Beyond the lure of war and glory, Philip was also motivated by revenge. He knew well enough the contempt the Greeks held for him and his people. Philip would avenge every slight and every injustice Macedonia had suffered at the hands of the Greeks. There, too, was a sense that Philip's envy of Athenian culture and past greatness drew him to reduce its power and reputation. As with the poor fellow who has finally made it rich, the achievement only has meaning when he is finally accepted by his betters into their club. Philip never hated Athens so much as he envied it, and this Macedonian rustic would force Athenians and the Greeks to accept him and his people as equals.

2 THE STRATEGIC ENVIRONMENT

In the fourth century BCE, Macedonia was the largest and most fertile area of Greece (see map 1).[1] Lower Macedonia comprised extensive alluvial plains at the mouths of its two great rivers, the Haliacmon and the Axius, that flowed into the Thermaic Gulf.[2] The Lower Macedonian plain was ringed by hills and mountains on all sides except to the east, where the Strymon River formed its natural boundary with Thrace. Along with Thessaly, Lower Macedonia comprised the largest area of alluvial plains on the Hellenic Peninsula.[3] West and northwest of Lower Macedonia were the smaller plains and pastures that lay at higher altitudes between the mountain ranges that made up the cantons of Upper Macedonia. Together, the territories of Upper and Lower Macedonia were able to support a population larger than that of any Greek state or combination of Greek states of the day.[4] Estimates of the country's population during Philip's era range from 500,000 to 1 million inhabitants.[5] Macedonia possessed a dual climate. Coastal Macedonia shared the Mediterranean climate of the rest of Greece, while inland the climate of Upper Macedonia was typical of the Balkans' continental climate with its harsh winters and cold temperatures.

THE LAND AND ITS PEOPLE

The plains of Lower Macedonia were well watered by the country's perennial rivers and streams, producing rich pasturelands ideal for raising horses, cattle, goats, and sheep. The alluvial soil was fertile, and extensive farming reaped large harvests of cereal grains that provided the staple diet of the inhabitants and a sufficient surplus to serve as a major export crop. The population of peasant farmers lived in the towns, villages, and cities scattered upon the plain. The Macedonian plain was almost devoid of rock, so the houses and town buildings were constructed of mud brick. Almost all cities and towns of Lower Macedonia were fortified with walls, a necessary means of defense against both the frequent raids conducted by the neighboring tribes and the military expeditions of the Greek city-states.[6]

Upper Macedonia was a very different place. Although substantial, its population was somewhat smaller than that on the plains, and life was much harder. The economy centered on the transhumant pastoralism of animal husbandry, mostly sheep and goats. The area's climatic severity forced the shepherds to transfer their livestock on a seasonal basis from winter to spring pastures. The mobility required by this mode of economic existence made it impossible to establish cities of any size, and people lived mostly in small hamlets and a few trading towns when not on the move or living in tents near their animals.[7] Living conditions were primitive. During his Persian campaign, when Alexander scolded some mutinous army units that had been drawn from the Upper Cantons, he reminded them of their lives in Upper Macedonia: "When Philip took you over you were nomadic and poor, the majority of you clad in skins and grazing sparse herds on the mountains, and putting up a poor fight for them against Illyrians, Triballians, and the neighboring Thracians. He gave you cloaks to wear instead of skins."[8]

Taken as a whole, however, Macedonia was the wealthiest area of Greece. Its people bred fine warhorses in larger numbers than anywhere else in Greece except, perhaps, Thessaly; so while elsewhere cavalry remained a secondary arm of Greek armies, the Macedonian cavalry became the primary combat arm of Philip's army. It was said that a Macedonian boy could ride before he could walk. Many of the Greek states had difficulty feeding even their small populations. Athens imported almost half its food, and malnutrition and sporadic famines were not uncommon in Greece. Macedonia, by contrast, had sufficient food for its own people and for export, with the result that Macedonians were a strong and hardy lot. They made excellent soldiers, and their ability to endure the rigors of the campaign, often in winter, amazed the Greeks.

Not all Macedonians were shepherds or farmers. With its large forests of pine and fir, Macedonia was also a land of lumberjacks and produced much of the wood for the ships of the Athenian and other navies of the Greek city-states. Macedonia was also rich in metals. Hundreds of mines produced iron and copper, and some of the largest silver and gold mines were found

The Strategic Environment 35

Map 1. *Philip's Greece*

there. Not surprisingly, over the centuries this rich land was targeted frequently by neighboring tribes, states, and nomadic peoples seeking access to its resources.

The settlement of Macedonia began at the end of the Bronze Age when a people scholars call "West Greeks" migrated south into Upper Macedonia. These people spoke Greek and their own Macedonian dialect.[9] Gradually, some of them drifted farther south, and by 700 BCE there were "Macedonic" tribes living on the edge of the lower plains as well. Among these were the Arestai, a powerful clan that traced their ancestors to the Argeadai, a family claiming descent from Argead of the Teminid kings of Argos in the Peloponnese, and through them to Herakles himself.[10] By the eighth century BCE, the Macedonian tribes had coalesced around the Temenid family, which became the royal house of the Macedonian kings and sustained an unbroken dynastic lineage until the death of Alexander the Great's son in 312 BCE. According to legend, the first of these Macedonian kings, Perdiccas I (whose name means partridge), followed a herd of wild goats through the mountains to level ground on the Macedonian plain, where he founded the first city in Macedonia. In honor of the goats that had led him there, Perdiccas named the city *Aegae* (Goat Town, now modern Vergina).[11] Aegae became the capital of the country and the sacred burial place of Macedonian kings.

Around 410 BCE, King Archelaus transferred the capital to the town of Pella. Being located on the open plain, the old capital was vulnerable to attack. Moreover, Macedonia had expanded eastward to the Strymon River so that Aegae was no longer centrally located, making administration and communication more difficult. The new capital was located on the shores of Lake Loudias. Surrounded by low-lying swampy terrain, Pella was more defensible from invasion by sea and afforded it access to the Thermaic Gulf.[12] The citadel sat on a fortified island in the lake called Phakos, rising from the marshes, while the city was built on nearby hills. Archelaus spent considerable sums on the new capital, and Pella was soon the largest city in Macedonia. Philip converted the lake into a spacious harbor by connecting it to the Axius River with an artificial channel that permitted direct access to the Thermaic Gulf. Artificial gates controlled the flow of the channel. It was the first harbor constructed on a river estuary in Europe.[13]

The city was heavily fortified from the beginning, and in Philip's day its walls, at eight kilometers long, were longer than the circuit wall of Athens.[14] The walls were constructed of mud brick set upon bases of stone.[15] The city itself was laid out in a regular urban grid with buildings and houses running along its streets. Main roads, thirty feet wide, ran east to west and north to south. Two wide roads connected the city to the artificial harbor. The city had a permanent water supply, which was evident in its many fountains, reservoirs, baths, and public sewers. The government compound and palace occupied fifteen acres and was the heart of the Macedonian government with offices for all financial, military, economic, diplomatic, and administrative activities. The Greek complaint that Macedonians were a primitive people was hardly believable after a Greek diplomat had visited Pella.[16]

The Teminids took over the transhumant society of pastoralists who moved their herds each season in search of pasture. Its social order was divided into pastoral groups, each led by a *tshelniku*, or "chief shepherd."[17] All land and livestock were held in common, and the tshelniku had wide authority to look after the group's welfare. He alone directed the timing of the group's seasonal movements, conducted its internal affairs, and negotiated with outsiders. He controlled the group's economic life by making decisions regarding when to cut timber, hunt, and slaughter livestock. To protect the group from attack and to enforce his decisions, the tshelniku surrounded himself with a group of warrior companions who carried out his orders. In these three elements of the first pastoralists—land owned in common, a powerful chief, and a group of companion warriors to protect the group—"we see the seeds of the constitutional monarchy that was the mark of the later Macedonian state."[18]

Another important legacy of Macedonia's pastoral past was the absence of the institution of slavery. Unlike the Greeks, whose societies rested upon a substratum of slave labor and whose wealthy households might contain as many as fifty slaves, slavery as a formal institution did not exist in Macedonia. The population did include serfs, whose labor could be commandeered, and under Philip it is likely that some slaves, criminals, and prisoners were forced to work in the mines. For the most part, however, Macedonian peasants and shepherds tilled their own fields and herded their own animals with their own hands and energy. Women cooked the meals, tended the children, and made the family's clothes. When Alexander the Great entered the Persian capital as its conqueror, he was dressed in simple homespun clothes that his sister had fashioned for him. There was no royal household to attend the Macedonian king; his wife and relatives performed all the chores of daily life. For most of the king's subjects, Macedonia was a relatively egalitarian society in which all people enjoyed the same basic rights.

Perhaps it was this sense of all subjects being part of the same society and the same people, without slaves, that made Macedonian cities and towns relatively peaceful places to live. The political purges, executions, factionalism, expropriations of property, and forced exile that so often characterized the political life of the cities of the "democracies" of the Greek states are noticeably absent from Macedonian history. Roman historian Quintus Curtius Rufus says as much when he tells us, "The Macedones were indeed accustomed to the rule of a king, but they lived in a greater semblance of liberty than any other who were subject to a king."[19] He might well have added that Macedonian subjects enjoyed greater liberty and freedom from fear than could be found in most other Greek city-states.

Without a substructure of slaves or foreign peoples living in Macedonian cities or on its farms, Macedonians came to think of themselves as one people, *Macedones*. This sense of belonging to the same societal group probably had its origins in the pastoral past when, indeed, everyone was part of the same pastoral group, everything was held in common, everyone contributed by working the land or tending animals, and everyone shared in the life and defense of the tribe. Occasionally, some new person would be added to the tribe by marriage or other circumstance, in which case he or she would be considered and become a Macedone. Over time the Macedonians came to live and work in cities and towns as well as tending their herds in the mountain pastures. Regardless of where they lived or how they earned their living, the people of Macedonia accepted the rule of a central royal house and its king and considered themselves one people.

Thus it was that the Macedonians were the first Europeans to develop a sense of national identity, defined as being members of a territorial state. To be a Macedon came to mean being anyone or any people who lived within the territory over which the king as the executive agent of the state exercised direct authority.[20] As Macedonia expanded over the years, and especially under Philip, each newly acquired territory was regarded as being part of Macedonia itself and its people regarded as Macedonians. In modern legal parlance, Macedonian "citizenship" was defined by the doctrine of *jus territoriale* and not jus sanguinis (right of blood, or having an ancestor who is a citizen).

The Macedonian idea of who constituted a Macedone was quite different from the idea of citizenship common in the Greek states. The Greek states were "citizen states"; that is, their fully enfranchised persons, whether they resided in Attica or in Athenian possessions overseas, were regarded as citizens of their home state, Athens. Whenever a Greek state conquered another territory, the Greeks planted some citizen-landholders (*kleroukhoi*) on the land but did not regard the conquered peoples as citizens. Citizenship was limited to residents of the city-state, and there was no way to accommodate large numbers of new inhabitants to full participation in the polity.

The Macedonian practice of extending the status of king's subject to newly conquered peoples made it possible to establish the first national territorial state in Europe. When new peoples were absorbed into the realm, the full rights of all Macedones were extended to them. The towns and tribes were mostly left to govern themselves in their own way, often retaining their own kings or assemblies. Conquered peoples were permitted to practice their own religions, laws, and customs; to speak their own languages; and to raise their own taxes. Even the military forces of local chieftains were permitted to remain, but they were sometimes retrained in the Macedonian army's new weapons and doctrines and were redefined as the king's militia. Particularly powerful and talented local barons and warriors were invited to Pella, where they became Companions of the king. Parmenio, Philip's most talented and trusted general and a Pelagonian by birth, was one of these men.[21] This said, the king of Macedonia, unhindered by local representatives, remained the ultimate authority on all matters. One-tenth of all produce or its cash equivalent was paid annually to the state, and the Macedonians demanded that segments of the population serve as soldiers or laborers.

Thinking of Macedonia proper and its acquired territories as one national unit permitted Philip to develop his kingdom along national lines. To this end, he established new cities, transplanted populations to live in them, drained swamps, constructed roads, fortified key passes through mountains, and even drew military units from specific geographical areas of the kingdom, permitting them to retain their local designations.[22] As Alexander reminded his troops, "He [Philip] brought you down from the mountains to the plains, making you a match in battle for the neighboring barbarians, trusting for your salvation no longer in the natural strength of places so much as in your courage. He made you dwellers in cities and graced your lives with good laws and customs."[23] The effect of Philip's policy was to bring under his command manpower and economic resources greater than those of any Greek state or alliance of states. Philip of Macedonia created the first nation-state in the West.

EXTERNAL THREATS

Napoleon Bonaparte is supposed to have remarked that "a nation's geography was its destiny." This observation was certainly true in Macedonia's case.

Geography rendered Macedonia particularly vulnerable to foreign invasion. Macedonia's invaders in the half century before Philip became king include Illyrians, Molossians (of Epirus), Paeonians, Thracians, Dardanians, Triballians, Chalcidians, Athenians, Thebans, Thessalians, Phokians, Spartans, and Corinthians. From 510 to 479 BCE, Persia invaded Macedonia twice and reduced the kingdom to a vassal state for more than thirty years. Later, Athens established colonies on the Macedonian coast of the Thermaic Gulf and forced the king to accept "Greeks resident in the kingdom," a euphemism for Greek troops garrisoned on Macedonian soil.[24] During the dynastic crisis following the assassination of Alexandros II, Macedonia was invaded by Athens. Thebes invaded the country twice in the year 367 BCE. It was Macedonia's unhappy lot to be surrounded by hostile forces that had relatively easy geographic access to the country and took frequent advantage of it.

Macedonia's coast was vulnerable to sea invasion along the Thermaic Gulf, a vulnerability Athens exploited all too often. On land, concentric rings of mountains encircled Lower Macedonia. The mountain passes served as routes through which invaders attacked the country. Controlling the strategic passes of each concentric ring of mountains was of paramount importance for Macedonia's security. The passes and mountains of the innermost defensive ring ran through Macedonia's four Upper Cantons—Elimea, Orestes, Lyncus, and Pelagonia—which served as buffers between Macedonia proper and Illyria. The peoples of these cantons were Greek-speaking Macedonians who continued to live the old transhumant pastoral life. As in the Macedonia of old, the people were divided into pastoral groups, each of which was governed by its own royal house or aristocracy supported by militia armies. The cantons' chiefs (or "kings") feared central Macedonian rule. Sometimes they forged alliances with the Illyrian, Paeonian, and Thracian tribes against the regime in Pella, permitting the invaders to traverse their lands on the way to Macedonia's interior. In some cases, the cantons even joined the fighting in return for a share of the loot or tribute. When Philip came to power, Pella's control over the Upper Cantons, where it existed at all, was tenuous. The weak central government, the uncertain allegiance of the Upper Cantons, the country's geographic vulnerability, and the constant threat of invasion combined to undermine any sense that Macedonia could be considered an independent and defensible political unit.

Among the most powerful, troublesome, and dangerous of Macedonia's enemies to the northwest were the Illyrians, a coalition of tribes that came together under the leadership of a single chief and formed powerful armies with which to attack their neighbors. A constant threat to the Upper Cantons, in 392 BCE, the Illyrians occupied them and then attacked and occupied parts of Lower Macedonia. They forced the Macedonian king, Amyntas III, from his throne and replaced him with their own cat's-paw. In return for his promises of tribute, Amyntas was able to regain his position. In 382 BCE, the year of Philip's birth, the Illyrians attacked again, defeated the Macedonian army, ravaged the kingdom, and withdrew after receiving promises of tribute. For nearly thirty years before Philip came to power, the Illyrians' ruler was a formidable chief named Bardylis, who led the raids against Macedonia and caused most of the trouble during this period. In 359 BCE, Bardylis attacked Macedonia again, this time annihilating its army and killing Philip's brother King Perdiccas III. Bardylis then occupied the Upper Cantons and was preparing for a larger invasion of Macedonia when Philip came to the throne.[25]

To the north the Paeonians occupied the wide lowland plain of the middle Axius River. They were not Greek-speaking people, but, just as the Thracians, were of Indo-Aryan stock. A fierce and warlike people, the Paeonians lived in tribes, each ruled by their own monarchy or royal house. Sometime around 550 BCE they expanded southward, drove the Macedonians back from the lowland plains, occupied the basin of the Strymon River, and later attacked Pella itself. They pressed eastward into Thrace as far as Perinthus (the Propontus in antiquity) on the Sea of Marmara. The Persian invasion of 510 BCE forced the Paeonians back beyond the Strymon River. When the Macedonians became vassals of the Persians, they drove the Paeonians from the lowland Macedonian plain and liberated Pella. For thirty years Macedonia's status as a Persian vassal was useful in deterring further Paeonian attacks. After the Greeks defeated the Persians at the battle of Plataea in 479 BCE, the Macedonian king, Alexandros I, switched sides, drove north and east, and removed the Paeonian threat.[26]

The Paeonian homeland sat astride the invasion route to Macedonia, and Paeonia was itself vulnerable to attack by the Dardanians and Thracian tribes seeking access to the route. No Macedonian king could consider the northern frontier safe as long as Paeonia was not subject to Macedonian control.[27] When Philip returned from Thebes, his brother assigned him to raise troops and guard the invasion route from Paeonia to Macedonia, sufficient evidence of the seriousness with which Macedonian kings regarded the Paeonian threat.

The most formidable and numerous of the Balkan peoples were the Thracians, who occupied the area eastward beyond the Nestus River and south of the Danube to the Black Sea. The Thracians had not forsaken their Indo-European heritage and remained a nation of fierce warriors living in fortified villages on hilltops. These tribes seemed to enjoy fighting one another year after year rather than forming a coherent nation and expanding westward. The Thracian cavalry was legendary for its numbers and combat power, and Philip adopted its wedge-shaped formation for his own cavalry's use. The lack of a central political organization and the frequent tribal wars prevented Thrace from becoming the major regional power it could have easily been given its resources. One consequence was that Thracian armies launched only one attempt to invade Macedonia between 452 and 359 BCE.[28] Thrace's strategic importance to Macedonian security interests was that it blocked Macedonia's attempt to expand eastward beyond the Nestus River and, in Philip's time, to gain a strategic advantage over Athens and its client states on the Sea of Marmara. Thrace presented no problem to Philip in his early days. From time to time, however, some high king would organize a larger coalition and create mischief for the Greeks. Ultimately, however, Philip would have to reduce Thrace by force if he was going to bring Athens to heel.

Thessaly was Macedonia's powerful neighbor to the south and the gate for Greek armies moving north into Macedonia. Thessaly was a wealthy and politically advanced kingdom similar to other Greek states in that it comprised a loosely organized union of independent city-states ruled by aristocracies. The country had large fertile plains from which to draw its food and was known for its fine horses. Thessaly also had good harbors on the Gulf of Pagasae and enjoyed a vigorous and profitable trade with Greece. Like Macedonia, the country was located on the coastal route between Athens and the coast of Asia Minor. Whenever Thebes intervened in Macedonia, its armies came through Thessaly. While the warlike tribes that occupied the mountains between Thessaly and Macedonia often caused problems for both countries, their presence in the highlands and passes served as an important buffer, reducing friction between the two countries along the shared frontier.

In addition to the obvious security concerns that Thessaly's geography presented to Macedonian kings, some of its city-states possessed powerful military forces that could be turned against Macedonia. In the 370s BCE, Jason of Pherae possessed an army of eight thousand cavalry and twenty thousand heavy infantry, most of whom were mercenary professionals.[29] Fortunately for Macedonia's security concerns, the other Thessalian states were masters of balance of power politics, often combining and recombining in alliances designed to prevent any one city or coalition from controlling the country and using it as a strategic platform from which to attack Macedonia. Moreover, Thessaly had security concerns of its own, and its strategic orientation was to the south toward Thebes and Athens and the other Greek states and not toward Macedonia to the north.

Of all its Greek enemies, Macedonia most hated or distrusted the coalition states of the Chalcidice region, which shared a common border with Macedonia along the Axius River. Olynthos was the most powerful and important Chalcidian city and led the Chalcidian League, a military alliance composed of thirty-two cities. The league constituted a major military alliance and a serious threat to Macedonia as it was only twenty miles from the Axius River to the outskirts of the Macedonian capital. In 382 BCE the league invaded Macedonia, attacking and capturing most of Macedonia's coastal cities before seizing Pella itself. The Chalcidians removed the king and attempted to install their own client on the throne. The Macedonian king appealed to Sparta, which intervened militarily, forcing the Chalcidians to return the Macedonian cities and permit the king's reinstatement.[30] A simmering hatred and distrust had existed between the two states ever since. In 367 BCE Chalcidice supported Pausanias, a pretender to the Macedonian throne, who attempted to capitalize on the civil war caused by the succession crisis in Macedonia. The Chalcidians backed the wrong horse, however, and Pausanias's efforts came to nothing. They tried again less than a decade later. When two of Philip's half-brothers fled Macedonia after their failed attempt to prevent his taking the throne in 359 BCE, Olynthos foolishly gave them refuge. Philip hardly needed more reason to distrust Chalcidice, especially when Macedonia was already under threat on other fronts.

Athens was a major menace to Macedonian security interests to the northeast and on the coast of the Thermaic Gulf. As the Athenian maritime empire grew in the fifth century, Athens pressed north, seeking to rule the gulf. In 437 BCE Athens established a colony at Amphipolis to control the lower Strymon River and the head of the gulf itself in an effort to dominate the maritime trade. Equally important was Athens' interest in securing access to the area's forests as its supplies of fir, pine, and pitch were vital to maintaining its powerful navy. Athens was also interested in seizing the large silver, iron, and gold mines located in the Strymon basin. The area was also important for fisheries and grain production in addition to accessing the hinterland's exports. Athenian economic interests extended to attempting to command the Macedonian coast, and in 434 BCE Athens established Methone, a trading colony on Macedonian territory.

The linchpin of Athens' ability to project power in the northern Thermaic Gulf was its alliance and relations with Chalcidice. Influencing Chalcidian policy was vital to keeping open the route through Thrace and to the cities along the Hellespont (modern Dardanelles) for trade and defense. In Macedonian eyes, an alliance between these strong regional powers constituted a serious national security threat to Macedonia itself. In 362 BCE Athens staged from the Chalcidian port of Potidea and attacked Macedonia, seizing Pydna and recapturing Methone. While the Macedonian king, Perdiccas III, countered by establishing a garrison in Amphipolis, Athenian control of Methone and Pydna allowed it to cut off Macedonia's primary route of ground communications to the south as well as interrupt its seaborne commerce. Athens also encouraged the Illyrian and northern tribes to cause mischief on the Macedonian frontier and interfered in Macedonia's dynastic quarrels whenever the opportunity arose. In 359 BCE, an Athenian army landed at Methone in support of Philip's half-brother, who challenged Philip for the Macedonian throne.[31]

Macedonia's geography, domestic politics, and economic wealth combined to make the country a tempting target for its numerous adversaries' national ambitions. Invasions, interference in domestic quarrels, attempts to install rival kings, the conquest and occupation of Macedonian cities, and frequent wars with powerful enemies had been Macedonia's curse for more than two centuries before Philip ascended the throne. An important element contributing to Macedonia's disadvantage in dealing with external threats was the primitive nature of the country's political institutions, including its military forces. Most important in this regard was the weakness of the Macedonian state and the monarchy itself.

THE MACEDONIAN STATE

The king and the Assembly of Macedones were the only official organs of Macedonian state government. The Macedonian monarchy's roots reached back to Homeric times. The original kings from Argos brought with them a Homeric view of kingship and imposed it upon the native peoples. Over time, however, this concept was modified with elements incorporated from Macedonia's own pastoral past, when the original society of pastoral companies was ruled by the chief shepherd, or tshelniku, whose position seems to have been largely confined to members of the same family and confirmed occasionally by the election of the warriors around him. The powers that the Macedonian king derived from both the Homeric and the pastoral traditions were extensive although not absolute.

The Homeric idea that the king was descended from the gods and embodied their favor was central to the Macedonian king's legitimacy. This embodiment was seen to reside in the physical person of the king, who passed it on to his son. Thus, Macedonian kings were always chosen from within the same bloodline if not from the same immediate family. By Philip's time, the Teminid dynasty had ruled the country for more than three centuries, and Philip himself was a direct heir. In some instances, the infant son of the previous king was anointed while a regent ruled until the child was old enough to assume his rightful position. For a Macedonian king to be legitimate, however, the Assembly of Macedones met and had to approve his appointment by formal election, a practice rooted in the pastoral past when the warriors around the chief shepherd were required to consent to a new chief. The Macedonian king's central obligation, as that of the ancient tshelniku, was to attend to his peoples' religious and material welfare.

As in the old pastoral system when the goods of the company were held in common, the Macedonian king claimed all the material goods of the country as his own. In practice, he disposed of all lands and all products of the land, mines, and stands of timber for shipbuilding that were not already taken with the obligation to use them for the good of his people. Any "spear-won" land outside the country proper also fell to his ownership and might be used as he saw fit. This arrangement made Philip the wealthiest king in all Greece, and he had few limits on how to use his wealth, certainly none as bothersome as those placed upon the rulers of the Greek states. The king awarded fiefs to important Companions and allies and gave grants of land to captured populations that were resettled in Macedonia. In other cases, he moved Macedonians to conquered lands, turning once foreign lands and cities into Macedonian territories. Philip used the income from taxes, custom duties, the sale of horses, and the output of the gold and silver mines to pay his army well, so much so that military service became a full-time profession at which a man could earn a proper living. The remuneration transformed the former militia force into a professional army. Philip paid for his infantry's equipment but required the cavalry to purchase horses, often from his own stud farms. Philip's great wealth enabled him to maintain large numbers of men and animals under arms year round, something no other Greek state could afford to do.

For all his power, however, Philip was by no means an absolute monarch, and his authority was limited by the Macedones who met in assembly to discuss important matters and advise the king.[32] The Assembly of Makedones was the embodiment of the Macedonian people and comprised serving soldiers and recent veterans of the king's army, or what Aristotle called the "citizens in arms." The assembly's military composition reveals its origins in the group of professional warriors that surrounded the tshelniku and protected the people during pastoral times. The king and his warriors in the assembly had created the Macedonian state, and as the only formal organs of state government, they remained responsible for protecting it.

The egalitarian atmosphere that usually attends a gathering of warriors was evident in the assembly's meetings. Aristotle noted that the assembly met "under arms"; that is, its members were in full military kit and had their weapons handy. Each Macedon was entitled to speak, and the Macedonians prided themselves on what Curtius called their "equal rights of speech." If a speaker addressed the king, he removed his helmet as a sign of respect and spoke freely, without fear. The king had only his single vote in a debate, the same as any other Macedon. While all spoke Greek, it was Philip's habit to use the Macedonian dialect during these meetings, yet another sign of military camaraderie and informality. The assembly's members were soldiers, comrades in arms, equals who bore the same risks and hardships in defending and protecting their people. One's standing therein was assigned not by birth or wealth but by one's demonstrated courage on the battlefield. It was with his comrades' help and advice that Philip governed Macedon.

The assembly did not sit permanently or even regularly, as in other Greek states, but was convened by the king, or by his representative if the king was on campaign, whenever important issues had to be discussed and decided.[33] These concerns included relations with other states, treaties, requests made by foreign governments, religious matters, payments of debts, and reports regarding finances. As already mentioned, the assembly was responsible for electing a new king and, if necessary, choosing a guardian for him. The assembly also heard trials in cases of treason and could sentence a person to death. Sometimes the sentence was carried out on the spot, with the assembly's members themselves throwing their javelins and spears.

Governing the Macedonian state and fighting its wars required more than an assembly of warriors that met only when important issues arose, however. To govern effectively, the king needed advice and expertise on a more regular basis. For this guidance, he turned to his Companions. The Companions were a group of the king's most trusted advisers, and he relied on their frank counsel and skills. The institution had its earliest roots in Homeric times when Achilles was said to have had his most trusted companions around him. It was also rooted in the Macedonian pastoral past when a small group of advisers (*parea*) was selected among the warriors and advised the tshelniku in carrying out the affairs of the group.[34] Under Philip were three types of Companions: the *hetairoi* (companions); the *philoi* (friends); and the *hegemones* (military commanders), particularly the unit commanders of the field army. The Companions not only comprised military men but also those who Philip thought important to have around him: Critobulus, the physician who treated Philip's eye at Methone; Eumenes of Cardia, the chief of Philip's intelligence service; and Polyeidos, the Thessalian engineer who directed Philip's military engineering department and was probably the inventor of the torsion catapult.[35] When Philip incorporated the Upper Cantons into Macedonia proper, he disbanded their local aristocracies but made their most important nobles Companions. Parmenio, a chief of the Pelagones, was one of these. Other Companions included a number of renowned mercenary officers who joined Philip, such as Demaratus of Corinth and Erigyius and Laemedon, two brothers from Mytilene.

Theopompus tells us that "there were not more than eight hundred Companions," and that number has been generally accepted as correct. When at war, the Companions provided the army's elite cavalry. But they could only have done so in the early years of Philip's reign when his cavalry force was about the same size as the Companions' group. Later, as his cavalry grew in numbers, it was unlikely that, in the strict sense, all his cavalrymen were Companions for they could not all be advisers to the king. Having hundreds of advisers is clearly not practical. Alexander's Companions numbered no more than 150 men. This difference suggests that a distinction arose between those Companions who were the king's closest advisers and the cavalrymen who were awarded the honorific of Companion Cavalry but who did not serve as actual advisers to the king.[36]

Although the Companions were an important part of the government, they had no constitutional or formal status. Without any restrictions, the king chose whom he thought could best serve him in time of war or in administering the state. The position did not pass from father to son, and the king's favor—and, with it, a man's status as a Companion—could be withdrawn at any time. While Philip provided his most important Companions with estates, there had never been a feudal landed nobility in Macedonia, even in pastoral times. The Companions did not constitute a landed feudal class such as that found in medieval Europe. They had no institutional, property, or independent power base from which to resist the king, and they did not command any element of the polity, such as militia troops or independent cavalry units raised by their own efforts.[37] They were a military nobility, and on the battlefield the Companions were Philip's best combat commanders, his elite cavalry, and his bodyguards, whom he relied on for his life.

In most important respects Macedonia was a military state. Its army was larger than any in Greece, and its complexity approached that of a modern military force. The country's far-flung and economically diverse conditions required a competent administration to function effectively and to provide the army with the necessary resources to carry out Philip's campaigns. The army also demanded capable combat leaders and generals to fight the battles and win the wars. It was a mark of Philip's genius that he recognized the need to train a cadre of qualified leaders to serve the army and the state. Philip turned to a traditional Macedonian institution, the Royal Page School, to identify, train, and develop new leaders.

The Royal Page School had existed since perhaps from as early as the fifth century BCE and certainly from the time of Archelaus (413–399 BCE).[38] In earlier times it had primarily educated the royal princes and, perhaps, the sons of allied tribal chiefs and Macedonian nobles. The school still served these purposes under Philip but was expanded to become the main educational and military training school for the sons of Philip's Companions and of other important friends and foreign allied nobles.

The school was located in Pella and served as the Macedonian West Point. It was a boarding school and required completion of a four-year-long curriculum of study and training for graduation. The cadets entered at the age of fourteen; moved through the curriculum in class years, just as in modern military schools; and finally graduated at age eighteen. Each class comprised about fifty students, so that some two hundred young men were enrolled at any one time.[39] The usual Greek curriculum was taught, and we might suspect some emphasis was placed on reading the many treatises of Greek military history that had appeared since the end of the Peloponnesian wars. The royal princes, including Alexander, all attended the school. Part of their education was also learning to associate with the sons of the other Companions who, when their time came, would be their own Companions while in the service of the country. Alexander later took several of his boyhood friends, with whom he had studied under Aristotle, as Companions; the most notable of whom was Ptolemy.

Besides the formal liberal Greek education, the students were put through rigorous military training. Rough living, fasting, endurance training, hunting wild animals with spears, riding, and other experiences central to Macedonian military training were required of all cadets, including the royal princes. Senior cadets were permitted access to the king. They served as guards when he slept, were allowed to sit at his table, and looked after his horses. Discipline was strict, and breaches were punished by caning, which the king himself often administered. It was said that Philip once beat a student to death for failing to carry out a military order.[40] The older cadets accompanied the king on campaign, where some of them fell in battle protecting their sovereign. If we are to believe Justin, some of Philip's "many sons" had been killed in battle this way. The Royal Page School was the training ground for Macedonia's future combat officers and administrators, and Aristotle was correct when he called it "a school for generals."

Few of Philip's accomplishments are understandable, however, apart from his tremendous accomplishments in the administration of his kingdom. Philip inherited a weak and geographically divided country with no central coherence or administration worthy of the name. By Greek standards of the day, its society was primitive, its standard of living low, its people poor, and the potential of its substantial economic resources either unrealized or exploited by others. From an administrative perspective, no central authority was sufficiently powerful to effectively govern the state, exploit its resources, and protect its territorial integrity. These circumstances changed under Philip, who transformed Macedonia into a large, wealthy, and well-managed state that remained a major economic and political force in Greece and the Eastern Mediterranean until the Romans dismantled it after the battle of Pydna in 168 BCE.[41]

Philip began reorganizing the Macedonian state almost immediately after he had defeated the Illyrians in 358 BCE and thereby reduced the most immediate threat of invasion. Philip restructured the frontier defenses by occupying the cantons of Upper Macedonia, abolishing their monarchies, and amalgamating their territories into the Macedonian state. He constructed fortifications to guard the important mountain passes, and in some places he forced the tribal peoples out of the mountains and resettled them in defensible settlements on the high mountain plains. Populations of Macedonians were transplanted and settled among them to teach agriculture and retrain their militias for self-defense along Macedonian military lines.[42]

In the northwestern areas facing the Illyrians, Philip established three new cities in strategic places to interrupt the invasion routes through the mountain passes. In the north, near Monastir, Philip established a new city that guarded the Paeonians' invasion routes and the approaches to the Iron Gates of the Axius River. Philip established this new city by removing the area's entire population and replacing it with Macedonians. In the northeast he created a new city called Philippopolis (modern Plovdiv) to control the routes of advance from Thrace to the Axius valley. According to Justin, Philip located cities such as these "on the very frontiers to face his enemies." Philip continued the same practices throughout his reign, founding "strong cities at key points that made it impossible for them to commit any further outrages."[43]

Philip took a tribal state and transformed it into a true territorial state for the first time in European history. To accomplish this feat, Philip imposed a policy of moving both Macedonian and captured populations to locations that provided the best defense and economic benefit for the state. This strategy met some resistance and, perhaps, even occasional violence. But Philip was involved in what we would today call nation building, and both disruption and resistance were to be expected. Justin explains how Philip went about transporting populations:

> In returning to his kingdom he transferred at his own pleasure populations and cities in accordance with his own idea of what places should be occupied or abandoned, even as shepherds move their flocks now to winter pastures and now to summer pastures. . . . He placed some populations on the very frontiers to face his enemies. Others he planted at the furthest limits of the kingdom. Certain populations that had been captured in war he divided and sent to supplement the inhabitants of his cities. And it was by these means that he created a single kingdom and a single people out of many tribes and races.[44]

In some cases the process involved transferring Macedonian populations to other cities to create "cities of Macedones." Sometimes half the population of a Macedonian city would be sent elsewhere to leaven a new site's population. Lower Macedonians were also sent to Upper Macedonia to create new cities and teach the former pastoralists law, order, and military training. "Some," as Justin tells us, "whom he had taken as prisoners of war, he distributed among certain cities to fill up the number of inhabitants."[45] We hear in one case of ten thousand Sarnousii (an Illyrian tribe) taken from their home and "led off to Macedonia." In Philip's Scythian campaign twenty thousand women and children captured in the war were marched off and resettled in Macedonian towns and cities.[46] Once, Philip had all the "thieves, informers, and false witnesses" in Macedonia, some two thousand of them, sent to a new town in Thrace to settle the area. He named the town *Poneropolis* (Rogue Town or Crooksville).[47]

Philip seems to have been the first Western ruler to recognize the need to tie the nation's economic and military infrastructure together with a series of national roads. Surely he was the first ruler in Greece to do so. Using corvée and serf labor, Philip constructed a number of all-weather roads to stitch the nation together. The army also worked on the construction projects, providing the critical building skills and engineering required.[48] Philip originally emphasized constructing military roads leading from the interior, up through the mountains, and into towns and forts that were key defenses of the mountain passes through which past invaders had so often traveled. Some of these roads led beyond Macedonia's own frontiers, no doubt as signals to the far tribes of Macedonia's intention to invade their homelands if attacked. In addition to military roads were those constructed for economic reasons. Major roads ran from Macedonia's ports to the capital, while others connected the mines and forests to important urban centers as well as the ports. Some of these roads were ten meters wide.

Philip also improved the country's agricultural base by draining swamps and building dikes to control the annual flooding of the lower plain, increasing the arable land available to farmers. In the highlands, he converted some of the pastureland to agricultural land, drawing the population out of the hills and sending Macedonian farmers to teach the pastoralists how to farm. He built towns and forts for them to live in, and he sent officers to train and equip them as militia so they could act as an early warning system against any surprise attack by tribal invaders.[49] He enlarged the city of *Crenides* (Gold

Town) and renamed it Philippi. He created new fiefs in spear-won lands, and as he did later in Olynthos, he razed the city and distributed its territory to Macedonians to settle there. Macedonian towns had been fortified since time immemorial. Philip embarked on a program to improve the old walls and forts, especially those nearest the coast and along the Thracian border, an area historically subject to attacks by Paeonians and Thracians. All new towns were also fortified.

Philip's effort to create an integrated national infrastructure was intended to accomplish more than military efficiency and economic integration. Philip was attempting to create a truly coherent national state in which all his subjects thought of themselves as one Macedonian people instead of being divided into scores of racial, ethnic, and tribal groups whose loyalty and effort extended no further than the group's self-defined identities. Moreover, as the Macedonian state extended its control to areas beyond its traditional geographic boundaries, Philip knew that Macedonia did not possess the resources to sustain the large army of occupation that would be required to maintain a harsh imperial rule. Instead, Philip ruled with a lighter hand than, say, the Persians would have in order to foster a realm in which coexistence, cooperation, and diversity were emphasized rather than domination. Philip's model of governance was somewhat similar to that later employed by Rome, but it was Philip who first attempted it in the West.

Creating a nation in which diverse peoples come to think of themselves as one people required far more than a coherent economic and administrative infrastructure. To convince different peoples that they were equals was in many ways more a psychological task than a physical one. Philip was building a nation of loyal subjects, not captives held against their will. To this end, all of Philip's subjects were free, even those taken in war and resettled in new cities. The captives and former slaves were transformed into yeomen who were free to work the land, fish the waters, herd cattle or sheep, or work in the forests and mines. Whenever Philip built a new city for resettlement, he made sure it had land to farm or mines to provide work. As previously mentioned, unlike the Greek city-states, Philip's Macedonia did not rely on a substructure of slave labor, and the new transplants were incorporated as free persons in the cities and villages.[50] For many of those who were captured in war or who watched their own lands absorbed by the expanding Macedonian state, their lives were often better and freer in a country that afforded them more food and economic opportunity.

One aspect of this increased economic opportunity was the ability of newcomers and transplants to serve in the Macedonian army. Each town and city raised its own militia for its defense and for maintaining law and order. These militia units were trained in Macedonian equipment and tactics, provided the strategic manpower reserve for the King's Field Army, and could be "called to the colors" if needed. Those militia soldiers who proved themselves attuned to military life were given the opportunity to join the King's Field Army and make a profession of military service. Philip may even have introduced a state system of education, at least for Macedonia proper and the Upper Cantons, that centered on infantry training for the young men in the cities and towns who might then qualify as members of the King's Field Army. It may have involved the creation of local "page schools" from which the best soldiers could then go on and serve as infantry, just as the graduates of the Royal Page School went into the cavalry.[51] Military service, as in modern times in nations such as Israel and Turkey, became a means of national identification for the various peoples within the country.[52]

Some of the peoples incorporated into the Macedonian state had specialized ways of fighting. The Thracian *peltasts* (light javelin infantry), Thessalian cavalry, Scythian horse archers, and Paeonian javelineers all provided specialized combat units for the King's Field Army. Then, as now, military service was an important avenue for diverse groups to raise their status in society and to demonstrate their loyalty to the nation-state. Philip used this dynamic to great advantage in acculturating many different peoples into an amalgam with a shared national identity.

Philip used the Greek language as another mechanism of national integration. The official language of the Macedonian state and its extended possessions was Greek, so many of the native peoples and tribes came under the Hellenic influence of Greek as the primary language of commerce and politics. One supposes that the specialized military units also had to learn Greek and that all military commands were given in Greek. For some of the more remote Balkan mountain peoples, Philip's adoption of Greek as the state's official language provided the first extended opportunity for exposing them to Greek values and culture. In this limited way, Philip deliberately fostered Hellenism in the hope that it would lead to increased social integration.

The oligarchies, aristocracies, tribal chiefs, and kings who ruled the tribes and lands that were now incorporated into Macedonia also had to be integrated into the nation-state. Philip recognized this problem from the beginning. Whenever he was forced to fight them, he made it a practice to kill as many of the leaders and aristocrats in battle as possible. Even with the battle won, he frequently ordered his cavalry to pursue and kill the enemy leadership. Philip understood that the more who fell on the battlefield, the fewer would be left to accommodate and gain their loyalty to the new order. Once the battle was over, Philip often took any surviving defeated chiefs and important nobles of conquered peoples into his court as Companions. This position awarded them an even greater status than they had previously possessed and afforded them an opportunity to demonstrate their loyalty to their king. It also allowed Philip to keep a close eye on them. Powerful Macedonian noblemen were also made Companions or given other respected positions at court for the same reasons. Philip aimed at reorienting their concerns and loyalties away from their regions, towns, or tribes and toward the nation-state.[53]

Philip's creation of the first competent corps of Macedonian infantry was not only an achievement of military genius but also an experiment in social engineering. Philip raised the infantry's status by calling them *pezhetairoi*, or "Foot Companions." The infantry was by far the largest of the combat arms, and men were drawn to the national standard from all walks of life, making it a truly national and democratic institution. As long as the infantry loved Philip, there was little even the most disgruntled group of noblemen might consider in attempting to resist the will of the king.

Thus it was that Philip transformed the power of the traditional Macedonian monarchy by changing the nature of social relationships of the old Macedonian society and by reorienting them away from tribal and local concerns and toward new *national* aspirations.[54] Proof of Philip's success at achieving a high level of national integration and identity in Macedonia can be inferred from the fact that although Philip's infantry and cavalry units were raised on a regional or territorial basis, they regarded themselves as national forces composing the King's Field Army. That Philip was able to instill a sense of national identity in such a diverse group of peoples in so short a time—or, indeed, to accomplish it at all—is testimony to his genius.

PHILIP'S STRATEGY

Philip was surely a great general. Seen in the larger context, however, it is clear that Philip was an equally great strategist. The ability to conduct war and win battles falls in the realm of the operational and tactical arts. Deciding whether to fight, when and where to fight, and in what political context and for what national goals to fight is the concern of the strategist and ought not be confused with those of the tactician. Strategy involves setting national goals and employing the appropriate means or combination thereof at any given time to achieve them. In this context, waging war is but one means among many available to achieve a nation's goals. Warfare is one instrument of national policy to be conceived and pursued only as a means to larger ends. This belief is the essence of Carl von Clausewitz's famous dictum that "war is the continuation of policy by other means."

The strategist of Philip's day might have implemented other means in the service of national goals: diplomacy, economic influence and pressure, intelligence gathering, bribery, fifth columns to undermine an adversary's political support within his own state, propaganda, assassination, and the threat or overt use of force. Whatever means were employed, however, they had to be used within the existing political context, for in the end strategy is about achieving national objectives as defined by political authorities. Such objectives are, therefore, ultimately political goals and have meaning within some identifiable political context. Philip was a supreme strategist in that he understood the place of war in policy, and he knew its limits. Even to a Homeric and Greek warrior such as Philip, the search for individual glory and heroism had no place in his strategic thinking. This position is in contrast to that of his son Alexander, who "seems to have been possessed of some sort of restless, almost irrational desire for glory unchecked by a larger political sense," that is, by strategic calculation or vision.[55]

Philip's emphasis on strategy is evident in his practice of using military force as little as possible when dealing with the Greek states; instead, he preferred to obtain his ends through diplomacy, threat, bribery, or any other means necessary. Diodorus tells us in this regard that

> he [Philip] is known to fame as one who with but the slenderest resources to support his claim to the throne won for himself the greatest empire in the Greek world, while the growth of his position was not due so much to his prowess in arms as to his adroitness and cordiality in diplomacy. Philip himself is said to have been prouder of his grasp of strategy and his diplomatic successes than of his valor in actual battle.[56]

This willingness to use force sparingly is one of Philip's most unusual traits as a strategist, especially since he possessed the largest and most effective army in Greece.[57]

The open debates, factionalism, and crippled executives characteristic of the politics of the Greek states gave Philip an important advantage when formulating and executing national defense strategy. Philip had the benefit of combining all government decisions in his person so that, as Demosthenes remarked, he was "master of all things public and secret, general, ruler, and treasurer all in one."[58] Philip also surrounded himself with excellent advisers, and his senior generals were first-rate combat commanders. After Philip, Antipater and Parmenio were probably the two most competent and battle-experienced field commanders in all Greece. They were also intelligent men in their own right. Antipater wrote a history of Philip's Illyrian wars, and Aristotle chose him to be the executor of his will. Parmenio's advice to Alexander to accept the Persian king Darius's offer of half the Persian Empire still stands as sound strategic advice.

This quality of leadership was important. The citizen armies of the Greek states had no professional generals, staffs, or noncommissioned officers, whereas the Macedonian army had a corps of experienced combat unit leaders at all levels of command that paid large dividends on the battlefield. Though the Peloponnesian wars had begun to change Greek military capabilities, the inability of most Greek armies to project and sustain force over prolonged periods and distances meant they were incapable of strategic application. The amateurism of Greek combat armies was compounded by the fact that few politicians or generals in these armies ever thought about strategy. When confronting a first-rate strategic thinker like Philip, the leaders of the Greek states were thoroughly outclassed.

Philip possessed numerous abilities that made his execution of grand strategy successful. He had unusual patience. He understood that not all the objectives of his strategy could be pursued at once and was always willing to defer to changed circumstances provided he could come away with at least some advantage. Philip could have forced the pass at Thermopylae almost anytime after 352 BCE, but he waited more than six years while he attended to other things. Philip never let temporary reverses dissuade him from continuing to pursue his objectives. Defeated in Thessaly in 353 BCE, he withdrew only to attack with more fervor the following year. Philip always kept his eye on the objective and did not permit operational success or failure to distract him from it or to force changes in the larger strategic equation. He could easily have reduced Chalcidice years before he did, but even in the face of provocation, he waited until he had attended to the more pressing threats from Illyria and Athens. Philip was able to set clear priorities in his strategic plan. He always focused on what was most important at any given time and never allowed minor reverses or political irritants to change his mind.[59]

Two of Philip's most useful qualities in executing strategic plans were his manifest preference for political solutions to military ones and his flexibility, which was demonstrated in his willingness to change course politically or militarily when events required.[60] Philip rarely found himself pursuing pointless adventures or trapped into a course of action whose cost exceeded the worth of its goals. When he laid siege to Perinthus and Byzantium in 340 BCE, for example, Philip expected quick success. When the sieges dragged on longer than he thought reasonable and events in Scythia promised greater gains, he broke off the sieges and marched north to attend to other matters. Similarly, he could have reduced Athens to ashes after his victory at Chaeronea, but Athens was too important to Philip's long-range plans. He reached a political accommodation with this most troublesome adversary and did not destroy the city or even punish those Athenian politicians who had vilified him for years. Revenge may be sweet, but in Philip's mind, there were times when other things were more important.

Philip's grand strategy had two aims: to unify the Macedonian state by integrating it socially, politically, and economically into a viable and effective national entity and to make it safe by reducing the military capability of Macedonia's neighboring states to invade the country. Philip also sought to expand Macedonia's control and influence over Thrace and the Balkans for both economic and political reasons and, in the process, create a power complex so strong as to enable him to influence events in Greece proper. Macedonia needed little in the way of resources from Greece. It sought political instead of military hegemony in order to prevent any Greek state or alliance of states from being able to threaten Macedonia's territorial integrity and national security interests.

Philip's grand strategy required different policies as means to his objectives in each zone of strategic interest. In the zone north of the boundary between Thessaly and Macedonia, Philip pursued a course of strong military action intended to intimidate, conquer, destroy, or annex Macedonia's immediate neighbors, including some of the Greek cities and colonies that had been established on Macedonian territory. His treatment of the populations in this zone was often rough and involved razing cities and selling their inhabitants into slavery. The goals of Philip's policies were to create the Macedonian state and secure it from attack, and he was prepared to use harsh measures to accomplish it.[61]

In dealing with the states in Greece proper, Philip employed policies that were very different. Here, he treated its population more leniently and did not annex territory. In Greece he resorted to force in far fewer instances and for the most part inflicted far less damage than he did in the north. This strategy was, of course, deliberate. Philip had no intention of occupying Greece. Instead, he wished to preserve the Greek states as political-military entities and keep them as a buffer against Persian ambitions both in Thrace and, ultimately, in Macedonia itself. Although by no means certain, it is also possible that from an early date Philip thought about a campaign against Persia.[62] If so, then he would have wanted to reserve for later use the military resources of the Greek states, particularly the Athenian navy, which could protect against a Persian counterattack once Philip's armies had landed in Ionia.[63] Philip spared Thebes, Sparta, and Athens when he could have destroyed them. He even intervened on behalf of Phokis to prevent its wholesale destruction by Theban hands at the end of the Fourth Sacred War.

To achieve the objectives of his grand strategic design, Philip needed an instrument of military force that was far different from the armies of the Greek states. Just as the Greek states' pursuit of limited political goals shaped the structure and capabilities of their hoplite armies, so, too, did Philip's strategic goals require a different military structure with greater operational capabilities to achieve them. An analysis of the Macedonian army is the subject of chapter 3. Here it is sufficient to note that Philip's army was very different from the armies of the Greek states. His army was a standing army, not a part-time army; comprised of professional soldiers, not citizen militia; highly trained in maneuver and not, as the hoplite phalanx was, virtually immobile; and made up of multiple combat arms instead of the single arm of infantry. Philip's army was also able to sustain itself for long periods in the field through a capable logistics train, while hoplite armies could sustain themselves for only short periods; to conduct strategic forced marches against armies with no comparable capability; to draw on large reserves of manpower; to employ the first professional siege train in a Greek army; and to confront its adversaries with new weapons, formations, and tactics, all employed in an integrated manner in battle.[64] Philip seems to have been the first general in the West to have had the opportunity to design his own military force and to have done so with clear strategic capabilities and objectives in mind. The objectives he wanted to obtain defined the required operational capabilities of the force structure needed to achieve them. The result was that Philip's army was the only army in Greece that, by itself, was capable of destroying not only the army of any Greek state but also the state as well.

Philip employed this new instrument of force in a manner that F. E. Adcock calls "the strategy of overthrow."[65] The culture of Greek warfare evolved armies capable of achieving only limited objectives that rarely involved the destruction or even long-term occupation of a city or state. Battles might be won or lost, but the states that fought them were relatively immune from wholesale destruction. The Macedonian army under Philip added a new dimension to Greek warfare, with its strategic capability to destroy entire Greek peoples, societies, and states. Philip first demonstrated this ability in his early campaigns against Macedonia's neighboring enemies. Any conflict between the Greek states and Philip now risked the possibility of the former's complete destruction, resulting in a fear that provided Philip with a considerable advantage in his diplomatic dealings with them. It is testimony to Philip's strategic genius that he won his most important victories in Greece through diplomacy, with his having to resort to force only rarely. One reason for his successful diplomatic overtures was that the threat of overwhelming force was always present in the minds of Philip's adversaries.

3 THE MACEDONIAN WAR MACHINE

The Macedonian army was born in crisis, and Philip II invented its structure, weapons, and tactics in a response to crisis. In the decade before Philip became king, Macedonia had suffered two foreign invasions, two hostage takings, the assassination of its king, and a succession crisis bordering on civil war. In 359 BCE, the Illyrians invaded Macedonia again. King Perdiccas III took the field against them with an army that could not have numbered more than six thousand infantry and, perhaps, only two hundred cavalry. The result was disasterous. The Illyrians crushed the Macedonians, killing some four thousand troops and Perdiccas as well. When Philip assumed power that year, for all practical purposes the Macedonian army had ceased to exist.

The Macedonian army had never been much of a fighting force, at least not since it had joined and fought with the Persians at Plataea (479 BCE) before switching sides and supporting the victorious Greek coalition that defeated the Persians. Unlike the Greek states, which had developed excellent hoplite infantry, Macedonia had no tradition of infantry combat. Macedonian infantry troops were little more than untrained peasants hastily assembled for the occasion and armed mostly with farm implements and work tools. The most important combat arm of Macedonian armies was the cavalry, comprising the nobility, who provided their own mounts and equipment. Early Macedonian cavalrymen fought as individual combatants and not in integrated combat units. Alexander II, Philip's oldest brother, seems to have made some tentative efforts to create infantry units that were armed and trained similarly to the hoplites of the Greek states. Like Philip, he may have called these units pezhetairoi to give them a measure of the prestige attendant to the elite cavalry Companions.[1] Alexander's reforms did not amount to much, and it is unlikely that the Macedonian hoplites, which served mostly as the king's guard on the battlefield, numbered more than a few hundred troops. Most were probably killed along with their king in the battle against the Illyrians, leaving Macedonia with its traditional untrained peasants for its infantry.

THE MACEDONIAN PHALANX

In 359 BCE, Macedonia needed an army and needed one quickly. The Illyrians were preparing for another invasion, this time aimed at occupying the entire country. The Paeonians had begun to assemble their armies along the Axius River for an attack on the lowland plains. Athens had demanded the return of Amphipolis and had assembled an invasion fleet to support the claim of Argaeus II, Philip's half-brother, to the Macedonian throne. Philip assembled what experienced troops he had left, and "he made the Macedonians confident by convening them in assembly after assembly and exhorting them by his eloquence to be brave."[2] At the same time he began to "reform the military formations to give them greater strength and equipped them with weapons suitable for these formations. He devised both the close array of the phalanx and their equipment, in imitation of the closed shield formation of the heroes of Troy, and he was the first to put together the Macedonian phalanx."[3] The infantry phalanx that Philip invented revolutionized infantry combat in Greece.

Why didn't Philip copy the traditional hoplite infantry of the armies of the Greek states? Philip surely was familiar with hoplite infantry, having encountered it in Thebes when he was hostage there and, perhaps, again when an elite hoplite unit served in Perdiccas's army. But the circumstances in which Philip found himself made the creation of hoplite infantry impractical in Macedonia. When Philip came to power, Macedonia was still a poor country and lacked an urbanized middle class that could afford the costly armor and equipment the hoplites required. The country's treasury was depleted as a consequence of the previous decade's events, and Philip was unable to purchase armor and weapons for his troops.[4] Even if Philip's foundries could manufacture the required equipment, the time required to do so would have left the country without an armed force for many months. More importantly, hoplites needed complex and extensive training to fight effectively in the phalanx, and Philip did not have the time to train new troops in this complex formation before the Illyrians, Paeonians, and Athenians attacked. The lack of an infantry tradition in Macedonia and the nobility's unwillingness to serve as ground troops virtually prohibited creating an adequate hoplite force soon enough to handle the threats facing Macedonia. Philip needed to find a way to take an assembly of peasants with little or no military experience and equip and train it quickly in a tactical formation that could hold its own against the hoplite infantry of the Greek states. The answer he devised was the Macedonian phalanx.

In a sense, Philip found himself in the same situation as Napoleon when the latter reformed the French army. Both needed large numbers of troops and had to quickly fashion them out of raw conscripts. Both solved their dilemma by creating new formations that were simple to assemble and control and required only limited training on the recruits' part to be used effectively on the battlefield. Napoleon's marching column and Philip's Macedonian phalanx were different solutions to the same problem.

The original Macedonian phalanx was a simple box, ten men in front and ten men deep, with each file commanded by a *dekadarch*, or "leader of ten," who led their files from the front.[5] These file commanders were the bravest and most experienced troops Philip had available and received double pay. The simple square was easy to control, especially in the attack when all it had to do was move forward. To control the formation, an experienced man in each corner of the square maintained its direction, and a few veterans were scattered throughout to maintain morale and cohesion by example. The square also lent itself to maneuver: it could turn in any direction while still presenting a strong front to the enemy. The crowding within the box increased the confidence and cohesion of the contained, marginally trained troops in the same way that the phalanx did for the trained hoplite.

Because the Macedonian phalangite's weapons made individual combat difficult, the Macedonian soldier relied primarily on the cohesion of the formation for protection. One on one against the hoplite, the Macedonian phalangite was almost helpless. Despite these circumstances, raw conscripts could be trained quickly to function effectively on the battlefield if their tasks were kept simple. Philip fashioned his phalanx to be ten men deep, thicker than the typical hoplite phalanx of eight men deep. This change probably reflects Philip's interpretation of Epaminondas's tactics that he had learned in Thebes. The key to an effective infantry on the ancient battlefield was not maneuver but the weight and power it could deliver straight ahead or with which it could resist the enemy's attack. Philip's original phalanx was designed for weight and power more than for maneuver. Later, it would also become the most maneuverable infantry formation to take the field until the legions of imperial Rome.

The phalanx did not need the hoplite's expensive equipment and armor; indeed, the compactness of the phalanx made them unnecessary and impractical. The cost of equipping the phalangite was much less than for the hoplite, an important factor in Philip's calculations since, as Diodorus tells, Philip had to bear the entire cost of equipping the infantry. The Macedonian phalangite originally wore no body armor at all; later leather breastplates were in use.[6] During Alexander's campaign, however, the phalangite seems to have acquired a linen cuirass of lamellar armor for upper body protection. To provide some body protection, the phalangite carried a small, twenty-four-inch circular shield made of wood and sometimes covered with bronze. The shield was almost flat, less concave than the *hoplon*, and weighed only twelve pounds.[7] The shield hung over the soldier's chest from a strap around his neck and provided some protection to his body just as the tower shield was used in the *Iliad*, serving more as a cuirass than a buckler.[8] When the phalanx formed in compact order, the men shifted their shields over their left shoulders as the files pressed together.

The Macedonian soldier wore the same iron helmet as the Greek hoplite and carried the same *xiphos*, or straight, double-edged, infantry sword. Greek armies widely used leg greaves during the seventh century BCE, but surviving equipment lists suggest that by Philip's day they were in common use among Macedonian infantry and cavalry but had fallen into disuse in most Greek armies.[9] The complete kit of the Macedonian phalangite weighed some forty pounds, almost ten pounds less than the panoply and weapons of the hoplite infantryman.[10] In the early days of Philip's reign, it is likely that only the front ranks were equipped with complete sets of armor.

The design of Philip's infantry formation and its minimal armor and protective equipment made sense only if Philip intended to equip his troops with weapons and tactics that were radically different from those traditionally employed by hoplite armies. We see Philip's brilliance clearly in his introduction of a completely new weapon to Greek warfare, the sarissa. The sarissa was a long spear fashioned of cornelian cherry, a wood that grew abundantly in the Macedonian forests and was thus easy and cheap to obtain. Characterized by its strength, hardness, and elasticity, cornel wood was a common material for making spears and javelins. Theophrastus, a contemporary of Philip's, tells us that the sarissa of Philip's day was twelve cubits, or some eighteen feet, long.[11] The sarissa's shaft weighed about 9.39 pounds, the iron spear point and socket about 2.7 pounds, and the butt spike some 2.4 pounds. The spear point was 20 1/4 inches long, with about half its length taken up by the socket and the other half by the point itself.[12] The complete weapon weighed around 14.5 pounds and was wielded with both hands.[13] The shaft of the spear came in two sections and was joined in the middle with a 7-inch iron coupling sleeve or metal joint fashioned from an iron tube into which both halves of the shaft were force fit to assemble the weapon.[14] This design allowed the infantryman to break the weapon down into two parts, wrap a strap around it, and carry it over his shoulder or across his back on the march.

An interesting question is, where did Philip get the inspiration for the sarissa? Just as numerous practices and rituals from the Homeric age survived in Macedonia after dying out elsewhere in Greece, it is possible that the sarissa derived from Homeric times as well. In the *Iliad*, Hector's spear is described as being eleven cubits, or about sixteen feet, long and wielded with two hands.[15] A miniature fresco from Akrotiri dating from 1450 BCE depicts Mycenaean warriors using long spears of the sarissa's length in battle. Later tomb paintings show men hunting wild boars with long spears.[16] It is likely that the Homeric battle spear survived in Macedonia in the form of the boar hunting spear. As mentioned in chapter 1, in Philip's day, a young warrior armed only with a long spear tested his courage by hunting the wild boar, a dangerous animal given to charging its tormentor. The long spear was an ideal weapon for keeping the animal at bay and, when wielded with two hands, retaining sufficient penetrating power to stab and kill the boar. In the same manner, Philip's phalanx was designed mostly to fend off the enemy long enough so his cavalry could attack its flank or rear. Later the phalanx developed an offensive role, but in the early days it was mostly a defensive formation. It is possible that Philip conceived of the idea of using the long spear to repel the enemy from the Macedonian boar hunt.

Even in its earliest form the phalanx was a powerful physical and psychological battlefield weapon force. Wielded with both hands, the sarissa had sufficient power to penetrate the hoplite's armor and shield. In describing the battle of Pydna against the Romans in 168 BCE, Plutarch tells us that "the Macedonians, wielding their pikes with both hands, drove them through their opponents, armor and all; for the door shaped shields and breastplates could not withstand the force of the pike."[17] The mere sight of the phalanx could be unnerving to the enemy. Aemilius Paulus, the Roman commander at Pydna, says, "At the sight of the bristling rampart of outstretched pikes, I was smitten at once with astonishment and terror; never before had I seen such a fearful spectacle."[18] By the time it fought at Pydna, the Macedonian phalanx had been in the field for almost two centuries. One can only imagine its impact on the morale of Greek hoplites who faced it for the first time against Philip.

In Philip's day, the phalanx advanced to contact in a formation called *pyknosis*, or "compact order," in which the interval between files was "two cubits," or about a foot and a half. In this phalanx formation, the last five ranks rested their pikes at an upward angle on the shoulders of the men in front of them and formed a barrier over the heads of the first five fighting ranks to protect against missiles.[19] When preparing to assume the defense or to penetrate a line of hoplite infantry, the phalanx assumed a *synapsismos*, or "locked shields" formation, which cut the interval between files in half. This configuration was accomplished in two ways. Either the files shuffled to the right, closing the distance between each man and shortening the length of the front, or the five rear men in each ten-man file moved forward to fill in the one-meter space between the files. This arrangement produced a thicker formation with a front of original length.[20] Either way, the phalanx could "inchworm" itself into adjusting the length of its entire front line. The Greek historian Polybius tells us that blades of the sarissae in the first five ranks extended beyond the first rank of pikemen, with the fifth rank protruding at least two cubits beyond the front rank.[21] When the sarissae were employed as long stabbing bayonets, the hoplite on the receiving end had to deal with five spear points coming at him at once. As long as the Macedonian infantry held their fear in check, the phalanx was impenetrable by hoplite infantry. In the attack, the phalanx could easily drive through a Greek infantry line. In the defense, its wall of pike points stopped cavalry in its tracks.

The term "Macedonian phalanx" properly refers to the entire infantry army. So, for example, the phalanx at Chaeronea numbered twenty-four thousand men. But the phalanx comprised individual regiments (to use modern military parlance), or *taxeis*, each having 1,536 pikemen. Each taxeis was composed of three battalions, or *pentakosiarchoi*, of 512 men. Each regiment and battalion had its own commander. The smallest combat unit was the individual file of ten men commanded by a dekadarch.[22] Infantry battalions and regiments were raised on a territorial basis from within Macedonia, and their titles reflected the region or canton from which they were drawn.[23] When Philip took the field against the Illyrians in 358 BCE, he deployed ten thousand men, or six regiments of pike infantry. Philip had raised that force almost from nothing within a single year after the Illyrians had destroyed the Macedonian army in 359 BCE. This achievement certainly suggests the rapidity with which raw recruits could be trained in Philip's new organizational and tactical system of infantry combat.[24]

It is often mistakenly believed that a major weakness of the Macedonian phalanx was its inability to maneuver and its lack of flexibility.[25] It is certainly true that Alexander increased the depth of the phalanx to sixteen men and that the Successor armies expanded its size and depth to where the phalanx could hardly maneuver at all. Thus, the phalanx's immobility dates after Philip's reign. As Adcock cogently observes, Philip's phalanx "had legs" from the beginning and was capable of much greater mobility than the hoplite phalanx was.[26] Within the long Macedonian phalanx infantry line, any given battalion or regiment could be ordered to take several formations (see figure 2). It could, for example, form itself into a solid triangular wedge to penetrate the enemy's line. Drawn up in tight compact order, the battalion could also form into a hollow wedge. This formation attacked the enemy with double the number of spear points of the solid formation, not only head-on but laterally as well, so that the individual hoplite could not rescue the comrade to his side.[27] At Gaugamela, Alexander formed his phalanx into a hollow outward-facing rectangle with orders that if it broke under attack, it was to reform itself into two similar rectangles.[28]

Macedonian commanders relied heavily on the mobility and flexibility of the Macedonian phalanx. Polyaenus recalls an incident when Philip was under attack by the Thracians: "He ordered the rear rank, when the trumpeter sounded the retreat, to lower its spears and remain in place, and the rest to retreat, in order to stop the enemy's pursuers, and to provide a head start for his own men."[29] This order required the front ranks to pass through the rear rank, no easy task when under attack from the front. At the battle of Gaugamela in 331 BCE, Alexander ordered his phalanx to open its files and allow Darius's scythed chariots to pass through harmlessly before the phalanx closed ranks and went into the attack.

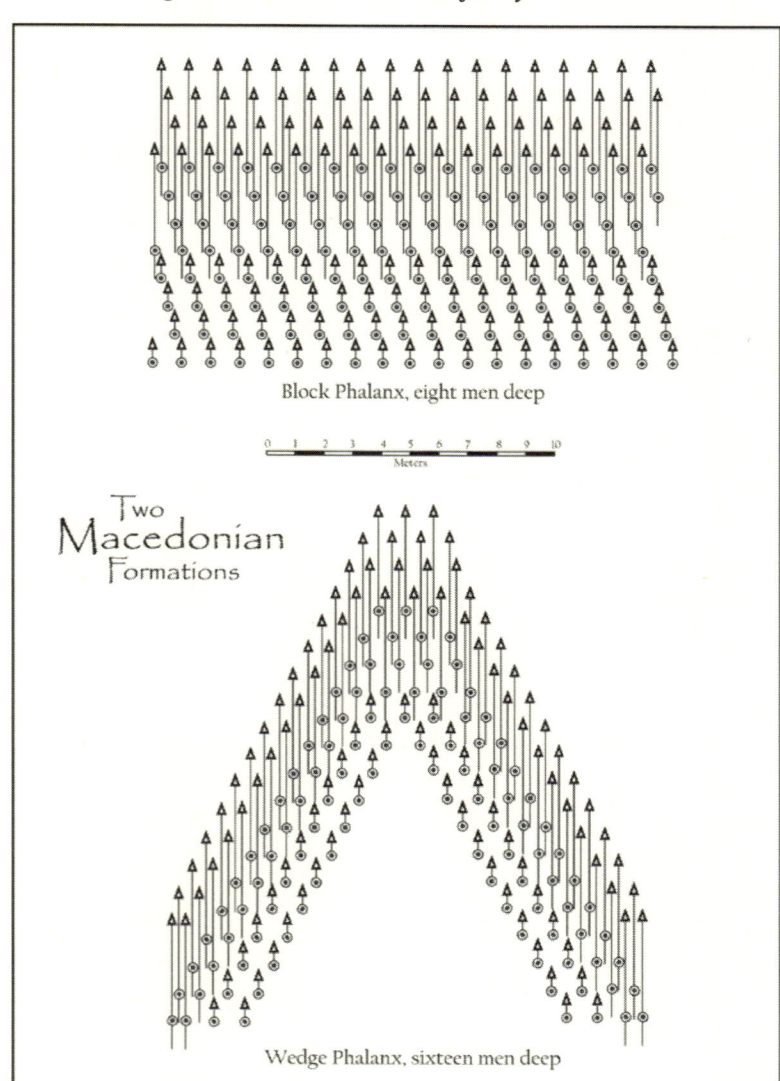

Figure 2. *Two Macedonian Infantry Formations*

Block Phalanx, eight men deep

Two Macedonian Formations

Wedge Phalanx, sixteen men deep

Unlike the hoplite phalanx, which tended to come apart or lose its directional thrust when maneuvering over uneven terrain, the Macedonian phalanx easily accommodated itself to this and more serious obstacles. At the battle of the Granicus in 334 BCE, Macedonian pikemen forded a shallow river in formation, forcing their way up a steep riverbank to engage the enemy. At Issus the next year, the phalanx again crossed a river and attacked through the gap that Alexander had created with his cavalry. Perhaps nowhere was the flexibility and maneuverability of the Macedonian phalanx more clearly demonstrated than during Alexander's Balkan campaign of 335 BCE undertaken against the tribes on the Danube. Alexander assembled his entire infantry phalanx of twelve thousand troops on an open plain and conducted a series of maneuvers and drills to frighten the enemy, watching from the hills. According to the Roman historian Arrian,

> Alexander drew up his phalanx with a depth of 120 men. He ordered the men to keep silent and act smartly at his word of command. The first signal was to raise their pikes upright; then at his word to bring them down for the charge; and then to swing their pike heads in close order now to the right and now to the left. Concurrently, he was moving the phalanx to one flank and then the other. After going thus through many formations and changing them in quick time, he formed as it were a wedge of the phalanx [open hollow formation] on the left. He began to lead it against the enemy.[30]

Philip's new infantry phalanx provided Macedonian commanders with far greater combat power, flexibility, maneuverability, and tactical opportunities than were available to hoplite unit commanders.[31] Philip's innovations had changed infantry combat completely, rendering the traditional hoplite phalanx obsolete. Philip's phalanx was lighter, more mobile, and more tactically flexible than Alexander's, as were the even heavier later formations of the Successors. Philip's tactical brilliance is revealed in the different ways in which he employed his new phalanx. Against the Illyrians, Philip used it offensively to drive through the enemy infantry square and open a gap through which his cavalry could attack. He used it in the same manner later against the Thracians.[32] At the battle of the Crocus Field against the Phokians (352 BCE), he employed the phalanx as a blocking force to fix the enemy infantry in place and as a platform of maneuver for the cavalry. At Chaeronea, Philip first used it as an attacking force against the end of the enemy line only to stop and retreat, drawing the enemy infantry after him. Then, precisely when his cavalry attacked the other end of the infantry line, Philip stopped his retreat and went over to the attack. He accomplished what Napoleon regarded as the most difficult maneuver for any army, to stop its retreat and regain the offensive. Philip was a brilliant tactician and relied heavily on the capabilities of the new combat instrument he had created and trained.

Not all of Philip's infantry were pikemen. Demosthenes notes that "you hear of Philip marching unchecked not because he leads a phalanx of heavy infantry, but because he is accompanied by skirmishers, cavalry, archers, mercenaries, and similar troops."[33] At Chaeronea, Philip deployed these "light armed" infantry to drive off the Athenian infantry that threatened his right flank. Philip's light infantry comprised Agrianian javelineers, Scythian archers, Thracian peltasts, and various tribal units used as skirmishers. These units were often drawn from subject peoples who were required to provide military service for the Macedonians and always fought under the command of Macedonian officers.[34]

Philip's great wealth also allowed him to hire contingents of mercenary troops on what Diodorus tells us was "an unprecedented scale."[35] After the Peloponnesian wars, Greece was crawling with unemployed experienced soldiers who sold their skills to various states, tyrants, and kings throughout the Mediterranean. Soldiers for hire were so common that mercenaries became an occupational group that Greek society recognized as legitimate. The Greeks had no word for mercenary that would convey its modern meaning as a soldier of fortune. Instead, these professional warriors were referred to as *epikouros* (fighter alongside), *misthophoros* (wage earner), or *xenos misthophoros* (foreign wage earner).[36] Mercenaries usually fought in small formations under professional commanders and commonly were light troops of peltasts, javelineers, slingers, and archers, although certainly some of them were hoplite infantry.[37] They could be hired for service year round and, as such, made excellent garrison troops. Philip used them often in this capacity.[38]

Polyaenus tells us that Philip used mercenary troops to attack besieged cities with scaling ladders, and once they breached the walls, mercenary infantry were often employed in the deadly hand-to-hand street fighting that followed. Curtius records a similar instance, in 352 BCE, when Philip held back his own Macedonian troops and sent his mercenaries inside to subdue the city of Pharcedon.[39] Mercenaries were, after all, expendable, and by using them in street fighting, he reduced the losses to his own Macedonian soldiers. Philip often sent mercenaries to the aid of pro-Macedonian cities that requested his assistance, and he used them to protect his line of communications on long campaigns.[40] Philip, of course, did not trust mercenaries and never used them in circumstances where their desertion could cause him difficulty. Still, mercenaries had their uses, and when Alexander left for Asia, he took five thousand mercenaries with him.

Philip probably obtained the idea for a permanent elite infantry force after encountering the Sacred Band while a hostage in Thebes. The idea of a standing force ran contrary to the traditional Greek practice of raising troops every campaign season and sending them "like good citizens" back to their homes when no longer needed.[41] Alexander II had formed a small unit of hoplites, probably mercenaries, to serve as his personal guard and named them the *hypaspistai*, or "shield bearers."[42] Philip created a professional elite force of Macedonian citizen-soldiers to serve as his personal guard, retaining the name hypaspistai for them.[43] W. W. Tarn describes them as "a standing foot guard, probably small, whose duty was to guard his person, not only in battle but at all times."[44] Philip must have formed this unit almost immediately upon taking power, for the men were in the field with him a year later in the war against the Illyrians when Theopompus described them as "picked men out of all the Macedonians, the tallest and strongest."[45] It was the first standing military force in Macedonian history.[46]

Initially the size of Philip's battle guard was small, but it grew after Philip incorporated the Upper Cantons of Macedonia, increasing the pool of military manpower upon which he could draw his army.[47] By the end of Philip's reign the hypaspistai numbered some three thousand troops divided into three thousand-man brigades. The first of these brigades was called the Royal Hypaspist Guard (*agema*) and were under the king's personal command. The Guard accompanied him all the time and seems to have been a standing, full-time professional force on duty year round.[48]

The Guard was also an elite fighting force, and it led the attack on the Athenians at Chaeronea. The question of its armament remains unclear, however. Probably early on the men were armed as the hoplites were, but by the time of the Illyrian war (358 BCE), they were certainly also armed with the sarissa. Historian George Cawkwell suggests that over time they became less heavily armed, like the peltasts, so they could act as the "hinge" between the phalanx and the cavalry, a mission that required rapid movement to stay in contact with both major combat elements.[49] We know that after Gaugamela, Alexander reconfigured some of these units with different weapons for special missions.[50] As an elite unit, it is not unlikely that, as G. T. Griffith has suggested, the hypaspistai were trained in the whole range of Macedonian weaponry just as modern elite units, such as the U.S. Special Forces and the British Special Boat Service (SBS), are similarly cross-trained.[51]

With the invention of the pike phalanx, Philip brought about a tactical revolution in Greek warfare. Until his day, hoplite infantry had been the primary combat arm and decided most battles. But for all its combat power and innovation, the Macedonian phalanx was not the combat arm of decision. Instead, the phalanx was designed to work in conjunction with cavalry, a combat arm that until now, in Greece proper anyway, had been largely underdeveloped. The revolutionary aspect of the Macedonian phalanx was its ability to penetrate or paralyze hoplite infantry in ways that made it vulnerable to cavalry attack. Philip's revolution in infantry combat made possible the transformation of Macedonian cavalry into the combat arm of decision.

CAVALRY

Cavalry remained a comparatively minor combat arm in Greece until Philip developed it into the Macedonian army's combat arm of decision. A number of factors retarded the growth of cavalry in Greece until after the Peloponnesian wars. The geography of Greece was largely unsuitable for raising horses. The rocky hills and glens afforded few open plains or sufficient surplus grain to feed and raise horses in significant numbers. Accordingly, little attention was paid to breeding horses or using the horse in warfare. Horses had to be imported from Thessaly and Macedonia at considerable cost. Purchasing and maintaining the animal were also expensive, so only the aristocracy could afford to own horses. The traditional Greek preference for hoplite warfare also worked against the development of cavalry. The Greek citizen saw himself first as an infantryman; service in the cavalry afforded no real status. For these reasons Greek states raised only small contingents of cavalry and employed them in limited combat roles such as protecting the flanks of the infantry phalanx or as a means of launching javelins against enemy infantry.

Circumstances were quite different in Macedonia, however, where cavalry developed early and played a major role on the battlefield from ancient times. Macedonia's large plains and surplus grain production supported horse breeding as a major industry. Macedonia's political culture and history worked against the development of the city-state with its attendant citizen militia infantry. Macedonia had no tradition of organized infantry, so the horse-mounted nobility became the primary participants in warfare. It was not until Philip introduced the pike phalanx in 359 BCE that Macedonian infantry became an important force on the battlefield. While Greece produced excellent infantry and poor cavalry, Macedonia produced excellent cavalry and poor infantry.

When the Theban general Pelopidas employed Greek cavalry as an assault force against the flanks of Alexander of Pherae's hoplite infantry at Cynoscephalae in 364 BCE, Greek cavalry began to emerge as an effective combat arm. Its traditional tactic was to assemble in a square formation, ride close to the enemy infantry, and launch its javelins, retiring to make room for the second rank's attack in a continuing caracole. Occasionally, the cavalry might venture closer and attempt to engage the infantry with stabbing spears. If the enemy ranks broke, Greek cavalry could be somewhat effective in the pursuit. By and large, however, Greek cavalry neither acquired the ability to engage infantry in close combat nor was a match for Macedonian cavalry in this capability.

Philip's heavy cavalry was drawn from his Companions (asthetairoi) and was organized into *ilai*, or "squadrons." This system by itself was one of Philip's major innovations. Before Philip, Macedonian cavalry had fought mainly as individual combatants rather than in organized tactical units. Philip ordered the squadrons on a territorial basis. A typical squadron contained two hundred horses or multiples of that number and sometimes comprised as many as 400 cavalrymen, depending on the formation. When formed into a solid wedge, a squadron numbered 120 men.[52] In 358 BCE, Philip put 600 cavalry in the field against Bardylis. At the battle of the Crocus Field in 352 BCE, Philip's cavalry numbered 3,000. At Chaeronea in 338 BCE, Alexander had two thousand horses under his command. When Alexander left for Asia, he took 3,300 cavalry with him.[53] It is unlikely, however, that Philip's Companion cavalry itself ever exceeded 800 or so troopers. Philip drew additional cavalry as needed from his allied states. Thus, most of the cavalry at the Crocus Field, some two thousand horses, was Thessalian. Philip also had four 150-man squadrons of light cavalry recruited from Thrace and Paeonia that he used as skirmishers and reconnaissance units and a regiment of Thracian lancers known as *sarissophoroi*, or "sarissa-bearing cavalry."[54] Philip was also the first to form the mounted cavalry scouts (*prodromoi*) that were found in Alexander's army.

Cawkwell suggests that Macedonian horses were larger and stronger and possessed greater endurance than the mounts used by Greek cavalry because the former were of different breeding stock. Between 510 and 479 BCE when Macedonia was a Persian vassal state, the Persians brought their larger Nisean horses to northern Greece and Macedonia but not to the states of Greece proper.[55] In addition, Macedonia had easy access to the horse-breeding areas of the Danube plain, where both the Scythians and the Triballi were excellent horse breeders. While Cawkwell poses an interesting argument, it is not likely correct. Horse breeding as known to the modern world was largely unknown in antiquity, and keeping a bloodline pure over time was unlikely to succeed.

It is, however, probable that Macedonian horses had superior endurance and strength than those of the Greek cavalry, if only because Macedonian horses enjoyed better nutrition. They were typically raised on stud farms, where their forage diet was supplemented with grain. Macedonians valued horses highly and, unlike the Greeks, took great care to see to their health and training.[56] It was likely that superior nutrition and care led to the Macedonian horse's somewhat larger size and, more important for war, greater strength and stamina. Given their love of horses, the Macedonian cavalryman chose his mount carefully to ensure that the animal had the proper spirit for combat. Each mount was chosen for its suitability for battle, unlike the cavalry armies of later periods when mounts were issued en masse with little regard for the animals' suitability for war. A typical Macedonian cavalry mount stood between fourteen and fifteen hands, or fifty-eight to sixty-two inches at the withers (where the neck meets the body of the animal), and weighed between 950 and 1,100 pounds. As we shall see, however, it was not the quality of the horse that made the Macedonian cavalry so deadly but its training, enhanced by the weapons, tactics, and ferocity of its rider.[57]

The Macedonian cavalryman's armor offers a clue to the tactical role that Philip set for him: his protective equipment was designed primarily to protect him more from attack by infantry than by cavalry. Xenophon provides a detailed description of this cavalry armor.[58] An iron breastplate protected the cavalryman's chest and back with some sort of loose-fitting collar to protect the neck "standing up from the breastplate and shaped to the neck . . . which if properly made, will cover the rider's face as high as his nose." The soldier's head was protected by an iron helmet.[59] "Since a wound in the left hand disables the rider," his left hand and arm were covered by a piece of equipment called "the hand," or gauntlet, which was a leather sleeve extending from the hand to the shoulder and secured under the breastplate. On the right side of the breastplate were thick leather flaps that ran under the armpit and protected the upper chest when the arm was raised to strike a blow. The rider's right forearm was covered with a metal greave attached to a leather sleeve that was attached under the breastplate at the armpit. His feet were covered in thick leather boots that went up to his metal leg greaves, for the great majority of wounds to cavalry were in the lower legs.[60] The cavalryman's thighs were protected by either leather or metal thigh pieces that served as greaves for the upper leg. Philip standardized armor for his cavalry, and the cavalryman had to bear the expense himself.

The primary weapons of the Macedonian cavalryman were the xyston (lance) and the *machaira* (saber).[61] It is likely that the Macedonians used their own word for lance, or sarissa, and this term has led to some confusion that the cavalry may have carried the same sarissa used by the infantry.[62] The xyston is also distinguished from the *dory*, the seven-foot ash spear the hoplite infantry used, and should not be confused with another cavalry weapon, the *palton* (javelin). The Macedonian cavalry lance was nine to ten feet long, fashioned of cornel wood that was "light and tough, with counter-balancing butt and a tip of metal, which he [the cavalryman] wielded with one arm."[63] The weapon was about one and a half inches around and weighed four pounds. Light and thin, the lance could be grasped two-thirds back from its point for thrusting, providing the cavalryman with a much longer reach than the much shorter dory afforded the hoplite. If the lance was broken, its butt spike was still a potent weapon in close combat. When aimed at a rival cavalryman en passant, the weapon was pointed at the rider's face and thorax so as to strike him high and unseat him more easily.

The lance was also an effective close combat weapon. N. de Lee offers an analysis of how the lance was wielded in close quarters after examining the Napoleonic manual for employing that period's cavalry lance. Interestingly, the Napoleonic lance was nine feet long and weighed four pounds, just as the Macedonian xyston did. The lance could be used to thrust, parry, and cut.[64] Held at the balance, the lance could be used to thrust in all directions—front to rear, side to side—with the thrust to the front being the most effective. When approaching another cavalryman, the lance was held in the "guard position," that is, straight forward with the shaft passing over the horse's head and the point level with its ears. Xenophon also mentions this technique. In the press of close combat, the lance or, if broken, its butt spike could be used to stab an adversary.[65] With the shaft of the lance pressed tightly against the trunk of the horseman's body for leverage, its blade could be swept horizontally to parry other weapons or to inflict deep cuts on both cavalry and infantry.[66]

The Macedonian cavalryman carried a murderous meat cleaver, or machaira, as his principle close combat weapon. Xenophon also referred to it as a *kopis*, and the names seemed to have been used interchangeably. Although by Xenophon's time the weapon was thought to be of Persian origin, there is some evidence that it was used by the Thessalians in sacrifice early in the ninth century BCE, making it, of course, of Greek origin. The machaira was about twenty-five inches long and weighed two pounds. Its two-and-one-half-inch-wide, single-edged blade was eighteen inches in length and curved backward. The weapon's weight was out at its tip, making it an excellent chopping sword but ineffective for stabbing or slashing. When the weapon was swung, its weight was carried toward the tip, where it would do the most damage as the cutting edge drove deeply into the target. It was especially destructive when gravity was added to the driving force, as when a cavalryman on his mount wielded it in a powerful downward chopping blow directed at the hoplite below him. Even without a saddle or stirrups to steady him, the Macedonian cavalryman could sufficiently grip his mount with his thighs to wield the machaira with great power. Arrian records that at the Granicus, Cleitus saved Alexander's life by striking a cavalryman about to attack Alexander from behind. The force of Cleitus's downward blow was so great that it completely severed the attacker's arm at the shoulder."[67]

Philip's greatest contribution to Greek cavalry warfare was to organize and train his cavalry units to do what no Greek cavalry had done before—to attack Greek hoplite infantry and destroy them in close combat. Until Philip demonstrated his cavalry's ability to effectively attack the infantry, Greek cavalry had played a limited role on the battlefield. Philip was the first Western commander to use his cavalry as his combat arm of decision. Philip accomplished this revolution by superbly training his cavalry, using appropriate combat formations, and employing new tactics.

Arrian tells us that "in imitation of the Thracians, Philip had trained his cavalry to employ in a wedge formation since the front tapering into a point made it possible easily to cut through every hostile formation."[68] Arrian was himself a Roman cavalry officer and the only one of our sources on Philip who had actual cavalry experience in combat. As such, he deserves to be taken seriously when he suggests that cavalry could penetrate Greek infantry formations.[69] Whereas Greek cavalry usually deployed in a square to launch successive waves of javelins from a safe distance or to use their weight to block maneuver on the infantry's flank, both of which were accomplished without engaging infantry in close combat, Philip's wedge formation was specifically designed to close with the infantry, break it apart, and exploit the breach by attacking through it. Philip brought about a revolution in cavalry tactics because he envisioned a new tactical role for his cavalry, one heretofore thought impossible.

Philip's new tactical vision for his cavalry was partially rooted in Macedonian history. Macedonian cavalrymen fighting as individuals had always attacked infantry at close quarters. Without infantry of its own to provide support, Macedonian cavalry had no other option. The ferocity and nerve required for cavalry close combat with infantry was already well established among Macedonian cavalry when Philip introduced the wedge formation and the standardized weapons that gave his cavalry greater effectiveness on the battlefield. It was the Macedonian cavalry's willingness and skill to engage infantry in close combat that distinguished it from Greek cavalry. Although Greek cavalry had begun to become more aggressive since the Peloponnesian wars, by Philip's day it had only timidly begun to develop a capacity for close combat, and Greek armies still relied on their infantry to carry the day. What Philip's cavalry brought to the battlefield was "an intimidating intimacy" that was able to disrupt, destroy, and pursue hoplite infantry with great effectiveness.[70]

The ineffectiveness of Greek cavalry has often been attributed to the fact that saddles, horseshoes, and stirrups were not yet invented, and the cavalryman could not obtain a secure enough seat upon his mount to wield his lance and saber. But as Robert Gaebel, himself an expert horseman, has demonstrated in his analysis of ancient cavalry, lacking a saddle or stirrups imposed no such limitation. He maintains,

> All else being equal, the bareback rider will be more skilled than one using a saddle. He will have a deeper seat with a lower center of gravity; he will of necessity develop a better sense of balance, since no security will be offered by the shape of the saddle or the lateral support from the stirrups, and he will have better control by virtue of the close contact between his legs and the sides of the horse.[71]

Xenophon in his *Art of Horsemanship* tells us that cavalrymen trained their horses for war by "springing across ditches, leaping over walls, rushing up banks, jumping down from banks. One must also try [the horse] by riding up and down hill and on a slope."[72] He also tells us that a good horseman could hold himself erect on the mount by getting "a better grip of his horse with his thighs,"[73] raising himself up as if he had stirrups to hurl his javelin. The Numidian cavalry that fought with Scipio at Zama were extremely effective in battle and had neither saddle nor stirrups. The American Plains Indians did have saddles but only used them when traveling. In war, they preferred to ride bareback because it gave them greater control of their mounts.[74] The success of Philip's cavalry testifies clearly that the absence of saddles and stirrups was not a significant hindrance in developing an effective cavalry in Greece.

The hoplite infantry's discipline in holding its ground against Greek cavalry gave rise to the belief that cavalry could not drive through an infantry line if the hoplites kept their courage and presented a solid wall of shields and spears to the charging horses. It is true, of course, that horses will not charge through what they think are walls and will pull up short before impact, sometimes throwing their riders to the ground. What probably happened in Greece is that after several failed attempts by cavalry to break the hoplite phalanx, the Greeks simply assumed that horses would not charge an infantry line with sufficient force to break it and gave up trying. It thus became an axiom of Greek military theory that cavalry was useless against disciplined infantry. It seems clear, however, that Philip's cavalry was successful at breaking through a line of infantry. We have Arrian's claim that Philip adopted the Thracian wedge to do precisely that, and Plutarch says that at the battle of Chaeronea Alexander was the first to assault the Sacred Band of Thebes.[75] Describing the same battle, Diodorus reports that "Alexander was the first to break the compact front of the enemy line."[76] How, then, did Philip's cavalry do it?

It was not the shock of the cavalry charge but the continuous push and press of cavalry horses and lance- and saber-wielding cavalrymen that broke the infantry line. A typical phalanx was eight men, or about twenty-four feet, deep. An average horse is between nine and ten feet long. A horse has to advance only about twice its length before it has reached the back of the phalanx. Given that the animal weighs about 1,000 pounds, even the slightest momentum is sufficient to carry it into the depth of the phalanx. An average

Greek hoplite of the day weighed about 145 pounds and stood some five feet, seven inches tall. Under cavalry attack, the hoplite had to face an armored cavalry trooper perched some five feet above him on a horse and armed with a nine-foot lance, affording the cavalryman advantages in the height and reach of his weapon. The greater height and weight of the cavalryman's mount moving however slowly or at an angle made it very difficult for the *individual* hoplite to hold his position in the phalanx.

Once even a single hoplite was killed or pushed out of position, the horse and rider would be inside the first rank. Once inside the phalanx, the sheer bulk, weight, and movement of the animal, accompanied by the damage the cavalryman's weapons inflicted, pushed against the ranks and forced them to move sideways and back. The pressure on the front infantry ranks would force them back on the others, rendering their weapons useless. Once an opening was made in the first rank, it was widened and deepened by the closely following second and third ranks of the wedge until the opening extended through the phalanx. At this point, the follow-on cavalry ranks of the wedge burst through completely, destroying the phalanx's cohesion at the point of attack. The press and push of horses and weapon-wielding cavalrymen initially pried the phalanx apart, and they expanded the opening by having the follow-on ranks of the cavalry wedge increase the pressure against the weak point in the line.

The Thracian wedge was perfectly designed to penetrate the infantry phalanx. When assembled in a wedge formation, the squadron comprised 120 troopers arranged behind a single leader at its point to command its direction and spot of attack. Each rank behind the leader had an increasing number of troopers in it, ranging from two in the second rank to twenty in the last rank.[77] The cavalry wedge approached the infantry at a canter or, perhaps, even a walk until the commander selected a point of attack. Using his lance to attack the hoplite directly in front of him, the first trooper urged his mount forward and used the bulk and weight of the animal to strike the hoplite down. Within seconds, the riders in the next rank of the wedge struck the hoplites on either side of the first victim. Quickly followed the next rank of riders, attacking behind the first two ranks to increase the assault's momentum. Even if the first attackers were killed, the confusion caused by the horse inside the phalanx weakened the cohesion of the phalanx's ranks. As more and more cavalry pressed into the opening, attacking with sword and lance, the pressure became intense until the phalanx came apart, allowing the follow-on cavalry ranks to burst through the infantry line.[78]

In comprehending the dynamics of the Macedonian cavalry attack, insufficient attention has often been paid to the horse's role. For an attack to be effective at close quarters, the cavalryman had to be in complete control of his horse, not only to use his weapons effectively, but to use the size, weight, and momentum of the animal itself as an integrated part of the attack. This integration was achieved through long training. Two natural traits of the horse, collection and shoulder barging, could also be enhanced by discipline and training to make the horse an effective partner in close combat.[79]

In his work *The Cavalry Commander*, Xenophon mentions collection when he advises, "To avoid being thrown the riders should throw the body back in charging, and collect their horses when wheeling, to keep them from falling."[80] A horse is "collected" when the hind legs are brought "under the body, whereby the horse brings up and arches the neck and bends the head downward from the poll, producing a shortening of the body."[81] The position resembles prancing. A collected horse is under control, is balanced between the bit and legs, has stability, and, most importantly, is able to move quickly in any direction because the animal's hind legs are positioned for maximum muscular effort. A collected horse affords the cavalryman a great advantage in close combat "where he must stop, start, change directions, and wheel about" to avoid attack or to bring his own weapons to bear upon the enemy.[82] Under these circumstances, the weight, bulk, and movement of the cavalryman's horse becomes an important element in breaking the cohesion of an infantry phalanx.

Shoulder barging is another natural trait that can be turned to the cavalryman's advantage with training. Barging is an aggressive action by one horse against another wherein the threatening animal bumps its rival with its shoulder and pushes it out of the way. It is similar to the technique of "riding off" used by polo players. Barging can be very effective in gaining position to strike one's opponent with a lance or sword. When ancient accounts report that a battle involved much "pushing of cavalry," the reference is probably to barging.[83]

Macedonians, cavalry warriors by nature and culture, were the best horsemen in Greece. Philip took this raw material and fashioned a new force. He organized individual fighters with their own weapons into squadrons equipped with standardized weapons, centralized the breeding and training of their mounts, and trained them to fight in a number of combat formations,[84] the most effective of which was the wedge. He thus produced the best cavalry in Greece. Most importantly, Philip harnessed the natural Macedonian cavalryman's ferocity for war to new tactics designed to engage Greek infantry at close quarters and break through or shatter their once impenetrable infantry phalanx. Employing his cavalry in conjunction with his pike infantry acting as a platform of maneuver, Philip revolutionized Greek warfare by transforming cavalry from an adjunct force on the battlefield into the combat arm of decision.

Once an enemy infantry line had been pierced, Macedonian cavalry could carry out lethal assaults on the infantry. If the infantry could be forced into flight rather than dying where it stood, Philip's cavalry engaged in prolonged and lethal pursuit, killing as many men as possible. Unlike Greek cavalry, which abandoned their formations and pursued as individual combatants, Macedonian cavalry retained their formations to avoid losses and to present a preponderance of combat power against groups of remnant infantry.[85] In one battle, Philip's cavalry killed 7,000 men of a force of 10,500 troops. In another, the Macedonian cavalry killed 6,000 Phokians in a single day.

Philip employed the lethal pursuit for political as well as military purposes. Many of the armies and tribes Philip fought were from warrior societies whose aristocracies and rulers fought as cavalry. The long and lethal Macedonian cavalry pursuit aimed at killing as many of these leaders as possible. The men of these armies' warrior classes were not much different from Macedonian warriors, sharing similar martial values and practices. With their leaders gone, it was easier for these classes to accept new roles as warriors in Philip's service. The demise of the old leaders presented Philip with the opportunity to create a loyal cadre of new leaders. By granting them fiefs and making some of them Companions, Philip transformed enemies into loyal allies, gaining additional military manpower in the process.

The key element in Philip's new tactics was using infantry and cavalry in concert rather than as individual combat arms. Philip's tactical array included several variations. The Macedonian phalanx could be used as a platform of maneuver to lock the enemy infantry or cavalry in place, while Philip's cavalry rode around the end of the formation and fell upon the enemy's flank or rear in close combat. Philip used this method against Onomarchus at the Crocus Field in 352 BCE. Philip used his forces differently against the Illyrians in 358 BCE when his infantry phalanx drove straight through the Illyrian infantry square, opening up a gap through which Philip's cavalry galloped to attack the infantry from inside its own formation. At Chaeronea (338 BCE), the Macedonian cavalry wedge drove through the allied line, creating a gap through which the main cavalry force exploded and fell upon the enemy rear and interior flanks at the same time with devastating effect. When the cavalry was not engaged in battle, it performed other functions, including reconnaissance, police duties, and mobile guerrilla operations. When undertaking these missions, the cavalry was equipped with a small round buckler, short spear, or javelins.[86]

Philip's Companion cavalry was a lethal bunch whose reputation for ferocity and willingness to engage at close quarters spread throughout Greece. Even Philip's enemy Demosthenes granted that the Companions "had a reputation as admirable soldiers, well-grounded in the science of war."[87] The reputation of Philip's cavalry also emerged in Greek plays. In a surviving fragment of Mnesimachus's propaganda play, *Philip*, one of Philip's cavalrymen describes the prowess of his comrades:

> Have you any idea what we are like to fight against? Our sort make their dinner of honed-up swords, and swallow blazing torches for a savory snack. Then, by way of desert, they bring us broken arrow-heads and splintered spear shafts. For pillows we make do with our shields and breastplates, arrows and slings lie strewn under our feet, and we wreathe our brows with catapults.[88]

Surely the actor was exaggerating, but the lesson was clear enough: Philip of Macedonia had created the most lethal cavalry force in the history of Greece. He intended to make good use of it.

MANPOWER, TRAINING, AND LOGISTICS

The manpower base of the Macedonian army was enormous, drawing as it did upon a general population base of between 500,000 and 1 million people from Macedonia alone and not counting military manpower that could be leveraged from spear-won lands. Prior to Philip's incorporation of the Upper Cantons (358 BCE), the Macedonian field army numbered 10,000 troops and 600 cavalry. With the annexation of the cantons, the military manpower base doubled, and a few years later (353 BCE) Philip was able to field an army of 20,000 men and 600 horses.[89] A year later, Philip destroyed the Phokian army with a force of 30,000 infantry and 3,000 cavalry, with 2,000 cavalry provided by his Thessalian allies. The Thracian campaign of 340 BCE required a force of 30,000 infantry, and at the battle of Chaeronea in 338 BCE, Philip's army numbered 30,000 heavy and light infantry and 2,000 cavalry. In 334 BCE, two years after Philip's death, Alexander's army had 24,000 infantry and 3,300 cavalry.[90]

The Macedonian military manpower base made it possible to raise large armies without causing dislocations in the country's economic or agricultural base, unlike in the Greek states, where putting an army in the field often severely disrupted the country's economy and food supply.[91] Only one in ten of Macedonia's military-age male population was needed to maintain the King's Field Army at full strength.[92] The rest were assigned to militias in the towns and villages where they lived and trained for military service. These militia units were called to national service only in an emergency and constituted the field army's national strategic reserve. Since both active and reserve units were raised and served on a territorial basis, integrating reserve units into the active force could proceed smoothly. Philip raised additional cavalry units by granting fiefs to Macedonians and important allies and thereby creating more Companions, who then raised cavalry that Philip could levy when needed.

In the early years of Philip's reign, when the army was raised annually, the troop levy could be rotated so that it didn't always take the same men away from their homes and farms for military service. But the lure of good pay, booty, social advancement, and victory soon transformed the annual levy into a standing military force of professionals.[93] To sustain an infantry force of twenty-four thousand men comprising mostly twenty-five-year career professionals required an annual levy of only a thousand men, most of whom were likely volunteers from the militias seeking the military as a career.[94] Army pay was good. A young infantryman earned twenty-five drachmas a month, while the more highly trained hypaspistai earned thirty drachmas a month. Bravery, competence, and length of service were rewarded with pay raises. "Ten-stater" men who had earned only ten staters then earned forty drachmas, and the "double-raters," the equivalent of Roman centurions or modern senior noncommissioned officers, earned fifty drachmas a month.[95] By comparison, a skilled bricklayer of the era made two and a half drachmas a day and his assistant one and a half drachmas.[96] Philip made much of giving his bravest troops honors and a share of the booty, further increasing the rewards for military service.

Philip's policies exploited the manpower base to create a full-time army of great size, paid and equipped by the king, that could be honed to a fine combat edge by discipline and training.[97] As the professional army of a powerful monarch, it could place more emphasis on discipline and obedience than was possible in the militia armies of the Greek states, where a citizen's social status and democratic values often made sound discipline and obedience difficult.[98] The weak discipline of the Greek militia armies also stemmed from their use of elected generals who could be prosecuted as public officials for their conduct. Macedonian officers were not elected officials but battle-hardened, experienced commanders who held their positions after demonstrating competence in war. Moreover, the long terms of service in the Macedonian army allowed Philip to develop a corps of young officers and noncommissioned officers of proven courage and ability to lead the ranks, something Greek militia armies always lacked.[99] Discipline and competent troop unit leadership are the marks of a good army, and we hear of no instances of mutiny among Philip's troops. Curtius describes the morale, discipline, and leadership of the Macedonian army when he says that it "was ready to stand and follow . . . intent not only on the signal of its leader, but even his nod."[100]

Good leadership and sound discipline are important elements in training the soldier for combat and for enduring the rigors of campaigns. Philip hardened his soldiers to the harsh conditions of the march. Diodorus tells us, "He was training the Macedonians before the hazards of battle. He made them take up their arms and march often thirty-five miles, carrying helmet, shield, greaves, sarissa, and in addition to their arms, their rations and all the gear for daily living."[101] Beyond endurance, the soldier needed to learn how to fight. In this regard, Diodorus says that Philip "held continuous maneuvers under arms and training exercises under combat conditions"[102] and goes on to say that the degree of training in the Macedonian army was unprecedented in the Greek world at the time.[103] Continuous arms drill under realistic conditions made the Macedonian infantry phalanx the most versatile and maneuverable infantry of the day. Cavalry, too, underwent continuous training and practiced the many roles Philip expected it to perform. Most important was its training for its use together with the infantry so that it would strike precisely when ordered by trumpet call to engage. As with professional armies in all ages, Philip's army trained, trained, and then trained again, a regimen that paid off handsomely when the time to kill in earnest finally arrived.

Another area in which Philip's brilliant military mind surpassed those of his contemporaries was logistics. Greek armies were designed to sally forth from their cities, travel short distances to the battlefield (its location often agreed upon in advance), engage in a single battle, and return to their cities, where their militia armies were disbanded until the next time they were needed. Greek armies had limited logistic capabilities and could neither remain in the field for an extended period nor support themselves over long marches. Greek armies were accompanied by hordes of attendants, women, slaves, sutlers, and other hangers-on to the point where the number of attendants often exceeded the number of combatants, all of whom had to be fed. The use of oxcarts and wagons slowed movement further. Lacking a sufficient logistics system made the Greek armies incapable of sustained field operations over long distances, rendering them useless as instruments of strategic warfare.

For Philip, however, war was all about gaining strategic objectives, and he set about creating a completely new logistics system that could support his army over long distances for long periods.[104] His first innovation was forbidding the use of carts. Sextus Julius Frontinus tells us that "when Philip was for the first time putting an army together, he forbade the use of carts for anyone."[105] Philip's early wars were fought in the Upper Cantons of Macedonia, Illyria, and Paeonia, all mountainous regions with few roads, steep trails, swift streams, and plenty of locations where his army might be ambushed. Carts would have been useless in this type of terrain. Equipped with a breast band, a horse would have been only able to pull light loads. Without an efficient horse collar that would have allowed horses to be used effectively as draft animals, only oxen could have pulled the carts. Macedonia, however, was a poor country with few oxen. Requisitioning them for military use would have created great hardship for its peasant farmers. Oxen are also very slow movers and usually unable to make more than seven or eight miles a day before becoming exhausted. Thus Philip replaced ox carts with horses used as pack animals. A horse can easily carry 250 pounds of cargo when outfitted with panniers. By comparison, an ox can move 1,000 pounds of cargo a day, but five horses can carry the same load thirty-two miles a day at twice the speed and on half the forage.¹⁰⁶ The Persian army used the horse as a prominent pack animal in a logistics train first, but Philip was the first Western commander to use the horse for this purpose.

To protect his army in the mountainous terrain in which Philip fought his first campaigns and to avoid an ambush, Philip's troops constructed a fortified camp every night, complete with protective ditches and a wall of sharpened stakes as a palisade.¹⁰⁷ In terrain without trees from which to cut palisade stakes, Philip's troops brought them on pack animals. Frontinus says that the later Roman practice of fortifying a night field camp with ditches and palisades was adopted from the Macedonians.¹⁰⁸

To lighten the load of his pack animals, Philip required every soldier to carry his own equipment, weapons, and rations. Polyaenus also tells us the Macedonian soldier carried his helmet, shield, greaves, sarissa, and utensils, along with personal possessions, in his backpack.¹⁰⁹ Curtius adds their sword, blankets, road-building tools, and medical supplies.¹¹⁰ The soldier's load from these items approached fifty pounds. Adding that to the thirty-day supply of flour each man carried, almost forty pounds, the Macedonian soldier carried between eighty and ninety pounds on his back.¹¹¹ A soldier can indeed carry some eighty pounds over the long haul without undue harm to his health. The Roman military historian Vegetius says the Roman soldier carried a seventy-five-pound burden, which is the same weight that Napoleon's soldiers bore at Waterloo in AD 1815. The British stormed Bunker Hill in AD 1775 with eighty-pound packs, and American troops landing at Normandy in AD 1944 carried eighty-two pounds on their backs.¹¹² It is possible that when Gaius Marius reformed the Roman army in 99 BCE and required his legionaries to carry their own weapons, armor, and equipment, turning them into "Marius's Mules," he was copying Philip's practice.

Philip lightened his logistics train further by reducing the number of its attendants and by prohibiting women, wives, and other civilian personnel from accompanying the army. Frontinus tells us that Philip "permitted the cavalrymen to have but one attendant each, and to the infantrymen one for each *dekas* [ten-man file] who might carry the mills [for grinding grain] and ropes."¹¹³ Thus, an army of ten thousand men would have an additional sixteen hundred men to act as porters, carrying food and equipment, and to help with such other tasks as cutting roads or foraging when the transported food supply was exhausted. The attendants also guarded the camp and took part in battles as light infantry.

Philip's reforms enabled his army to move faster and farther in a single day than any other Greek army, and it sustained itself in the field for weeks dependent only on its own resources. Each cavalry horse required ten pounds of forage and ten pounds of grain a day. Forage was gathered from the fields along the march, and each horse carried 230 pounds of grain, or enough for twenty-three days.[114] The forty pounds of flour each soldier carried could feed him for a month. The pack animals, horses, and mules were used to carry bulky items, such as tents, ropes, mills, and the prefabricated parts of the siege engines, as well as their own food. Donald Engels estimates that the pack animals could carry the bulky items at a ratio of one animal to fifty men.[115] Thus, Philip's army in the Illyrian campaign required only two hundred pack animals for a force of 10,000 men.

The strategic range of Philip's army was greater than that of any army in Greek history. In a single day, Philip's column could usually cover fifteen miles, and it could go twenty miles on a forced march. He could make these distances even though he had to stop every hour and rest the pack animals and horses for ten minutes and then every three hours halt, remove the animals' packs, and rest their backs for thirty minutes. The cavalrymen walked alongside their mounts. At a rate of march of fifteen miles a day with a twenty-five-day supply of food, Philip's army could cover three hundred miles before it had to replenish its supplies and still have five days' reserve of food for the men and animals.

The operational implications of Philip's logistical reforms were staggering. An examination of map 2 demonstrates that Philip's army could reach the Illyrian and Paeonian areas of operation in only ten days' march. The shaded circle represents the distance Philip's army could cover in ten days of marching, or some 150 miles. Once within the theater of operations, Philip's army could sustain itself for another two weeks on its own supplies or, if required, continue the march. To the east, the distance from Pella to the Nestus River in Thrace was also within a ten-day march. From Philippi to Byzantium (240 miles) or north to Scythia (200 miles) was longer, but it was still within the army's strategic range. Staging from Philippi, he could reach the Triballi and Getae within ten days' march. When Philip moved south against Athens, he staged from Pherae in Thessaly, bringing all the Peloponnese and Athens itself within a ten-day march. As the Macedonian sphere of influence increased in all directions, Philip established forts and towns at key locations that he turned into supply depots for future use. This system permitted his army to move along interior lines of communication and supply to the empire's farthest stretches with adequate logistical support. Philip could also increase his army's size by absorbing the militia units in these forts and towns as he marched toward his objective.

It is interesting that in all Philip's campaigns, we hear nothing of any difficulties in crossing rivers. Given that Philip's overall theater of operations was crisscrossed with major rivers—Nestus, Strymon, Axius, Orion, Haliacmon, Aspus, Peneus—and scores of swift-running mountain streams, it is puzzling that no mention is made of river-crossing techniques. Once the river areas were incorporated into the Macedonian state, it is reasonable to assume that ferries and bridges were used at regular crossing points to move trade goods, but there is no mention of crossing river obstacles under combat marching conditions. If Alexander's crossing of the Hydaspes River is any indication, however, Philip's troops may have used boats, rafts, or straw-filled tents for flotation devices and swam across rivers.

The Macedonian army's lethal combination of speed, logistical support, and combat power was clearly demonstrated in 335 BCE when Alexander took the army into the Balkans. The army set out from Amphipolis, crossed the great Balkan Range, fought south of the Danube, crossed the river, and fought again before returning by way of Sofia in modern-day Bulgaria. It then marched into what is now eastern Albania, where it did battle again south of Lake Prepsa. It next moved through Thessaly to suppress the revolt in Thebes, arriving in surprise in Boeotia. Alexander's fighting march and logistical supply effort covered some two thousand kilometers, the last five hundred or so in only thirteen days.[116] In introducing a completely new system of logistics to Greek warfare, Philip accomplished what no Greek general had done before: he made it possible for his army to strike with speed, logistical support, and combat power against any adversary from the Danube River to the Adriatic Sea.

SIEGECRAFT

Philip was the first Western general to create a permanent engineering corps with a siege capability as an integral part of his army.[117] Early on, perhaps before 350 BCE, Philip established a department of military engineering under a talented engineer's direction to research and develop new weapons and their applications. The department was established at Pella, where

THE MACEDONIAN WAR MACHINE   89

Map 2. *Logistical Range of Philip's Army*

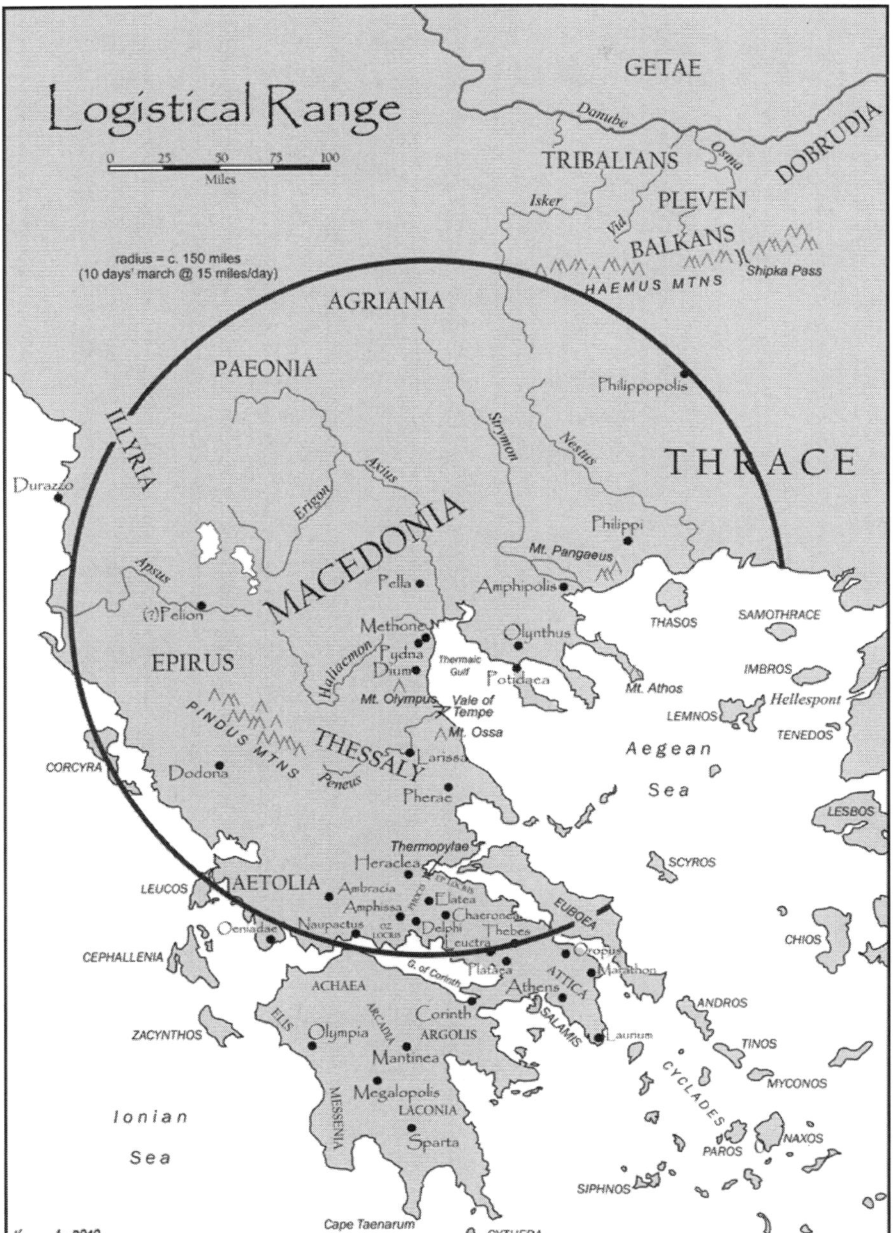

Philip constructed magazines, workshops, and training facilities for his army. The engineering department was part of the military administration of the army.[118] While the identity of Philip's chief engineer remains lost, under his guidance, and that of his successors, Philip's military engineering department ushered in a period of astonishing technological development.[119]

As with all Philip's innovations, this one was also designed to serve specific tactical and strategic ends. The hoplite culture of limited war retarded the development of siegecraft in Greece in that its armies usually did not seek to destroy their adversary's cities. Siege machinery, the engineers to construct it, and the large numbers of trained technicians needed to conduct sieges were expensive and generally beyond the financial ability of many Greek states. By the fourth century BCE, Persian influence led to towers being added to the Greek cities' simple curtain walls from which counterfire could be directed at attackers, making a successful siege an even more uncertain proposition.[120] During the Peloponnesian wars, sieges were undertaken with the objective of starving out the defenders, sometimes taking years to succeed, and until the last decade of the fifth century BCE, no one had taken any Greek city by assault. As long as Greek armies did not seek to project their force over great distances and to capture their opponents' cities by storm, Greek armies did not need the capability to conduct sieges.

Philip had other ideas, however. Philip's army was designed precisely to project force over great distances, and his political objectives often required the capture and even permanent occupation of enemy cities. As noted, Philip intended to incorporate some cities into the Macedonian state after deporting their native populations and replacing them with Macedonian settlers. Speed was essential to Philip's campaigns, and he could not afford to spend time and energy in protracted sieges. Bypassing hostile cities exposed his line of communications to attack. He could achieve none of these objectives without the capability to overcome enemy cities relatively quickly. To solve the problem, Philip created a professional corps of engineers to conduct sieges.

The walls of Greek cities were constructed of either sun-dried brick or stone, depending on where the city was located. Walls of sun-dried brick covered with plaster were waterproof and fireproof and less likely than stone walls to collapse during minor earthquakes. However, only a few places in Greece had the proper clay and water supply to produce bricks in sufficient quantities, making these bricks expensive.[121] In much of Greece plenty of limestone was available in easily quarried outcrops, so the walls of many

Greek states were fashioned of stone. In Macedonia, where stone was not plentiful, city walls were fashioned of mud brick. A typical wall of either type would be constructed upon a low socle, or base, that was two and a half meters wide and rose one meter above the ground. The socle was made of an inner and outer skin of dressed masonry, and the space between its skins was filled with earth or rubble. This base could support a stone or brick wall seven to eight meters in height.[122]

In the three years between 357 and 354 BCE, Philip successfully conducted six sieges against fortified cities. In a little less than twelve months (357–356 BCE), Philip took Amphipolis, Pydna, and Potidea, and in 354 BCE he took Methone, Pagasae, and Olynthos.[123] He captured Amphipolis in five months and took Olynthos in three. The speed with which these sieges were accomplished was nothing short of amazing by Greek standards. Philip's siege train possessed the usual machines that had been used in the Levant for centuries. The Persians probably introduced them to Greece, but, as noted, they received little use except, perhaps, among Greek armies operating in Sicily. Rather than the machines themselves, the key to Philip's success was his employment of trained and experienced professional engineers who planned and executed the sieges.[124] Furthermore, Philip personally oversaw siege operations. He was wounded in the eye at Methone after venturing too close to the walls while checking on the siege's progress.

Diodorus's description of Philip's siege of Perinthus in 340 BCE mentions siege towers "80 cubits (120 feet) high," battering rams, bolt-shooting artillery, and scaling ladders.[125] Sappers, miners, and assault troops, while not mentioned, were no doubt present as well. The siege towers were prefabricated in sections and assembled at the siege site.[126] The bolt-shooting artillery were *grastraphetes* (belly-shooters), large laminated bows mounted on a wooden frame that shot large arrows with triple-barbed arrowheads. They also were capable of firing small stones.[127] The wood for battering rams was usually obtained on the spot, with only their metal heads and handles being transported, although in some cases fully assembled rams may have been transported. Protective sheds that shielded the miners and other equipment operators from counterfire from the city walls as the miners were filling in ditches and constructing approaches for the rams could also be constructed on the spot.

Transporting siege machinery was no easy task and required wagons, which slowed the army's rate of march. There was no reason why, however, the wagons couldn't make their way at the tail of the column at their own speed and catch up several days after the army arrived at the siege site. Except for the sieges of Perinthus and Byzantium, to which the Macedonian navy transported the siege train, all of Philip's sieges took place within fifty miles of Pella; so the distance and speed of transport did not present problems. In Philip's day, stone-shooting catapults were too weak to batter down walls and were used instead to shoot at the defenders on the walls.[128] These catapults were traction machines that derived their power not from twisting hair or sinew but from bending metal or wood, usually in the form of bows. By the end of Philip's reign, however, Polyeidos the Thessalian, Philip's chief engineer since 340 BCE, developed the prototype of the more powerful torsion catapult that could shoot larger stones and arrows over greater distances.[129] Surviving documents refer to this new type of catapult as *katapeltai Makedonikoi* (Macedonian catapults).[130] Philip's use of their early models at the sieges of Perinthus and Byzantium was the first time that any army in the world deployed fully operational torsion catapults.

Polyeidos trained two of his students, Diades and Charias, to continue his work, and in 334 BCE Diades succeeded him as Alexander's chief engineer. The two engineers appear to have completed the development of the torsion catapult, producing machines capable of throwing stone shot large enough to batter down city walls. Alexander used these new, powerful catapults first at the sieges of Halicarnassus and Tyre in 334 BCE and 332 BCE, respectively.[131] Without Alexander inheriting the ability to subdue cities quickly from Philip's engineers, his Persian campaign would not have been possible.

PHILIP'S INTELLIGENCE SERVICE

Roman politician Marcus Tullius Cicero remarked, "Philip used to say that all strongholds could be stormed provided an ass laden with gold could get up to them."[132] Given Philip's strategic perspective that war was always subordinate to political direction and that much more could be achieved by politics than by war, it is hardly surprising that Philip became a superb intelligence officer who knew the value of information and how to use it. Philip was famous as an affable host who threw the most expensive parties, was a great conversationalist, and gave expensive gifts and honors to many of his friends. And Philip had hundreds of friends throughout Greece whom he turned into valuable intelligence assets.

The relationship between guests (*xenia*) and guests-friends (*xenia kai philia*) in ancient Greece was actually institutionalized.¹³³ Originating in a tie of shared hospitality between two people, their "friendship" developed into almost kinship bound by gifts and mutual assistance and was similar to the Roman *clientele* system. A powerful man might inherit some friends, but most were established in person. Philip's friends received gifts of money, timber, grain, land, cattle, horses, and gold. Philip really had no tangible gifts in return. In these circumstances, the distinction between a gift from a powerful friend and a bribe became blurred. Philip used his gifts to extend his influence and patronage abroad to friends in the Greek states.¹³⁴ In this way, Philip created a stable of intelligence assets, many of them agents in place who could be used as needed.

What Philip needed most from these friends was information. His foreign friends were ideally placed to keep him informed about a state's domestic politics, the nature and relative strengths of their domestic factions, the size and morale of their armies, the state of their economies, and other important data that allowed Philip to assess the political context within which his own politics and strategy had to operate. Some of these friends became agents of influence within their target states. The success of Philip's intelligence operations can be gauged from the fact that when Philip entered Greece in force after his victory at Chaeronea, most of the Greek states already possessed factions that were openly or clandestinely pro-Macedonian.¹³⁵ It was the result of years of Philip's propaganda to convince their populations that he was a benevolent king and years of cultivating friendships with important political players to create what amounted to fifth columns that could be used to his advantage. Once the Greek states had recognized Philip's hegemony, these fifth columns were employed to replace existing state governments, exile the old rulers, and execute opponents. Their work made it unnecessary for Philip himself to carry out these harsh policies and enabled him to avoid the hatred that they engendered. Philip's "conquest" of Greece was, after all, a masterful *political* achievement that followed on a single military victory, and it was made possible by Philip's agents successfully preparing the political environment.

We hear again and again from such sources as Demosthenes and Theopompus that Philip's successful "enslavement" of Greece was owed more to treachery on the part of the Greeks themselves—allowing Philip to "purchase" their consciences—than to Philip's own abilities. If so, Philip's capitalizing on the Greeks' cupidity was testimony to his successful intelligence operations. And these operations may have been extensive indeed. During the siege of Olynthos in 348 BCE, the city's two cavalry commanders, Lasthenes and Euthycrates, defected to Philip and took their commands with them, making it easier for Philip to complete his assault.[136] In 343 BCE, as relations between Athens and Philip were deteriorating, an Athenian citizen named Antiphon, who had been forced to leave the city, returned to Athens. There he was caught red-handed trying to set fire to the Piraeus dockyards. During his trial, he was charged with having been sent by Philip to set the fire.[137] Both of these operations may have been put in motion by Philip's "friend" or even by Philip himself.

Philip's numerous friends, along with their locations, weaknesses, and assessments of their value as agents, were simply too much information for one man alone to retain in his memory or utilize effectively over time. The official diplomatic representatives (*proxenoi*) also had to be managed. To effectively exploit these intelligence assets, some form of organized intelligence service was required. Early on, Philip created a secretariat who was responsible for keeping a journal of his activities and for reading, drafting, recording, and delivering all diplomatic and royal correspondence.[138] The name of Philip's first chief of intelligence is lost to us. But in 343 BCE Eumenes of Cardia became chief of the department. It was probably in the secretariat that Philip's intelligence service operated. Upon Philip's death, Eumenes retained his position and went on to serve Alexander in the same capacity.

THE MACEDONIAN NAVY

Another of Philip's innovations was the Macedonian navy, the first national naval force in the country's history. Macedonia proper, Chalcidice, and Thrace from the Strymon River to the Hellespont had exposed coastlines that had to be defended from Greek naval attack. The combination of geography and the Athenians' naval power and history of seaborne invasions of Macedonia forced Philip to develop a naval force in self-defense. In 357 BCE, he captured the Athenian colony of Amphipolis at the head of the Thermaic Gulf. Amphipolis had extensive shipbuilding yards, a seafaring tradition of competent sailors, and proximity to fir and pine forests that were the sources of wood for ships. Philip now had his own shipyard. Next he seized another Greek colony on the Macedonian coast, Pydna, which possessed a fortified harbor and a seagoing population that could be used to man the new ships.

By 353 BCE Philip had a small fleet operating from the Thracian coast. In 352 BCE he gained control of the Magnesian coast and the Gulf of Pagasae from which he raided Athenian shipping. While the numbers are uncertain, Philip probably had less than a half dozen or so triremes and a few *penteconter* (fifty rowers) and *triaconter* (thirty rowers) galleys.

By 348 BCE Philip controlled the ports of the Chalcidian Peninsula and drew on its seafaring population to supply oarsmen for his fleet.[139] Philip's attacks on Perinthus and Byzantium in 340 BCE were supported by his fleet, which transported his siege machinery through the Sea of Marmara. When Philip shifted his attack from Perinthus to Byzantium, he moved some of his troops by sea. And in one of the more daring naval operations in Greek history, Philip captured the Athenian grain fleet intact.[140]

The Macedonian navy was not a match for the Athenian navy, but Philip never let events come to that. The Macedonian navy was basically a defensive force tasked with protecting the country's coastline and preventing hostile amphibious landings across the Macedonian army's line of communications whenever it was in the field. From time to time, however, Philip used the navy to raid Greek shipping or to carry out minor harassing raids. By the time of Philip's death, the navy had grown to twenty-two triremes and thirty-eight penteconters or triaconters.[141] Their crews were mostly Macedonian sailors and not Greeks. Some of these ships were used to transport Alexander's army to Asia.

4 THE UNIFICATION OF MACEDONIA

When Philip assumed responsibility for governing Macedonia in the late spring of 359 BCE, the country was barely recognizable as a political entity (see map 3). The Macedonian king, Perdiccas III, had been killed in a battle against the Illyrians. The Illyrian army occupied the country's Upper Cantons, the important geostrategic barrier between Macedonia's heartland and Illyria, and was replenishing its forces for another attack, this time to seize the Macedonian plains.[1] The Macedonian army had been destroyed, and for all practical purposes it no longer existed. Only a skeleton force of survivors stood between the Illyrians and the sea. Macedonia's cities on the coast of the Thermaic Gulf, from the Strymon River to the Thessalian border, were under foreign control. The Paeonians, a people living on the upper reaches of the Axius and Strymon rivers, sensed Macedonia's weakness and began raiding the Macedonian lowlands.[2] Athens and the king of Western Thrace were each supporting rival claimants to the Macedonian throne. While Thrace threatened the small Macedonian garrison in Amphipolis, Athens was readying a fleet and an invasion force to land on the Macedonian coast and march on Pella itself. "These were the perils threatening them," Diodorus says, "and the Macedonians were reduced to the greatest despair."[3]

To be a great leader, one must live in challenging times, and these were certainly challenging times for Philip II and Macedonia. Philip needed a break in hostilities to rebuild the army so it could at least handle the threats from Paeonia and Thrace. To counter the imminent military threats from Illyria and Athens, Philip turned to diplomacy. The goal of Philip's strategy was to prevent both adversaries from invading Macedonia. Shortly after Perdiccas's funeral, Philip opened contacts with Bardylis, the Illyrian king. The Illyrians were not a politically united kingdom but a coalition of large tribes. Bardylis was probably the king of the Dardanians, living near what is now Kosovo in modern Serbia.[4]

The meeting was concerned with forging a peace. Philip had precious little to offer. We have no account of the negotiations, but it seems likely that Philip agreed to formally recognize the Illyrians' occupation of the Upper Cantons and some Macedonian cities and to pay tribute in cash or in-kind goods. One source says that Bardylis may have imposed his daughter or granddaughter, Audata, on Philip as his wife to guarantee Philip's future good behavior, but this is unlikely.[5] It is possible that some sort of domestic concerns caused Bardylis to postpone the invasion, but we have no information in this regard. Philip clearly came away from the meeting, however, convinced that the Illyrian king would not immediately attack Macedonia.

Philip moved quickly to defuse the threat from Athens. The root of the problem was Perdiccas's installation of a Macedonian garrison in the city of Amphipolis sometime in 359 BCE. Amphipolis had been founded by Athens in 437 BCE but was lost to the king of Western Thrace in 424 BCE. The city was situated on the banks of a horseshoe bend of the Strymon River and controlled the river's only bridged crossing point on the mainland route from Byzantium to the Adriatic Sea. The city had a good port at Eion and easy access to the trade in raw materials with the interior. The shipyard had access to Macedonian timber and pitch, although most of the raw materials for shipbuilding were exported to Greece. Part of the population was employed as shipwrights and sailors. Amphipolis was close to significant gold and silver mines in the area, although they seem for the most part to have been only marginally exploited at the time. Perhaps for reasons of national prestige, the Athenians had never formally recognized the loss of Amphipolis but made its recovery a driving force in determining foreign policy issues with Macedonia and Thrace.[6]

No doubt aware of Philip's difficulties, Athens pressed its case for Amphipolis and used its military force to support Argaeus's claim to the Macedonian throne. Argaeus was a member of an older branch of the Macedonian royal house—perhaps the son of Archelaus (who reigned 413–399 BCE)— whom the Illyrians had installed on the throne as Argaeus II from 393 to 391

Map 3. *Macedonia and Its Occupied Territories (359 BCE)*

BCE. To further complicate matters for Philip, Pausanias, who seems to have been Argaeus's brother, gained the support of Cotys, the powerful Odrysian king of Thrace, to support his claim to the kingship.[7] In return for their support against Philip, no doubt both brothers had promised to relinquish Amphipolis to their respective patrons after assuming the throne. Archelaus, one of Philip's three half-brothers, also seems to have made a half-hearted claim against Philip and had the support of the Chalcidian League. Philip nipped this plot in the bud by having Archelaus murdered. His two remaining half-brothers, Arrhidaeus and Menelaus, fled and were given refuge in the city of Olynthos. Philip saw Olynthos's offer of sanctuary as support for the conspiracy and would in good time take his revenge.

Meanwhile, the Paeonians began raiding south along the Axius River, while the Thracians were becoming more vocal supporters of Pausanias. Once more Philip turned to diplomacy. Philip understood that the Macedonian garrison in Amphipolis was a bone in the Athenians' throat. To remove any casus belli with Athens and, perhaps, to persuade it to abandon its support for Argaeus, Philip "withdrew of his own accord from the city and left it independent."[8] The Athenians interpreted Philip's withdrawal as a sign of weakness, however, and continued to assemble their naval force for an invasion of Macedonia in support of Argaeus.

A military confrontation with Athens was now a certainty, and Philip moved diplomatically to try and neutralize the threats from Paeonia and Thrace beforehand. Diodorus explains Philip's gambit this way: "Next he opened up negotiations with the Paeonians, and, having corrupted some with bribes and others with generous promises [the Paeonians, like the Illyrians, were not a united people but a coalition of tribes with their own rulers] he made an agreement with them to remain at peace. Likewise he induced by presents the king [Cotys of western Thrace] who was intending to restore Pausanias and so thwarted his return."[9] We do not hear of Pausanias again and may reasonably assume that he was killed.

In a few short months, Philip had achieved what might have first appeared impossible. Without the means to protect Macedonia by force, Philip relied on diplomacy to reduce the dangers facing his country. In this way he had delayed an invasion by Illyria, and he had discovered and neutralized several plots to remove him, including at least two that had the support of foreign powers. Gifts, bribes, and promises had purchased a temporary peace from the Paeonians and ended their harassing raids. Only his attempt to pacify Athens by withdrawing the Macedonian garrison from Amphipolis had failed. As the summer wore on, Philip prepared to deal with the Athenian invasion that would surely come. The question was then whether Philip's new army was ready for a fight.

THE BATTLE AT LIVAHDI RIDGE

Under the command of Athenian general Mantias, an Athenian fleet of some forty triremes and additional support ships carrying three thousand mercenaries, Macedonian exiles, a small contingent of Athenian citizen-hoplites, and some official observers landed at Potidea on the Chalcidian Peninsula in early autumn, 359 BCE. The city was under Athenian control, and its port served as naval base to protect Athenian interests in the Thermaic Gulf. A few days later, the invasion force sailed the twenty miles across the gulf and made a surprise landing at Methone on the Macedonian coast. Methone had been an Athenian ally since 363 BCE when it was captured by an Athenian army.

With the troops safely ashore, Argaeus formed up the mercenaries and began his march to Aegae, the old Macedonian capital. It is interesting that Mantias stayed behind in Methone with the Athenian hoplites and sent only the exiles and observers to accompany Argaeus. Not having Mantias in command of the land operation suggests that Athens may have been satisfied with Philip's withdrawal from Amphipolis, at least to the degree that it wished to separate itself diplomatically from Argaeus's attempt to drive Philip from the throne. Should Argaeus succeed, Athens was still in a position to reap the benefits of its support. Should Argaeus fail, however, Athens could claim that it had not sent its citizen-soldiers but only provided transportation for a band of mercenaries in the pay of a renegade prince. Its involvement could all be chalked up to a mere commercial venture. If Argaeus failed, though, Athens would still have to live with Philip.

The marching distance from Methone to Aegae was eighteen miles over a ridge and through the pass at Livahdi. Once over the ridge, the ground to Aegae was open and flat and remained so until one reached Pella, twenty-four miles distant.[10] Philip and his new army remained in Pella to prevent any landing by a second invasion force sailing up the Ludias River and an attack on the capital itself. Argaeus reached Aegae without opposition and approached the city, whereupon "he proceeded to call upon the citizens of Aegae to welcome his return and to become the founders of his kingship. However, since nobody paid any attention to him, he returned to Methone."[11]

By now Philip knew that Argaeus had been in Aegae and was returning to Methone. Under cover of night, Philip and his army marched from Pella to the Livahdi ridge, where they waited in ambush for Argaeus. This was dicey business. Philip's new army had no combat experience, and he could only hope it would perform as it had been trained. While details are lacking, Philip likely chose the terrain most advantageous to his new phalanx formation, or flat and even ground. The same would apply for Philip's cavalry. Although composed of experienced horsemen, the cavalry would face its first fight in squadron formations. Philip knew that Argaeus had no cavalry with him and planned his tactics accordingly. It might be conjectured, then, that Philip formed his infantry at the exit of the Livahdi Pass across Argaeus's line of march and deployed the Macedonian cavalry on the flank. Once the mercenaries became aware of the Macedonian infantry, they would form in their usual phalanx formation and await the Macedonian charge, leaving their flanks exposed.[12]

Diodorus tells us that "when Philip appeared on the scene with his troops, he joined battle with the mercenaries and killed many of them. The remainder, who had taken refuge on a hill, he let go under truce, but received from them the exiles whom they surrendered to him."[13] The account suggests that the new phalanx worked perfectly. The mercenaries had never seen the Macedonian phalanx in action before, and they must have been terribly surprised by its ability to kill by driving the sarissa points right through their armor and shields. High casualty rates in Greek infantry battles were unusual. That an inexperienced force killed so many professional mercenaries speaks to the effectiveness of Philip's new phalanx. That those who were not killed "took refuge on a hill" suggests that the mercenary formation came apart under the Macedonian attack and that Philip's cavalry prevented the men's escape by surrounding and entrapping them at one location.

With Philip's victory at Livahdi ridge, a new day had dawned on the battlefields of Greece. An army of untested infantrymen wielding new weapons in new combat formations with new tactics had defeated an army of Greek military professionals and had done so while inflicting unusually heavy casualties and shattering what until now had been the strongest infantry formation in Greek history. No one knew it then, but warfare in Greece would never be the same. The battle at Livahdi ridge was the first in a twenty-three-year-long series of combat engagements in which the Macedonian phalanx was victorious in all but one. Philip had discovered the terrible secret heretofore concealed by centuries of Greek history, culture, and tradition: battle was less about observing ritual and demonstrating individual heroism and more about killing.

Philip's new army had drawn its first blood and, in doing so, changed Greek warfare forever. It had, of course, also transformed the soldiers who fought under Philip's command that day. They had tasted their first victory, and they realized that their beloved Macedonia was no longer without protectors. Diodorus wrote that "as a result of his victory in his first battle Philip made the Macedonians more confident in facing subsequent conflicts"[14] and in meeting the challenges he planned for them. Philip now had the instrument he needed to safeguard Macedonia.

As important as the victory at Livahdi was to Philip, it did not change the situation with Athens regarding Amphipolis. Philip used his victory as an opening to seek a diplomatic solution to the problem and offered lenient terms for those he had captured. He proposed that the mercenaries be permitted to depart Macedonia under truce, that the Athenian observers recover anything they had lost, and that they should go free. Argaeus and his exiled supporters, however, were to be turned over to Philip. Mantias had little choice but to accept. Soon after, the Athenian naval squadron put to sea for its return to Athens. Philip had given Mantias a letter in which Philip proposed a peace with Athens in return for his renouncing his claim to Amphipolis. Diodorus tells us that Athens accepted the proposal and that "Philip sent envoys to Athens and persuaded the people to make peace with him now that he was no longer laying claim to Amphipolis."[15] Interestingly, Philip had proposed the agreement not in his own name but in the name of Amyntas IV, his infant nephew, who was still the legitimate king of Macedonia at this time.[16] Argaeus and the exiles were brought before the Macedonian Assembly and charged with treason. They were found guilty and executed.

Philip's victory against a three thousand–man force of military professionals raises questions of when the battle took place and the size and composition of Philip's army. It is most likely that the battle took place sometime in early autumn. Throughout the summer months the barometric pressure over the eastern Mediterranean falls dramatically, causing steady northerly winds of twenty to twenty-five miles an hour to blow almost constantly. Known in antiquity as the Etesian winds, they blew from the north in the central Aegean and from the northeast in the eastern Aegean.[17] The winds made navigation upwind from Athens to the ports on the Thermaic Gulf very difficult. Accordingly, it was unlikely that the Athenian naval force transporting Argaeus and the mercenary army arrived in Potidea before the winds had lessened or late September or early October 359 BCE. The battle occurred shortly afterward.

The size and composition of Philip's army remains a matter of conjecture. In the early spring of 359 BCE, the Illyrians had destroyed the Macedonian army in a battle that killed four thousand Macedonians and their king. Whatever force Philip had with him at Livahdi ridge had been assembled and trained over a period of only seven months. The centerpiece of this force was Philip's battle guard, which he had assembled and trained in the new weapons and tactics while he was governor of Amphaxitis. Assuming his battle guard had not grown, it numbered at most 1,000 men. It would, as a matter of course, have had a cavalry contingent since the Amphaxitis region was an open plain and best patrolled adequately with cavalry. A locally raised cavalry force of 120, or a single squadron, seems appropriate. Philip might have salvaged perhaps another 2,000 men from the remnants of Perdiccas's shattered army and probably another 200 or so cavalry from the king's Companions. This combination accounts for a force of 3,000 infantry and 300-plus cavalry.

While Philip organized, trained, and drilled this small army into a combat-ready field force, he recruited additional soldiers into the ranks before he faced the Illyrians in the early spring of 358 BCE. During the previous winter, Philip had campaigned in Paeonia. Marching into Paeonia, waging the battles, returning to Pella, replenishing the army, and marching some sixty-five miles south to Elimiotis, where he began his march to engage the Illyrians, all must surely have taken at least two months or longer. Diodorus tells that after the Paeonian campaign, Philip "was eager to subdue them [the Illyrians] also,"[18] so it is surmised that the Illyrian campaign followed closely upon the Paeonian campaign. It is unlikely that Philip was able to recruit and train more troops during either campaign, so the size of his army must have been the same for both campaigns. Diodorus tells us that when Philip marched against the Illyrians, he did so "with no fewer than ten thousand foot soldiers and six hundred cavalry."[19]

Thus we are faced with the following information. Philip had some ten months from the time of Perdiccas's defeat in 359 BCE until his attack on Paeonia in early 358 BCE, to rebuild the Macedonian army. Some seven months passed before the battle of Livahdi ridge took place, and that was sufficient time to train about a thousand new recruits each month. Cavalry recruitment from among the nobility would have been somewhat easier since it involved offering new cavalry, perhaps the sons of those men killed in the battle with the Illyrians, the status of Companions. All things considered, Philip may have been able to put nine thousand to ten thousand infantry and seven hundred cavalry in the field at Livahdi ridge.

Philip's success at Livahdi ridge and the negotiated peace that followed removed the Athenian threat at least for the moment. Never one to miss an opportunity, however, Philip turned his attention to the Paeonians. Although he had reached an agreement with them only months before, Philip marched against Paeonia. The Paeonian king, Agis, had died in early 358 BCE. Philip may have reckoned that Agis's succession would cause domestic turmoil and that an untested king would need time to consolidate his control over the other tribes. Philip saw an opportunity to take his army into battle against a relatively weak opponent and give it additional combat experience. Another victory would boost Macedonian morale before the army had to confront the more formidable Illyrians.[20]

Philip must have had the Illyrian threat in mind and known that sooner or later he would have to deal with it on the battlefield. When Philip "marched therefore into Paeonia and defeated the barbarians in a set battle, he compelled the tribe [actually the tribal state and not a single tribe] to obey the Macedonians."[21] Here we have Philip's first winter campaign, an unusual occurrence in Greek warfare. Greek armies usually took to their homes and barracks during the winter months, permitting Philip's army to move without hindrance and affording him significant strategic and tactical advantages. Philip's army appears to have been the first Western army to develop the capability to fight in all seasons of the year. Philip conducted other, more extensive winter campaigns, but the campaign in Paeonia was the first.

THE ILLYRIAN WAR

In less than two years, either by diplomacy or by force, Philip had neutralized the dangers facing his country. Only the very real danger of a large-scale invasion by Illyria remained. Philip's military and diplomatic successes could hardly have gone unnoticed in Illyria, which may now have thought its pact with Philip a strategic mistake. A year earlier Philip was at its mercy. Now he had rebuilt the Macedonian army and could forcefully resist any Illyrian incursion. For forty years Illyria had exercised military ascendancy over Macedonia, and the "Illyrians, gathering large forces, were making preparations for an invasion of Macedonia."[22] But Philip struck first.

Philip moved his army from Pella to Elimiotis on the bend of the Haliacmon River and staged his advance against the Illyrians there. In 358 BCE Perdiccas had arranged a diplomatic marriage with Phila, the daughter of the ruler of Elimiotis, for Philip. There is reason to believe that some Elimiotian troops, most probably cavalry, accompanied Philip on this campaign. Diodorus tells us that "Philip convened an assembly, exhorted the men with suitable words to go to war, and led his army . . . into the territory of the Illyrians."[23] Philip's movement seemed to have caught the Illyrians by surprise while making their own preparations, and they attempted to buy time by opening negotiations. According to Diodorus, "Bardylis, the Illyrian king, on being apprised of the enemy presence, immediately dispatched ambassadors concerning a settlement on terms that allowed both parties to remain masters of the cities that they at the time controlled."[24] This proposal was hardly credible in light of the Illyrian occupation of the Upper Cantons of Macedonia. Philip rejected it out of hand, demanding that the Illyrians withdraw from "all the Macedonian cities" as the price of peace. The negotiations collapsed.

Philip arrived first and chose the battlefield for the tactical advantages it afforded his forces, in this case, level ground for the phalanx and plenty of room for the cavalry to maneuver. His advance took him through the Kirli Dirven Pass and on to the open plain of Lyncus.[25] Diodorus says Bardylis, "confident in his previous victories and the prowess of the Illyrians, with ten thousand picked infantry and about five hundred cavalry was on the way to meet him."[26] We have only Frontinus[27] and Diodorus as sources for the ensuing battle, and both accounts are incomplete. The Illyrians, armed and trained as hoplites, fought in typical Greek infantry fashion in phalanx with their flanks protected by cavalry.[28] But our sources do not mention the Illyrian cavalry in their accounts. It is not reasonable to assume that Bardylis arrived on the battlefield without it since Diodorus tells us that the cavalry were with Bardylis when he went out to meet Philip in battle. Where, then, was the Illyrian cavalry and what happened to it?

A clue is provided by the fact that the Illyrians "formed themselves into a square."[29] The formation that Diodorus describes, however, is not a square but a rectangle, and the word used in the text is *plinthion*, derived from the Greek term for an oblong wooden frame used for making bricks.[30] As described in Asclepiodotus's *Tactics*, this rectangular formation was used only in desperation when the infantry's supporting cavalry was driven from the field, exposing the flanks of the phalanx to attack. In these circumstances, the phalanx formed itself into a rectangular box to "have a body in all directions," that is, to protect itself on all sides from cavalry attack.[31] It seems reasonable to conclude, then, that the Illyrian cavalry was driven from the field before the infantry engagement commenced.

In all likelihood, the armies formed up facing each other in the usual way with the Illyrian cavalry divided into two sections, and each protected a flank of the phalanx. Illyrian cavalry, like Illyrian infantry, was organized, trained, and armed in traditional Greek fashion. The cavalrymen's role was usually to use their weight to protect the infantry. In the offense, their task was to launch their javelins or engage enemy cavalry with the short stabbing spear. They were, however, neither trained to deal with the ferocious Macedonian cavalry armed with the longer-reaching xyston nor willing to engage in the "intimidating intimacy" of close combat. Under these circumstances, the Illyrian cavalry probably broke quickly under the shock of the Macedonian cavalry attack, fled the field, and left the infantry to their fate. After the cavalry escaped, the Illyrian infantry line reformed in a plinthion in a desperate effort to save itself from annihilation.

The Illyrian infantry, formed in a rectangle, was now immobile, and the tactical initiative shifted to Philip, who recalled his cavalry and repositioned it to the right of his infantry line. Philip himself led the "tallest and strongest men, men who served as the King's Guard and were called *pezhetairoi*" into battle.[32] It is of great interest that Philip fought with the infantry and not on horseback with the cavalry as was usual for Macedonian kings. Philip's presence with the infantry on the battlefield was symbolic of the infantry's rise as an equal branch with the cavalry in the Macedonian army. Since Macedonia had possessed no respectable infantry before Philip, its development was a major revolution in military culture. Moreover, Philip's infantry was more lethal in close combat than any hoplite phalanx was, and although the cavalry

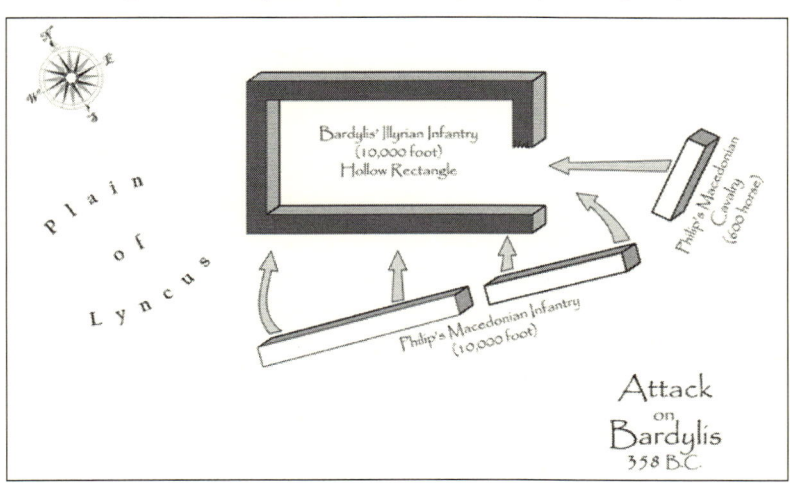

Figure 3. *Philip's Attack on Bardylis's Illyrian Infantry*

became the combat arm of decision, it was the infantry that still inflicted the greatest number of casualties.

The King's Guard comprised Philip's oldest comrades, those who had served as his bodyguard while he was provincial governor, and became the elite of the new army. Philip placed these men on the extreme right wing of the infantry line under his personal command. The rest of the infantry line was held back at the left oblique as it advanced, a variation on Epaminondas's tactics employed at Leuctra. Diodorus describes Philip's movement: "Philip, who directed the right wing and the pick of the Macedonians involved in the conflict, ordered his cavalry to ride past the enemy and attack them on the flank, while he himself assailed the enemy in the front and brought on a fierce struggle."[33] Frontinus has Philip's right wing leading out toward the enemy's left side beyond the corner formed by the front and left sides of the Illyrian formation:

> The Illyrians . . . threw themselves into the engagement with all their might. At first the battle was equally balanced for a long time because of the surpassing valor of both sides, and, while many were killed and still more wounded, the battle inclined first one way and then the other, as the bravery of the contestants caused the outcome to swing backwards and forwards.[34]

Philip massed his cavalry to the far right of his own position on the right wing and ordered it to advance at the walk, or at the speed of the infantry's advance. When Philip's guard overlapped the corner of the rectangle, one part of Philip's infantry turned left while the other attacked straight on. Thus both sides of the corner came under attack by the compacted ranks of Philip's elite infantry, which drove through it, opening up a gap at the left corner of the rectangle. At about the same time, units of the Macedonian infantry line began to contact and engage the Illyrian infantry at the front of the rectangle, pinning it in place. Philip ordered his cavalry to attack through the opening in the angle, exposing the entire enemy formation to simultaneous attack from the rear and front. Diodorus tells us that "as the cavalry forced their way onwards both from the flank and from the rear with Philip fighting heroically alongside the best of his troops, the bulk of the Illyrians were obliged to take flight."[35] Philip's coordinated cavalry and infantry strikes against the enemy in the flanks and the front simultaneously were in imitation of the tactics employed by the Theban general Pelopidas at the battle of Cynoscephalae (364 BCE) against Alexander of Pherae.[36] The shock of the Macedonian cavalry attack shattered the Illyrian phalanx, scattering its soldiers across the Lyncus plain as they fled the ferocity of the killing. Philip's cavalry rode them down mercilessly, leaving seven thousand infantrymen dead upon the bloodied plain in addition to however many Illyrian cavalrymen had already been killed.[37] Bardylis, said to have been ninety years old when he took the field against Philip, escaped.[38] At Lyncus we see the first recorded instance of Philip's policy of using lethal pursuit after the battle to kill as many of the enemy's leadership corps as possible and to weaken the survivors' position in the negotiations that followed. Philip not only intended to drive Illyria out of Macedonia, he intended to fix it so that it could not threaten his country again.

Its army destroyed and its ruling aristocracy destroyed, Illyria was in no position to resist Philip's demands.[39] The Illyrians were forced to relinquish "all of Macedon's cities" that they occupied, and "Philip made all the inhabitants as far as Lake Lychnitis [modern Lake Ohrid] subject to himself."[40] This decree led to pressing the old Macedonian frontier farther north and west, incorporating some minor Illyrian tribes, and using a double line of mountains as the new border of Philip's kingdom. Philip now controlled the mountain passes and the routes around the lake that the Illyrians had used as invasion routes in the past.[41] The area's tribal states were permitted to administer their own affairs, and militia units of infantry were established under the command of Macedonian officers to guard the passes. The new Macedonian border lay directly against Illyria proper, with no intervening buffer states. To formalize the new Macedonian-Illyrian relationship, Philip married an Illyrian princess named Audata who, like Philip's own mother, took the Macedonian name Eurydice.[42] A year later (357 BCE), Philip made an alliance with Arybbas, the king of Molossia (of Epirus), to further strengthen his position against Illyria. The pact was sealed with a diplomatic marriage between Philip and Arybbas's niece Olympias.[43]

Meanwhile, Philip annexed the Upper Cantons and abolished their royal houses. Their former rulers and aristocrats were taken into Philip's court, became Macedones, and served as Companions. He made their sons eligible for admission to the Royal Page School. The cantons' populations were now formally considered Macedonians with the same status of the original Macedonians. They could serve in the King's Field Army and qualify for elite citizenship. Annexing the Upper Cantons doubled the territory of Macedonia under Philip's control and increased the population from which Philip's military manpower could be drawn.[44] Philip immediately set about recruiting more men for his army by establishing bases for training the militia that would protect the towns. The best of the militia soldiers were moved into the King's Field Army. In time, three of the six phalanx battalions of Philip's army were drawn from Upper Macedonia, including several new squadrons of cavalry.[45] Within a year, Philip "was master of a greater force thanks to his victory over the Illyrians."[46] His defeat of the Illyrians on the Lyncus plain was one of the most decisive battles in military history because it achieved the unification of Macedonia and expanded the manpower and resource base available to Philip to realize his strategic vision of Macedonian hegemony over the Greek states. Had Philip been defeated, the military history of the West would have been markedly different.

THE SIEGE OF AMPHIPOLIS

During this time, Philip's actions were guided by four strategic objectives: to secure his hold on the throne; to protect Macedonia from threats of invasion; to increase, battle test, and refine the Macedonian army into a military force capable of obtaining additional national goals; and to finance and sustain these efforts by gaining access to much-needed sources of wealth.[47] Philip's success thus far had been premised on his speed and decisive actions. After a year spent organizing his conquests in Upper Macedonia and doubling the size of the Macedonian army, Philip was ready to attempt his next objective.

With the Upper Cantons integrated into Macedonia proper and the threats from Illyria and Paeonia reduced, the remaining security problem concerned Macedonia's narrow waist at the head of the Thermaic Gulf that separated eastern and western Macedonia and offered easy access for invasion from Thrace or by a Greek naval force. The key to controlling this strategic area was the fortified city of Amphipolis. The city maintained the only crossing point with a permanent bridge over the lower Strymon River,[48] and Athens had tried on several occasions to retake the city. Athens saw Amphipolis as an important base from which it could project power in the Thermaic Gulf, protect its source of shipbuilding materials, and guard the land route to Byzantium over which a hostile army could march and disrupt its vital supply of imported grain. From Philip's perspective, the city blocked any Macedonian attempt to expand east into Thrace and obtain access to its gold- and silver-producing regions. Strategically Amphipolis was a door that swung both ways.

Compounding Philip's security concerns were the pro-Athenian cities along the Macedonian coast and on the Chalcidian Peninsula that could serve as naval and land bases for a large-scale invasion of Macedonia. Chief among these cities was Methone, located thirty miles southeast of Pella. It had been an Athenian possession since 364 BCE, and its population had resisted efforts at incorporation into Macedonia. Philip had not forgotten that Methone had served as a base of operations for the Athenian invasion force that supported Argaeus's claim to the Macedonian throne. Its excellent fortifications, pro-Athenian population, and strategic location made the city a significant threat to Macedonian security. Pydna, another coastal city five miles south of Methone, had been an Athenian possession since 364 BCE as well after it was captured by Timotheus. Its population remained mostly Macedonian; however, the people were subject to the authority of Athenian settlers, who remained strongly pro-Athenian in their sympathies. Twenty miles across the gulf from Methone was Potidea, located on Pallene, the narrowest part of the western Chalcidian Peninsula. Originally a Corinthian colony, it had been won for Athens in 364 BCE. In 361 BCE the city requested that Athens send in settlers who could help strengthen Potidea against retaliation from the Chalcidian League. An Athenian garrison followed, and Potidea became an important Athenian naval base in the Thermaic Gulf. To secure Macedonia from seaborne invasion, Philip would have to neutralize these cities.

By 357 BCE, his army having increased to twenty thousand infantry and six hundred cavalry, a force sufficient to deal with any seaborne force landing at his back, Philip went after Amphipolis. He first made diplomatic overtures, trying to bring the city into the Macedonian orbit without violence; however, the city's ruling faction feared Macedonia more than it did Athens and refused.[49] Philip brought up his engineers and siege train and took Amphipolis under assault in the spring. The city's walls were massive. The Athenians, themselves having tried and failed to take the city twice by isolation and starvation, thought it was impregnable.

The city's governors appealed to Athens for help. By the time the city's envoys reached Athens with their appeal and considering the time it would take for Athens to raise a sufficient relief force, it was already late summer. The Etesian winds began to blow, making it impossible for Athenian ships to sail against them and reach Amphipolis. Athens did, however, send two envoys to negotiate with Philip, although it is unclear what they discussed. According to Theopompus and Demosthenes, a secret pact was struck with Philip: once he had taken Amphipolis, he promised to it turn over to Athens in return for Pydna.[50] Whatever Philip promised is unknown, but the Athenians thought they had a deal in betraying Pydna.

Amphipolis fell in five months.[51] Diodorus tells us that "having applied siege engines to the walls and launched continuous and vigorous attacks, he knocked down part of the wall with his battering rams. Entering the city through the breach and slaying many, he won control of the city. He exiled those who were ill-disposed towards him but treated the remainder with lenience."[52] In the autumn of 357 BCE, Philip "straight away reduced Pydna." The Athenians waited for Philip to turn Amphipolis over to them. It would be a long wait.

EXPANSION TO THE EAST

The Chalcidians greeted Philip's capture of Amphipolis with mixed emotions. On the one hand, the fall of Amphipolis and Pydna had greatly reduced Athenian power in the Thermaic Gulf, thereby increasing Chalcidian influence there. Only Methone in Macedonia and Potidea on the Chalcidian Peninsula remained as bases of Athenian support. On the other hand, Athenian power had been largely replaced by Macedonian power, and Philip's intentions were less than clear. In the 380s BCE, the Chalcidian League, led by the powerful city of Olynthos, had captured parts of the Macedonian coast and occupied Pella.[53] There was no reason to suspect that Philip had forgotten the incident.

In Philip's view, Olynthos and the thirty-three cities of the Chalcidian League that it led had to be handled carefully. Olynthos alone had ten thousand hoplites and a thousand cavalry at its disposal, including numerous light infantry and warships that could transport troops across the gulf to attack the Macedonian coast.[54] When combined with the military forces of the league's cities, Olynthos and its allies presented a significant military threat to Philip. Moreover, whatever ambitions Philip might have for Thrace, he had to consider the geographic reality that Olynthos and its allies sat on his line of communications to Thrace, essentially making any Macedonian expansion into Thrace dependent on the acquiescence of Olynthos and the Chalcidian League. In some manner, then, Philip had to secure good relations with

Olynthos, if only in the short run until a more permanent solution could be found.

After the fall of Pydna, Philip opened negotiations with Olynthos and proposed an alliance. In return, Philip offered to capture the Athenian naval base at Potidea and turn it over to the league.[55] The basis of the proposal was that both Olynthos and Philip had a mutual interest in driving the Athenians completely out of the Thermaic Gulf. Once accomplished, Olynthos and Macedonia could work things out between them. Behind Philip's proposition was his fear that Athens, having lost Amphipolis and Pydna, might enter a military and political alliance with Olynthos and the league that could block Philip's ambitions in Thrace. In proposing a pact with Olynthos, Philip hoped to deprive Athens of any future help from Olynthos in the Thermaic Gulf. The agreement was signed in the winter of 356 BCE, and that spring Philip attacked Potidea.

According to Demosthenes,[56] when Athens learned that Philip was attacking Potidea, it made preparations to come to the city's aid. That help never arrived, however, and by July Philip had taken the city.[57] The speed and efficiency of Philip's besiegers and the Etesian winds again made it impossible for Athenian help to arrive in time. Diodorus tells us that, just as he had done after the battle of Livahdi ridge, "when Philip reduced Potidea, he brought the Athenian garrison out of the city and, treating them humanely, sent them back to Athens,"[58] probably in an effort to influence Athenian public opinion favorably. Philip sold the citizens of Potidea into slavery, however. Since he had promised the city to Olynthos, he imposed this harsh fate on the captured population to recover the costs of the siege. True to his word, Philip handed the city "over to the Olynthians and at the same time gave them in addition the properties in its territory."[59]

The Athenians' inability to respond militarily to the seizure of Amphipolis and Pydna encouraged them to seek other ways to damage Philip. To this end, Athens had been scheming to convince a number of tribal kings to attack Philip simultaneously on two fronts. The tribal alliance into which Athens entered as a passive partner included Grabus, an Illyrian king probably of the Taulanti; Lyppeios, the Paeonian chief who had succeed Agis; and Ketriporis, the king of Western Thrace who had succeeded Berisades.[60] Word of the Athenian plot reached Philip as the siege of Potidea was ending. As luck would have it, the citizens of Crenides, a gold-mining town some thirty-eight miles east of Amphipolis, appealed to Philip for help after Thracians in the service of Ketriporis attacked it.⁶¹ Faced with challenges on two fronts, Philip attacked both.

We have no account of the siege of Potidea and, therefore, no knowledge of the disposition of the Macedonian army. In all likelihood, however, some significant part of it was garrisoned around Pella to protect the capital while Philip was away, and the rest accompanied Philip to lay siege to Potidea. When Philip learned about the Athenian plot, he ordered the forces around Pella to march immediately against Illyria and engage Grabus. Plutarch tells us that in August 356 BCE the Macedonian general Parmenio won a great victory over the Illyrians,⁶² and he gained a second victory over the Paeonians shortly afterward. Diodorus tells us that the Macedonians struck while the enemies "were still in the process of assembling their armies."⁶³ Once again, Macedonian speed and logistical reach had been decisive. At about the same time, Philip marched north and east from Potidea to Crenides, attacked Ketriporis's Thracians, and occupied the town. The alliance with Athens had ended in disaster for all three kings, with Philip triumphing all around. It is noteworthy that Philip entrusted Parmenio and the troops raised in the Upper Cantons to deal with the Illyrians alone. His decision suggests that Philip's policy of integrating the Upper Cantons' peoples and aristocrats into the Macedonian nation-state was already succeeding.

Crenides was a valuable prize. Its location gave Philip a foothold in Western Thrace and control of the area as far east as the Nestus River, which itself was protected by a deep gorge farther east. Olynthos and the Chalcidian League now found themselves caught between the Macedonian fortresses at Amphipolis and Crenides and Macedonia proper. Any future attempt to deal with Philip by force was now fraught with the risk of military disaster. Crenides had great potential economic value. It was the center of the gold and silver mining area situated north and west of the mines of Mount Pangaeus. Until the capture of the town, these mines "were wholly paltry and unimportant."⁶⁴ When Philip resettled large numbers of Macedonians in the town, he sent along miners and other experts to improve the mines, and "by means of new equipment he augmented their production to such an extent that they were able to produce for him a revenue of more than one thousand talents,"⁶⁵ or some 300,000 gold pieces annually.⁶⁶ He used these gold staters, which he called Philips (*Philippeioi*), to pay and equip his army, which included mercenaries for the first time.⁶⁷ Philip fortified the town with walls and towers and later drained the marshy plain, transforming it into productive agricultural land. Philip ordered the construction of ships for the new Macedonian navy, which would protect Crenides from Athenian assault by sea.[68] The importance of Crenides to Philip's larger strategic design in Thrace was evident in the new name he chose for the place. He called it Philippi, after himself.

In three years Philip had unified Macedonia; inflicted crushing defeats on the Illyrians and Paeonians; put down two attempts by his rivals, with the aid of foreign governments, to depose him; freed the Macedonian coast of all but one of its foreign bases; captured the fortress of Amphipolis; destroyed the Athenian naval base at Potidea; neutralized the Chalcidian threat; driven Athenian influence from the Thermaic Gulf; and pushed into Thrace, extending Macedonian power east to the Nestus River. Incorporating the Upper Cantons had doubled the size and population of Philip's kingdom, and his addition of Amphipolis, Pydna, and the western areas in Thrace by 355 BCE increased his kingdom by another third. To bring Thrace within his operational reach, Philip began to construct and outfit the first navy in Macedonia's history. Finally, he began to place Macedonia itself on a sound economic footing by developing its infrastructure and integrating its towns and cities into a single economic entity.

In July 356 BCE, Olympias presented Philip with a son. Philip named him Alexander.

5 THESSALY AND THE SACRED WAR

The year 358 BCE had already been an eventful one for Philip, having fought battles with an untested army against Argaeus and his mercenaries, then Lyppeios and his Paeonians, and finally the critically important campaign against Bardylis of Illyria. Now he was deeply engaged in rebuilding the Macedonian army and assimilating the population and aristocrats of the Upper Cantons into the Macedonian national state. His battlefield successes, along with the fear that a major conflict with Athens might be brewing over Amphipolis, created uncertainty in the Macedonian Assembly over whether the country could afford the continued reign of the infant king, Amyntas IV. Philip was surely aware that important nobles wanted to replace Amyntas with Philip, who, in all his public actions, continued to act as regent. Philip even went so far as to sign diplomatic agreements in the infant king's name and never in his own. Given the sometimes violent nature of Macedonian politics, Philip may have feared that the boy, who was his nephew after all, might be murdered. These considerations and planning the attack on Amphipolis must have weighed heavily on Philip's mind.

THESSALY

One of Macedonia's curses was its assailable position vis-à-vis its potential enemies. Thessaly, to the south, had easy geographic access to Macedonia in times of conflict and, on a number of occasions in the recent past, had attacked and occupied parts of the country. The coast road from the Valley of Tempe in the north left Macedonia's coastal cities and its sacred shrine at Dium vulnerable to invasion, as did the Cambunian Mountains' eastern passes at Meluna and Volustana that debouched on the open plains of the Haliacmon River valley. Thessaly was the gateway to invading Macedonia from the south and the route that Thebes, Athens, or any hostile coalition of Greek states could use to attack the country.[1] It was vital to Macedonia's southern defenses to prevent Thessaly from becoming a strategic platform from which Thebes or Athens could assault Macedonia.

Thessaly was an important power in its own right and had enough resources to threaten Macedonia. Thessaly was among the largest and richest of the Greek states, with sufficient agriculture, natural resources, and an outlet to the sea at Pagasae that permitted a substantial and lucrative trade. It was also capable of raising large cavalry armies from its many cities. Estimates of the number of cavalry that a united Thessaly could raise range from three thousand to six thousand horse warriors.[2] Thessalian cavalry had been the best in Greece until eclipsed by the Macedonian cavalry, but it was still widely admired and equally feared throughout Greece, even in Macedonia. Thessalian horses were excellent mounts known for their size and endurance and were highly prized despite their often tremendous cost. Bucephalus, Alexander the Great's famous Thessalian horse, was said to have cost thirteen talents, a staggering sum.[3]

In the past two centuries, the political situation in Thessaly had been favorable to Macedonia in that the country was divided into numerous cities ruled by aristocracies whose rivalries had effectively prohibited the establishment of a strong national government. This political fragmentation sometimes caused the powerful aristocratic families of rival cities to ask outside parties for diplomatic and military help in handling their competitors. In 401 BCE, the city of Larissa asked Macedonia's king, Archelaus, to intervene in one of its disputes, and in 369 BCE Alexander II intervened again on Larissa's behalf against the tyrants of Pherae. Sometimes, however, the opposite occurred, with Macedonia requesting Thessaly's intervention. Thus, Thessalian force of arms restored Philip's father to the throne after the civil war, and, at least for a time, Macedonia was functionally a Thessalian protectorate. It was, therefore, not without precedent when in October 358 BCE Cineas, the head of the powerful Aleuadae family that ruled Larissa, requested that Philip intervene in his quarrel with the tyrants of Pherae.[4]

Macedonian policy toward Thessaly had always been to play one city against another and prevent the rise of a powerful national state governed

Map 4. *Thessaly*

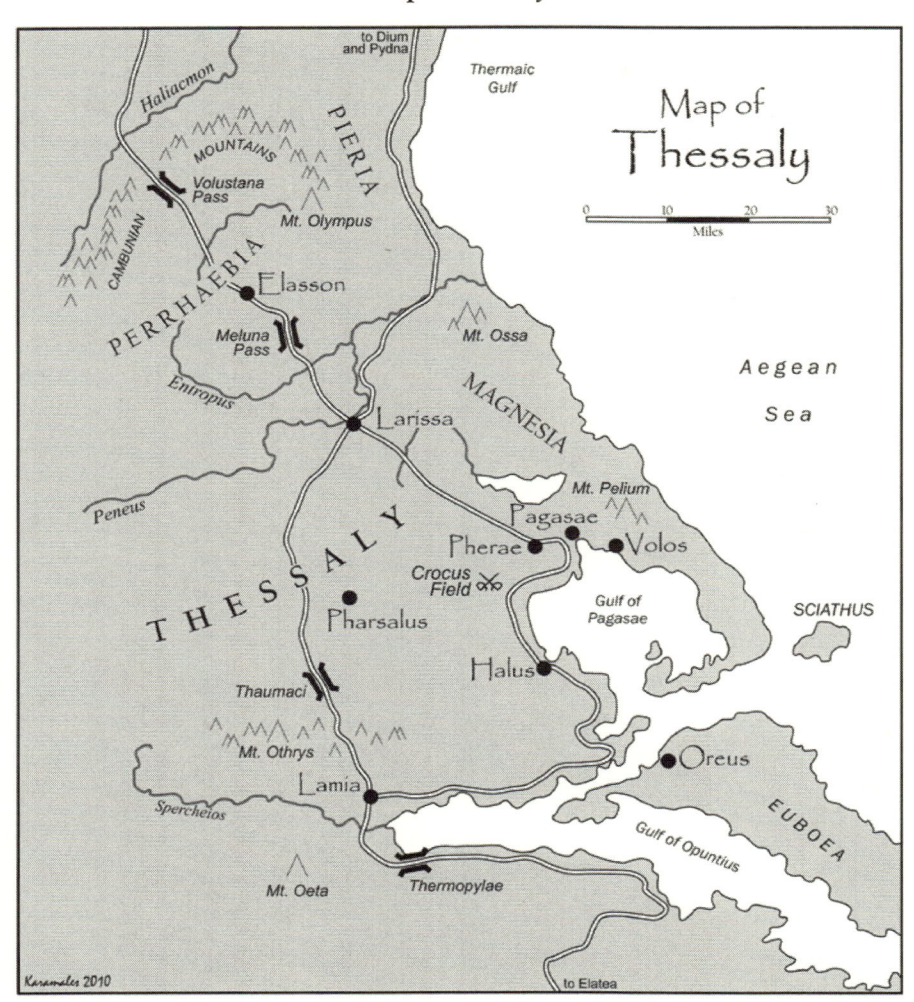

effectively from the center. To this end Macedonia had occupied parts of Thessaly for significant periods, as when King Archelaus seized the important border province of Perrhaebia and took ten sons of Larissan aristocrats as hostages.[5] The policy of encouraging domestic division and turmoil began to fail around 380 BCE when Jason of Pherae raised a powerful army and tried to unify the country. Jason's army was said to number eight thousand cavalry and twenty thousand hoplite mercenaries, a force large enough to encourage Philip's father to seek a nonaggression pact with him. Jason was assassinated in 370 BCE and replaced by his nephew, Alexander II, who actually exceeded his uncle's tyrannical behavior. In reaction, the leaders of the traditional aristocratic families of the other Thessalian cities formed a military alliance, the Thessalian League, to oppose the tyrant of Pherae. The country divided into two camps—one led by Larissa and comprised the cities of the inland plain, and the other led by Pherae, which controlled the coastal towns and cities, the most important of which was the port of Pagasae. In the late summer of 358 BCE, an assassin cut Alexander of Pherae down. In an effort to exploit the opportunity, Cineas of Larissa invited Philip to intervene in Thessaly.

Philip hardly had the time or the resources then to intervene in Thessaly in any decisive way, however, and it is probably not accurate that, as is sometimes claimed, he occupied the passes at Perrhaebia and sent mercenary troops to help Larissa.[6] Diodorus says that Philip "entered Thessaly and, by overcoming the tyrants and regaining freedom for the cities, showed much goodwill to the Thessalians."[7] But Jason's sons were still in power in Pherae when Philip attacked them in 353 BCE, suggesting that Diodorus's assertion that Philip overcame the tyrants in 358 BCE is probably false and that he is confusing Philip's later assault with answering Cineas's request.[8] It is more likely that in the meantime Philip was able to intervene diplomatically and to effect some temporary resolution between the warring factions. Certainly, the intervention settled little, for the civil war in Thessaly continued for six more years until Philip and his army finally put an end to it.

Philip's intervention at the request of Larissa was an important diplomatic achievement for Macedonia, however, for it established Philip as a legitimate player in Thessalian politics and one to whom the cities of the Thessalian League could turn for advice. Philip exploited this position brilliantly over the next six years. He never intervened in Thessaly without invitation and played the role of honest broker and honest man. Philip threw extravagant parties for his Thessalian friends[9] and acquired friends among the aristocracies of all the important cities. As would become his standard practice, he conferred expensive gifts and honors upon important nobles and even extended his largesse to people of the lower classes.[10] To demonstrate his sincere commitment to Thessaly, Philip married a Thessalian girl, Philinna of Larissa, in 358 BCE.[11] As noted in chapter 1, she was the mother of Arrhidaeus, Philip's first son.

Here we see Philip at his diplomatic best, ingratiating himself with the powerful for their future usefulness while always keeping his own interests uppermost in mind. Philip had substantial long-term interests to attend to in Thessaly. Good relations with Thessaly meant security for Macedonia because the invasion routes through the Thessalian passes to Macedonia could be protected perhaps even by Macedonian garrisons or, at least, by forces friendly to Philip. Philip's allies in Thessaly could also be called upon to provide him with contingents of cavalry during his campaigns. Politically, a substantive involvement in Thessalian politics brought Philip into contact, if only at first tangentially, with the Greek states to the south. Over the long run, a Macedonia allied with Thessaly presented a strong barrier to Theban or Athenian attack from the south. Alternatively, of course, such an alliance presented a future gateway for Philip's forces to invade Greece. Philip's policy of gradually ingratiating himself with Thessalian rulers was a long-term bet that Philip hoped one day to collect.

Over the next six years, and even after he had gained Thessaly's submission, Philip always employed diplomacy and reasonableness instead of war to gain his ends. Polyaenus thus described Philip's efforts to win Thessaly:

> Although he wanted to acquire Thessaly, Philip did not openly wage war against the Thessalians. But when the Pelinnaeans were at war with Pharsalians, the Pheraeans were at war with the Carissaeans, and the other Thessalians had taken sides, he always responded positively to requests for aid. When he won he did not exile the losers, take away their arms, or knock down their walls. He supported rather than destroyed factions, took care of the weak, brought down the more powerful, was a friend to the people, and cultivated the popular leaders. By these stratagems Philip mastered Thessaly, not by arms.[12]

Philip became a familiar figure in a number of Thessalian cities and befriended important nobles who saw him as someone to be trusted and relied on for his judgment and good will. By 355 BCE everyone loved Philip.

THE SIEGE OF METHONE

Philip's interest in Thessaly was heightened in 356 BCE when Phokis occupied the sacred shrine at Delphi and seized the temple's treasure. Besides genuine religious concerns, Thebes had its own political interests at stake and threatened to declare war on the defilers of the temple. In 355 BCE both Phokis and Thebes sent ambassadors throughout Greece, seeking allies in the dispute. Locris and Thessaly declared for Thebes and Athens and Pherae for Phokis. The Athenian commitment brought Athens into the Pherae–Thessalian League dispute that had waxed on and off for six years and raised the possibility that Athens and Phokis might provide military support to Pherae, involving them in what Philip regarded as a Macedonian sphere of interest. An Athenian army might come overland through Thessaly or by sea. If by sea, it would likely use the city of Methone, its remaining ally on the nearby Macedonian coast, as a place for its invasion force to come ashore. Philip might even have come into some intelligence to that effect. Diodorus tells us, "When Philip saw that the inhabitants of Methone were offering their city as a base for his enemies, he initiated a siege."[13] Sometime in the fall of 355 BCE, Philip attacked Methone.

Besieging Methone in the autumn forced Philip to conduct the siege over the winter months, not exactly ideal conditions for such an endeavor. And unlike when Philip besieged Potidea, a winter siege also meant no Etesian winds to prevent Athens from sending a relief force. Why did Philip take Methone under siege at a time so disadvantageous to him? The answer probably is that the conflict over Delphi between Phokis, Athens' ally, and Thebes was about to turn into open warfare, bringing with it the prospect of military aid to Pherae, Philip's adversary in Thessaly. If Philip anticipated having to come to the Thessalian League's aid, he could not afford to leave Methone at his back when he took his army into Thessaly. Methone was located close to the strategic communications route that ran to the Macedonian border, through the Vale of Tempe, and into Thessaly itself. Methone also blocked the route to Dium, Macedonia's main religious shrine in the foothills of Mount Pieria. Philip accepted the disadvantages of a winter siege to remove any hindrance to his future movement into Thessaly.

Philip offered Methone the chance to surrender, but it refused.[14] Methone had good defenses, and the siege went on for months. With all their bases in the Thermaic Gulf already gone, Athens decided to fight to keep control of Methone and assembled a relief expedition to try and raise the siege. By December, an Athenian force of unknown size was ready to set sail for Methone.[15] Just when the relief expedition arrived is unclear, but it must have been around the time when Philip was wounded in his eye. Philip's wound was serious enough that it might have killed him, and with him out of action, or because of unusually inclement weather, military activity around Methone came to a temporary halt. During this time the Athenian relief force came ashore, breached the Macedonian line, and made its way into the city.[16] Once it was clear that Philip would not succumb to his wound, however, the siege continued until the city surrendered, probably in late spring or early summer.

Diodorus tells us that "for some time [about six or seven months] the Methoneans endured the siege, but were eventually overcome and compelled to surrender their city to the king on the condition that they should depart from Methone with one garment apiece. Philip razed the city to the ground and apportioned its territory among the Macedonians."[17] It is interesting to note that the city surrendered and, apparently, was taken without violence.[18] Why the defenders and the Athenian relief force did not put up greater resistance is unknown. Perhaps Philip's offer of leniency instead of slaughter convinced the defenders that discretion was indeed the better part of valor. Justin seems to reinforce this idea when he describes Philip's mood after recovering from his wound at Methone: "The wound did not make him slower in war or angrier with his enemies, so much so that a few days later he granted them peace at their request and was not only restrained but mild to the vanquished."[19]

It is unclear whether the city was actually "razed to the ground," as Diodorus says, for it would have made no military sense to capture such a well-fortified and prosperous city on Macedonian land only to destroy it. Diodorus's claim "that Philip apportioned its territory among the Macedonians" suggests that the city was not destroyed and that parcels of land were distributed among those of Philip's soldiers who had distinguished themselves during the siege.[20] It is also unlikely that the city's entire population left with only the clothes on their backs. Many of the local Greeks owned property and land there and would have been encouraged to remain to keep the economy functioning. Under these circumstances, Methone became a city of the Macedones, where the locals continued to work the land and shops and paid part of their produce and incomes to the new owners, Philip's veterans, who, presumably, were settled in the area as a military colony.[21] With Methone in his possession, Philip controlled all the ports and harbors on the west and north shores of the Thermaic Gulf.

Of equal importance, the road from Macedonia to Thessaly was open, which would allow Philip's army to move quickly into Thessaly at the

Thessalian League's request. And this avenue opened none too soon. Diodorus suggests that the league's plea for help came while Philip was still besieging Methone,[22] which might account for Philip's offer of leniency in return for the city's quick surrender. At the request of the Thessalian League, Philip marched south into Thessaly and "reduced Pagasae and compelled it to submit."[23] Pagasae, the port city of Pherae and the only good harbor in Thessaly, was under the control of Jason's two surviving sons—Lycophron and Peitholaus. Philip attacked Pagasae to prevent an Athenian naval relief force from using it. Philip probably assaulted the city in midsummer and captured it by the autumn of 354 BCE.[24] We have no details regarding his attack on the city, but, in any case, the political consequences that followed are more important. In acting on the league's behalf, Philip had cast his lot with it and against Pherae. The problem was that Pherae was closely allied with Phokis and Athens, which were fighting with Thebes and Locris in the opening phases of what came to be called the Sacred War. The league had also joined the alliance against Phokis and Pherae. By acting on the league's behalf, Philip was drawn into the Sacred War.

For the remainder of 354 BCE, Philip let the league handle events in Thessaly while he attended to Macedonia's interests in Thrace. In 360 BCE, Cotys, the king of Thrace, had been assassinated and the region divided among this three sons. Cersobleptes ruled the easternmost section, which controlled the Chersonese (now the Gallipoli Peninsula); Ketriporis governed the westernmost area, which included the Nestus River valley and Crenides; and Amadocus ruled the region in between. It was Ketriporis who in 356 BCE had foolishly joined the Illyrian-Paeonian alliance to oppose Philip, which had ended in their defeat and Philip occupying Crenides and Western Thrace. From the autumn of 354 BCE to early 353 BCE, Philip undertook an expedition into Thrace. Accompanied by a small naval force (the first operational test of the new Macedonian navy), Philip pressed east beyond the Nestus into Amadocus's kingdom of middle Thrace.[25]

The point of the expedition may have been to test the resistance of Amadocus, the Athenians' ally, and to feel out Cersobleptes, who was also on good terms with Athens but not its ally. Athens regarded the latter's area, the Chersonese, as vital because it could be used as a base for those looking to interrupt its annual wheat shipment from the Black Sea. Philip and Cersobleptes seemed to have established some sort of alliance that Cersobleptes saw as a counterweight to Athenian influence in Eastern Thrace, while Philip regarded it as a means of demonstrating his influence in an area Athens considered significant.[26] Nothing seems to have come of the expedition except Philip despoiled the territories of Abdera, Maronea, and Neapolis, Greek cities allied with Athens, to demonstrate his ability to strike across coastal Thrace and potentially threaten Athenian interests in the Chersonese.[27]

THE SACRED WAR

Philip's alliance with the Thessalian League drew him into the Sacred War and embroiled Philip for the first time in the politics of the major Greek states. The Sacred War began in October 355 BCE when the Amphictyonic Council, acting at the request of Thebes, declared a "sacred war" against Phokis.[28] The Amphictyonic Council was originally an ancient assembly of Greek tribes—the *Amphictyones*, or "dwellers around"—that had, in the distant past, lived close to the great shrine at Delphi and were charged with its care and protection. By the 360s BCE the council had been formalized into an organization of twelve members representing the Greek states and tribes of Phokis and Thessaly,[29] each possessing a certain but unequal number of votes. By 362 BCE the council was under the control of Thebes and its allies, a fact symbolized by Thebes having been granted the formal right of precedence in consulting the oracle at Delphi.

The war had its origins in the Phokians' refusal to send troops and help Thebes at the battle of Mantinea in 362 BCE. Angry Thebes sought to punish Phokis for its treachery. No doubt other issues of long standing also fed Theban fury. Phokis was not a major power. It had far less territory than Thebes had, and its population, settled in twenty-two cities, was small and incapable of raising a large army. In any conflict with Thebes, Phokis was almost certain to be defeated. Phokis thus sought safety in alliances with Sparta, Athens, and the tyrants of Pherae in Thessaly. In 357 BCE Alexander of Pherae was assassinated, removing a key Phokian ally. In April 356 BCE Thebes moved quickly to have Phokis sanctioned by the Amphictyonic Council.

The charges were preposterous and clearly only a pretext for further action against Phokis. It was alleged that Phokis had violated the Delphic sanctuary by farming the land on the plain below the shrine. For good measure, Sparta was charged with having occupied the citadel of the shrine twenty-five years earlier. Thebes and the council imposed a heavy fine on Phokis and Sparta. The Phokian leader, Philomelos, refused to pay. In the summer of 355 BCE, the council doubled the fine. Philomelos seized the Delphic shrine and hired a large contingent of mercenaries. In October, the council declared a "sacred war" against Phokis, meaning that the desecrators of the Delphic shrine would be executed without mercy.[30] Once more the Greek states plunged into a self-destructive war. "For all their attempts to impose their rule on each other," Justin tells us, "they only succeeded in losing their ability to rule themselves. With no restraint they rushed into mutual destruction and realized only in subjection that what they forfeited individually constituted a loss for them all."[31]

Over the winter, Philomelos assembled a large army of mercenaries, which he paid for by pillaging the temple treasure at Delphi. In the spring of 354 BCE, he marched into Locrian territory at the head of a ten thousand–man army and defeated the Locrians and their Boeotian allies in a large cavalry battle.[32] The Thessalians sent a contingent of six thousand men and horses to relieve the Locrians, only to be defeated in turn by Philomelos's army. At this point the Thebans arrived, collected the remnants of the other two forces, and assembled them in a force of thirteen thousand men. The Boeotians captured a number of Philomelos's mercenaries while they were foraging and, considering them defilers of the shrine, "promptly shot them down with javelins."[33] Outraged, the Phokians sent out patrols and "captured many of the enemy who were roaming over the countryside and took them back to Philomelos, who had all of them shot down."[34]

The armies broke contact and began to maneuver away from one another. "After this [it is unclear how much later, perhaps days or even a week] when the armies were invading another area and were passing through wooded and rough places, the two vanguards suddenly encountered one another," Diodorus continues.[35] The engagement was followed by a "severe battle" in which the Theban-led army defeated the Phokians. Pausanias says the battle took place at Neon, the ancient name for the city of Tithorea, whose citadel retained the older name.[36] Philomelos was trapped on the edge of a cliff, "and because of a fear that he would be tortured after capture, he threw himself down from a rock and in this way paid the penalty to the god and terminated his life."[37] Meanwhile, during the summer of 354 BCE, Philip captured the besieged Methone. It was then that Pausanias says Philip "joined the alliance of Thebes."[38]

Battles rarely settle wars and almost never end wars fought over religion. Thebes forgot this lesson. Its tactical victory against the Phokians had settled nothing as far as the Phokians were concerned. Thebes, however, believed that it had and let its economic needs determine its national security strategy. Desperately short of money because of the war, it hired out one of its generals, Pammenes, and five thousand soldiers to aid the rebel satrap Artabazus in his campaign against the Persian king. In the spring of 353 BCE, Philip allowed Pammenes and his army safe passage through Macedonia and Western Thrace while he accompanied them on his way to deal with Amadocus in Central Thrace. Philip entered a friendship agreement with Cersobleptes, the king of Eastern Thrace, who extended permission for Pammenes to cross into Asia unimpeded. Philip was acting out his role as a loyal ally of Thebes. With much of the Theban army now in Asia, the Phokians prepared to continue the war against Thebes and its Boeotian allies.

The Phokians elected a new general "with full powers" to replace Philomelos.[39] His name was Onomarchus, and he was a brilliant field general. His brother, Phayllos, was elected his second in command. Onomarchus raised an even larger army of mercenaries and bribed his allies to continue the war. He immediately took the offensive, forced the Locrians out of the war with a series of sharp battles, marched into Boeotia, and besieged Chaeronea, tying down what was left of the Theban home army. Philip was by now back in Macedonia and in possession of Pagasae, which he had seized after the successful siege of Methone the previous year. At the Thessalian League's request, Philip marched into Thessaly and prepared to attack Pherae, Phokis's ally in Thessaly. Philip was now deeply involved in the conflicts of the major Greek states, and there was no turning back.

AMBUSH AND DEFEAT

Lycophron, the tyrant of Pherae, responded to Philip's threat by asking his Phokian allies for help. Onomarchus sent Phayllos north with seven thousand troops to intercept and stop Philip, only to meet with a crushing defeat.[40] The significance of Philip's threat to the Phokian-Pherae alliance was evident in Onomarchus's reaction to his brother's defeat. He immediately broke off operations in Boeotia, turned his army northward, and marched into Thessaly, where he linked up with Pherae's troops and waited for Philip to do battle. Diodorus tells us that "when Philip and the Thessalians ranged themselves against the Phokians, Onomarchus, who was superior in numbers, defeated him in two battles and destroyed many Macedonians."[41] Onomarchus inflicted the only battlefield defeats that Philip ever suffered.

The only account of these events comes to us from Polyaenus, who describes just one of the two battles Diodorus mentioned.

> In deploying against the Macedonians with a crescent shaped mountain at his back, Onomarchus concealed on the summits on each side infantry and stone-throwing artillery and advanced his force into the plain lying beneath. When the approaching Macedonians began to skirmish, the Phokians pretended to flee into the central area of the mountain. The Macedonians, pursuing with zestful vigor, pressed them, but those shooting stones from the summits began to crush the Macedonian battle line. At that very moment Onomarchus signaled for the Phokians to turn and engage the enemy. While some were shooting from behind, others from the front, the Macedonians were being crushed by the stones and retreated.[42]

Figure 4 illustrates Polyaenus's description of the ambush of Philip's army.

Onomarchus had set the trap for Philip beforehand. Onomarchus had the stone-throwing catapults (traction machines) with him because he had marched directly from besieging Chaeronea to the battlefield in Thessaly. Armies traveling with siege machinery do not carry their stone shot with them. Onomarchus needed time to assemble his catapults, to conceal their firing positions, and to find enough stones and haul them up the ridge where the catapults had been hidden.[43] The ambush, therefore, must have been planned well in advance.[44]

The most likely location of the ambush was in the foothills of the mountains some sixteen miles south of Pherae. Onomarchus had moved north along the coastal road, and the mountains to his left were the last significant high ground before he had to cross the wide plain between there and Pherae. Crossing the open plain risked attack by the Macedonian cavalry and being caught in the column of march. We have no information as to how many cavalry Onomarchus had with him, but he certainly knew that Philip's cavalry would likely be strongly reinforced by the Thessalian League, which was famous for its ability to deploy large cavalry contingents. It is likely, then, that Onomarchus chose the foothills of the nearby mountains as his ambush site and lured Philip into the trap.

But how was Philip drawn to the ambush site? Once again, we can only speculate. First, Philip's army probably had a large cavalry contingent provided by his Thessalian allies. Cavalry is best used on terrain similar to the open plain

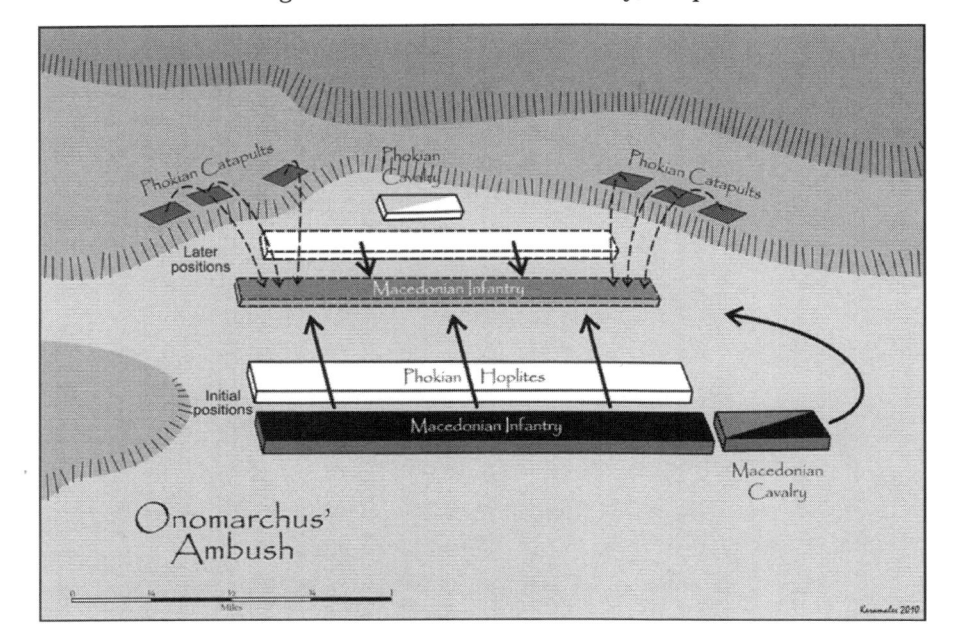

Figure 4. *Onomarchus's Ambush of Philip*

between Pherae and Phokis. Philip probably intended to intercept Onomarchus's route of march on the open ground and was already moving south when he was enticed into the ambush. But what drew him to the mountains? The answer may lie in Diodorus's claim that Philip suffered *two* defeats at the hands of the Phokians. Once Onomarchus set the ambush, he may have sent his cavalrymen forward on reconnaissance to locate Philip's army, skirmish with it, and draw it after them as they retreated toward the mountains. Polyaenus's use of the phrase "approaching Macedonians" suggests that Philip's army was still in marching column when the first skirmishing began. Polyaenus also uses the term "battle line" instead of "phalanx," implying that the Macedonians may have first been attacked while still in a column of march. It may be that Diodorus, drawing on an earlier source, counted the first skirmish as a separate battle and called it a defeat for Philip. If there were really two separate defeats for Philip so close together, it is curious that no ancient historian has recorded the other one.

Onomarchus's ambush showed he was a brilliant tactician, and his use of catapult artillery against enemy troops in the field appears to be the first tactical use of field artillery in Western military history. Traction catapults were commonly used against defenders when besieging a city. Catapult fire was designed to make it difficult for the defenders to fire on the miners and sappers who were bringing the rams, towers, and tunnels ever closer to the city's walls. Onomarchus's use of catapult fire against troops in the open, however, represents a truly brilliant military innovation. It is the first evidence of artillery as an effective combat arm, earning Onomarchus the distinction of being the father of field artillery.

The ambush shows that Onomarchus understood the different tactical dynamics and capabilities of hoplite infantry and Macedonian infantry. Although Greek hoplite infantry usually fought in phalanx formation, it is often overlooked that they were quite capable of effective individual combat, which they frequently demonstrated when engaged in individual combat with adversaries before the main battle. Because of his unwieldy sarissa and his lack of body armor and individual combat training, the Macedonian phalangite had a much more limited ability to fight effectively outside the phalanx. Polyaenus emphasizes this vulnerability when he says, "But when the phalanx is dissolved, and its strength becomes a matter of individuals, each of the combatants perishes."[45] The key to Onomarchus's successful ambush was finding a way that his hoplite infantry could engage the Macedonian infantry out of its combat phalanx formation.

Onomarchus also needed to neutralize Philip's cavalry. Thessalian cavalry had a reputation as excellent fighters. Onomarchus surely knew that Philip had Thessalian cavalry contingents with his army, even if he knew little about the close combat capabilities of Philip's own cavalry squadrons. By now, the Macedonian army could put twenty thousand infantry and six hundred cavalry in the field, and it is likely that Philip might have had another thousand Thessalian horses with him. Arranged for battle, Philip's infantry took up two kilometers of frontage and his sixteen hundred cavalry another five hundred meters, or some two and a half kilometers for the entire army.[46] It is curious that there is no mention of cavalry in the ambush, suggesting that Onomarchus had neutralized Philip's cavalry advantage perhaps by deploying his infantry across the front of a semicircle of open ground between two hills whose distance across was sufficient only to accommodate Philip's infantry. This tactic would have taken Philip's and Onomarchus's cavalry out of the fight because there was no room for either to deploy or maneuver. In choosing this terrain and depriving Philip of the use of his cavalry, Onomarchus forced Philip into an infantry battle and rendered the Macedonian combat arm of decision useless.

Onomarchus took a position on level, open ground that ran between the two horns of a semicircle of hills that probably had no rear exit. Choosing a site without an exit served two functions. First, with no place to run, Onomarchus could expect his mercenary hoplites to fight fiercely to the end if need be. Second, seeing no exit might have enticed Philip into the fight by letting him think that he could trap the hoplites against the hills and slaughter them. The battle opened as the Macedonian infantry advanced slowly against the Phokian line and began to skirmish with it. After putting up some resistance, the Phokians began to give ground at first slowly and then, turning completely around, fled to the rear. The Macedonians continued their disciplined advance deeper into the cul-de-sac between the hills. At some point, Polyaenus says, the Macedonians began "pursuing with zestful vigor" while still maintaining their phalanx formation.

Once deep inside the cul-de-sac, the phalanx came under heavy shelling from the catapults located on the hills in front and on the sides of the battlefield. The packed Macedonian phalanx offered the Phokian artillery a target-rich environment, and a large number of phalangites must have been struck and injured or killed by the one- to two-pound stones the catapults fired over a range of more than two hundred yards.[47] As the artillery pummeled the Macedonians, the hoplites stopped their retreat, reformed their units, and counterattacked, at which point, one assumes, the catapults stopped firing on the Macedonians. The impact of the shelling had already loosened the cohesion of the Macedonian phalanx, and it shattered under the Phokian infantry assault. The fight resolved itself into a swirling battle of individual combatants, precisely the kind of fight at which the hoplite excelled and had the advantage against the Macedonian infantry. Without body armor and encumbered by the long spear, the Macedonian infantry was unable to meet the attack effectively.

Only Philip's cavalry, stationed behind his infantry, prevented a complete slaughter. By acting as a covering force for his infantry as it fled to the rear, his cavalry foiled an effective pursuit by Onomarchus's cavalry. This fight was no minor engagement, and the Macedonians suffered heavily. Diodorus describes the situation following the ambush: "Philip was now in the midst of the greatest dangers and deserted by his despondent troops, but he encouraged the majority of them and with difficulty rendered them obedient."[48] The disciplined Macedonian army came apart, and all Philip could do was stop the panic, gather his troops, and withdraw to safety.

It is an axiom of strategic thinking never to permit an operational success to drive changes in the overall strategic plan. This premise, of course, presupposes that there is an overall strategic plan in the first place. And here Onomarchus failed to turn his brilliant tactical victory into a significant strategic one. Philip's army was broken and in full retreat. Onomarchus could have gathered his army, set it on the march, thrown his cavalry forward, and chased Philip out of Thessaly and all the way back to Macedonia, picking off the stragglers and forcing Philip to conduct a fighting retreat and suffer the attendant losses. This option would have denied Philip the respite he needed to reconstitute his force. Moreover, Onomarchus could have used his army to break the back of the Thessalian League or at least its more powerful members, thus ensuring Pherae a stronger position in Thessaly. Instead, Onomarchus turned around and marched back to Boeotia to resume his sieges and operations there, defeating the Boeotians in another battle and capturing the city of Coronea. Allowing Philip to escape was a serious strategic error, one that Onomarchus would regret. Philip understood how fortunate he was to have escaped with his army to fight again another day. In thinking about Onomarchus's ambush, Philip is supposed to have remarked, "I didn't run away, but like a ram I pulled back to butt again."[49] Philip never fell into another ambush.

THE BATTLE OF THE CROCUS FIELD

Events on the battlefield often have important political consequences, and it was certainly the case when news of Philip's defeat arrived in Greece. The Athenians made much of it and sought to gain an advantage. They pressured Cersobleptes, the king of Eastern Thrace, to renounce his recent alliance with Philip and renew his former agreement with Athens, guaranteeing Athenian access to the Chersonese. The Chersonese was an important choke point on the approaches to the Sea of Marmara through the Hellespont from where it could threaten Athenian grain shipments from the Black Sea. Cersobleptes reckoned that Philip's defeat might open opportunities for his own interests in Thrace and renewed his alliance with Athens. Cersobleptes "handed the cities of the Chersonese apart from Cardia over to the Athenians, and the people [Athenians] sent out settlers to the cities."[50] Cersobleptes still remained technically allied with Philip, but the new arrangement clearly threatened Philip's interests in Thrace.

Olynthos also attempted to weaken Macedonian influence by seeking an alliance with Athens. Olynthos's perfidy was of much greater concern to Philip. As noted earlier, Olynthos was of strategic importance to Philip because of its location and military might. After Philip's capture of Amphipolis, the two powers had signed a treaty of alliance, which Philip regarded as their solemn guarantee against Athenian influence in the Thermaic Gulf. Philip attached such importance to this treaty that he had insisted that the treaty oaths be sworn at Delphi and that the treaty's documents be deposited there. In Philip's eyes, both parties were bound by a sacred oath. When Olynthos opened negotiations with Athens, Philip saw it as a betrayal. A treaty between Olynthos and Athens would threaten Macedonian interests in Thrace, at the head of the Thermaic Gulf, and even in the coastal cities of Macedonia itself.

Philip's defeat had cost him dearly in military and political terms, and he moved quickly to reverse the situation. He spent the winter rebuilding the Macedonian army, replenishing it with men drawn from the militia units, restoring its equipment, and building its morale. Reversing the political situation, however, would require more time. Philip's most immediate concern was to restore his military reputation and regain his position in Thessaly. Fortunately, Onomarchus had failed to remain in Thessaly or significantly increase Pherae's troops there, so the military balance in the country remained about what it had been before the ambush. Philip still had an opportunity to recover his position with the help of the Thessalian League. In the spring of 352 BCE, Philip and the Macedonian army marched into Thessaly and made straight for the city of Pherae.

Philip took Pherae; its tyrant, Lycophron; and his two thousand defenders under siege. Lycophron immediately appealed to his Phokian allies for help. It would have taken at least four days for a messenger to reach Boeotia, where Onomarchus and his army were besieging its towns. Onomarchus would have required several more days to ready his army for the march north and another week or so to cover the hundred miles from Boeotia to the Crocus Plain in Thessaly. Philip used this time to strengthen his army and bring the cavalry units of the Thessalian League under his command. Diodorus tells us that "Philip, having persuaded the Thessalians to prosecute the war in common, gathered them all together, numbering more than twenty thousand foot and three thousand horse."[51] The number Diodorus recorded for Philip's infantry was normal for the Macedonian army whose

Companion cavalry numbered about six hundred. Thus, we might reasonably conclude that Philip's allies provided him with an additional twenty-five hundred cavalry.

Onomarchus's army marched north from Boeotia, through the Thermopylae Pass, and entered Thessaly along the coastal road before venturing upon the plain between the border and Pherae. His army was made up of twenty thousand infantry, mostly hoplite mercenaries, and five hundred cavalry. Off the coast and moving along a parallel course was an Athenian fleet under the command of Chares. Diodorus tells us only that Chares "was by chance sailing past with many triremes."[52] It is inconceivable that Chares' fleet just happened to be in the area. Athens was a Phokian ally, and it is more reasonable that Athens had sent troops to support Onomarchus. Chares' ships might have staged from an Athenian naval base at Neapolis in the northern Aegean. The normal complement of Athenian ships at Neapolis was twenty triremes,[53] but twenty ships hardly count as the "many triremes" Diodorus mentioned. Each trireme could transport a hundred soldiers. If there were only twenty ships, the Athenian naval infantry contingent amounted to two thousand additional troops, although the possibility that the number of ships was greater and their troop numbers greater cannot be excluded.[54]

The Athenians probably intended to land their troops in support of Onomarchus once the rival commanders had chosen a battlefield. That is probably why Onomarchus remained close to the coast once he entered Thessaly. Using the naval infantry to support the Phokian army relied on two assumptions: some suitable landing place could be found near the battlefield, and there would be sufficient time before the battle to allow the troops to disembark and assemble at the battle site. If either of these assumptions proved to be false, the Athenian fleet and its naval infantry would be of no use to Onomarchus.

Philip had stumbled into Onomarchus's ambush because he neglected to use his cavalry and conduct a thorough reconnaissance of the area of operations. As a result, Philip had no idea where Onomarchus was before his vanguard stumbled upon him. Philip did not make this mistake at the Crocus Field. Philip's reconnaissance assets picked up Onomarchus as soon as he entered Thessaly. Philip was aware of Onomarchus's progress and position at any given time. Moreover, Philip's reconnaissance discovered the relative strength and composition of the Phokian force, so Philip knew he held a great advantage in cavalry. This intelligence allowed Philip to choose the battlefield and surprise Onomarchus.

Philip planned to fight where his cavalry had sufficient room for maneuver and where he could take Onomarchus by surprise. Philip's army was still besieging Pherae when Onomarchus entered Thessaly and began his march north along the coastal road. He encamped somewhere near a place that came to be called the Crocus Field by later historians. The name is taken from Strabo's account in which the Greek historian says that crocuses grew in abundance there. The battlefield's exact location is unknown, but it was probably close to where the International Airport of Central Greece is currently located, or some eight miles south of Pherae. There was a good reason why Pagasae was the only usable port on the Thessalian coast: the entire coastline is rocky and cliff ridden, with few shallow beaches upon which ancient ships could land. The underwater terrain drops off quickly a few feet from shore, offering no gradual slope and shallow water for ships to beach themselves.[55] Xerxes' ships had come to grief on these rocky shores when he attempted to invade Greece in 480 BCE. Without a suitable beach for them to put in for the night, the Athenian triremes remained at sea the evening before the battle with Philip.

As night fell, Philip assembled his army under the cover of darkness for the eight-mile march to the Crocus Field.[56] He left behind his engineers and some small troop units, probably Thessalian infantry and some supporting cavalry, to continue the siege and keep Pherae's garrison contained in the city, where it could not threaten Philip's line of communications. It was the Macedonian army's first combat action since it had been badly mauled by the Phokians the year before, and Philip may have been concerned that the defeat had eroded his men's confidence. To stiffen his troops' morale, Philip probably delivered one of his famous orations on courage. In addition, "Philip, as if he was the avenger not of the Thebans but of sacrilege, ordered all his soldiers to wear crowns of laurel and he proceeded to battle, under the leadership, as it were, of the god."[57] The Amphictyonic Council, in whose name Philip now fought, had declared the Phokians "temple defilers," and the laurel wreath was the symbol of the god Apollo. Delphi was the spiritual center of the Greek world, and Philip cast himself as the defender of Greek religion. He called his troops "the saviors of Apollo."

It would have taken Philip only a few hours to reach the Crocus Field, where he took up positions across Onomarchus's line of march at some short distance (perhaps a mile or so) from the Phokian camp (see figure 5). The army assembled. No fires were permitted, so rations were eaten cold. The troops slept on the ground already assembled in their unit phalanxes. Every effort was made to maintain night and sound discipline. As the sun came up over the Gulf of Pagasae, one can only imagine the panic in the Phokian camp when they discovered Philip's army to their front, blocking the route north, and ready for a fight. It would have required two or three hours for Onomarchus to assemble his army for battle. Meanwhile, the Athenian fleet bobbed helplessly offshore, unable to land its troops to support the Phokians. By midmorning, both sides were ready to do battle.

Onomarchus found himself facing the best infantry in Greece on an open plain with no terrain that could be used to his advantage. Without hills upon which he could anchor his flanks, Onomarchus had no way to protect the flanks of his infantry. Philip's advantage in cavalry spelled disaster. An honorable surrender, too, was out of the question. The Amphictyonic Council's declaration of a sacred war against the Phokians permitted the summary execution of the defilers of the Delphic temple.

Onomarchus must certainly have known that he was doomed. Still, he had no choice but to fight, and he tried to make the best of a bad situation. He placed the right flank of his infantry line on the steep, rocky shore that dropped off sharply into the sea. From there his infantry line ran inland for two kilometers, its left flank completely unprotected by any obstacles or favorable terrain. He stationed his five hundred cavalry on his left to protect the infantry's flank, but it was little more than a symbolic gesture in the face of Philip's huge cavalry force.

Every advantage fell to Philip. His infantry formed up facing the Phokian hoplites. Though equal in numbers, the Phokian mercenaries were no match for the Macedonians in killing power. Arranged in its wedge formations, Philip's infantry could easily punch through the Phokian infantry line, a tactic Philip often used when he wished to create a gap into which his cavalry could rush and attack the enemy's rear. In this case, however, Philip's infantry was arranged in its standard rectangle formation. Its task was not to penetrate the Phokian line but to fix it in place so the cavalry could attack it from the flank and rear. The Macedonian infantry was the anvil against which the Macedonian cavalry would hammer the enemy to death.

Far to Philip's right, the Macedonian and Thessalian cavalry formed up in squadrons opposite the Phokian cavalry. Five hundred Phokian cavalry

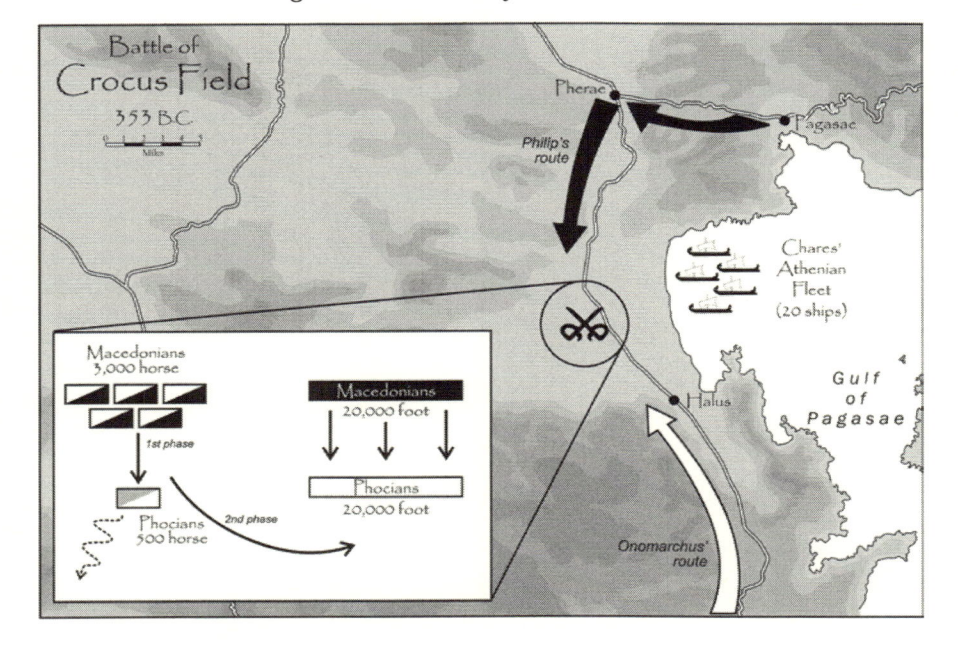

Figure 5. *The Battle of the Crocus Field*

were no match for Philip's three thousand, and no matter how bravely the Phokians fought, their defeat was certain. Philip's advanced cavalry squadrons attacked the Phokian cavalry head-on, while other squadrons struck their flank. There was no need to drive the Phokian cavalry from the field before the Macedonian cavalry attacked the Phokian infantry. While a few squadrons attacked the Phokian cavalry, the remainder of Philip's cavalry swept around the end of the line and fell on the rear and left flank of Onomarchus's infantry. Trapped between the Macedonian pikemen to their front and the machaira-wielding cavalry at their back, the Phokian infantrymen were stabbed and hacked to pieces.

The battle could not have lasted long, perhaps only an hour or so. In the end, six thousand Phokian soldiers were killed, and another three thousand taken prisoner.[58] While these casualty rates are high, they are not as great as we would expect had Philip ordered his cavalry to undertake its usual lethal pursuit. There was, of course, nowhere to escape the Macedonian hammer, and most of the dead and prisoners were likely taken in a small area. Some of the Phokians fled to the sea, where they drowned while trying to swim to the Athenian triremes floating offshore.

Onomarchus's fate is unclear. Pausanias says that he was slain by his own men as punishment for having failed them so miserably,[59] but this is an unlikely fate for a general competent enough to have defeated Philip the previous year. The historian Eusebius says Onomarchus was drowned while trying to swim to one of the Athenian ships.[60] Diodorus tells us only that "Philip hanged [crucified] Onomarchus" but does not tell us if he was killed this way or if only his corpse was crucified to symbolize Philip's new role as the punisher of sacrilege and the avenger of the gods. In all likelihood, Onomarchus perished in the battle and then his corpse was crucified. On Philip's orders, the three thousand prisoners were put to death by drowning, the traditional punishment for sacrilege.[61] Their weapons were collected and later smashed and thrown over the Phaedriadae cliffs at Delphi, an act that symbolized that they had been polluted by sacrilege.

THE SUBMISSION OF THESSALY

The great victory on the Thessalian plain destroyed the Phokian army and isolated Pherae and the other Thessalian cities that had supported the Phokians. With Pagasae firmly in Macedonian hands, Athenian naval forces were unable to use the port and come to Pherae's aid. Pherae was already under siege and at Philip's mercy. Philip could have marched south, linked up with his Theban allies, and destroyed Phokis before its new leader, Phayllos, had time to hire more mercenaries and rebuild the Phokian army. Instead, Philip turned around and marched against Pherae. The Pheraean tyrants, Lycophron and Peitholaus, Jason's surviving sons, had little choice but to surrender. Philip permitted the tyrants, the merchants, and two thousand mercenaries to leave the city under a truce. The brothers and the mercenaries left Pherae, marched south, and joined Phayllos, who had already set about rebuilding the Phokian army.

Why didn't Philip march immediately against Phayllos? The answer seems to be that Philip was prepared to take the long view of events. First, Philip's strategic center of gravity was the security of Macedonia, which meant that his concerns with the regions surrounding the country—Illyria, Thrace, Epirus, and Thessaly—were of greatest importance to him. Compared with Thessaly and its cavalry, abundant agriculture, large population, and lucrative port, the small, poverty-ridden states of Greece had little to offer Philip.[62] From a strategic perspective, Thessaly was by far the greater prize. Second, Philip had no interest in destroying Phokis and bringing an end to the Sacred

War. From Philip's vantage point, the war had set the Greek states at each other's throats. The longer it went on, the more resources it consumed and the more trouble it caused. Over the long run, the war would weaken all the major Greek states, as well as keep Athens occupied and reduce its ability to oppose Philip in Thrace. Third, whatever Philip's long-term objectives, he judged that it was not the time for him to become deeply involved in the politics and conflicts of the Greek states. That day would come, of course, but for now Philip remained aloof, content to allow the Greeks to hack at one another.

Diodorus tells us that after "Philip suppressed the tyranny at Pherae and restored freedom to the city . . . he arranged all the other affairs of Thessaly."[63] These affairs were some of Philip's most important political achievements. As he had done in the past, Philip set out to gain the goodwill of the Thessalian people and rulers. He did not carry out reprisals against the population of Pherae; instead, he was content to attribute their resistance to the fear of their tyrannical leaders. Philip offered further proof of his regard for the Thessalian people by marrying a Thessalian girl named Nicesipolis, a niece of Jason of Pherae. Later, when she bore him a daughter, Philip named the child Thessalonice (Victory in Thessaly).[64] Philip's lenient treatment of Pherae concealed the more important concessions he obtained from the city. Pherae formally transferred the port of Pagasae to Philip's control along with the subject territory of Magnesia. Pagasae was Thessaly's only major port, and its substantial revenues now fell to Philip.[65] There is no evidence that Philip moved Macedonian naval ships to Pegasae, which had served as a base for Pheraean ships under Alexander of Pherae, but Philip's control of the port denied its use to Athens as a future base.[66]

Philip now called into account the numerous Thessalian cities that had gone over to Pherae and its Phokian protectors. Philip punished those that had renounced their loyalty to the Thessalian League following Philip's defeat in 353 BCE. Some of their leading citizens were banished from the country forever and some of their populations sold into slavery. Gomphi's population was sold off in this manner, its lands resettled by Macedonians, and the town renamed Philippopolis.[67] It is interesting that Philip did not formally carry out these reprisals as the king of Macedonia but in the name of the Thessalian League with Philip acting as its legal chief. Philip's actions on the league's behalf reconstituted the Thessalian League as the main institutional mechanism for national unity.

To the Thessalian aristocrats, Philip of Macedon was no longer a foreign king called upon to save Thessaly from civil war. Philip was now regarded as the savior who suppressed the Pheraean tyranny and rescued the league, something the league alone had been unable to do. Philip was seen as the only person capable of guaranteeing the future unity of the country. In an event that was completely without precedent in Greece, a foreign king was chosen by free election and without compulsion or intimidation to be *archon* or "ruler of a league of Greek cities."[68] What made Philip's election even more astonishing is that the office was conferred for life.[69] Not only was it Philip's greatest diplomatic victory, it also changed the history of Greece.

As archon, Philip was commander in chief of the military forces of a united Thessaly and controlled the taxes and revenues from the country's harbor and markets to defray the costs of running the league. He had some measure of supervision over the country's constitution, which he used later to reorganize its regional governments. Philip also exploited his position to station Macedonian garrisons in key Thessalian cities and settled Macedonians on the lands of those cities that had supported Pherae. Thessaly had been an original member of the Amphictyonic Council, where it held a disproportionate number of seats. These seats now fell under Philip's control. Philip could draw upon Thessaly's population and resources, which were at least the equal of Macedonia's at the time, for his future wars.[70] Philip could now put thirty thousand infantry and three thousand cavalry in the field, a military force of unparalleled power in Greece. For all practical purposes, Philip's election as archon made Thessaly a part of the Macedonian kingdom. It would remain so for the next hundred and fifty years.[71]

Arranging his affairs in Thessaly took some time. It was not until midsummer that Philip marched south toward the pass at Thermopylae, as Diodorus tells us, "with the aim of making war on the Phokians."[72] When Philip arrived at Thermopylae, he found a large force defending the pass. Phayllos had reconstituted the Phokian army with new mercenaries, and the troops from Pherae and a large contingent of Athenian troops had joined him. Athens had sent five thousand troops transported by fifty triremes at a cost of two hundred talents,[73] a clear indication of the seriousness with which Athens regarded Philip's advance toward Thermopylae. Athens feared that the armies of Macedonia, Thessaly, and Boeotia would invade Attica and attack Athens itself. Sparta, fearing an invasion of the Peloponnese, also sent troops.

According to Diodorus, when Philip saw the size of the allied army blocking his way, he turned back to Macedonia without attempting to force the pass. At that time Thermopylae was a far more formidable obstacle to invasion than it appears in the present day. Since ancient times, silting from the Sperchius River has created a wide, flat area through which troops might more easily pass. In Philip's day, however, there was only room at its two narrowest points, between the almost sheer mountainside and the sea, for a single cart to pass at one time. A wall with a gate had also been constructed across the path to further control passage.[74] Under these circumstances, Thermopylae could not be forced. Troops could only bypass it over the formidable mountainous terrain on either side along routes that the Phokians easily defended. Philip's decision to retire was a wise one.

But why march on Thermopylae at all? Philip surely had no intention of invading Greece at this stage. Things were still too uncertain in Thessaly and needed his full attention. At the same time, events in nearby Olynthos and Thrace were turning serious and demanded his consideration. Nor had Philip sufficient time to prepare his army logistically for a long campaign, and he still had to integrate the Thessalian cavalry into his army and train it in Macedonian tactics. As noted earlier, Philip had no interest in bringing the Sacred War to an end. Left to their own devices, the Greek states, including his Boeotian and Locrian allies, would continue to weaken themselves in a long war, all to the benefit of Macedonia's long-range interests. An invasion of Greece at this time made no strategic sense.

Perhaps Philip marched south to satisfy his Thessalian allies, whose longstanding animosity for Phokis was well known and who may have wanted to use their new strength to punish their longtime enemies. In this case, as newly elected archon, Philip could hardly refuse. And if Thermopylae's defenses were found to be too strong, as might have reasonably been expected in light of the Phokians' continuing public efforts to hire more mercenaries, then Philip had a convenient excuse not to try and force the pass. Thessalian vengeance would have to wait another day. Under these circumstances, the expedition became more a reconnaissance in force intended to discern what political reaction it might provoke than an attempted invasion. The strong Athenian and allied response gave Philip his answer.

6 THE ROAD TO EMPIRE

After returning from Thermopylae, Philip spent several weeks in Thessaly putting the affairs of his new possession in order. Afterward, he returned to Pella, where the army rested and was replenished for the next campaign. Philip's victory at the Crocus Field had reestablished his military prestige. His defeat at the hands of Onomarchus the previous year had led to important changes in the political configuration of Macedonian power in Thrace, Chalcidice-Olynthos, and Illyria-Paeonia as these states' rulers sought to take advantage of Philip's weakness and loosen his grip on their affairs. With his military prestige now restored, Philip set about reestablishing Macedonian political influence in the recalcitrant territories.

THRACE

Philip first turned his attention to Thrace, where events had seriously altered the previous power balance between Athens and Macedonia in Eastern Thrace. During the year following Philip's defeat, the Athenian general Chares had captured Sestus in the Chersonese as part of a more aggressive Athenian policy to obtain control of the Chersonese and to protect its access to the sea route leading through the Sea of Marmara to the Black Sea. Chares executed all the adult males in Sestus and sold the remainder of the population into slavery.[1] Athens sought to take advantage of Philip's weakened position and his occupation with events in Thessaly. Chares opened negotiations with Cersobleptes, who promptly abandoned his alliance with Philip and ceded to Athens all the cities of the Chersonese with the exception of Cardia. Athens promptly sent settlers to occupy the cities and lands.[2] Cersobleptes also formally recognized the Athenians' claim to Amphipolis.³ (Athens was still waiting for Philip to honor his promise and deliver Amphipolis into its hands.) Shortly thereafter, Cersobleptes tried to offset his losses in the Chersonese by attacking those territories in Eastern Thrace claimed by Perinthus and Byzantium and Amadocus's kingdom in Central Thrace.

These changing circumstances occurred at the expense of Macedonian economic and security interests in the region, and Philip quickly grasped the threat. Especially troubling was the increase in Athenian power, which would inevitably bring it into conflict with Macedonian aspirations in Thrace. In September 352 BCE, Philip and the Macedonian army left Pella for the three hundred–mile, twenty-day march to Eastern Thrace. The ships of the Macedonian navy accompanied them, moving along the coast and carrying Philip's siege equipment, the army's heavy baggage, and additional food. Philip's route took him through Amphipolis and Philippi before reaching Heraion Teichos (modern Tekirdag/Karaevlialti), which was Cersobleptes's westernmost fort on the coast of the Sea of Marmara and eighteen miles west of Perinthus. In November, Philip brought the fortress under siege.⁴

When Philip arrived in Thrace, he found willing allies in Amadocus and the cities of Perinthus and Byzantium who were already engaged in hostilities with Cersobleptes. They joined forces with Philip. Philip was likely aware of the conflict in Eastern Thrace before he left Pella and sought to exploit it for his own ends. When the Athenians learned that Philip was in Thrace besieging Heraion, the assembly voted to protect its newly won acquisitions in the Chersonese and aid Cersobleptes. The assembly agreed to send forty triremes and a large levy of citizen-soldiers to Thrace and approved sixty talents for expenses.

On the face of it, the expedition might have been successful if it had only had to deal with Philip's army. But against Philip and his allies, the Athenian attempt to rescue Cersobleptes faced almost certain failure. The Athenian force would have required forty triremes to transport some four thousand hoplites and numerous transports for their supplies. We have no figures for the number of troops Philip had with him, but it must have been at least half the Macedonian army, or some ten thousand infantry and three hundred cavalry. With the military forces of Perinthus, Amadocus, and Byzantium, the allied troops far outnumbered the Athenians. Moreover, Philip's allies all possessed naval forces, and when joined with Philip's own ships, the alliance effectively controlled the sea in the zone of military operations. The Athenian convoy would have risked being attacked and sunk before it made landfall in Thrace. All in all, the Athenian expedition would have been a disaster.

As things turned out, the Athenian expedition never put to sea. The initial Athenian decision to support Cersobleptes in Thrace seems to have been made soon after hearing the news that Philip was besieging Heraion Teichos in November 351 BCE. The Athenian plan was based on the assumption that Philip was campaigning alone. Under these circumstances, giving Cersobleptes aid made some sense. But when new intelligence reached Athens that Philip had joined an alliance with Amadocus, Perinthus, and Byzantium, it must have been abundantly clear that the proposed Athenian relief force would have stood little chance against the forces now arrayed against it in Thrace. Cooler heads prevailed and cancelled the expedition.[5]

For almost a year Philip campaigned in Thrace, fighting several battles and capturing numerous towns and cities. Justin tells us that Philip "cast out some of the rulers and others he placed on their thrones,"[6] something Philip could only have done by capturing their territories first. There are no extant accounts of Philip's combat operations, but it might be reasonably inferred that several engagements took place over ten to eleven months. It is also significant that Philip campaigned during the winter. Winter weather in Eastern Thrace can be truly uncomfortable for an army in the field and present a serious logistical challenge. Philip's successful winter campaign in Thrace again shows that the Macedonian army possessed an all-weather, all-season combat capability that no other army in Greece had. In July or August 351 BCE, with the campaign completed, Philip fell seriously ill. Rumors reached Athens that he was dead.[7] The news must have raised hopes in Athens that with Philip gone, the Thracian alliance might disintegrate, and Athens would be in a position to recover its position there. In September, the Athenians authorized Charidemos, "with ten empty ships and five silver talents [for expenses]," to sail to Thrace.[8] The term "empty ships" refers to the fact that no citizen-hoplites were sent and that Charidemos had to recruit his own troops for the voyage. But if Philip was still thought to be in Thrace and the alliance intact, Charidemos's little fleet would likely have been either sunk at sea by the allied navies or crushed immediately by the allied ground forces upon landing. Under these circumstances, Charidemos's venture was suicidal.

His voyage suggests that word had reached Athens sometime in the late summer that Philip had recovered from his illness and was marching back to Pella and that the members of the alliance against Cersobleptes had returned to their territories and disbanded their armies for the campaign season. Under these circumstances, Charidemos's expedition made sense. Athens needed a thorough assessment of the damage Philip's campaign had done to its interests in Thrace as well as an assessment of the political environment Athens would face when rebuilding its position in Eastern Thrace. Charidemos was essentially leading a reconnaissance operation to appraise the strategic military and political situation in Thrace.[9]

Meanwhile, Philip's campaign had restored both his military and political reputation and prestige in Thrace and increased Macedonian influence in the region. Cersobleptes had been forced to come to terms, which permitted Philip to place friendly rulers in some cities and towns. To ensure Cersobleptes observed the conditions of the truce, his son was taken to Pella as a hostage. The cities of Perinthus and Byzantium remained on good terms with Philip and saw Macedonian influence in the region as an effective counterweight to Athens. Whatever latent threat Cersobleptes and the Athenians had posed to Philip's possessions in Thrace was, for the time being at least, greatly diminished.

Amadocus was now in his eighties and effectively reduced to the status of a client king, just as Ketriporis in Western Thrace had been. With Perinthus and Byzantium friendly to Philip, there was little to stop a Macedonian army from marching from Philippi to the Bosporus. Philip's Thracian campaign had opened the road to a strategic strike at the Athenian food supply for Philip could close the Bosporus to the Athenian wheat fleet that moved from the Black Sea through the narrow waterway each spring to Athens. Athens depended on this route for 40 percent of its food, which was now at great risk.

EPIRUS

Philip stopped briefly at Olynthos on his way back from Thrace, for reasons that will be explained shortly, before arriving at Pella sometime in November 350 BCE. The army went into winter quarters and gathered its strength for Philip's next campaign. In the spring of 350 BCE, Philip ordered the army into action again, this time taking it west into Illyria, Paeonia, and Molossia. There are no accounts of Philip's actions in Illyria and Paeonia, and we have only Demosthenes' mention of them as evidence that they occurred at all.[10] Illyria and Paeonia had been brought under Macedonian control in 358 BCE after their crushing defeat by Philip. When Onomarchus drove Philip from Thessaly in 353 BCE, Illyria and Paeonia may have attempted to lift the Macedonian yoke either by local revolt or by embarking upon diplomatic approaches to gain Athenian support. Athens had supported the previous revolt by Illyria, Paeonia, and Thrace against Philip, and something similar may have been afoot again, causing Philip to use the army to remind them who was master in the new Macedonia. Demosthenes says Philip was fortifying cities in Illyria during this time.[11]

The reasons for Philip's attack on the Molossians of Epirus are unclear. The kingdom of Epirus was a coalition comprising of four major tribes under the leadership of Arybbas, the high king. Arybbas was the uncle of Philip's Epirote wife, Olympias, whom he had married in 357 BCE as the price of an alliance with the Molossian coalition. Until 350 BCE, there seems to have been no difficulties with the alliance, and why Philip moved against his allies is puzzling. The tribes of Upper Macedonia were related more to the Molossians than they were to the Macedones in dialect, origin, and way of life, and perhaps Philip saw these cultural loyalties as a potential threat to Macedonian control and integration of the Upper Cantons.[12] It is also possible that, as others had, Arybbas had sought to exploit Philip's defeat in some way that made Philip doubt his loyalty. Once more no accounts of Philip's battles survive, but given what happened to the Molossian king and the coalition, it seems certain that some sort of armed conflict took place that resulted in Arybbas's surrender and acceptance of relatively harsh terms.

Whatever Arybbas's offense was, it must have been serious for it cost him the throne he had occupied since 360 BCE when his brother, Neoptolemus (Olympias's father), died. Philip reduced Arybbas to the status of regent for Arybbas's nephew and Olympias's younger brother, Alexandros, thus creating a new line of succession. The twelve-year-old Alexandros was removed from the country; taken to Pella, where he would remain for the next eight years; and educated in the ways of the Macedonians.[13] Philip suspended the king's right to issue coins, and the Molossian currency was replaced with Philip's bronze currency for domestic exchange. He then annexed the remaining tribal kingdoms of Tymphaea and Parauaea, the easternmost regions of the Molossian tribal state, and extended Macedonian influence to the coastal areas of Epirus. Philip encouraged some of the residents to build towns and forgo their pastoral existence for a more settled life. Over time this transition seems to have occurred, and then Philip established militia units there and introduced the use of the sarissa and the phalanx.[14] Philip intended to integrate the people of Epirus into the Macedonian national state just as he had integrated Macedonia's Upper Cantons.

THE WAR WITH OLYNTHOS

Philip had been concerned with Olynthos and the thirty-two cities of the Chalcidian League that it led from the beginning of his reign. Its strategic geographic location at the head of the Thermaic Gulf, its economic power and large population, and its considerable military forces constituted a potentially serious threat to Macedonian security. The Macedonian ports were off the main shipping lanes; so much of Macedonian trade moved through Chalcidian ports.[15] In 356 BCE Philip had concluded an alliance with Olynthos to deprive Athens of a possible ally in the gulf and guarantee him freedom of action in Paeonia, Illyria, and Thrace. As proof of his sincerity, Philip had not only captured the Athenian naval base at Potidea and turned it over to Olynthos, as promised, but he had also insisted that the treaty be sworn at Delphi and the articles of agreement be deposited at the shrine. Philip's ability to conduct his military campaigns between 358 BCE and 351 BCE depended on Olynthos observing its obligations under the treaty and remaining aloof from Philip's affairs. Most important was Olynthos's obligation not to seek an alliance with Athens. The treaty's equally important but unwritten diplomatic understanding was Olynthos's obligation to no longer interfere in Macedonia's domestic affairs. By 351 BCE, both of these commitments were in doubt.

On his way back from the Thracian campaign in the fall of 351 BCE, Philip stopped at Olynthos with the Macedonian army not far behind, no doubt so the Olynthians might feel its presence. There is no information as to what had raised Philip's suspicions, but if Olynthos had again been exploring an alliance with Athens, as it had following Philip's defeat in 353 BCE, it is not unreasonable that Philip's intelligence network may have gotten wind of it. Olynthos had openly been in contact with Athens since 353 BCE and had, Demosthenes tells us, already concluded a peace treaty with Athens to repair relations strained during Philip's siege of Amphipolis. Olynthos may have become concerned with the expansion of Macedonian power in Thrace and begun more serious discussions with Athens regarding a military alliance. Olynthos's treaty with Philip prohibited such a deal and would have been of great concern to Philip.

Justin suggests that the cause of Philip's concern was the presence of his two half-brothers, Menelaus and Arrhidaeus, in Olynthos. The city had given them sanctuary following their attempt to prevent Philip's rise to the Macedonian throne.[16] In addition, Demosthenes implies that strong anti-Macedonian factions in Olynthos regarded Philip as a threat and wished to conclude an alliance with Athens.[17] Philip may have concluded that Olynthos was planning some sort of intervention in Macedonia, perhaps with Athenian help, aimed at removing Philip by military means and replacing him with one of his half-brothers. Olynthos had a long history of intervening in Macedonian politics, and a renewed attempt along these lines to weaken or replace Philip could not be reasonably discounted.

We have no account of Philip's discussions with Olynthos except Demosthenes' cryptic statement that Philip "made a move against" Olynthos.[18] That there was no military action seems certain, and Theopompus is probably correct that Philip delivered a stern warning to the city's leaders while the Macedonian army was encamped close by.[19] As serious as the potential threat from Olynthos was, Philip was in no position to deal with it at present. On his return from Thrace, Philip had learned that events in Illyria, Paeonia, and Epirus demanded his immediate attention. As he had done often, Philip used his diplomatic skills to deal with Olynthos by reminding its leaders in serious tones of their treaty obligations but taking no further action. The discussions seem to have had some effect, and the Olynthians expelled Apollonides, the leader of the anti-Macedonian faction, from the city.[20] In addition, two "friends" of Philip's, Lasthenes and Euthycrates, were elected to the important military posts of commanders of the Olynthian cavalry.[21] The question of Athens, however, was not addressed. The Olynthians were trying to allay Philip's fears with diplomatic gestures. The realities remained, however, and Philip was a man who always dealt in realities.

After settling the problems in Illyria, Paeonia, and Epirus, Philip turned his attention to Olynthos and the Chalcidian League. In the spring of 349 BCE, Philip demanded that Olynthos surrender his half-brothers to him. Olynthos refused, and in midsummer Philip attacked Chalcidice. Justin's suggestion that Philip went to war because Olynthos would not turn over his half-brothers to him is probably incorrect. More serious reasons of state were at hand. Philip simply could not tolerate Olynthos's attempted rapprochement with Athens, for if it were to succeed, Macedonian security would be gravely at risk. Philip moved against the Chalcidians to prevent the alliance.

Map 5. *Chalcidice*

In midsummer 349 BCE, Philip's army moved overland through Macedonia on a route that took him north of Lake Bolbe and allowed him to enter Chalcidice far to the east of the capital of Olynthos. Philip held the military advantage. He was fighting close to his home base along internal supply lines against an enemy whose forces were dispersed among thirty-two cities, all located on open ground. From the beginning of the invasion, Philip held the initiative and the Chalcidians always the defensive. He quickly overran a small fortress guarding the northern approaches to the city of Stagirus, Aristotle's birthplace, and attacked the city. Philip's engineers went about their work, and the city fell in a relatively short time. Philip then ordered Stagirus completely destroyed. There is no record of what happened to the city's population, but rather than sell it into slavery, Philip likely turned it loose to wander throughout Chalcidice and tell others what would happen if they resisted Philip's advance.

Philip's policy of striking terror in the hearts of the league's cities paid quick dividends, and a number of small towns—Stratonica, Acanthus,

Apollonia, and Arethusa—surrendered without a fight to save themselves from destruction. Philip had no intention of meeting the armies of Olynthos and the league in open battle where he might be at a disadvantage. His strategy was to isolate the smaller cities in the east of the country, by either attacking them or frightening them into surrender, while Olynthos itself was left unmolested. Philip's strategy was succeeding handsomely, when events forced him to abandon his campaign and return to Thessaly in the late fall of 349 BCE.

Even before Philip's successes, Olynthos had appealed to Athens for military help against Philip. In July, an Olynthian delegation reached Athens and concluded a military alliance with the Athenians. Athens assembled a fleet of thirty-eight ships carrying a force of two thousand *peltasts* (light javelin infantry) under the command of Chares. The Etesian winds delayed the fleet's departure for a few weeks and did not reach Mecyberna, the port of Olynthos. By that time, however, Philip had halted his campaign and marched into Thessaly to deal with his difficulties there.

Pherae had broken into open revolt, perhaps as a consequence of the return of Peitholaus, one of the deposed tyrants. The Pheraeans had taken steps to prevent the Macedonians from fortifying Magnesia and had demanded the return of the port of Pagasae. Pagasae itself had also withheld the harbor and market taxes that were due Philip as their archon.[22] By themselves, these events would not have required Philip to cease his campaign in Chalcidice. But the Pheraean revolt occurred as the Phokians won a series of victories over the Boeotians in the still-simmering Sacred War to the south, and it appeared that Phokis might try to restore its alliance with Pherae and march into Thessaly in support. This greater fear of a Phokian invasion prompted the Thessalians to recall Philip to Thessaly and deal with Peitholaus. The Pheraean armed forces were likely a small mercenary contingent in the pay of Peitholaus and no match for Philip's army. Though no accounts of the battle exist, it is certain that Philip made short work of the resistance and drove Peitholaus and his mercenaries from Thessaly. The much-feared Phokian invasion did not materialize, and Philip decided to remain in Thessaly for the winter to quarter his army.

While Philip was in Thessaly suppressing the Pheraean revolt, another revolt broke out in the island of Euboea in February 348 BCE that greatly concerned Athens. That island was of vital strategic importance to Athens. In concert with its allies Sparta and Phokis, Athens had already demonstrated its ability to block Philip's advance through the Thermopylae Pass in 352 BCE, and as long as the alliance remained intact, Athens felt secure enough from land invasion. Athens was less confident about Euboea, however. The island's western shore ran close to Attica and was connected to the mainland by a narrow bridge controlled by Chalcis.[23] If Philip could reach the northern end of Euboea by sea, he could then march down the island, cross into Boeotia, link up with his Theban and Boeotian allies, and attack Athens itself. The key to any invasion was Chalcis and its control of the bridge.

Relations between Athens and the states of Euboea had been generally cordial until the winter of 348 BCE when Callias, the leading politician of Chalcis, led a rebellion against the Second Athenian Confederacy to which many states of the island belonged. Callias proposed the formation of a pan-Euboean league instead, and a number of states joined him. What had been a relatively secure border for Athens was suddenly threatened by political instability, while Athens was already deeply engaged in supporting Olynthos in the Chalcidice against Philip.

Athens responded to the Euboean uprising by sending troops to support the pro-Athenian faction, while Callias "summoned additional forces from Philip."[24] As early as 351 BCE Philip had already established a strong diplomatic correspondence with the Euboeans and may have had a hand in encouraging Callias in his rebellion.[25] That Philip sent additional forces to support Callias once the revolt began suggests that Philip was prepared to exploit the situation in Euboea if only to distract Athens from its efforts in Chalcidice. The pro-Athenian faction suffered a series of defeats. In the resulting negotiated truce, all of Euboea became independent, leaving Carystus the only Athenian ally on the island. Under the influence of Callias, Chalcis was now openly pro-Macedonian, and the threat of a Macedonian invasion from the island was a stark possibility for Athens. It forced Athens to maintain a large naval presence in the area to guard against Philip landing his army on the island's northern sector, tying down more Athenian naval assets precisely when it needed them to transport troops and cavalry to support Olynthos.

In the spring of 348 BCE, Philip was again in the Chalcidice, this time campaigning against the western cities and much closer to Olynthos itself. He took Apollonia and, not long after, Torone. Chares' fleet, which had been based in the key port of Mecyberna, had returned to Athens, perhaps in early spring. By summer, Mecyberna fell to the Macedonians, greatly reducing Olynthos's ability to receive reinforcements from Athens. If they were sent at all, Athenian ships would be forced to disembark their troops and cavalry at much greater distances from Olynthos itself, giving Philip plenty of time to react.

The Olynthians had already appealed for Athenian aid when Philip reentered Chalcidice. The Athenians had responded by outfitting a relief force of eighteen ships carrying four thousand light infantry and 150 cavalry under the command of Charidemos.[26] This force joined the Olynthians and attacked those cities in the west that had already gone over to Philip, putting the Olynthians in the position of attacking the cities of members of their own alliance. These operations accomplished nothing, except they occupied the Olynthians and Athenians in areas where they could do little to threaten Philip, who was ready to attack Olynthos itself.

Meanwhile, the Macedonian navy had intercepted and looted a number of merchantmen off Euboea and had even captured the Athenian Sacred Trireme at Marathon.[27] The navy also conducted successful raids on the harbors of Lemnos and Imbros. Philip's improved naval capability placed the considerable Olynthian sea trade at risk, and the Macedonian navy's raids could not have gone unnoticed in Athens, Greece's preeminent naval power.

Philip tightened the noose around Olynthos's neck, and in June he was outside its walls, preparing to bring the city under siege. Olynthos had anticipated this move a few weeks earlier and had sent an emissary to Athens asking for additional military support. Once more Athens assembled a relief force. Seventeen ships carrying two thousand troops and three hundred cavalry were prepared for transport. The importance that Athens placed on its support of Olynthos can be inferred from its decision this time to send citizen-hoplites instead of mercenaries. The three hundred cavalrymen were also citizens and made up 30 percent of the entire Athenian cavalry force.[28] Once again, command of the relief expedition was awarded to Chares. But it was now late June and the Etesian winds had begun to blow, making the transit from Athens to Olynthos impossible. As he had done before, Philip had timed his final assault on Olynthos to coincide with the season of the Etesian winds. The transports carrying the Athenian relief force were unable to put to sea for forty days.

Philip's army was only seven miles from Olynthos when the city's defenders sent a messenger asking Philip for terms. Philip's reply reflected his contempt for Olynthos and the way its rulers had betrayed him: "For the rest of time it is not possible for you to live on in Olynthos and me in Macedonia."[29]

Philip had no intention of coming to terms with Olynthos. Doing so would not solve the strategic problem Olynthos and the Chalcidice presented to Macedonia. His only solution was to destroy Olynthos and annex the entire Chalcidian Peninsula, making it an integral part of the Macedonian national state. Philip's ultimatum left Olynthos little choice and did nothing to diminish the resolve of the city's defenders. Philip was forced to bring the city under siege. The assault began sometime in July, and by September 348 BCE it was over. Olynthos was a large city with good fortifications and high walls. Its garrison must have been at least four thousand strong, counting some of the Athenian mercenaries who had arrived earlier, and seems to have initially put up stiff resistance. A two-month siege, however, was very short as Greek sieges went and short even by the new standards set by Philip's siege engineers. Diodorus tells us that the fighting was heavy, and that "in the course of a constant series of assaults, he [Philip] lost many of his troops in the battle for the walls."[30]

The reports of heavy Macedonian casualties "in the course of a constant series of assaults" suggest that Philip had pressed hard to take the city quickly. Perhaps he had been informed that the Athenian relief force was ready to put to sea as soon as the Etesian winds subsided. If so, Philip had until early October to vanquish Olynthos before the Athenian relief force landed at his back. After two months of fighting, heavy casualties, and perhaps with no end in sight, Philip may have found another way to take the city. Diodorus tells us that "eventually he bribed Euthycrates and Lasthenes, two of the Olynthian [cavalry] commanders through whose agency he took the city by treachery."[31] As noted, Euthycrates and Lasthenes were both friends of Philip's and openly pro-Macedonian in their political sentiments. They had both only been appointed to their military commands when the Olynthians sought to placate Philip's suspicions of Olynthian loyalty. Once more Philip's policy of making friends he one day hoped to find useful paid off. Demosthenes says that the two commanders brought their five hundred cavalrymen and their weapons over to Philip.[32] But this defection, by itself, could hardly have caused the city to fall into Philip's hands in the treacherous manner that Diodorus says it did. While we have no details, there must have been much more to the "agency" of the two officers that brought about the capture of Olynthos.[33]

Because Olynthos had betrayed Philip, he forced upon it the harsh fate he reserved for traitors. He turned the city over to his army, which went on a bloody rampage, killing the civilian population indiscriminately. A small number of the people escaped, but most were either enslaved and forced to work the mines of Macedonia or, as Diodorus says, were sold into slavery. Philip gave some of the Olynthian women as gifts to his guest-friends and supporters in other Greek states.[34] Among those captured were members of the Athenian relief expeditions. Their numbers were probably small, but according to Demosthenes, they, too, were sent to the mines.[35] Larger numbers of Athenian soldiers were captured throughout the campaign and after the fall of Olynthos. Philip had always released captured Athenians in the past. This time he kept them, and they were not released until the peace with Athens was sealed in 346 BCE. Philip sold off the booty taken from the city, and "as a result of this action he secured an abundance of money for waging war and alarmed the other cities which were at war with him."[36] Presumably the Chalcidian cities that had not yet surrendered to Philip did so now, and the Chalcidian League, with its history of interference in Macedonian affairs, was disbanded.

Philip ordered Olynthos razed to the ground.[37] Demosthenes claimed that Philip destroyed many of the cities of the Chalcidian League, "all of which he destroyed so brutally that it is hard for a visitor to tell if they were ever inhabited."[38] The claim is false, and neither Justin nor Diodorus mentions such destruction. Only Stagirus seems to have been destroyed and was done so early in Philip's campaign as an example of psychological warfare. It apparently was a success, since many of the Chalcidian cities surrendered to Philip without resistance. Moreover, Philip had come to annex Chalcidice for its natural resources, ports, taxes, timber, and other revenues. Important gold and silver mines at Stratonica also added greatly to his wealth. It would have made no sense for him to destroy Chalcidice only to have to rebuild it later.

Olynthos, however, was destroyed brick by brick, reduced to two flat-topped mounds of rubble.[39] The once-powerful city of ten thousand ceased to exist. Philip distributed Olynthian lands to his Companions and other important persons, distributed cash gifts to important men in the other cities of Chalcidice, and "in this way secured the services of many men willing to betray their city."[40] Philip intended to integrate the whole of Chalcidice into Macedonia, and establishing friendships with the powerful in the country's cities reassured them that their positions were not threatened. It was the first step in winning their loyalty. Philip did not import large numbers of

Map 6. *Macedonia and Its Conquests (348 BCE)*

Macedonians into Chalcidice as he had done in other places. With the fall of Olynthos and the surrender of Chalcidice, the Macedonian state expanded farther to the east, making it the most powerful and largest of the Greek states. Before leaving for Pella, Philip attended to one last detail. He had his half-brothers executed.

The collapse of Olynthos and the Chalcidice was a severe blow to Athens, which had no allies left in the Thermaic Gulf and northern Aegean Sea. In the east, only the fickle Thracian king Cersobleptes stood in the way of Philip's advance toward the Hellespont. Philip's brilliant execution of Macedonian grand strategy was eroding Athenian power (see map 6), and there was little Athens could do to stop it.

THE END OF THE SACRED WAR

While Philip was fighting in Chalcidice, the Sacred War raged on to the south. After the defeat at the Crocus Field in 352 BCE, Phayllos, the Phokian commander who had replaced the executed Onomarchus, set about recruiting more mercenaries and allies to the Phokian cause. In late 352 BCE, Phayllos succumbed to a "wasting disease"[41] and was replaced by Phalaecus, who held the Phokian command with two other generals. Phalaecus recruited additional mercenaries and in 349 BCE went over to the offensive, delivering the Boeotians a series of defeats and capturing the cities of Coronea, Corsiae, and Orchomenus. By 348 BCE, the Phokians controlled much of southwestern Boeotia. It was the high-water mark of the Phokian military effort thus far, and Thebes was near exhaustion.[42] The Phokian allies, Sparta and Athens, were occupied with their own problems. Athens had just suffered considerable reverses in Thrace and the Chersonese at the hands of Philip, and Sparta was bogged down in a war in the Peloponnese.

Had Philip wished to do so, he could have easily forced the now only lightly defended pass at Thermopylae, joined with Thebes, and defeated Phokis, bringing an end to the Sacred War. But again Philip had no desire to end the war so long as it continued to weaken all the major Greek states except Macedonia. Philip spent 347 BCE in Thessaly, resting his army and attending to calming down the Thessalians, who pressed him to march south and exterminate the Phokians in revenge for ancient wrongs. A dispute broke out between the Thessalian cities of Pharsalus, a major contributor to the Thessalian League, and the small port city of Halus, the last city in Thessaly with pro-Athenian sympathies. Philip set the Macedonian navy to work protecting the Thessalian coast and raiding Athenian shipping. He watched from afar as the Greek states wore themselves out dealing with their own problems.

Phalaecus's offensive and his capture of Boeotian cities in 348 BCE sent fear up the Thebans' spines. Diodorus tells us, "The Boeotians, who were under pressure in the war and suffering from the loss of many troops and from the lack of financial resources, sent envoys to Philip with a request for aid."[43] He dates the Theban request to early 346 BCE. Until now, there had been no formal alliance or cooperation between Philip and Thebes. Only their common interest in defeating the Phokians had placed them on the same side in the war. But Philip was still technically the commander of the forces of the Amphictyonic Council arrayed against Phokis and could hardly ignore the Thebans' request. Strategically, however, Philip had not worked to reduce Athenian power in Greece only to see Thebes replace it once the war with Phokis ended. Thus, "the king [Philip], delighted to witness their [Thebes'] humiliation and eager to deflate their Leuctric arrogance [a reference to Theban behavior after its victory at the battle of Leuctra], sent only a few troops, for he took pains to avoid being seen by public opinion as one who looked on impassively at the plundering of the oracle."[44] The war went on and the stalemate continued.

Meanwhile, events in Phokis began to spin out of control. In the summer of 347 BCE, Phalaecus was removed from command of the army and charged with plundering the Delphic treasury. We have no information about the nature of the factional politics that were at play, but clearly Phalaecus was removed in some internal power struggle and charged with stealing the Delphic treasure, an accusation that could have led to his execution. A triumvirate of generals took command of the Phokian army in his place.

Philip dispatched troops to the Thebans in early 346 BCE. When they joined the Thebans and attacked the city of Abae, which the Phokians were attempting to fortify, the Phokians were convinced that Philip intended to attack south with his Thessalian allies. Phokis appealed to Athens and Sparta for help. The Spartans sent a thousand hoplites under the command of Archidamus III, their king. Athens sent general Proxenus to take over the forts controlling the road from Thermopylae to central Greece. These three fortified towns—Alponus, Thronium, and Nicaea—were the keys to blocking Philip's access to the Thermopylae Pass and to preventing his movement into Phokis. Athens also voted to send fifty triremes and their crews along with a large number of troops.[45] The allies intended to block Philip's southern advance at Thermopylae, as they had done after his victory at the Crocus Field in 352 BCE. In addition, the Athenians decided to commit a small force to assist Halus in its dispute with Pharsalus.[46] Philip could hardly ignore the Athenian provocation, and in February 346 BCE, Philip sent troops under Parmenio to take Halus under siege.

Having made arrangements to block Philip's advance, Athens turned to restoring its position in Eastern Thrace and the Chersonese. In 347 BCE, Athens had sent an expedition under the command of Chares to Thrace, where it joined up with the wily Cersobleptes. Having changed sides again,

Cersobleptes established several garrisons along the coast of the Sea of Marmara. In response, Philip dispatched Antipater and a small force to keep an eye on events in Thrace. Antipater set up a base on the coast to monitor Athenian movements in Thrace and the Chersonese but did not engage the troops.

Prior to these events, Philip had taken the first steps toward a negotiated peace with Athens immediately after his capture of Olynthos in 348 BCE. After taking the city, Philip retired to Dium and celebrated the autumn festival in honor of Zeus. The games associated with the festival were accompanied by the Olympic Truce, a period when those traveling to and from the games were protected from attack or capture. That summer, Macedonian privateers had captured an Athenian citizen named Phrynon and held him for ransom. Athens sent an embassy to Philip demanding the man's release. Philip agreed that the seizure was illegal and the man was released. More importantly, Philip sent back a message with Ctesiphon, the Athenian emissary, that the king regretted the war with Athens, that he had been forced into it, and that he now wanted to end it and conclude a peace with Athens. Athens should have accepted the offer given its own weakened position in the Thermaic Gulf, Thrace, and the Chersonese. As always, Philip was trying to obtain by diplomacy what he had not yet achieved by war.

The factionalism of Athenian domestic politics, however, made it impossible for Athens to accept Philip's overture. Instead, Demosthenes warned that Philip could not be trusted and that the danger he represented to all of Greece was greater than ever. Arguing that war with Philip was inevitable, Demosthenes urged Athens to seek a great alliance of Greek states to oppose Philip. Philip's peace overture collapsed, and Athens sought allies for war. In 346 BCE, Philip made another attempt to settle things diplomatically. The fate of the Athenians captured by Philip at Olynthos and being held prisoner was an emotional issue in Athens, and in early 346 BCE the Athenian Assembly sent Aristodemus, an actor and an old friend of Philip's, to Pella to determine what Philip intended to do with the prisoners. Empty-handed, Aristodemus returned with the news that Philip wanted peace and an alliance with Athens.[47] This time Athens was in no position to refuse.

While Philip was trying to arrange a peace with Athens through diplomatic means, he was simultaneously engaged in efforts to erode the military arrangements Athens, Phokis, and Sparta had assembled to protect the Thermopylae Pass. The results of Philip's labor reached Athens just as Aristodemus returned from Pella with news of Philip's desire for peace. The Athenians also learned to their great dismay that Phalaecus, the commander of the Phokian mercenaries, had seized power with the aid of his mercenaries and was now in command of the Phokian army.[48] He had imprisoned the Phokian ambassadors who had promised Athens control of the fortresses of Alponus, Thronium, and Nicaea controlling Thermopylae, and the Athenian general sent to assume control of the forts was told to keep out. Phalaecus turned on the Spartans next and warned the Spartan king not to enter Phokis.[49] The carefully crafted military arrangements Athens made to prevent Philip from advancing through Thermopylae collapsed.

The question is, why did Phalaecus expel his Athenian and Spartan allies at a critical time and leave himself vulnerable to an attack by Philip? One can only speculate. First, it is obvious that Phalaecus's position was less than secure. He had imprisoned his enemies and forcefully taken power with the support of mercenaries. Phalaecus had every reason to suspect that Athens and Sparta might support his enemies in a countercoup and thus kept them out of the country. Second, Phokis was financially exhausted. Even the melted-down treasures seized at Delphi had been spent. Phalaecus could hardly expect to keep his mercenaries' loyalty without the money to pay them. Third, even with sufficient allies and money, Phokis was doomed if Philip decided to attack in force. Finally, Phalaecus knew that the Thessalians were thirsting for a violent revenge on their Phokian enemies. The only person who could restrain the Thessalians and prevent Phokis's destruction and enslavement was Philip. Thus Phalaecus may have decided that the only way to save himself and Phokis was to reach some sort of accommodation with Philip.

The Athenians sent a delegation to Pella to begin negotiations with Philip. It arrived in mid-March 346 BCE. Athens continued to insist on its right to Amphipolis and to support Halus in Thessaly. Philip rejected both positions out of hand, but he suggested that Athens and Macedonia recognize each other's possessions in Thrace (at that time), that both parties cooperate in fighting the rampant problem of piracy in the Aegean, and that they conclude a formal peace and defensive alliance. As a sign of his good faith, Philip offered two things—to release the Athenian prisoners taken at Olynthos immediately and without ransom and to recognize Athenian influence in Euboea.[50] He also promised not to attack Athenian possessions in the Chersonese as long as the negotiations were in progress.[51] The Athenian envoys returned to Athens and presented Philip's proposals to the assembly.

As soon as the Athenian envoys left Pella, Philip and his army marched into Thrace to settle affairs with the treacherous Cersobleptes. Before leaving, however, he had sent an embassy to Athens to confirm his terms, to reassure the Athenians that he was sincere in his effort to conclude a peace, and to continue the negotiations. In 347 BCE Athens had supported Cersobleptes again and had helped him construct some coastal forts.[52] In response, a small Macedonian advance force under Antipater had been sent in February 347 BCE to monitor Athenian movements. Philip's army now linked up with this advance force, and on April 20 attacked Cersobleptes's fortress at Heraion Orus and defeated him.[53] Philip spent another two months reducing the independent coastal Thracian forts, completing his operations around mid-June.[54] Philip allowed Cersobleptes to remain king but reduced him to a vassal while taking some of his sons as hostages to guarantee the Thracian king's good behavior. Philip then forced Teres II, the successor to Amadocus in Central Thrace, into the same vassal relationship. With Western Thrace virtually integrated into the Macedonian state as far as the Nestus River, Philip's Thracian campaign of 346 BCE created a double buffer zone between the new eastern Macedonian border and the Black Sea and Persia beyond.[55] By the end of June, Philip arrived in Pella by ship ready to deal with the Athenians and what remained of the Sacred War.

While Philip was campaigning in Thrace, the Athenian delegation had returned to Athens and began debating Philip's terms for peace and an alliance with Macedonia. On the first day of the debate, Philocrates, a member of the delegation to Pella and a proponent of a peace with Philip, arose to address the assembly.

> Bear in mind, that this is not the time to engage in contentious rivalry, that the affairs of the state are not in a good situation, that many grave dangers surround us. For we know that the Boeotians and the Megarians are at enmity with us, the Peloponnesians are courting some of the Thebans and others the Spartans, the Chians and the Rhodians, and their allies are hostile to our state, and they are negotiating with Philip for his friendship.[56]

He might have added that Phokis was exhausted and had all but ceased to be an Athenian ally by exposing the Thermopylae Pass, that Cersobleptes had been defeated, that Athens no longer had possessions in Thrace,[57] and that Philip was in a position to attack Athenian interests in the Chersonese at will and to block the grain shipments through the Hellespont. Athens was isolated, exhausted, broke, and easy prey for the Macedonian king should he join with Thebes and invade Attica. While others argued that Athens should attempt a grand coalition of Greek states to oppose Philip, the realists prevailed. A few days later the Athenian Assembly agreed to the Peace of Philocrates.

The agreement called for a peace treaty between Philip and Athens along with an alliance, which amounted to a mutual nonaggression pact. Athens had to swallow the bitter pill of renouncing its claims to Amphipolis, which had become an integral part of the Macedonian state.[58] It is significant that the agreement did not address continued Athenian support for Phokis, Halus, or Cersobleptes. In one sense the issue of Athenian support for Phokis and Halus would be resolved when the Sacred War was officially over. In another, however, Philip's approaches to Phalaecus, his siege of Halus, and his recent successes in Thrace had already, in fact, decided these issues. Their formalization in a later treaty concluding hostilities could wait. For the moment, Athens was seeking to protect itself from any future Macedonian attack by concluding a peace and nonaggression pact with Philip. Phokis, Halus, and Cersobleptes were on their own.

On April 29, the Athenian delegation set out for Pella to meet with Philip, to seal the agreement with formal oaths, and to secure the release of the Athenian prisoners taken at Olynthos. Since Philip was campaigning in Thrace, the delegation traveled at its leisure and arrived in Pella twenty-three days after leaving Athens. They waited another twenty-seven days until Philip returned from Thrace on about June 17. The Athenian delegation must have been surprised to find diplomatic delegations from most of the important Greek states, including Thebes, Sparta, and Phokis, already in Pella.[59] By now the Athenians must have suspected that Phalaecus and Philip had entered some sort of arrangement, even though they could not have known the details. A Phokian delegation's presence at the talks is circumstantial evidence that Philip had already made an arrangement with Phalaecus, the details of which were soon to be shockingly evident to all. The Athenians had come to Pella to conclude a bilateral agreement only to find themselves in the middle of the larger negotiations addressing how Philip intended to settle the Sacred War.

Much was at stake for Phokis, Thebes, and Sparta. On the one hand, if Philip had the support of Thebes, the Theban allies in the Peloponnese, the Thessalians, and the Athenians and destroyed the Phokians, the effect would be to confirm Theban power in central Greece at Athenian expense. On the other hand, if Philip joined Sparta, Athens, Thessaly, and Phokis in an alliance, then Theban power in the region would be broken. Sparta, for its part, feared that Philip would invade the Peloponnese, using the Theban subject states to foment rebellion as an excuse to come to their aid. Athens was safe from Philip's wrath as long as he swore his allegiance to the peace. It was the fate of Phokis, Sparta, and Thebes that hung in the balance. As expected, Thessaly and Thebes wanted Phokis destroyed, while Athens and Sparta argued that the Phokians could not be held collectively responsible for the actions of their blasphemous leaders. Philip, always the diplomat, listened carefully to all sides and led each to believe that he supported its position.

While the negotiations continued, Philip did nothing to hide the obvious signs of the large military buildup taking place in Pella. The Thessalians openly boasted that the army was aimed at an invasion of central Greece. Philip dismissed the delegations' concerns and explained that the troops were needed to bring the siege of Halus to a successful conclusion. Under Parmenio's capable command, the siege had been under way since February. It seems to have occurred to no one how remarkable it was that such a small town had held out for so long against Philip's engineers. Nor did anyone seem to notice that the Macedonian army at Halus was only two days' march (forty-four miles) from the vital pass at Thermopylae.

The Athenians were eager to have Philip swear the oaths that would bind him to the peace and the alliance before events got out of hand. Philip delayed the oath swearing, pleading that not all of his allies were present. Philip then said he was needed at Halus and that the Athenian delegation would have to accompany him and his army as it marched to Halus.[60] When the parties reached Pherae, Philip swore the oaths, and the Peace of Philocrates came into being. The Athenian delegation boarded its ship for home at Pagasae. Once more, no one seems to have noticed that Philip and his army were uncomfortably close (sixty-two miles, or four days' march) to Thermopylae.

The peace with Athens concluded, Philip marched his army south toward the Thermopylae Pass, "making ready to determine the outcome of the war in pitched battle."[61] On the march, Philip "picked up the Thessalians en route and arrived in Locris with a large force."[62] It is unlikely, however, that the force that accompanied Philip and the Athenians to Pherae was the entire Macedonian army. By this time Philip could put twenty-four thousand infantry and three thousand cavalry, including the Thessalian cavalry, in the field. The Athenians, already suspicious of Philip's intentions in central Greece and fearful that he would indeed march on Thermopylae, could hardly be expected to believe that a force of this size was needed to bring the siege of Halus to an end. Thus, the army that accompanied Philip and the Athenians to Pherae was probably a much smaller force, one whose size could convince the Athenians that it was really targeted at Halus. One might venture the guess that a force of some eight thousand to ten thousand infantry and a thousand cavalry might have sufficed to convince the Athenians.

Twenty-two miles south of Pherae and forty-four miles from Thermopylae, Parmenio was still besieging Halus. The size of his force is unknown, but it could hardly have been less than six thousand men if the siege was to have seemed credible by the Athenians who passed Halus en route to the Pella negotiations with Philip. Halus was located on the coastal road leading to Thermopylae. Since the city was no longer Philip's concern now that the Athenians had abandoned their support for it, Parmenio's troops were no longer needed there. They joined Philip on the way south. Diodorus tells us the Thessalians, who probably provided large contingents of cavalry, also linked up with Philip. These units were either stationed at Lamia on a regular basis, or they could have been sent there from Larissa before Philip's march to Pherae. Lamia was only nine miles from Thermopylae, and its strategic location made it likely that at least some Thessalian units were regularly stationed there to act as a screen against Phokian incursions. Philip may also have sent the rest of the Macedonian infantry to Lamia in advance. If Diodorus is correct that Philip expected a pitched battle, it made sense to have the entire Macedonian field army at his disposal, especially so if, after the battle, Philip's threat to invade central Greece was going to be credible. Philip's force, augmented by Parmenio's troops, probably met up with the rest of the Macedonian infantry and the Thessalian cavalry coming from Lamia just outside the Thermopylae Pass. When Philip reached Thermopylae (see map 7), his army probably numbered twenty thousand infantry and twenty-five hundred cavalry.

Philip's arrival caught the Phokians by surprise. They had been misled by Philip's promises that he intended to settle the Sacred War peacefully. It is unlikely, however, that Philip's arrival surprised Phalaecus and the mercenaries

Map 7. *Thermopylae*

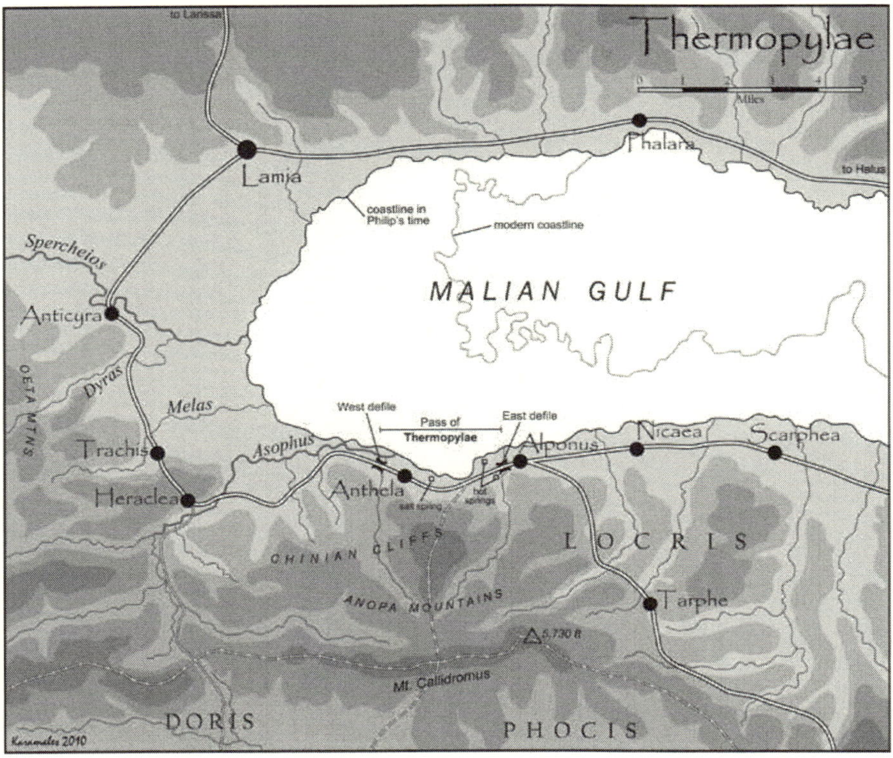

guarding the pass. Phalaecus's army, numbering only eight thousand men,[63] was deployed in the three fortress towns south of the pass from where they could quickly assemble at the pass itself and throw up a defense. Diodorus tells us that when Philip arrived, "Phalaecus, who was lingering at Nicaea and saw that his numbers were unequal to the task of taking on Philip, entered into negotiations with the king with a view to concluding an armistice."[64] It is unlikely, however, that Phalaecus was cowed by Philip's army. Philip and Phalaecus had already reached some sort of agreement several months before. That agreement resulted in Phalaecus refusing the troops Sparta and Athens offered to defend Thermopylae against Philip. Part of that agreement may have been that in exchange for his own life, his men's lives, and the fair treatment for the people of Phokis, Phalaecus agreed to deliver the pass to Philip. Phalaecus kept his part of the bargain and surrendered Thermopylae to Philip without a fight. "An agreement was made permitting Phalaecus to depart with his troops wherever he wished, and he retired to the Peloponnese with his mercenaries, who were around eight thousand in number."[65] Philip's army poured through the pass and occupied the fortress towns. All of Greece from Attica to the Peloponnese was now at risk of Macedonian attack.

7
WARRIOR DIPLOMAT

Philip's seizure of the Thermopylae Pass was more a victory of diplomacy and intelligence than of arms. As in most successful diplomatic efforts, the threat of force played an important part in Philip's calculations, and it was no accident that Philip arrived at Thermopylae prepared to fight a pitched battle. But it was Philip's diplomatic skill that convinced Phalaecus to deliver the pass without Philip having to fire a shot, the latest gambit in a decade-long political game that Philip played exquisitely to his advantage. The major Greek states were kept at each other's throats while Philip furthered his own national ambitions first in Thrace, Amphipolis, and Thessaly and then in Thrace again. In those instances when Philip might have intervened to end the war or lessen its burden on his own allies, he did nothing. Philip wanted the Sacred War to continue, and continue it did.

Macedonia's emergence as a major power was possible in large part because the most important Greek states were busy fighting each other at the center of the Greek world while Philip expanded Macedonian power at its periphery. Isocrates' observation that Greece "was filled and obsessed with war and revolutions and massacres and innumerable evils"[1] did not escape Philip's notice, and he manipulated these circumstances to his advantage with great skill. When eventually Philip was ready to strike at the center of Greece, no state or combination of states was left that could stop him. Philip's ability to use force successfully in conjunction with diplomacy marks him as one of the great warrior diplomats of the ancient world.

Philip and the Macedonian army were now less than thirty miles from Elatea with no substantial enemy forces between them and the Phokian capital. To the southeast, Thebes and the armies of the Boeotian League were preparing to move north with the dual mission of crushing Phokis and positioning the Theban army across Philip's line of march to prevent his further advance into central Greece. Phokis's ally, Athens, had already signed a peace with Philip, and Sparta had withdrawn its troops at Phalaecus's order. Phokis was now trapped in a vice by two major armies without any prospect of aid. "The Phokians, their hopes now completely shattered, surrendered to Philip"[2] in June 346 BCE.

THE AMPHICTYONIC PEACE

The Macedonian army quickly occupied the fortress towns guarding Thermopylae and sent armed contingents to other Phokian towns as a show of force. Philip was well aware that Thebes and Thessaly wished to impose great suffering on Phokis, and his quick occupation of the country's key towns was designed as much to protect the Phokians from Theban vengeance as to demonstrate the Macedonian army's control of the country. But for all the military force at his disposal, Philip was by no means a free agent in determining Phokis's fate. Thebes, Thessaly, the Boeotian League states, and Athens all had important interests in what happened to Phokis and were determined to press them on Philip. Having fought the Sacred War as the leader of a religious coalition, Philip could hardly abandon that role now and impose his own peace without taking the risk of shattering the alliance and frightening the rest of Greece into a grand coalition against him. His intentions in central Greece were now even more suspect. It was imperative, then, that Philip act in concert with and as a representative of the Amphictyonic League's wishes and allay Greek suspicions. After some initial discussions with the Thessalians and Boeotians, which probably revealed the depth of the allies' disagreement, Philip "determined to summon a meeting of the delegates of the Amphictyonic League and to entrust to this body the resolution of the whole issue" of the Phokian peace.[3]

Philip's main problem was restraining the allies' desire for revenge. Thessaly's hatred for Phokis had its roots in the ancient past, and the Boeotians wanted reparations, territory, and revenge for the damage that the war had caused in Boeotia. What had begun as a minor slight over Phokis's refusal to send troops and support Thebes at Mantinea had embroiled Thebes in a decade-long war. Thebes wanted to recover its considerable costs at Phokian expense. At some point in the discussions, the Oetaeans, a Thessalian people living on the border with Phokis, demanded that the entire adult Phokian male population be regarded as temple robbers and suffer the traditional punishment for sacrilege—that is, they wanted them thrown off the Phaedriadae cliffs at Delphi.[4] The Boeotians, somewhat less harshly, suggested that the Phokian populations of the captured Boeotian cities be "andrapodised," or enslaved where they were taken or sold abroad as slaves.[5] Philip had his hands full dealing with his allies, for it was not in Macedonia's long-term interest that Phokis be destroyed.

The Amphictyonic League met in July and pronounced a harsh fate upon the Phokians, but it would have been much worse without Philip's calls for moderation. It seemed to many that in reaching a separate peace and an alliance with Athens, Philip had cast his lot with the Athenians at the expense of Thebes. Now Thebes had to be prevented from becoming a threat to Macedonian aspirations. Destroying Phokis would have increased Theban influence in central Greece and removed an important geographic buffer between Macedonian power in Thessaly on the one hand and Thebes and the Boeotian League on the other. Moreover, Theban gains in Phokis would inevitably increase its influence in Boeotia. Still, while Philip's own religious sentiments required that Phokis be punished for its grave sacrilege, at the same time his considerations of Macedonian national interest demanded that its existence be ensured. This said, the allies still meted out a harsh peace.

The Amphictyonic League's delegates "resolved to destroy all the Phokian cities,"[6] and Pausanias names twenty cities that suffered this cruel fate.[7] Only Abae, with its oracle to Apollo, was spared because of its previous opposition to the Delphi sacrilege. Three Boeotian cities that the Phokians held at the end of the war—Orchomenus, Coronea, and Corsiae—had their walls pulled down and were returned to their rightful owners. The league left the treatment of their defenseless populations to the Boeotians, however, who promptly enslaved them or sold them off abroad.[8] The Thessalians enslaved and deported the population of Halus at the same time.[9] The buildings of the Phokian cities were destroyed, and the population "split up into villages which should be separate from one another by not less than one stade and each of which should contain no more than fifty houses."[10] The Phokians were "denied the use of horses and weapons until such time as they paid back to the god the money which had been embezzled."[11] However, the Phokians were "to possess their land and to pay every year to the god an indemnity of sixty talents until they had repaid the amount which had been entered in the inventories at the time of the sacrilege."[12] Those Phokians who had fled into exile and were implicated in the sacrilege were declared accursed and liable to seizure wherever they were found. Presumably, they could then be executed by being thrown from the cliff at Delphi. Harsh as it was, Phokis was not subjected to the wholesale extermination or enslavement of its population that at times had followed other states' defeat. Phokis was at least allowed to live.

The armed forces of Macedonia, Thessaly, and Boeotia carried out the Amphictyonic League's decisions, but they were apparently under Macedonian command. Philip was the obvious choice to direct the troops' actions since he had commanded the league's troops in the campaign. Any Phokian town that refused to surrender was attacked and destroyed.[13] Macedonian troops played the largest role in implementing the league's decisions, permitting Philip to diminish the severity with which its dictates were carried out while still claiming that he was faithfully fulfilling the league's orders. Thus, the fine of sixty talents was not implemented until 343 BCE, and in 341 BCE it was reduced to thirty talents at Philip's suggestion.[14] Within two years, Philip began to call for rebuilding some of the Phokian cities, and by 339 BCE the country's capital, Elatea, was being rebuilt. Philip was taking pains to ingratiate himself with the Phokian population.

Theban troops are not mentioned in any of Philip's efforts to execute the league's dictates, and Philip likely tried to minimize their participation. Philip knew of the Theban desire for a dominant role in Phokis and worked to block its influence when he could. Although Philip returned the three cities the Phokians had captured to Thebes, he did not put the Thebans in charge of Phokis as the Athenians feared he would.[15] It was said that Philip wanted Thebes to be Boeotian and not Boeotia to be Theban. Thebes must have recognized that it had gained little for its long war with Phokis, which had cost it considerably in men and treasure. Thebes found itself caught between Philip and his new ally, Athens, and the Macedonian army was on the Boeotian border, capable of striking directly at Thebes should Philip wish to do so.

The league "decreed that Philip and his descendants should be members of the League and should have the two votes which had formerly belonged to the Phokians."[16] Combined with the six Thessalian votes that he controlled as archon of Thessaly, Philip now had a virtual majority over the league's decisions. The votes awarded to Philip were awarded to him personally, so he now became a member of the league in his own right.[17] The Phokians were stripped of their seats as punishment and had "no share in the shrine of the Amphictyonic Council."[18] For supporting the Phokians, Sparta was also expelled from the league. Athens, however, was not expelled even though it was as much an ally to the sacrilegious Phokians as Sparta had been. The only punishment imposed on Athens was the loss of its right of precedence (*promanteia*) in consulting the oracle at Delphi, a privilege now awarded to Philip. Philip's lenient treatment of Athens could only deepen Theban resentment that it had been poorly rewarded for its part in the Sacred War. Moreover, Philip's preeminent position in the league came at Theban expense, but it had been Thebes that persuaded the league to declare the Sacred War in the first place. Theban distrust of Philip grew more ominous.

Philip took great pains, however, always to appear to be operating within the context of the league and not as the king of Macedonia, that is, furthering the alliance's interests first and not those of his own country. In his negotiations with league members, "he dealt generously with everyone."[19] To calm Theban fears, Philip pulled his own Macedonian garrison out of the important fortress town of Nicaea, which controlled the road to Thermopylae, and replaced it with a garrison from Thessaly.[20] Philip was also elected president of the Pythian Games, which had not been celebrated for the last twelve years because of the war. Along with the Boeotians and Thessalians, he was to organize the music and athletic festival as an offering of gratitude to Zeus for the liberation of Apollo's shrine. It was ironic that the Greeks chose this barbarian king to become a member of the Amphictyones, that most august of Greek institutions, and to preside over the Greek Olympic games. But Philip was still Philip, and "he had not only made a name for himself for his piety and talented generalship, but had also built a sure foundation for the future increase of his power."[21]

ATHENS

Because of his important role in ending the Sacred War, Philip was inextricably involved in the great power politics of Greece. The political and economic isolation from Greek affairs that had attended much of Macedonia's history was now a thing of the past. Macedonian policy had once sought to protect the country from invasion by the major Greek states of Athens, Thebes, and Sparta. To this end, Philip had become the champion of the Sacred

War in order to balance Athenian power with Theban power. Athens was by far the greater of the threats to Macedonia insofar as its powerful navy could project force against Macedonian interests in Thrace and the Thermaic Gulf. Containing and eroding Athenian power were central to Philip's strategy. On the one hand, his alliance with Thebes in the Sacred War had forced Athens to keep substantial ground and naval forces in Attica to counter a possible Theban attack.[22] Sparta's alliance with Athens, on the other hand, forced Thebes to deploy substantial military resources to protect against a possible Spartan attack. It was classic balance of power politics, and Philip proved himself a master at the game.

By the time Philip proposed an alliance and truce as early as 348 BCE, Athens was already on its last legs. For the previous century, Athenian power had been built on its control or predominant influence in four areas. Its alliance with the cities of Euboea provided an important geographic buffer to invasion by making it impossible for Thebes or Macedonia to use the island as a strategic platform to attack Attica. Second, Athenian control of the Thermopylae Pass, often in alliance with others, was vital to preventing any hostile power to the north—Macedonia and Thessaly, in particular—from invading central Greece as a prelude to an attack on Athens itself. Third, the Athenian alliance with the cities of Chalcidice and the pro-Athenian cities and naval bases in the Thermaic Gulf allowed Athens to protect its access to vital strategic materials—timber, silver, gold, and iron—and economic markets in the northern Aegean. The Athenian presence at the head of the Thermaic Gulf also permitted Athens to defend its interests in Thrace from ground attack by cutting off the land route to the region. Finally, Athenian power depended heavily on its control of the Chersonese and the coast of Eastern Thrace so that an enemy could not close off the sea route the Athenian grain fleet sailed to reach the Black Sea ports and their vital supplies of grain.

By the end of the Sacred War, Philip had weakened the Athenian hold on Euboea, driven it from Chalcidice and the Thermaic Gulf, seized and occupied the Thermopylae Pass, and reduced much of Thrace to a Macedonian satellite from which he was able to attack Eastern Thrace and the Chersonese. It was precisely Philip's success in reducing Athenian national power that compelled him to seek an alliance with Athens. Athenian power had been so successfully reduced that Athens could no longer serve as an effective check on Thebes or Sparta. Having allied Athens with Macedonia, Philip now aimed to reduce Theban and Spartan power in the central Greece region.

Sparta had lost its leading position in Peloponnesian affairs when it was expelled from the Amphictyonic League. Philip soon began to support pro-Macedonian factions in the city-states of the Peloponnese to weaken Spartan influence even further. Demosthenes says that by 344 BCE Philip was providing Argos, the ancestral home of the Temenid dynasty of which Philip was a direct descendant, and Messenia with both money and mercenaries.[23] Philip also reestablished diplomatic contact with the Arcadians, who "set up a statue of him [Philip] in bronze and crowning it with garlands, and, to cap it all, they have passed a decree to welcome him in their cities if he should come in the Peloponnese. And the Argives are doing just the same."[24] Philip supported a bloody but successful uprising among the Eleans, who then concluded an alliance with him.[25] Within three years (343 BCE), Philip had so successfully eroded Spartan control of the Peloponnesian states by political means that the only states in the region that remained aligned with Sparta and were not on friendly terms with Philip were Achaea and Corinth. As a consequence, Sparta's ability to interfere with Philip was greatly reduced.

Some similar efforts at domestic subversion may have gone on in Boeotia, where Philip, as he did elsewhere in Greece, had hundreds of guests-friends in whom he had invested over the years and who could now be used to good effect. When civil strife broke out in Megara on the Boeotian border, Philip supported the oligarchs with money and mercenaries, increasing the already substantial resentment the Boeotians felt over having not gained territory from their efforts in the Sacred War while watching Philip award Thermopylae to the Thessalians.[26] There is no doubt that the Thebans, too, were growing more suspicious of Philip by the day. When civil strife broke out in Euboea in 345 BCE, the rival city-states called for help from Philip and Athens but not from Boeotia or Thebes, forcing Thebes to suffer directly the result of its loss of national prestige. Nor could it have escaped Thebes' attention when Philip argued for a reduction of the punitive fine that the Amphictyonic League had imposed upon the Phokians or when he supported the rebuilding of some Phokian cities, most noticeably Elatea. Phokis lay between Thessaly and Boeotia, an important geographic buffer as long as Phokian power remained reduced. But with Philip already occupying most of the Thermopylae fortress towns, the possibility of even a moderately rebuilt Phokis friendly to Philip represented a military threat to Boeotian and Theban security.

It was in 346 BCE that Philip may have begun contemplating an invasion of Persia. Diodorus tells us that after he had arranged the Amphictyonic peace, Philip returned to Pella, where "he was eager to be nominated commander-in-chief of the Greeks with full powers and to conduct the war with the Persians."[27] Long a supporter of a Greek-Persian war as a means of uniting Greece and reducing its civil wars, Isocrates had urged Philip in his treatise *To Philip* in 346 BCE to contemplate such an undertaking. A year later in his *First Epistle to Philip*, Isocrates again urged Philip to action, this time upbraiding him for risking his life and being seriously wounded in a battle with the Illyrians. Just before his death in 338 BCE in his *Second Epistle to Philip*, Isocrates reported that friends had asked whether he had put the idea of waging a Persian war in Philip's head or if Philip had had the idea himself. Isocrates suggested that Philip had already thought about invading Persia and that Isocrates' pleas had merely encouraged Philip to contemplate it seriously.[28]

The case for Philip having considered an invasion of Persia at this early date is not overly persuasive. It is based on the fact that Philip did not attack Athens after he seized Thermopylae but had honored his alliance with Athens instead. Once beyond the Thermopylae gates, Philip had asked his new ally to send troops to assist him. Athens had refused, providing Philip with an excuse to attack Athens if he had wished. Moreover, Philip was still allied with Boeotia, Thebes, Thessaly, and most of its cities, including Pharsalus, Pherae, and Pagasae. In the east, Byzantium, Perinthus, and king Amadocos of Thrace were Philip's allies.[29] Philip's armies could have easily cut Athenian defenses and taken its remaining possessions in Thrace and the Chersonese. Thus some argue that Philip did not attack Athens when he could have done so because he wanted to use its navy during a Persian invasion, implying, of course, that he was already contemplating invading Persia.[30] Philip may well have had that idea in mind, but the primary reason he did not attack Athens was that he needed Athens as a check against Thebes and Sparta to maintain the balance of power in central Greece and not because he needed the Athenian navy to invade Persia.

Assuming Philip considered undertaking a Persian war, it could not have been more than a vague idea in his mind in 346 BCE and certainly not a premise upon which to base Macedonian strategy in the near future. A good general, Philip must have recognized that the conditions for waging a successful invasion were nowhere on the political horizon. First, an invasion of

Persia would have to be launched from Eastern Thrace, which Cersobleptes still held with Athenian help. Athens itself continued to control the Chersonese and the Hellespont, and Philip understood that a major military campaign would be required to force Cersobleptes to terms. Second, Philip needed the Athenian navy not so much for transports, which were readily available for hire, but for its naval combatants to protect the invasion force against the Persian fleet during the crossing. Once accomplished, Philip would need the Athenian navy to remain at sea, bottling up the Persian ships in its Phoenician and Ionian ports and preventing a Persian seaborne attack on Greece itself.

The problem was that Athens was unconvinced that its true interests lay in an alliance with Philip. When news reached the city that Philip had captured the Thermopylae Pass, the population was thrown into a panic. The assembly voted to evacuate the city, to take up positions in the countryside, and to man the fortifications in the city's defense.[31] Philip was outraged at the Athenians' behavior and sent a letter protesting that their actions were hardly consistent with those of a true ally. Nonetheless, Athens continued to regard Philip with suspicion, urged on by an anti-Macedonian faction led by Demosthenes, who sought every means to oppose Philip and to increase Athenian influence at Philip's expense. In 346 BCE, it was unclear whether Athens would cooperate with Philip in anything, much less allow its navy to support an invasion of Persia.

Third, Philip could dare to take the Macedonian army out of Greece and into Persia only if he were absolutely certain that the major Greek states would not attack Macedonia while he was away on campaign.[32] But in 346 BCE, while Philip was busy undermining Thebes, Boeotia, and Sparta, his efforts did not go unnoticed and increased these states' suspicions regarding Philip's intentions. The day might come when these states could be trusted, but that day was still quite distant. Philip could have given only passing consideration to the idea of an attack on Persia in 346 BCE.

It is interesting that Athens remained consistently opposed to Philip's apparent genuine desire to reach an accommodation with it. If Philip's strategy to reduce Theban power was to succeed, then Athenian power and influence in central Greece had to increase in order to serve as an effective check on Thebes. To this end we might surmise that Philip was genuinely interested in making Athens the dominant power in central Greece with his cooperation and military support.[33] Athens mistakenly saw Philip's ambitions as taking control of all Greece, with itself playing a subordinate role. The issue swings, of course, on whether in 346 BCE Philip was indeed trying to bring about the conditions necessary for an invasion of Persia.

It could be argued that Philip was looking to the long term and that an invasion of Persia was what he wanted. Control of Greece, after all, had little to offer Philip. Most of the Greek cities were small, poor, and barely able to feed themselves. Macedonia would derive little wealth and perhaps significant expense from their conquest. Control of Greece south of Thessaly was of no strategic use except to prevent the larger states from combining against Philip during his absence in Persia. If Philip was seeking glory and wealth, then an invasion of Persia made the most sense.[34] The Athenians, however, remained unconvinced. No matter how logical the argument for Philip's Persian policy could be made to sound, in the end the Athenian experience with Philip, the vastly different cultures and histories of the two states, and the nature of Athenian factional domestic politics left many with a genuine fear and suspicion of Philip.[35] The opportunity for a lasting peace and alliance between Philip and Athens slipped away.

ILLYRIA AGAIN

Philip's respite from war and the affairs of state did not last long after his return to Pella. The following spring (345 BCE) Philip took his army into Illyria to deal with the growing threat of rebellion. As noted in chapter 1, the Dardanians and the Ardiaei had formed an alliance that forced Philip to move quickly to prevent them from assembling on his borders. Philip's previous defeats of the area's tribes may have encouraged the remaining tribes, particularly the Ardiaei, to move south into the now-weakened territories and to encroach on Philip's new security perimeter.[36] Diodorus, however, says that the reason for Philip's campaign was "an ancestral enmity with the Illyrians and [he] found the quarrel to be unreconcilable."[37] If Diodorus is correct, then Philip's problem was with the Dardanian king, Bardylis, who had invaded Macedonia when Philip was a young man and with whom the Macedonians had an "ancestral" quarrel. It is possible, however, that the stimulus for the revolt came not from the Dardanians but from the Ardiaei and King Pleuratos, who may have been directing events for the tribal confederation.[38] The Ardiaei occupied the lower valley of the Drin River area, located near the Rhizon Gulf on the Dalmatian coast in northern Albania.

Diodorus tells us that Philip invaded Illyria "with a large army," from which we may conclude that he brought the full strength of the Macedonian army to bear. Philip's previous campaigns in Illyria had taught him the difficulties inherent in fighting against such fierce tribal warriors in terrain that was hostile to an invading army. These circumstances and the size of the tribal armies noted by Theopompus—"three hundred thousand strong"—led Philip to ensure his forces would be adequate for the task. We are unclear as to which of the tribes, the Dardanians or the Ardiaei, was Philip's primary target. Justin claims that Philip campaigned against Cleitus, the son of Bardylis of the Dardanians,[39] but Didymus tells us that Philip fought against Pleuratos, king of the Ardiaei.[40] We are probably not too far wrong if we conclude that Philip attacked Cleitus first and then Pleuratos, prohibiting the kings from assembling their forces against Philip. The battle must have been a major engagement. Philip himself was almost killed, but the soldier Pausanias saved the king by covering his body with his own and shielding him from further blows. Philip was badly wounded along with 150 of his officers. It was in this battle that Philip suffered the broken leg that laid him up for perhaps a year.[41]

Philip's victory broke the Illyrian rebellion, and "after pillaging the land and securing many of the townships he returned to Macedonia with large quantities of booty."[42] It is at this time that Justin, our only source for the incident, says that Philip "capriciously transplanted whole peoples and cities as he felt regions needed to be populated or depopulated."[43] Curiously, Justin says that Philip pursued this strategy after "he returned to his kingdom," meaning that the forcefully moved populations were Macedonians already living in the country. Undoubtedly, Philip had begun taking measures to develop Macedonia, and some movement of peoples within the country had already occurred. Philip continued this policy throughout his reign, with the result that Macedonia's infrastructure and economy became among the best in Greece.

I think it unlikely, however, that Justin was speaking about the forced movement of Macedonian populations. The cruelty with which Justin implies the deportations were carried out stands in stark contrast to Philip's usual treatment of his countrymen. Justin notes the despair and fear of the displaced populations: "Everywhere it was a dismal picture, almost of desolation . . . there was silent, forlorn dejection, as men feared that even their tears might be taken to signify opposition. . . . The evacuees looked wistfully now at the tombs of their forefathers, now at their ancient family deities, now at the houses in which they had been born and themselves produced children."[44] That Philip could be cruel is beyond question, as his enslavement of Olynthos shows, but his treatment of his own countrymen usually stood in marked contrast to the manner in which Justin says Philip treated the deported populations.

It is possible that Justin was instead describing Philip's deportation and transplantation of the tribes he had just defeated, moving them away from their homelands and mixing them with other peoples to dilute their tribal identities so that they could not trouble him again. Justin tells us that during this campaign, Philip captured and transplanted to Macedonia "more than ten thousand Illyrians, named Sarnousii."[45] Philip's campaign of 345 BCE was his third in Illyria and the tribal areas in less than a decade. Perhaps Philip decided to put an end to the problem in Illyria once and for all. Justin's description of what happened to the transplants lends itself to this interpretation: "Some of these people settled right on his borders as a bulwark against his enemies, others he set on the remote frontiers of the empire, and some, who were prisoners-of-war, he distributed to supplement the populations of his cities."[46] Perhaps some of these tribal populations were mixed with Macedonians whom Philip had encouraged to move with grants of land and other inducements, as he had already done in Thrace and Chalcidice. If Philip hoped deporting the tribes would solve the Illyrian problem, he was to be disappointed. In 337 BCE, Philip was allegedly back in Illyria, this time campaigning against a tribal king named Pleurias.[47]

TROUBLE IN THESSALY

While Philip was in Pella recovering from his fractured leg, sporadic civil strife broke out in several Thessalian cities. The causes of the disorder are unclear. Some in the country were disappointed that Thessaly had only gained Magnesia and Nicaea for its efforts in the Sacred War, but it is unlikely that the turmoil was directed at Philip. The violent factional politics of Thessalian cities had frequently led to such conditions in the past. Pagasae's grievances probably were related to its having to pay some of its port duties to Philip. Meanwhile, Pherae seems never to have lost its resentment of Philip for having deposed its previous rulers, who were plotting a return. Larissa's rebellion must have taken Philip by surprise, however. The Aleuadae clan, to whom Philip was related by marriage, still ruled the region. Philip's primary concerns in Thessaly were maintaining its stability, preserving his access to its taxes and dues, and, above all, ensuring that the Thessalian cavalry was available when he needed it.

It was probably Larissa's issuance of currency in its own name that pushed Philip to put an end to the instability in Thessaly. In the summer of 344 BCE the Macedonian army marched into Thessaly, seized Larissa, and removed Simus, the leader of the Aleuadae, from power. Pherae was captured next and its renegade leaders imprisoned or driven from the city.[48] The Macedonian army then continued to quash the disorder in some other cities, although Demosthenes' claim that all of them were occupied can be rejected.[49] It is unclear if Philip himself led the army or if he put Parmenio or Antipater in command. The soldier-scholar N. G. L. Hammond, citing Demosthenes, says that Philip led the incursion, while Cawkwell believes that Philip was still recovering from his wound and had remained in Pella.[50] In either case, relative tranquility was restored to Thessaly in short order.

To prevent any future civil disturbances from getting out of hand, Philip established Macedonian troop garrisons in several cities. In addition, he reorganized the administrative structure of the major cities by placing power in the hands of a ten-man board (*decadarchy*), whose members he appointed. As its archon, Philip next strengthened the administrative structure of the Thessalian League, the all-important military alliance of Thessalian cities that provided him with cavalry and money. The league had traditionally been organized into four quarters (*tetrades*) or regions whose origins were tribal,[51] but this form of organization had been previously discarded. Philip now reintroduced it. He reinstated each of the four original tribal areas—Thessaliotis, Pelasgiotis, Hestiaeotis, and Phthiotis—and, in each, appointed a military governor, or *tetrarch*, who was answerable only to him.[52] Every tetrarch was placed in command of the troop levies drawn from his area.[53] With these reforms, Philip's control of Thessaly's vital military resources was strengthened but not unduly so. The Thessalians seemed to accept the new order as the necessary price of civic peace while Philip always treated Thessaly as a free country and not a mere possession of Macedonia.

EPIRUS

In the early spring of 342 BCE, Philip moved against the Molossian ruler, Arybbas, who was the uncle of Olympias, Philip's Molossian wife. In 350 BCE,

Philip had removed Arybbas as king; reduced him to the status of regent for Alexandros, Arybbas's nephew and son of the former king; and thereby established a new line of succession. Alexandros had been sent to Pella, where he was educated and prepared to assume the Molossian throne when he reached the age of majority. Now Philip took an army into Epirus, removed Arybbas,[54] and placed Alexandros on the throne. Diodorus tells us that "Arybbas the king of the Molossians died after a reign of ten years, leaving a son Aecides the father of Pyrrhus. However he was succeeded by Alexandros the brother of Olympias thanks to the involvement of Philip."[55] Diodorus is incorrect, however, in saying that Arybbas died. In fact, Arybbas was an honorary Athenian citizen and fled to Athens, where his citizenship was confirmed. The Athenian generals were instructed to recover Arybbas's throne for him and his children.[56]

Why did Philip move against Arybbas? Since the peace in 346 BCE, the anti-Macedonian faction in Athens had been gaining influence. Delegations were sent to the various Peloponnese states and elsewhere in Greece, stirring resentment against Philip. Arybbas had attempted to use Athens against Philip once before, after Philip's defeat at the Crocus Field, and this flirtation had cost Arybbas his throne once Philip regained his position. Arybbas was possibly attempting to secure the succession for his son and sought Athenian support for his plan. Philip was aware of the sentiment in Athens and may have removed Arybbas to forestall any Athenian military support for the old Molossian king. The southwestern border had always been a problem for Macedonia, and Philip may have hoped to solve the problem once and for all by installing a loyal vassal king there.

Philip was always cognizant of the political context in which he operated, and before invading Epirus he had sent several proposals to Athens to demonstrate his reasonableness and open-mindedness in dealing with the Athenians. Philip proposed that the Peace of Philocrates be expanded into a common peace that was open to any Greek state that wished to join. He offered to submit Athenian claims to the Thracian fortresses and the island of Holonnesus to arbitration. Finally, Philip proposed a joint expedition to rid the Aegean of piracy and offered to bear all costs associated with it if Athens provided the ships and crews.[57] Given that Athenian commerce and its wheat supply were vulnerable to piracy, Athens should have easily accepted the offer. While these proposals were being debated in Athens, Philip marched into Epirus and removed Arybbas.

Still in the field, Philip decided to strengthen the southern border of Epirus by pushing it to the Ambraciote Gulf, which the Cassopaeans then controlled. The Ambracians had trading stations on the peninsula and monopolized the trade to Ambracia and Corinth. Demosthenes tells us that Philip "destroyed by fire the territory of the three city-states in Cassopia—Pandosia, Boucheta, and Elatria, colonies of Elis—forced his way into the cities, and handed them over to his kinsman Alexander to be his slaves."[58] The whole operation could not have taken very long, and by early summer Philip moved south toward the Corinthian colonies of Leucas and Ambracia, the chief exporter of Epirote timber and animal products to Corinth.[59] The colonies appealed for military help to Corinth, which in turn appealed to Athens for troops.

Philip's decision to move toward Ambracia seems to have been one of the few instances when he failed to consider the political context in which he was operating and as a result may have been surprised by the reaction he encountered. Athens answered Corinth's appeal by sending troops to reinforce Acarnania, and Corinth sent troops to reinforce Ambracia. Philip wisely withdrew rather than risk a direct confrontation with Athens over a minor border dispute. The event was enough, however, for the Athenian Assembly to reject Philip's proposals, and Demosthenes, the leader of the anti-Macedonian faction, increased the delegations visiting Greek states to stir up trouble against Philip. In the summer of 342 BCE, Demosthenes himself led a delegation visiting "Thessaly, Ambracia, the Illyrians and the kings of the Thracians."[60] The Athenian diplomatic efforts against Philip were successful. An Athenian delegation visiting the Peloponnese was able to convince Philip's allies of Argos, Messenia, and Megalopolis to enter alliances with Athens. Mantinea and Achaea did likewise.[61] Philip had miscalculated badly, with the result that Athens was able to reduce Macedonian influence in the Peloponnese and to convince three of the region's states to break openly with Philip.

THE THRACIAN CAMPAIGN

Since the Peace of Philocrates Athenian responses had been almost entirely negative to Philip's attempts to reach a genuine accord with Athens. They refused Philip's proposal in 344 BCE to expand the Peace of Philocrates into a common peace. Philip had hoped that a common peace would bind the Greeks together, leaving him free to campaign in the east. But the Athenian willingness to check Philip's moves in Ambracia with force, their rejection of his proposals on piracy and arbitration, and the brazen attempts by the anti-Macedonian faction in Athens to suborn Macedonian influence in the Peloponnese and elsewhere had finally convinced Philip that a rapprochement with Athens was now impossible. With his southern and northwestern borders secured against any further disruptions by the tribes, the Greek states still too weak to form a coalition against him, and Athenian interests in the region no longer of his concern, Philip attacked Thrace in July 342 BCE.

He had good reasons to do so. The treacherous Cersobleptes had once more moved closer to Athens and again accepted its help in expanding his kingdom. Diodorus, who is the only source for Philip's Thracian campaign, says, "The king of the Thracians, Cersobleptes, was continually making subject to himself and ravaging the territory of the [Greek] city-states which were his neighbors by the Hellespont. Accordingly, because Philip wished to put an end to the assaults by the barbarians, he campaigned against them with large forces."[62] Cersobleptes and Teres, the king of Central Thrace who had joined him, submitted. Philip could now remove the last vestiges of Athenian influence in the region, threaten their bases in the Chersonese, and block the route the Athenian wheat ships used. Removing Cersobleptes was the prelude to a major strategic strike at Athens.

Just as all Greeks, Philip was acutely aware of Persia and the threat it presented to his ambitions in Thrace. Three times in the last 150 years, Persia had invaded Greece by crossing the Hellespont and moving its armies overland through Thrace. Philip saw his occupation of Eastern Thrace as necessary to block any future Persian move against him. With Thrace in his possession, Philip would be able to meet any Persian forces early and perhaps prevent their landing. Even if he failed to do so, he could at least confine much of the fighting to Thrace rather than face it in Macedonia itself. Finally, if Philip was contemplating a future invasion of Persia via Ionia, he would lead that invasion from Eastern Thrace, with the region serving as the strategic platform for the attack. The size of Philip's "large forces" suggests that he intended nothing less than the complete subjugation of all Thrace.[63]

With its three geographic zones, Thrace is a forbidding region in which to wage war. First, the Aegean coastlands run from Philippi to Byzantium and are bordered by the sea to the south and the Rhodope mountain range to the north, separating the coast from the interior. Philip's previous incursions into the region had been confined to operations in the coastal area, which was the heartland of Cersobleptes's kingdom. Next, beyond the first range of mountains to the north was the Hebrus River valley (modern Maritza River in Bulgaria), which ran parallel to the coast down to the Aegean and led to a region of fertile plains that went north from the Aegean to the Black Sea coast. This agricultural region was the source of the grain shipped to Athens each spring. The third zone was separated from the fertile plains by the Great Balkan Mountains (the Haemus Mountains in antiquity), running west to east almost to the Black Sea coast, and included the valleys running north down to the Danube basin. This area was accessed through the Shipka Pass some ninety miles north of Philip's base at Philippopolis. The heartland of the Getae kingdom was located some 150 north of the pass near the headwaters of the Danube. Passages over the mountains were few and difficult, and much of the region was heavily forested, slowing military movement and affording great risk of ambush. The Balkan winters are notoriously harsh, but some of Philip's campaign was conducted in the winter months.

The Thracians were a formidable foe whom the Greeks feared as ferocious warriors. Herodotus says that "to live by war and plunder is of all things the most glorious [to them]" and "to till the ground the most dishonorable.... The Thracians are the most powerful people in the world, except of course the Indians; and if they had one ruler, they would be irresistible and far the strongest of all peoples in my belief."[64] The Thracians' weakness was their social structure in which each tribe or clan had its own ruler or king and nothing in the way of a national authority for waging war against an invader. Moreover, the tribes regularly fought one another from their isolated hilltop kingdoms. These circumstances allowed Philip to engage the Thracian tribes piecemeal, usually with numbers being in his favor. Thracian tribal forces were usually a mix of cavalry and infantrymen, or peltasts. Named for the small shield (*pelta*) they carried, the peltasts were light infantry skilled in mobility and in using a longer spear than that of the Greek infantry against both infantry and cavalry. By Philip's day, it was not unusual to find peltasts in the armies of the Greek states, although they usually appeared in small numbers. These units brought a modicum of mobility to the battlefield that heavy Greek hoplite infantry lacked.

The magnitude of Philip's Thracian campaign in 342–340 BCE should be appreciated. Thrace was an enormous region, comprising seven times the area of Macedonia and the Upper Cantons from which Philip drew his

Map 8. *Philip's Zone of Operations in Thrace*

army.[65] The population was at least five times greater than that of Macedonia and the Cantons. Thrace's difficult terrain—mountains, thick forests, and swift running streams—and terribly harsh winter climate worked against the invader. In these conditions, Philip's army, as usually configured with heavy pikemen and cavalry, would have been at a disadvantage against the more mobile tribal forces that knew the terrain well. Drawing upon his allies and subjects, however, Philip could reconfigure his forces to the operational environment. Referring to Philip's armies in Thrace in 340 BCE, Demosthenes tells us that "you hear of Philip marching wherever he wishes not by leading a phalanx of heavy infantry, but by being equipped with light infantry, cavalry, archers, mercenaries, and such soldiery."[66] The mercenaries included Cretan archers, traditional Greek hoplites for hire, and some Greek light cavalry. From his allies and subjects, Philip drew Thessalian cavalry, light infantry from Thessaly and the mountain tribes of central Greece, and javelin men from Illyria.[67] Both the terrain and configuration of enemy forces required that Philip be able to tailor his forces to the tactical circumstances he was facing. The addition of new, more flexible units gave the traditional pike phalanx and Macedonian heavy cavalry that constituted the bulk of Philip's expeditionary force the tactical flexibility he required.

In July 342 BCE, Philip's army marched out of Pella, crossed the Strymon River, turned north along the borders of the Maedi, and then headed northeast to Philippopolis, where the army rested before beginning the combat phase of the campaign. At Philippopolis, Philip built a fort to serve as his army's main operational and logistics base. From there Philip could take two different routes. He could go down the Hebrus River valley; strike into Odrysae (modern Edirne), Cersobleptes's stronghold; and then go on to the Aegean coast, a march of some 160 miles. Alternatively, from Philippopolis, Philip could march due north 40 miles to the Shipka Pass leading through the Great Balkan Mountains and debouche on the Danubian plain in the land of the Getae, a march of 110 miles. Philip marched down the Hebrus River valley, attacking and defeating the forces and allies of Teres and Cersobleptes "in several battles" as he went.

Ten months later, in April 341 BCE, Philip had subdued the area from the Hebrus River valley to the Black Sea coast. In a speech delivered in the spring of 341 BCE, Demosthenes says that as a result of Philip's winter campaign, Philip had "destroyed and reorganized" the cities of Drongylus, Cabyle (near modern Yambol), and Masteira,[68] indicating that Cersobleptes and Teres had been driven from their kingdoms.[69] Philip's army roamed at will the great plain between Byzantium and Odessus (modern Varna), a Greek city on the Black Sea coast, and a number of Greek cities in the area made alliances with him.[70] During the year that followed, Diodorus tells us that Philip founded "significant cities in advantageous [strategic?] localities."[71] Diodorus probably means Philip built forts and points of military control rather than cities per se. Athens must have been greatly concerned that Philip's army now had access to the great plain and the source of much of Athens' imported grain and that he was forging alliances with those cities that made their living shipping that grain to Athens. Philip was in an excellent strategic position to cut off the food supply to Athens.

One of these Greek cities was Odessus on the coast of the Black Sea, about a hundred miles north of Byzantium. As Philip approached the city with his army, he discovered that it was occupied by a garrison of Getae, a seminomadic people who lived between the Great Balkan range and the Danube River. What they were doing there is unknown, but their presence indicates that the king of the Getae, Cothelas, controlled the area of the southern bank of the Danube from the middle of the Great Balkan range and east to the sea. Theopompus records that as Philip was preparing to assault the city, the gates opened and white-robed Getic priests playing lyres and singing prayers marched out toward the Macedonians. The priests wanted peace and offered to negotiate a truce. A treaty was quickly concluded.[72] The inhabitants of Odessus welcomed Philip as a liberator.

Philip seems to have marched into the Getic heartland shortly thereafter. Marching north from Odessus, Philip crossed the Thracian lowlands between the easternmost foothills of the Great Balkan range and the sea before turning inland and reaching the Getic kingdom that lay between the Shipka Pass and the Danube some 140 miles from Odessus. There, Philip made an alliance with Cothelas, who offered his daughter, Meda, to be Philip's wife to seal the alliance. Philip took Meda as his wife, his sixth marriage after a gap of ten years.[73] Philip's alliance with the Getae secured the loyalty of the only major population left in Thrace that had the means to oppose Philip or to join with Athens against him. Philip had already enlisted most of the coastal cities, including Perinthus and Byzantium, as allies, and many of the city-states from the Sea of Marmara up the coast of the Black Sea were under Philip's influence. Philip returned to Philippopolis through the Shipka Pass and posted a Macedonian garrison there to control its access.

By the summer of 341 BCE, Teres and Cersobleptes had formally surrendered, and Philip controlled Thrace from the Great Balkan range in the north to the Aegean Sea in the south and from the Nestus River east to the Black Sea. He had concluded alliances with most of the "independent" tribes, which agreed to provide soldiers for Philip's armies. He began to construct a number of military towns and strong points to fortify the approaches from Thrace to Macedonia. He constructed the towns of Drongylos, Cabyle, and Masteira to control the eastern approaches through the vital Hebrus Valley, and Beroe (modern Stara Zagora) and Philippopolis at the west end of the valley commanded the southern approaches to the Shipka Pass.[74] Philip imposed a 10 percent tax on all agricultural produce coming from Central and Eastern Thrace. No tax was imposed on Western Thrace, which, in any case, had been incorporated into the Macedonian national state. To administer the region, Philip appointed a military governor with the title General of Thrace.[75] The region's mines were opened for exploitation, and Thracians were allowed to serve in the Macedonian army.[76]

Recruiting Thracian troops into the army was important since Philip needed the tactical capability that the Thracian peltasts, archers, slingers, and other light infantry could provide to maintain control of the region and to participate in a possible campaign against Persia. Philip's activities in Thrace must have depleted Macedonian military manpower to some degree. Early in 340 BCE Philip ordered Antipater, whom he had entrusted with the governance of Macedonia in 342 BCE when the Thracian campaign began, to join him with additional forces.[77] Philip's son Alexander, now sixteen years old, was appointed regent in Antipater's place. Philip's use of specialty military units drawn from the various tribes and peoples of the empire created the multiethnic army that established Macedonian supremacy in eastern Europe and that Alexander later took with him into Asia.[78]

While Philip was busy in Thrace, events in Greece had taken an interesting turn. Almost immediately after Philip left for Thrace, civil strife broke out once again between the pro-Macedonian and pro-Athenian factions on the island of Euboea. Macedonia and Athens both sent generals and mercenaries to support their respective clients. Callias, the leader of the important city of Chalcis, had been an ally of Philip's, but by early 341 BCE he had switched sides in return for Athens' support for the creation of an independent Euboean Confederacy under Chalcis's leadership. That summer, Athens provided Callias with ships that he used to attack Macedonian cities on the coast of the Gulf of Pagasae. As allies of Philip's, these cities fell under the protection of the Peace of Philocrates. Athenian complicity in the raids—the Athenian Assembly publicly thanked Callias for his efforts and made him an Athenian citizen—constituted an act of war against Philip.

Meanwhile, to counter Philip's activities in Thrace, Athens strengthened its position in the Chersonese by sending both more settlers (*cleruchs*) to the area and a general in command of ships and a force of mercenaries. Athens also attempted to insert a group of its colonists in the city of Cardia. The expedition's commander, the Athenian mercenary captain Diopeithes of Sunium, raised the money to pay his troops by demanding protection money from merchant ships, engaging in piracy against merchantmen bound for Macedonia, and ravaging the lands around Cardia and holding its citizens for ransom.[79] Diopeithes also attacked Cabyle and Tiristasis and carried off hostages. All three cities were allies of Philip's. When Philip sent an envoy, Amphilochus, to petition for the relief of the captured civilians, Diopeithes tortured him and demanded ransom for his release as well. After he also threatened to attack Cardia, Philip sent a Macedonian garrison to protect the city. Diopeithes' actions against Philip's allies constituted another casus belli under the terms of the Peace of Philocrates.

Still Philip took no military action. Instead, he sent letters to the Athenian Assembly, asking it to recall Diopeithes and punish him. Demosthenes and the anti-Macedonian faction convinced the assembly to refuse Philip's request, however, and to send reinforcements and a fleet of forty ships under General Chares' command to aid Diopeithes. To further insult Philip, Demosthenes and Callias undertook a tour of the Peloponnese that autumn and winter to encourage the states there to join the general alliance against Philip. All of these actions were technically acts of war under the peace. Still Philip did nothing.

Persia made Philip cautious. Persia had been distracted by internal problems for most of Philip's reign. By 340 BCE, however, Persia had succeeded in establishing control over Egypt, Cyprus, and Phoenica and remained on good terms with the Greek cities in coastal Asia, gaining access to their fleets. Philip knew that, for all its bluster, Athens was making little progress in attracting other Greek states to its anti-Macedonian cause and that alone Athens was in no position to fight a war against Philip. Philip's most important strategic concern was that Athens would seek an alliance with a resurgent Persia, and their combined naval forces could seriously threaten Philip's hold on Thrace.

Philip had anticipated such a possibility. In the summer of 342 BCE, before embarking on the Thracian campaign, Philip and the Persians had signed a nonaggression pact in Pella in which Philip promised not to intervene in Asia and Artaxerxes, and the Persian king agreed not to cross into Thrace or interfere with Philip at sea.[80] When an Athenian delegation arrived in Susa in the early summer of 340 BCE seeking a defensive alliance against Philip, the Persian king declined the offer and sent them packing with financial gifts.[81] The failure of the Athenian delegation to secure Persian aid removed the last restraint on Philip. That summer, Philip prepared for war with Athens.

8 THE WAR WITH ATHENS

Philip had concluded that a genuine peace with Athens was no longer possible. The recent events of the fall and winter of 341 BCE convinced him of the soundness of his judgment. In the spring of 340 BCE, he began reinforcing his army in Thrace. Antipater and Parmenio arrived from Greece with more troops, probably Thessalian cavalry, while the Macedonian fleet carrying supplies and Philip's siege machinery arrived off the Thracian coast near Cardia. In response to the Athenian provocations regarding Cardia, Philip sent a letter to Athens complaining of its actions. Philip wrote that "having made the gods witness, I shall deal with you about these matters."[1] But Philip still did not declare war, even though the Athenians' actions were clearly hostile acts under the Peace of Philocrates. Philip enjoyed the high regard of Greek public opinion and was determined to maintain the Greeks' esteem by not being the one to break the peace. Instead, Philip set about goading Athens into declaring hostilities.

THE CHERSONESE

Philip had already sent a garrison to defend Cardia against further predations by Chares and his mercenaries who were supporting the Athenian settlers on the Chersonese Peninsula. The Chersonese is a narrow strip of land extending southwesterly from the Thracian mainland into the Aegean Sea. Forty-eight miles in length, the peninsula is fifteen miles at its widest point and only three and a half miles across at its northern neck, where a wall ran completely across the isthmus. The peninsula comes closest to the Asian mainland at the city of Sestus, located about two-thirds of the way down the eastern coast and was the main crossing point of the Hellespont that separated Europe from Asia and linked the Aegean with the Sea of Marmara. Command of the Chersonese was vital to controlling the sea route from the Aegean to the Black Sea. Its location also offered a strategic platform from which to launch attacks into Asia or farther along the Marmara coast to Byzantium.

The peninsula offered fertile soil to its settlers, and in antiquity the area was known for its wheat production. The Athenians settled the peninsula in the sixth century BCE and founded twelve cities there. Although the peninsula had changed hands several times since then, in 357 BCE Athens again took possession of the Chersonese. The main city of Cardia controlled the route from the peninsula to the mainland and refused to join the Athenian League. In 352 BCE, Cardia concluded a treaty of friendship with Philip. In 346 BCE, this treaty also fell later under the provisions of the Peace of Philocrates. The outrages that Athenian mercenaries perpetrated against Cardia thus constituted a breach of the peace accord, and Philip was well within his rights to defend his allies and blame Athens.

After warning Athens of its violation, Philip sent his army into the Chersonese in the spring of 340 BCE. Antipater had arrived with more troops, and Philip's army numbered thirty thousand soldiers. While his fleet sailed alongside his route of march, Philip entered the isthmus on the west side, marched completely around the peninsula, and arrived back at Cardia. It was a dramatic demonstration of Philip's military strength. He could have attacked any of the Athenian settlements, seized Athenian ships, or announced the annexation of key parts of the peninsula. Instead, Philip took no military action against the Athenians settlers. Nonetheless, the message was clear: Philip could reduce the Chersonese to Macedonian control at any time.[2] The Athenian ships were away from the peninsula at the time of Philip's raid, and Chares made no effort to interfere with Philip's fleet. The march through the Chersonese may have had the strategic purpose of provoking Athens into declaring war, perhaps by igniting a military incident between Philip and Chares, but Athens did not react. Philip sent another letter to Athens offering to submit the matter to arbitration.[3]

THE SIEGE OF PERINTHUS

In the early summer of 340 BCE, Philip marched seventy miles along the coast from Cardia to Perinthus on the Sea of Marmara and took Perinthus under siege. The puzzle is why Philip attacked Perinthus. Along with Selymbria (modern Silivri) seventeen miles farther down the coast and Byzantium, located thirty-seven miles beyond Selymbria, Perinthus had been an ally of Philip's since 352 BCE when the Thracian king, Cersobleptes, attacked the city and Philip came to its aid.[4] Diodorus says Philip marched against Perinthus, "which was opposed to him and which [was] inclined to the Athenians."[5] Demosthenes suggests that Philip's attack was a result of the city's refusal to supply Philip with troops for his most recent campaign.[6] There is no evidence in any Athenian speeches of a rapprochement between Athens and Perinthus. The city was not of any known strategic value; indeed, no evidence is available that Athenian grain ships had ever called at Perinthus.[7] If Philip wanted to interrupt the Athenian grain route, taking Perinthus was of little use. Why, then, did Philip attack Perinthus?

The answer may lie in Philip's grand strategic plan for Thrace. By 340 BCE, Philip controlled all of Thrace south of the Great Balkan Mountains and as far east as the Black Sea coast. He also established alliances with many of the Greek cities along the west coast of the Black Sea, with the Scythians in the Dobruja region of the Danube delta, and with the Getae farther west. He also made alliances with many of the Greek states along the Aegean coast. All that was left beyond Philip's command was the coast of the Sea of Marmara, from the Hellespont to the Bosporus, where the independent cities of Perinthus, Selymbria, and Byzantium controlled access through both straits.

Philip's Thracian policy aimed at creating a deep military defensive zone to protect Macedonia from a possible Persian attack. Philip could also use the zone as a strategic platform from which to invade Persia in the future. His concern was that the three cities, in alliance with Persia, could do much to neutralize Macedonian power in Thrace and to disrupt any invasion of Persia. Moreover, Athens was a maritime power whose large navy could project force over long distances. If Philip did not occupy the coastal cities of the Sea of Marmara, Athens could use them to land troops there and threaten Macedonian control of Thrace. Athenian troops could then march east, destroying Macedonian cities in Thrace until the Athenians were in range of Macedonia itself. Thus, Philip's Thracian strategy required that he take the three cities eventually. The assaults on Perinthus and Byzantium, therefore, should be understood as Philip's attempt to complete the subjugation of Thrace with a view toward consolidating a Macedonian strategic defense perimeter there.

Philip apparently did not believe that his existing alliances with the cities were sufficient to guarantee their loyalty, and there is probably some truth in Diodorus's claim that Perinthus had begun to "incline" toward Athens as a means to check Philip's increasing influence in the region.[8] The same was probably true of Byzantium. If Philip thought that Perinthus's "inclination" was sufficient for Athens to come to that city's aid and declare war on Philip, he was disappointed. Athens correctly assessed Perinthus's lack of strategic importance to its grain route and did nothing. For the time being, Perinthus was on its own.

Diodorus tells us that Philip brought his force of thirty thousand soldiers against Perinthus. The Macedonian navy had also arrived, carrying "a store of missiles and siege engines as well as a quantity of machines of other kinds that could not be bettered."[9] The number of Macedonian ships was necessarily small, perhaps no more than twenty or thirty, and thus could not command the sea off Perinthus. The navy beached its fleet a mile or so down the coast. Philip's army was enormous by Greek standards of the day and comprised specialty units from his allies and subject peoples around a core of Macedonian pikemen, infantry, and cavalry. If Philip intended to bring the cities under his control, he certainly had the manpower and resources to do it.

But Perinthus was no soft target. "Perinthus lies by the sea on what might be called the neck of a high peninsula which is a stade [about 200 yards] in breadth,"[10] with the city wall running completely across the isthmus. The city rested on the side of a steep hill about 160 feet high. The houses and buildings inside its walls were built on terraces, one behind the other up the steep hillside, and "are densely packed together and conspicuous for their height. These houses are constructed in such a way that they invariably project one above one another along the slope of the hill and endow the entire city with the appearance of a tiered theater."[11] Once inside the main wall, the attacker found himself confronted by rubble and additional defenses as the defenders, who blocked the narrow roads in front of and in between their houses, retreated upward to the next terrace.[12] "The besieged . . . kept barricading the alleys, making use of the lower tier of houses on each occasion as a substitute for strong walls."[13] Any invader faced bloody hand-to-hand combat with the defenders. Complicating Philip's plan, Perinthus was open to the sea. While Philip could prevent reinforcements and supplies from reaching the city by land, his small navy could not prevent aid from arriving by ship.

Finally, if Philip intended to capture Byzantium as well, then Perinthus had to be captured quickly. Philip could not afford a protracted siege.

Philip threw the full weight of his siege engines and engineers against the two hundred–foot wall blocking the isthmus. Diodorus tells us:

> Having constructed towers eighty cubits in height [about 35 meters, or 116 feet] which rose far above the towers of Perinthus, he contrived from the commanding heights of these machines to reduce the besieged. In like manner his battering rams shook the walls, and his mining operations which dug underneath them threw down a large portion of the wall . . . the king had large quantities of artillery of different types and sought to use it to destroy those who were fighting from the parapets . . . dividing his forces into several parts he maintained unremittingly his attack on the walls in relays by day and night.[14]

Philip's engineers succeeded relatively quickly in overcoming the main city wall, only to have the Perinthians retreat and blockade the alleys and doorways of the next layer of terraced houses, "quickly erecting another wall against him." The fighting was intense on both sides, and "some unbelievable contests took place in the course of the fighting for the wall."[15]

Both sides suffered heavy casualties, and the Perinthians were on their last legs when help arrived by sea from Byzantium and the king of Persia. Byzantium sent "troops, missiles, and other implements of weaponry," including "the best of the commanders and soldiers they had at their disposal."[16] Of grave significance was the Persian king's support. Persia had come to regard Philip with suspicion, and the king ordered the satraps closest to the city to send aid to the Perinthians.[17] The satraps "sent to Perinthus a force of mercenaries, abundant supplies of money, and adequate stocks of missiles and everything else that would be of use in the war."[18] A short time later a second Persian force went directly into Thrace to support Diopeithes, who was again active in the Chersonese.[19]

Persia had not intervened in Europe since Xerxes' invasion, and its policy reversal demonstrates how seriously the Persians now regarded the threat Philip posed. Philip's rationale for attacking the cities along the Marmara coast was to keep the Persians from using them against his defense perimeter in Thrace; however, events had turned Philip's strategy on its head. Philip's actions had now driven these cities into Persia's camp and precipitated an armed Persian incursion in Thrace, precisely the circumstances Philip had sought to prevent.

The Byzantine and Persian reinforcements evened the odds between the besieger and the besieged. Philip pressed the attack, however,

> by launching constant strikes against the walls with his battering rams, kept trying to knock them down. Moreover by thrusting back the enemy on the battlements, he sought simultaneously to force his way in with his troops in compact formation through breaches in the walls and to use ladders to climb over the parts of the wall that were denuded of defenders. Accordingly, a hand to hand struggle took place in which some were killed and others fell only after succumbing to many wounds.[20]

The fighting continued for weeks with heavy casualties on both sides. Philip was getting nowhere.

BYZANTIUM

Never one to stay the course of failure, Philip shifted tactics. According to Diodorus, Philip "divided his troops into two parts and, putting half under his best commanders, left them behind to prosecute the siege, while he himself suddenly made an assault with the remainder on Byzantium and instituted a close siege."[21] Presumably these "best commanders" were not Antipater and Parmenio, who, if we can believe Theopompus, were commanding their own columns elsewhere in Thrace and attacking the Tetrachoritae for supporting Diopeithes' outrages against Cardia.[22] At first glance, Philip's shift in tactics seems foolish. How could he hope to take Byzantium, with its walls and fortifications, with only half of his force and one that had failed to take Perinthus at that?[23] On the contrary, the attack on Byzantium was a reasonable course of action and had at least a moderate chance of success.

Philip would not have undertaken his plan without first sending his cavalry to conduct a thorough tactical reconnaissance of the route to Byzantium and the city's defenses. Byzantium lay fifty-four miles east of Perinthus along a good coastal road. Seventeen miles from Perinthus lay the city of Selymbria. Although fortified, the small city lacked the ability to seriously interfere with Philip's march. Still, Philip could hardly leave it unmolested across his line of communications. Justin's claim that Byzantium possessed massive fortifications is an exaggeration.[24] In fact, Byzantium in Philip's day was much smaller than the great city Constantine built later. It occupied only the high ground at the most eastern part of the headland, jutting into the Bosporus south of the Golden Horn, or approximately the area where Topkapi and Hagia Sophia sit today. Its walls were built to repel the attacks of Thracian tribes and not to resist the more advanced techniques of Philip's siege engineers.[25] At best, its walls may have been no more substantial than those of other Greek cities that Philip's engineers had already overcome. It is even possible that the walls were less substantial since they were designed only to keep out Thracian tribesmen, who did not possess any appreciable siege capability.

Finally, Philip was all too aware that Byzantium had sent substantial numbers of troops, artillery, and "their best commanders" to support the Perinthians. Philip reckoned that their deployment might have left Byzantium so weakened that a sudden surprise assault might have a good chance of succeeding. Of particular interest to Philip were the Byzantine catapults and large quantity of missiles that had been sent to Perinthus. These stone and arrow throwers were crucial to Byzantium's defense, and without them it had no way to keep Philip's engineers and assault groups away from the walls. Diodorus confirms Philip's insight was correct: "Since the Perinthians already had the Byzantine troops, missiles, and other implements of weaponry within their city, the people of Byzantium found themselves in severe difficulty."[26]

Philip's force of some fifteen thousand men could cover the distance to Byzantium in three and a half days' forced march, arriving outside the city ready to attack and take Byzantium by surprise. A substantial cavalry force riding a day ahead of the main body could reach Selymbria quickly and take up positions as a blocking force. Once Philip's army passed, a small Macedonian force would remain and, perhaps, even make a feigned attack to bring Selymbria under siege.[27] As he had done before, Philip used the cover of night to dismantle some of his smaller artillery pieces and prepare them for transport while setting his army on the march.[28] The heavy siege towers were left behind. Philip hardly needed to get bogged down in another long siege. This next attack required mostly light forces such as his Greek mercenaries and Thracian peltasts using scaling ladders. Slingers, archers, and the light artillery could drive the defenders from the walls while Philip's assault teams scaled them. With many of their soldiers in Perinthus, the Byzantine defenders would find it difficult to protect the walls against simultaneous attacks from several directions. All things considered, Philip's plan was bold but reasonable. If it succeeded, he would capture one of the most strategically important cities in the ancient world.

It is uncertain what happened when Philip arrived outside Byzantium, but he may have come within an ace of seizing the city by a coup de main. Philip's army reached the approaches to Byzantium sometime around dusk, apparently having made slower time than anticipated. Philip may have held his troops far enough away from the city so as the defenders would not discover them. Under cover of night and with the sound of their movement muffled by a rainstorm, Philip's assault teams approached the walls in a daring attempt to storm the city. Unfortunately for Philip, barking dogs alerted the defenders, who were able to repel the attack.[29] The surprise attack failed, and Philip was forced to take the city under siege. Here at the siege of Byzantium the Macedonians first used the new, experimental torsion catapults invented by Philip's chief engineer, Polyeidos.

While Philip's tactics in attacking Byzantium were sound, his strategy failed to appreciate the environment in which the attack took place. If the Greek states and Persia had come to the aid of Perinthus, it was simply reasonable to expect that they would also come to the aid of Byzantium, which was of much greater commercial and strategic importance. Even if Athens and the maritime states somehow failed to respond, Philip could hardly expect that the Persian king would allow Byzantium to fall into Macedonian hands. Once Philip failed to take Byzantium quickly, he found himself bogged down in another long siege against a city that promptly sought and received military support from Athens and the maritime states of Chios, Rhodes, and Cos. Persia, too, provided food and arms to Byzantium's defenders and at one point conspired with Chares to coordinate military actions. As Philip's small fleet could not command the sea around the Bosporus, Byzantium continued to be easily supplied by sea.

It is interesting to note the size of Philip's forces at this time. While Philip's army of thirty thousand Macedonian, Thracian, and allied units besieged Perinthus and Byzantium and blocked Selymbria, Antipater and Parmenio were commanding columns against Greek mercenaries and Thracian rebels in the Chersonese. Back in Macedonia, Alexander was mounting a substantial military operation against the Maedi tribes on the upper Strymon River (that he completed successfully). Alexander's force probably drew heavily from Macedonian militia units assembled around a core of professionals of the King's Field Army and must have numbered at least ten thousand troops.

Whether Philip succeeded in capturing Byzantium, the Greeks must have noticed that no state by itself, including Athens, could hope to survive an attack by so large a Macedonian army. Macedonian military power was already great enough to conquer Greece.

Philip began his siege of Byzantium around early September. Although Chares and the Athenian fleet were active in the Bosporus, the fleets of the maritime states and the Athenian reinforcements had yet to arrive, so Philip's fleet was still able to move freely around the Sea of Marmara and even the Bosporus. The weather around the Bosporus–Black Sea region often turns bad for several days in mid-September, and the Athenian grain fleet of 230 ships returning from the Black Sea ports was forced to put in at Herion, a small port on the Asiatic shore of the Bosporus where it enters the Black Sea. Denied entrance to the Byzantine harbor because of his reputation for brutality, Chares and his fleet of forty ships were deployed off Byzantium and waited to escort the grain ships once they put to sea again. Chares was then called to a meeting of the Persian satraps who supported the Byzantines to plan their counterattack to Philip's siege. The meeting probably took place somewhere on the Asiatic coast. While Chares was away, Philip struck.

The Macedonian fleet under Demetrius attacked and blocked the Athenian grain fleet resting at its Herion anchorage. Meanwhile, Philip ferried a ground force over the Bosporus and captured the Athenian crews ashore at Herion. The grain fleet was taken back across the Bosporus. Philip kept only 180 Athenian ships and released the other fifty. He dismantled the captured ships and used their timbers to construct siege towers, and he sold some of the grain while keeping the rest to feed his army. Selling the grain and ship's hardware brought Philip a profit of seven hundred talents, or more than a year's revenue for the city of Athens.[30] Chares rushed back to his fleet and drove the Macedonian ships into the Black Sea, trapping them there.

Philip must have known when he seized the Athenian grain fleet that nothing would outrage Athens more than an attack on its food supply. Demosthenes and others in Athens had been arguing for more than a year that Philip was already at war with Athens, and there was little left to do but to declare it formally. Meanwhile, Athens had begun assembling a large fleet to aid Byzantium, and when Philip seized its grain fleet, Athens formally declared war on Philip.[31] Within weeks, a large Athenian fleet sailed for Byzantium to join Chares' fleet. Other allies—Chios, Cos, and Rhodes—also sent warships. In symbolic response, Philip "with his bravest men" ravaged a few Athenian towns in the Chersonese.[32]

As long as Perinthus and Byzantium were open to the sea and supplied by powerful allies, Philip could not bring either siege to a conclusion. Philip recognized his limitations, and by the end of November he pulled his troops back from both cities and assembled them on the Thracian plain, perhaps at Cabyle, for rest and replenishment. His fleet, however, was still trapped in the Black Sea. It was probably after Philip had begun to withdraw his army from around Byzantium that he tricked Chares into lifting his blockade of the Bosporus. Philip sent a bogus letter to Antipater ordering him to send troops to Thrace immediately and subdue a great rebellion there. Philip had decided, the letter said, to end the siege of Byzantium, march directly into Thrace, and put down the insurrection. As Philip intended, the Athenians stationed at the Bosporus intercepted the letter. Always eager to support any revolt against Philip, Chares and the Athenian fleet set sail for Thrace to help the rebels. Thinking Philip was already leaving Byzantium, Chares' fleet no longer needed to guard the city. The blockade was lifted, allowing Philip's fleet to exit the Black Sea.[33]

It is tempting to see Philip's efforts at Perinthus and Byzantium as failures, and surely from a tactical perspective, they were indeed. Strategically, however, the outcome was far less negative. If Philip wanted to provoke Athens into declaring war, his attack on Byzantium and the grain fleet had accomplished it.[34] Now he could shift the burden of public opinion against Athens as the ones who wanted war. In this way, Philip hoped to retain the positive feelings most Greeks already had for him. Moreover, once the war with Athens was over, Byzantium and other Greek cities would have little choice but to come to terms with him.

As Philip was preparing to abandon the sieges, he opened negotiations with some of "the Greeks opposed to him," and if we can believe Frontinus, some sort of talks were held.[35] While it does not appear that Athens took part, some evidence shows that Philip made peace with the Chians and Rhodians and, perhaps, even the Byzantines and Perinthians.[36] If he indeed reached such agreements, it was a classic maneuver of Philip's to use diplomacy and shore up his military position when other more pressing matters required his attention. The peace negotiations with his former Thracian adversaries would remove any threat to Philip's rear and leave him free to deal with Athens and other issues.

THE SCYTHIAN CAMPAIGN

In the spring of 340 BCE when Philip was concluding his conquest of Thrace, the rulers of Apollonia, a trading town on the Black Sea coast, approached him with an offer of alliance from Atheas, king of the Scythians. His people occupied the area known as Dobruja, which is located between the lower Danube River, including the delta, and the Black Sea. Beginning in the marshy Danube delta, the terrain to the south is initially hilly until it gradually runs into the coastal Thracian plain. Dobruja afforded the Scythians easy access to Philip's possessions and allied cities on the plain and the Black Sea coast. When King Atheas suggested an alliance, Philip saw the opportunity to neutralize the Scythians' potential military threat to his back while he was besieging Perinthus and Byzantium.

When Atheas took the initiative for the alliance and used the Apollonians as intermediaries, he was engaged in a war with the king of the Histriani, a native people who lived in and around the Danube delta to the north. Indeed, he was "being distressed by the war," that is, getting the worst of it.[37] Atheas had recently expanded his kingdom southward and was concerned that Byzantium might use its influence with the Black Sea coastal states to oppose him later. Thus, he welcomed Philip's efforts to reduce Byzantium to a Macedonian protectorate. The offer that the Apollonians presented to Philip suggested that in exchange for a military alliance and the provision of Macedonian troops, the Scythian king was prepared to "adopt Philip for his successor to the throne of Scythia."[38] The offer would be sealed by Philip's marriage to Atheas's daughter.

It is unlikely that Philip believed Atheas was prepared to deliver his kingdom in exchange for a few troops. Atheas, after all, had much in common with Philip: he had spent his life conquering and uniting a coalition of tribes from the Maeotian marshes to the Danube and creating a state that the Greeks later called Scythia Minor.[39] Although he was in his nineties, Atheas was probably not about to relinquish his claim to his life's work. In the short run, though, an alliance, however temporary it may prove to be, would remove any Scythian threat to Philip while he was attempting to subdue the coastal cities of the Marmara coast. Philip thus agreed to the alliance and sent an unknown number of troops, probably mercenaries, to Atheas.

While the troops were en route to the Danube, events took a positive turn for Atheas. The king of the Histriani died and "relieved the Scythians both from the fear of war and the want of assistance."[40] When the Macedonian troops arrived, Atheas sent them back to Philip, and they arrived some time during the siege of Byzantium. Had Atheas left the matter at that, nothing more might have come of it. But Atheas sent a message to Philip that Atheas "had neither sought his aid, nor proposed his adoption; for the Scythians needed no protection from the Macedonians, to whom they were superior in the field, nor did he himself want an heir, as he had a son living."[41] Atheas claimed that it was all a misunderstanding and that the Apollonians had apparently been mistaken when they presented the original terms of Atheas's proposed alliance. Philip was still occupied with the Byzantium siege and replied reasonably that he would be satisfied if Atheas, as his ally, would defray at least a portion of the siege's expense and the costs of the mercenaries that Philip had sent to Atheas. All this back-and-forth would have taken several weeks and avoided an open break with Atheas.

It is difficult to see what Atheas hoped to gain by straining relations with Philip, but his reply to Philip's request was an insult. Claiming that Scythia was a poor country with poor soil and a harsh climate, Atheas said that "he had no treasury to satisfy so great a king, and that he thought it less honorable to do little than to refuse altogether." Then came a veiled threat. "The Scythians," Atheas said, "were to be estimated by their valor and hardiness of body, not by their possessions."[42] By this time the siege of Byzantium was winding down as Philip had decided to abandon it. He moved his army inland, gathered his troops from Perinthus and Selymbria and those campaigning under Parmenio and Antipater, and replenished his army for further action.

While he rested his army, Philip sent a message to Atheas saying "that while he [Philip] was besieging Byzantium, he had vowed a statue to Heracles, which he was going to erect at the mouth of the Ister [Danube] requesting an unobstructed passage to pay his vow to the god, since he was coming as a friend of the Scythians."[43] The wily Atheas saw the request for what it was, an attempt to get inside Scythian defenses. Atheas replied that if Philip sent him the statue, Atheas would gladly install it on the Danube. He refused "to allow an army to enter his territories." Moreover, if Philip "should set up the statue in spite of the Scythians, he [Atheas] would take it down when he was gone, and turn the brass of it into heads for arrows."[44] Sometime in early winter, perhaps late December or early January, Philip and his army marched north into Dobruja to deal with the Scythian king.

Justin tells us that a great battle was fought between Philip's army and the Scythians. There is no reason to think that Philip's army was any fewer than the thirty thousand men with whom he had conquered Thrace and besieged Byzantium. But Justin says that the Scythians "were superior in courage and numbers," implying that Atheas's army was even larger.[45] If so, the battle was one of the largest between two combatants recorded in antiquity. The evidence does not indicate where the battle was fought, but it is possible that Atheas moved his army south out of the hilly country and onto the flat inland plain to give his horse archers every advantage in speed and mobility. It would have made sense for Philip to stage through Odessus for logistical purposes and to give himself a redoubt upon which to withdraw should things go badly. At some point almost midway between Odessus and the Danube, possibly modern Dobrich, the two armies met.

Carved images on an electrum cup found in a *kurgan* (tomb) at Kul-Oba offers some idea as to the composition of the Scythian army that fought Philip. Most Scythian warriors were archers, as befits a people who called themselves *skolotoi*, derived from the Indo-European word for archer. Armed with the composite bow, Scythian archers rode horses and perhaps were drawn mostly from the horse-breeding segments of the society. Herodotus tells us that Scythian cavalry did not use saddles.[46] Curiously, the horse archers wore heeled boots, but no stirrups have been found in the graves explored by archaeologists. Other archers served as light infantry and probably came from the society's agricultural elements. Scythian arrowheads were often barbed, were sometimes poisoned, and caused terrible wounds. The cup also depicts heavy infantry armed with the short spear, sword, and wood and leather shield.

We know little about the tactics of the Scythians of Philip's day, but when Alexander fought them in 329 BCE, they relied heavily on lines of horse archers attacking his infantry, one after another, firing their arrows and then retreating. When their opponent had been sufficiently weakened, the Scythian horse archers rode around the enemy in a circle, firing their arrows as they went. The role of the spear infantry and regular archers is not known, but one might reasonably surmise that the archers opened the battle with volley fire to inflict casualties on packed infantry. The spear infantry closed in on the enemy once it was on its last legs, having been leveled by the horse archers, and engaged in close combat.

How Philip dealt with the Scythians was not recorded, but it is clear that his pike infantry with their small shields would have been vulnerable to the Scythian archers' volley fire. His peltasts, Thracian javelineers, and mercenary hoplites, deployed in spread formations or covered with their large *hoplons* (shields), were less exposed. Philip's heavy cavalry, with iron helmets, armor, and leather arm and neck protectors, were the most protected. In swirling combat with the horse archers, the Macedonian cavalry had the advantage with its long lances. Close in, the Macedonian machaira was likely to be more effective than the Scythian straight sword. It is likely, then, that Philip's cavalry may have played the decisive role in the battle. Perhaps, as Alexander did later, Philip waited until the horse archers formed their circle and then sent his cavalry in to smash the enemy formation and chop it up in close combat. The cavalry could engage in a long pursuit, using the superior reach of the cavalry lance to inflict heavy casualties.

However it was done, Philip's army carried the day, killing Atheas in the process. The Scythians in the Dobruja were horse-riding nomadic pastoralists who engaged in agriculture (growing wheat and cannabis for export), horse breeding (Homer called them the "mare-milkers," and an extensive slave trade. The agriculturalists lived in stable towns and villages, while the horse breeders moved their herds with the seasons, returning to the permanent settlements on a regular basis. The populous society that Philip encountered after his victory was extensive and decentralized. Philip spent the rest of the winter rounding up the young men, women, children, horses, cattle, grain, and other booty, which he took with him when he returned to Macedonia.

According to Justin, "twenty thousand young men [meaning boys] and women [which included girls] were taken, and a vast number of cattle, but no gold or silver.... Twenty thousand fine mares were sent to Macedonia to raise a breed."[47] It is interesting that he does not mention any grown Scythian men. Some of them would surely have been killed in battle, but Philip must have captured substantial numbers of males, including elderly males. What happened to them? The Scythians represented a serious security threat to Philip's control of Eastern Thrace. He may have set out to eradicate that threat completely by resorting to the Greek practice of killing all the adult males and carrying off the women and children into slavery or resettlement. It is likely that Philip married Atheas's daughter to obtain legal title to the Scythian lands, and it was probably this woman who is buried with Philip in his tomb. There is no information as to what befell Atheas's son and heir. If he was not killed in battle, he was probably executed. We know from Strabo that after Philip's victory, Atheas's kingdom literally ceased to exist. Philip gave its lands to the Getae and the Histriani.

The column that left the Danube delta in the early spring for the return trip to Macedonia was enormous, consisting of more than 50,000 human beings, 23,000 horses, and a greater number of cattle, sheep, and other farm animals. Other booty was carried in captured Scythian carts and wagons. The column must have been several miles long and could hardly have covered more than four or five miles a day. Philip's route took him west along the south bank of the Danube and around the western end of the Great Balkan Mountains, where he turned southwest. His route brought the column within the territory of the Triballi, a fierce tribal people known for their cavalry and the use of the long cavalry lance. As noted in chapter 1, the Triballi refused to allow Philip to pass through their territory unless he gave them part of the Scythian loot. When Philip refused, Justin tells us that the Triballi waged a battle in which they severely wounded Philip and killed his horse, and "the booty was lost."[48] Given the enormous size and composition of Philip's column, his troops would have had a difficult time defending it. The Triballi could have dispersed the column with a few attacks and made off with whatever they could grab. The nature of Philip's wound suggests a wild melee more than a set-piece battle,[49] and while Justin says "the booty was lost," it is likely that only some of it was.

From the land of the Triballi, Philip made his way south to the banks of the Strymon River and on to Amphipolis. At Amphipolis he turned due west for the journey's final leg to Pella. The trek from the Danube delta to Pella is almost five hundred miles, and it probably took the slow-moving column two and a half months to complete. Philip and the army arrived in Pella sometime in midsummer 339 BCE. Philip's campaigns between 342 and 339 BCE had created a cordon sanitaire, or a military district, that ran from the Adriatic to the Black Sea, making Macedonia free from the threat of foreign invasion for the first time in its history.[50]

The area Philip conquered in the twenty years since assuming the throne of Macedonia represented the first large land empire in Europe. As head of the Macedonian state, Philip could dispose of the spear-won lands as he and the Macedonoi saw fit. A 10 percent tax on all produce was levied on the conquered lands as tribute to Macedonia, and as the empire's *hegemonoi*, the Macedonoi could demand service and obedience of their subjects in the form of labor or military service. Beyond these stipulations, the tribes, towns, and cities of the empire were permitted to govern themselves, keep their own laws and customs, practice their own religions, speak their own languages, and levy their own taxes. They even raised and trained their own troops, although in the larger cities Macedonian military formations, weapons, and tactics were introduced. Some tribes and cities received favored treatment because of their importance, but most peoples were direct subjects who had to keep the peace and accept Macedonian rule.[51]

THE PRELUDE TO WAR

When Philip arrived in Pella he confronted two major problems. First, just prior to his return, the Thebans ejected the Macedonian garrison at Nicaea, the key town controlling the route through the Thermopylae Pass, and occupied the town themselves.[52] Philip had controlled Nicaea since the peace of 346 BCE, and Thebes and Macedonia were still considered allies. Thebes' sudden and ominous seizure of Nicaea blocked the direct land route to Attica and Athens. Thebes took the strategic town out of concern that, with Athens and Philip now officially at war, Philip was bound to act sooner or later. The road to Attica ran through Boeotia and Thebes, and the Thebans already had good reason to distrust Philip's ambitions. They occupied Nicaea so they could bargain with Philip to ensure their own security. If Philip had designs on Thebes as well as Athens, the Thebans were in a better position to resist with Nicaea in their hands.

Philip's second problem concerned the Amphictyonic Council, which had been engaged in a yearlong dispute with the Locrian town of Amphissa over some supposed illegal and sacrilegious cultivation of sacred lands. After much maneuvering, Amphissa was fined, and Cottyphus, a Thessalian, was appointed commander of the Amphictyonic forces to enforce the fine. When Cottyphus arrived in Amphissa with only a token force, the Amphissans refused to pay, and he was driven off by Amphissan troops.[53] At the autumn meeting of the Amphictyonic Council, a Sacred War was declared against Amphissa. It removed the ineffective Cottyphus from command of the league's forces and appointed Philip in his place, with the expectation that Philip would punish Amphissa with military force.

The Macedonian army, however, had been in the field for more than a year before returning to Pella in the summer of 339 BCE. It was in no condition to wage war with Amphissa and certainly not to engage in a major campaign against Athens. Throughout the summer and early fall of 339 BCE, Philip recuperated from his leg wound and rested and replenished his army. Philip's primary strategic concern was the war with Athens, and he needed to carefully assess the politico-military environment in which the war would be fought. Philip had spent years casting himself as a reasonable man who fought war only reluctantly. The fact that Athens had declared war on Philip now served him well. Athens found itself almost politically and militarily isolated. Not a single Peloponnesian state supported Athens. Its allies in Euboea also refused to help. A few of the maritime states in the east stood with Athens but only in spirit since it was unlikely that the allies in the Hellespont region could do much militarily in mainland Greece. Acarnania remained faithful, but its contribution was offset by the stance of its more powerful neighbor, Aetolia. The Aetolians supported Philip because he promised to liberate Naupactus from the Acarnanians and give it to them. The Locrians, for their part, had no love for Athens, and Phokis was already in the Macedonian camp. The Athenians' only hope for a military alliance lay with Thebes, its traditional enemy.[54]

The strategic situation was complicated, however, by Persia. Philip's attack on Byzantium had provoked a Persian military response into Thrace, a clear indication that Persia now regarded Philip as a long-range threat to its security. Although withdrawing troops once Philip broke off the siege of Byzantium and rebuffing an earlier Athenian request for an alliance, the Persians sent money to Athens to prosecute its war with Philip. Persia's actions made it very difficult for Philip to assess its intentions. If Philip marched into Athens, would Persia march into Thrace? And if so, would the Persian army, as it had done before, march overland through Thrace and attack Macedonia itself? With the Macedonian army tied down in Attica and Persia marching through Thrace, what would Thebes do? Philip's answers to these questions resulted in a military campaign based on precise timing and strategic deception.

Philip was appointed commander of the Amphictyonic League's armies in the early autumn of 339 BCE. In November, the Macedonian army, the league's forces, and the Aetolians assembled at Lamia, nine miles from Thermopylae, and prepared to move south. Legally, Philip was commanding an Amphictyonic alliance in service to the league council's mandate to punish the Amphissians for their sacrilege and refusal to pay the council's fine. That most of the alliance's troops were Macedonian and Thessalian did not raise any alarm in either Thebes or Athens. Apparently both saw Philip's march south as a limited and temporary military operation against Amphissa. Marching in the name and authority of the Amphictyonies was a brilliant strategic deception on Philip's part, and it lulled the only two states capable of opposing his ambitions in Greece into taking no steps to oppose him. At the same time, Philip also deceived the Persians, who were closely watching his actions.

The Thebans may have believed that their control of Nicaea and the Thermopylae Pass would protect them should Philip reveal a hostile intent. To further this illusion, Philip did not try to force the pass or seek permission to use it. Instead, marching west from Lamia, Philip's army ascended the narrow pass between Mount Oeta and Mount Callidromos and entered the territory of the high canton of Doris, which was a member of the Amphictyonic League and Philip's ally. Philip marched quickly to the city of Cytinium, where he established his logistics base. Cytinium was only six miles from the Gravia Pass, which led south to Amphissa, Philip's presumed objective. Philip did not, however, seize the mouth of the pass.[55] To this point, Philip did exactly what he said he would do.

Suddenly, Philip's army swung east, marched into Phokis, down the Cephissus River valley, and occupied Elatea, the Phokian capital. The Amphictyonic League had disarmed and split up Phokis at the end of the Sacred War, thus it was in no position to resist Philip's occupation of the city. More importantly, however, Phokis strongly sympathized with Philip for, after all, he had been the one on the Amphictyonic Council who had kept the country from being destroyed and its males exterminated. Philip had also reduced the council's heavy fines and lifted the restrictions on rebuilding the Phokian cities. By this time, Elatea itself was almost completely rebuilt. Philip's reasonable treatment of Phokis after the Sacred War now paid huge dividends. Philip counted on Phokis to provide the winter quarters and supplies his army needed while it was in the field.

Philip's deception permitted him to place a large army close to the Boeotian border. He also controlled the road that led through Boeotia to Attica and onto Athens. Philip's army was only three days' march from Athens' walls. Philip had caught Athens and Thebes completely by surprise. Neither had called up their citizen levies, and it would take several days at the earliest for them to do so. Neither was in a position to stop Philip. For his part, Philip could march through Boeotia, bypassing Thebes; ravage Attica; and drive the

Athenians inside their walls, where they would be completely cut off from outside aid. In a matter of a few weeks, he could have destroyed Athens.

Despite holding every advantage, however, Philip did not advance beyond Elatea. Instead, he sent a delegation comprising Macedonians and members of the Amphictyonic League to Thebes to negotiate his free passage southward. The delegation's composition makes clear that Philip presented his actions as representing the will of the Amphictyonic League, which was conducting a Sacred War. Philip's envoys proposed that Thebes relinquish its hold on Nicaea and return the town to the Locrians, its proper owner. The Thebans offered to consider the idea. Philip's envoys then requested that the Boeotians join the league in attacking Athens. In return, Thebes would receive all the booty taken from the city. If Thebes and the Boeotian League did not wish to participate in the demise of Athens, Philip proposed they remain neutral but allow his army free passage through their territory on his way to Athens.[56] The choice was simple, at least in Philip's view.

Philip approached Thebes diplomatically because he understood that the situation was militarily complex. Thebes and the Boeotian League commanded the largest and best-trained army in Greece. Acting in concert, they could put twelve thousand infantry and eight hundred cavalry in the field.[57] Without their consent, a march through Boeotia and an attack on Athens would leave a powerful military force at Philip's back and across his line of communications. Although Thebes and Macedonia were technically allies, there were hard feelings between the two, and neither completely trusted the other. If Philip besieged Athens, he would be particularly vulnerable to a Theban attack that could crush him between the Theban army and the walls of Athens. Philip halted his march because he dared not proceed without first learning what Thebes' intentions were.

The news of Philip's occupation of Elatea sent Athens into shock, and a hastily convened meeting of the assembly resulted in Demosthenes leading a delegation to Thebes to seek an alliance against Philip. The delegation reached Thebes to discover that Philip's envoys were already there. The Athenians must have been stunned by Philip's offer to allow Thebes to pillage Athens and keep all the booty in return for Theban support. Both sides presented their cases. Thebes held the future of Greece in its hands. If it supported Philip, Athens was doomed. Sooner or later, however, Macedonia and Thebes would have to fight for preeminence in Greece. A future war was inevitable. For Thebes to support Athens required that it break its alliance with Philip. Should it choose the losing side, Thebes would likely face the same harsh fate that Olynthos suffered when it broke its treaty with Philip, went to war with him, and lost: it saw its entire population enslaved and its city obliterated. Thebes could expect no less if it chose poorly. Nonetheless, the Theban leaders reached the conclusion that they had a better chance of defeating Philip in an alliance with Athens than facing him alone after Athens was destroyed. They renounced their treaty with Philip and voted to ally themselves with Athens.

But Thebes did not risk its existence cheaply. It demanded numerous conditions as the price of its support. Athens was to forgo any future support for the autonomy of any Boeotian city, in effect recognizing Theban hegemony over Boeotia. Regarding the war effort, Thebes would bear one-third of the land war's cost, and Athens would assume the rest. Further, Thebes demanded sole command of the allied land armies. Although Athens would bear the entire cost of all naval operations, both states would share this command. Finally, the combined armies' headquarters was to be located at Thebes, not Athens.[58] To have any chance of survival, Athens had to pay the Thebans' price.

Philip was now at war with Athens and Thebes, and the alliance changed his military calculations considerably. His attempt to neutralize Theban military power through diplomacy had cost Philip the elements of surprise and momentum he had gained with his rapid march and seizure of Elatea. He may also have believed that if he had been able to achieve an alliance with Thebes or at least its neutrality, then Athens would have had little choice but to come to a diplomatic arrangement to avoid the defeat that would certainly follow a war with Philip. Philip's diplomacy failed, and with it went his military advantages. Athens and Thebes were rapidly mobilizing their armies and had begun deploying them into forward positions to block Philip's advance.

It was December and winter was setting in. If Philip attacked now, he would have to fight a winter campaign against an enemy that had the advantage of interior supply lines. Thebes and Athens could retreat before him, taking refuge in their fortified cities, while Philip's army operated at the end of extended lines of supply. If Philip stayed in Elatea with his logistic base at Cytinium, both supplied by the friendly Phokians, he could wait out the winter in relative comfort and security. His remaining in Elatea would force the Thebans and Athenians to deploy their forces forward, placing them at the end of an extended supply line. It made sound military sense for Philip to wait until spring to begin the war's combat phase. Waiting also served Philip's interest in that the slow pace of unfolding events worked to calm Persian anxieties over Philip's ambitions. Whatever was happening in Greece was happening gradually, reducing any Persian perception that things were getting out of hand. To Persian eyes, Philip appeared to be just another Greek king pursuing his interests in the same manner Greek kings, tyrants, and oligarchs had done for centuries.

Both the Thebans and the Athenians called up their troop levies while Philip was still conducting negotiations with them. Once the sides were drawn, allied units began to take up positions to block Philip's advance. The Boeotian and Athenian troops deployed on the Boeotian frontier near the town of Parapotamii, where the Cephissus River flowed through a narrow gap between a spur of Mount Parnassus on the west and Mount Helicon on the east. This deployment effectively barred Philip's route to Chaeronea, for the narrow pass made using his cavalry impossible. Two smaller passes connecting these positions with the allied garrisons protecting Amphissa to the east were also fortified. Six miles from Philip's main logistics base at Cytinium was the opening to the Gravia Pass and the road over the mountains that led to Amphissa twelve miles away. A force of ten thousand mercenaries led by the Athenian general, Chares, was deployed to protect Amphissa. Operational command of the mercenaries, however, rested with Proxenus, a Theban general.[59]

The allied forces effectively blocked the only two routes leading south that were available to Philip. There were difficulties, however. The allied supply lines were long, running from Thebes to Amphissa and Parapotamii through mountains and narrow passes easily closed by foul weather. Two narrow passes at the base of Mount Parnassus connected the allied deployments and permitted the two sides to reinforce each other. The allied deployment had a major weakness, however: if either position fell to Philip, the other one would be immediately exposed on its flank, a circumstance that would force the exposed force to withdraw farther south. Such a move would relinquish control of the Cephissus valley and expose Chaeronea to attack. Nonetheless, the allied defensive plan was tactically sound.

The most immediate threat to Athens was Philip's ability to carry out a ground attack against the allies, and Athens acted correctly in deploying its ground forces to stop it. What was lacking in the Athenian strategy, however, was any naval component to augment its ground operations. Athens was still the preeminent naval power in Greece and could send more than three hundred triremes transporting significant land forces, or easily five thousand hoplites, to war.[60] With Philip's army ensconced around Elatea and his route of advance blocked, one wonders why Athens did not bring its navy into play by mobilizing its manpower reserves and using its ships to strike at Philip's strategic rear. Athens had the capability to conduct naval assaults in the Thermaic Gulf and against Philip's ports in Chalcidice. Athenian naval infantry could have even attacked the coast of Macedonia itself. With Philip's army in the field, the Macedonian coast was defenseless. Naval attacks might have forced Philip to break off his campaign and return home to defend Macedonia itself.

The subject of naval operations must surely have been raised when Thebes and Athens discussed their alliance agreement, and Athens agreed to bear the entire cost of naval operations and to share the command of naval assets with Thebes. The concord implies that some sort of naval operations were at least considered, if not actually planned. While winter in the Aegean is not an ideal time to mount naval operations, it is not impossible to do so. The allies might have been waiting for spring before sending their naval assets into action. It may also have been the case that many Athenians were obsessed with the past glory of Athens when it was a great land power. By this time, however, its population and wealth had declined to where Athens relied more on mercenaries than on its own citizen-hoplites.[61] Its cavalry arm was small and trained in the old ways of Greek cavalry warfare. It was no match in either numbers or quality for the Macedonian cavalry. Still, old ideals die hard, and it is possible that Demosthenes and other Athenians saw the war with Philip as an opportunity to restore their national pride and reputation by fighting and winning that most traditional form of Greek warfare, a great infantry battle. If so, theirs was a mistake of enormous proportions.

Over the winter of 339–338 BCE, both sides made efforts to increase their strength and sought support from their respective allies. Neither side was particularly successful, and only a small number of new troops accrued to either side. On the one hand, Philip was disappointed that those Peloponnesian states that were friendly to him did little to help. On the other hand, the large coalition of Greek states that Philip feared might join Athens against him did not materialize either. Over the winter, both armies skirmished with one another across the Cephissus valley, conducting raids on each other's strong points, which were hastily constructed forward of their main lines. Unless they were dispatched to secure food, there seems to have been little point to these guerrilla raids except to keep the army busy and maintain camp discipline through the long winter months.

As spring approached, Philip made a last attempt to reach a peaceful settlement with Thebes and Athens.[62] Philip probably knew that the die was cast and that no diplomatic solution could be had. Accordingly, he used these discussions to cast himself as the one who did not want war and who attempted to avoid it until the last possible moment. He reminded them that he was acting legally in the name of the Amphictyones, one of Greece's oldest and most venerable institutions, in punishing Amphissa for its sacrilegious actions. Philip was already looking beyond the battlefield to the public support he would need to unify Greece without bloodshed once Thebes and Athens had been defeated. The allies, of course, recognized Macedonian imperialism when they saw it and viewed the war as a defense of Greek liberty against Macedonian servitude. The Boeotian and Athenian assemblies rejected Philip's last offer of peace, and both sides resigned themselves to war.[63]

The spring of 338 BCE came and went, and still both sides held their positions. Philip refused to attack. The spring and early summer offered Athens an opportunity to launch naval operations against the Macedonian coast, but unbelievably it did not do so. A few more allies trickled in small troop contingents to support Thebes and Athens, so that their force now outnumbered Philip in infantry, if not in cavalry. Then, in early summer, Philip opened hostilities with an attack on the Gravia Pass.

According to Polyaenus, our main source for the incident, Philip tricked Chares and Proxenus, the allied commanders of the ten thousand hoplite mercenaries guarding the pass, with a fake letter. Philip concocted a letter to Antipater in Macedonia "saying that he was postponing the campaign against Amphissa but was hurrying to Thrace, since he had learned a revolt had begun there."[64] The courier was captured "going through the narrow passes" and the letter seized by the Greek commanders who "believed it and abandoned their guard over the passes."[65] Later, "Philip found the passes deserted and unguarded, burst through, defeated the generals when they turned around, and captured Amphissa."[66] Philip used an identical ruse to the one he had employed to free his fleet during the siege of Byzantium. Chares again fell for a captured bogus letter to Antipater saying that Philip was breaking off his campaign to put down a revolt in Thrace. Chares was an experienced soldier and captain of mercenaries, so it is difficult to believe that he was as gullible as he is portrayed—twice. Polyaenus's account takes on the appearance of a literary device offered to explain an event for which no other explanatory evidence is offered.

The Gravia Pass connects the northern Cephissus valley with Amphissa twelve miles to the south. It traverses mountainous terrain for some five miles before debouching on a gradually widening plain leading to Amphissa six and a half miles farther south.[67] The modern road running through the pass is only thirty-five yards wide on average with canyon-like walls rising steeply on either side. No level section of the pass is wide enough to accommodate an encampment of ten thousand troops. Nor is there any place where even a much smaller number of troops—say, a thousand—could deploy for battle. Small units acting as lookouts and pickets might find sufficient space, but the steep walls of the pass would force them to take up positions on the road itself and leave them exposed to attack. It is very unlikely that Chares deployed his mercenaries within the pass itself.

Only the mouth of the pass opening on the Cephissus valley or the far exit leading to Amphissa could have accommodated Chares' troops. On the one hand, this site placed his troops only six miles from Philip's main force, exposing them to attack by a much larger force. The narrow road to Chares' rear effectively prevented a controlled retreat. Finally, supplying ten thousand troops over a narrow mountain pass for six months and over the winter would have been a logistical nightmare for a Greek army. The rear exit of the pass, on the other hand, offered a gradually widening plain more than a thousand yards wide that could accommodate Chares' camp if it deployed some five hundred yards from where the narrow road exited the mountains. His army could easily be supplied from Amphissa, which was less than seven miles away. Amphissa also provided a redoubt to fall back on in case of a rout. It is more probable that Chares' army was encamped here and not in the mouth of the Gravia Pass.

Polyaenus tells us that Philip found the pass "deserted and unguarded," ostensibly as a result of Chares having believed Philip's bogus letter and ordering his troops to withdraw. And it may have happened that way. If so, Parmenio caught Chares by surprise while he was withdrawing because Parmenio "defeated the generals when they turned around, and captured Amphissa."[68] If we remember, however, that Chares' army had been living in tents for six months, much of it during the winter, it is possible that the camp's strict military discipline of posting pickets within the pass had been eroded

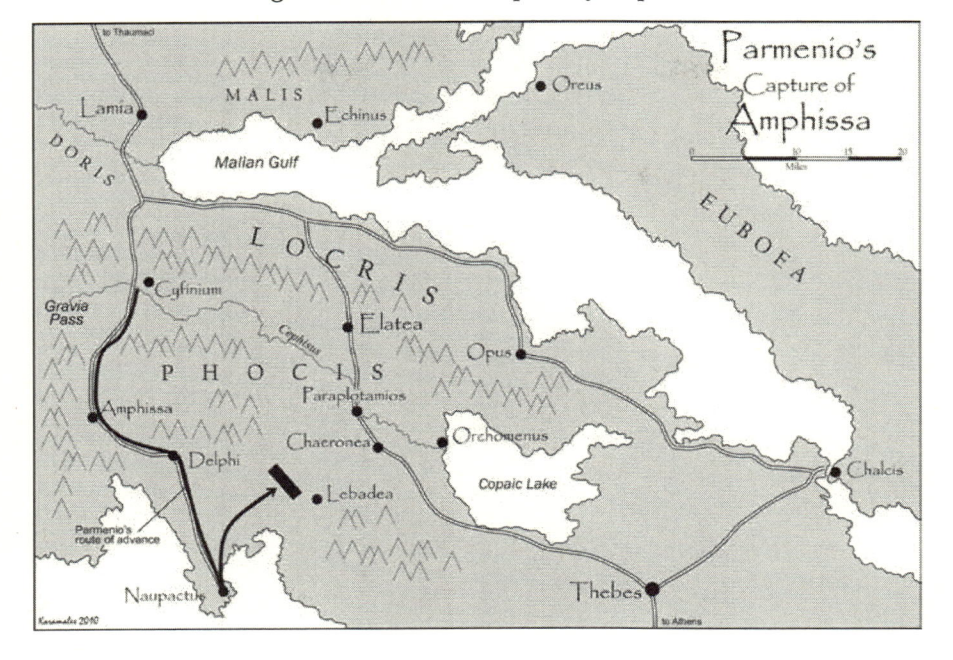

Figure 6. *Parmenio's Capture of Amphissa*

by the harsh living conditions. Under these circumstances, Parmenio's cavalry column may have attacked down the road, brushed aside the pickets, and attacked Chares' camp, catching his troops at night in their tents.[69] Chares' army was annihilated in less than three hours.[70] Once Parmenio's lead units had gained the pass's exit, follow-on units would have quickly traversed the pass, reinforced the advance force, and perhaps participated in the slaughter of Chares' mercenaries.

With Chares out of the way, Paremenio and his army—probably mostly cavalry, light infantry, and some mercenary hoplites—advanced south and captured Amphissa (see figure 6). The city formally surrendered to Parmenio, and those deemed guilty of sacrilege were banished. The mandate of the Amphictyonic League had been carried out and the Sacred War was officially over. Parmenio continued his advance to the southwest, however, capturing Naupactus. The Achaean garrison surrendered on the promise of free passage across the Corinthian Gulf to Achaea. On their arrival there, however, the commander and his men were executed. Parmenio handed Naupactus over to the Aetolians as Philip had promised when they joined his alliance.

In a single stroke, Parmenio's rapid advance had rendered the allied defenses vulnerable. If Parmenio crossed the Corinthian Gulf, linked up with

Philip's allies in the Peloponnese that were now willing to help since victory was in sight, and cut off the Athenian and Theban retreat as Philip attacked from the north, the allied forces would be crushed between two Macedonian field armies. In a less sweeping movement, Parmenio could turn east, capture Delphi, and seize Labadea. He could arrive behind and outflank the allied defenses at Parapotamii, and if Philip attacked south from Elatea, they could trap the allied armies between them. Parmenio chose the latter course and sent cavalry columns to occupy southern Phokis, capturing Delphi, Cirphis, and Anticyra before taking up positions outside Labadea. From there, Parmenio could ravage the central Boeotian plain and cut off the allied armies' retreat at Parapotamii.

The Theban commander at Parapotamii realized the danger and ordered his army to retreat five miles south and take up new defensive positions on the three-kilometer-wide plain between the acropolis of Chaeronea and the Cephissus River. Once the allied armies were in motion, Philip moved south to join Parmenio coming from the west. The two armies linked up just south of Parapotamii, setting the stage for one of the most important battles in Western military history, the battle of Chaeronea.

THE BATTLE OF CHAERONEA

The armies moved into position a few days before the battle to prepare themselves for what lay ahead. Philip himself assumed the field command of the Macedonian army, accompanied by Antipater, Parmenio, and the eighteen-year-old Alexander. Theagenes, a Boeotian general, was the overall commander of the allied armies. Based on his design of the allied defense and his use of terrain, Theagenes was a competent tactician. It was August, a time in Greece when the days can be suffocatingly hot and bring an army to its knees with heat stroke and exhaustion. The armies rose early and armed themselves in the comforting cool of the predawn twilight. As the sun rose, Philip's army went into the attack.[71] The exact date of the battle is uncertain, but it was probably fought on August 1 or August 4, 338 BCE.

The armies that faced each other that August morning were mismatched. The infantry contingents of the allied armies totaled thirty-five thousand troops, of which some thirty thousand were hoplite heavy infantry and the rest light infantry. There is no record of allied cavalry being present at the battle, perhaps because Theagenes' defensive infantry deployment covered the entire battlefront, leaving no place for cavalry to maneuver. The twelve thousand Boeotians were the most experienced and well trained of all the allied soldiers and included the famous Sacred Band of three hundred Theban elite heavy infantrymen. Athens had issued a dire call to its citizenry, and its contingents included infantrymen as old as age fifty. The Athenians numbered ten thousand citizen-soldiers along with an additional two thousand mercenaries serving under their own commanders as independent units. Corinth and Megara may have contributed two thousand hoplites each, and some smaller contingents from Corcyra, Leucas, Acarnania, and Euboea may also have participated.[72]

Only Diodorus provides an estimate of Philip's combat strength: thirty thousand infantry and two thousand cavalry.[73] Philip's army comprised the twenty-four thousand Macedonian pikemen of the King's Field Army; five thousand to six thousand light infantry; specialty units—peltasts, archers, bowmen, javelineers, and so on—drawn from the subject peoples of the empire; and two thousand Macedonian cavalry. Philip seems to have made no use of the Thessalian cavalry at Chaeronea, probably because the Thessalian cavalry was neither trained nor equipped to carry out the important tactical role that Philip had in mind for his cavalry. Diodorus tells us that Philip's army was larger,[74] but Justin says that "when the battle was joined, the Athenians [the allies] were far superior in numbers of soldiers."[75] Justin's source is Theopompus and is probably correct.

The size of the armies at Chaeronea was less important to the battle's outcome than their composition and combat experience. The allied army was made up entirely of infantry, which limited its tactical options to the defense and rendered it incapable of pursuit. Accordingly, the tactical initiative went to Philip. Because the allied army could not conduct a lethal pursuit and destroy Philip's army, he could retreat and fight another day. Thus, the allies could not effect a strategic decision even if they were victorious. If the victory went to Philip, however, he was capable of using his cavalry to completely annihilate the allied armies. In preparing to fight a traditional Greek infantry battle, Theagenes apparently did not understand that Philip brought a new dimension to Greek warfare. Unlike other Greek armies, Philip's army was capable of fighting a battle of annihilation.

The Macedonian army was superior in combat experience, power, and training, although the Boeotians were probably their equals in infantry. With the exception, perhaps, of some of the mercenaries, none of the allied contingents had ever seen the Macedonian phalanx in action, much less fought against it. The same was true for cavalry. The allies' combat experience against cavalry was against Greek cavalry, with its short spear and its inability to deliver effective shock against the front of the infantry phalanx. They had no conception of the murderous killing ability of the Macedonian cavalry, which was equipped with the saber and the long lance and was trained to employ the wedge formation to break though an infantry line. From the moment the allied armies took the field, they were vulnerable to combat capabilities and tactics that most had never experienced or even imagined existed in a Greek army.

The Chaeronean plain is three kilometers wide at the battle's site. Standing in the center of the allied line and looking north, one sees that the plain to the right (east) terminates on the steep banks and marshy ground of the Cephissus River. A brook—probably the Haemon, which the Chaeronean native Plutarch mentioned and identified with the modern Lykuressi stream—marked the western (left) boundary of the battlefield. Forward of the brook and to the left, the terrain sloped upward to a rise, atop of which sat the acropolis of Chaeronea. The Karata Pass behind the battlefield provided a route of retreat for the allied units located on the left and center of the line. The allied force of thirty-five thousand infantry, deployed eight men deep, ran the entire length of the battlefield. Its left flank was anchored on the Haemon stream, its light infantry deployed to control the sloping ground leading to the acropolis, and the Sacred Band positioned on the extreme right. The Athenian phalanx, some ten thousand strong, occupied the ground on the left of the line and the Boeotian contingent of twelve thousand men deployed to their right. With the allied infantry occupying the entire battlefront, Theagenes may have reckoned that he had taken Philip's cavalry out of the fight, since it had no room in which to maneuver on the flanks, and that he had transformed the battle into a pure infantry contest. The idea that the Macedonian cavalry could attack dead-on from the front was simply beyond Theagenes' tactical imagination.

Philip's tactical deployment was offensive in nature, designed to take the battle to the allies with shock and maneuver. At the extreme right of the Macedonian line, Philip placed his light infantry whose mission was to sweep the allied light infantry off the acropolis hill and protect Philip's main units. The first infantry unit on the right of the line was the King's Guard, consisting of five hundred elite Companion infantry who were recruited from the Macedonians of the old kingdom and spoke the Macedonian dialect as a sign

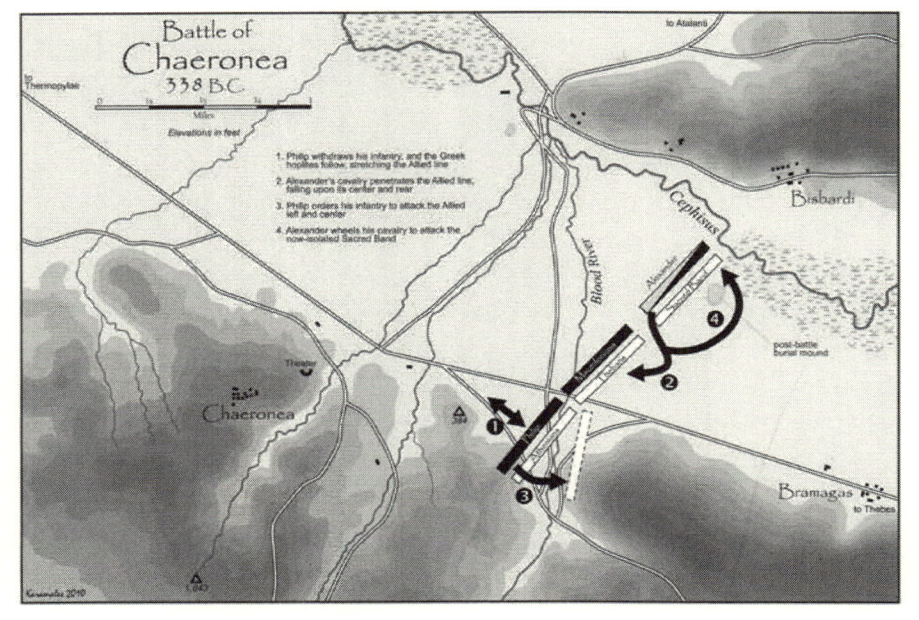

Figure 7. *The Battle of Chaeronea*

of their elite status and loyalty to the king. Next was Philip's Royal Hypaspist Guard, one thousand strong and recruited from Macedonians drawn from the Upper Cantons. Two additional brigades of these troops were posted near the king. The rest of the infantry line comprised fourteen infantry brigades, each fifteen hundred men strong, with half drawn from the old kingdom (*pezhetairoi*) and half from the Upper Cantons (asthetairoi). Each of the brigades was named for its commanding officer. All of Philip's infantry that day was armed with the sarissa.[76]

Philip's infantry line took up two and a half kilometers across the plain. Except for the units directly across from the Athenians, the Macedonian line deployed in its traditional array of ten men deep. Philip placed his two thousand cavalry far to the left and directly opposite the Sacred Band and the rest of the Theban-Boeotian line. Diodorus tells us that Philip placed Alexander in command "on the left" but "stationed alongside him the most important of his commanders,"[77] presumably Parmenio and Antipater. Philip "himself, keeping his specially selected men by his side (i.e., the King's Guard and elite infantry units), had charge of the other wing. He also placed the individual units wherever the circumstances required them (light infantry)."[78] Philip was protected by his *somatophylakes*, or "bodyguard" of seven senior cavalrymen whom he sometimes also used as messengers to carry orders to units along the line.

No ancient source mentions the presence of cavalry at Chaeronea, and while Diodorus implies Alexander was in command of cavalry, he does not expressly say so. Although the sources are silent on this issue, we can conclude from the evidence that the cavalry was involved in the battle. First, we know from the sources that Philip had two thousand cavalry with him at Elatea before the battle. Second, Parmenio's raid on the Athenian camp, his capture of Amphissa, and his outflanking of the Athenian line at Parapotamii were accomplished with a mixed force including cavalry. Thus, Parmenio had cavalry with him when he linked up with Philip prior to the battle. Third, no sane commander would have neglected to use his cavalry and leave his infantry considerably outnumbered by the enemy infantry. Without his cavalry, Philip would not have been able to extend his line completely across the allied front, and one or both flanks would have been left open to envelopment. Fourth, Philip sent Parmenio and Antipater to assist Alexander on the left of the line. Both senior commanders were cavalry officers. It would have made no sense to send them if Alexander was in command of only infantry. Finally, the speed with which the battle developed after Alexander's force penetrated the allied line implies the use of cavalry both to encircle the Sacred Band and to block the retreat of the Theban and Boeotian elements of the allied line. If Alexander's force was infantry moving in phalanx formation, they could hardly have moved into position in time to bar the Thebans' flight. For these reasons, modern scholars have tended to agree that Alexander was in command of cavalry at Chaeronea.

Philip opened the attack by sending his light infantry forward to clear the acropolis hill to his right. The infantry of Philip's right wing and under his command began to advance toward the Athenian left, which was commanded by Stratocles. The rest of Philip's line, the center infantry, and Alexander's cavalry began to advance only after Philip moved, with the result that the entire line was going to contact at the oblique. To ensure maximum coverage across the front of the Athenian phalanx, Philip's infantry was arranged in the rectangle formation. Polyaenus tells us, however, that Philip's phalanx was "contracted."[79] When the ten-man-deep phalanx contracted, the men of the last five ranks moved into the spaces between the men of the first five ranks, effectively doubling the spear points directed at the enemy while keeping the length of the phalanx front constant. The hedgehog of spears became thicker, making the phalanx "heavier" and more difficult to penetrate. Philip advanced just short of making contact with the Athenians and then halted. "As Philip's line faced the Athenians, he gave way and while the Athenians advanced hot-foot, retired step by step with his phalanx contracted and his men protected by a hedge of spears."[80] As Philip retreated, the Athenians moved forward out of the line and followed.

Philip withdrew slowly back and to his right until "gaining some high ground, he attacked the Athenians vigorously."[81] This high ground was probably "the elevation of a dyke that enclosed the waters of the Lykuressi stream when it was in flood."[82] Philip's retrograde movement lasted about thirty minutes and covered 150 meters to the rear and 50 meters to his right.[83] The time was enough for the Macedonian infantry advancing in the center and Alexander's cavalry advancing on the left, both of which lagged behind Philip at the oblique, to reach the allied line. Thus, when Philip stopped his retreat and began the attack, his infantry and cavalry made contact simultaneously all along the allied line. The entire allied front was suddenly engaged.

As soon as Alexander's cavalry came on line, it went immediately into the attack. According to Diodorus, "Alexander and his men were the first to force their way through those arrayed against them and put them to flight,"[84] and "first opened up a gap in the enemy line with the support of the many brave men contending by his side."[85] As they had done many times before, the fierce Macedonian cavalry cut through the infantry line, gaining the enemy rear in short order. Arrian, himself a Roman cavalry officer, tells us that Philip had trained his cavalry to employ the Thracian wedge formation, "the front tapering into a point that made it possible easily to cut through every hostile formation."[86] A Macedonian cavalry squadron in wedge formation had 120 horsemen.[87] A squadron was twenty ranks deep, with the last rank being the widest at twenty cavalrymen across, or a length of fifty meters.[88] Alexander could have deployed five cavalry wedges across the five hundred–meter front afforded him, or a force of six hundred horses, with adequate space between them for maneuver. This tactic left some fourteen hundred cavalrymen to be arranged in rectangular formations behind the line of wedges. Once the wedges had punched through the infantry line, the follow-on cavalry burst through in strength. We may reasonably take from Diodorus that Alexander commanded one of the cavalry wedges.

The preceding description of the battle of Chaeronea diverges from the usual descriptions offered. I have suggested that the reasons for Philip's advance, retreat, and counterattack were to loosen and disrupt the Athenian phalanx, rendering it easier to shatter upon counterattack, and to afford the rest of his infantry and cavalry the time to take their positions to attack the allies simultaneously all along the line. Instead, the traditional view is that Philip's maneuver was intended to draw the Athenian line forward and to the left and stretch the allied infantry line so that a gap opened at its far end. When this break occurred, the Sacred Band did not abandon its strong positions along the banks of the Cephissus to close it. Alexander's cavalry attacked through this breach, gaining the allied rear.[89]

The traditional explanation probably arose for two reasons. First, Diodorus's phrase "Alexander . . . first opened up a gap in the enemy line" establishes that a gap was created in the allied line. Second, our main sources for the battle, Diodorus and Polyaenus, were not military men and accepted the Greek and later Roman conventional wisdom that the cavalry could not penetrate the infantry phalanx by frontal assault. Thus, something other than Alexander's cavalry attack must have caused the break in the line. Neither Diodorus nor Polyaenus offers an explanation as to how the gap was created. The argument that it happened because the allied infantry line extended in response to Philip's tactical withdrawal appears to be a result of modern scholarship and not based on the evidence of the ancient texts.[90]

An analysis of the dynamics of an expanding infantry line shows that the length of Philip's tactical retreat was insufficient to create a gap in the three-kilometer allied infantry line. If Johannes Kromayer and Georg Veith are correct, Philip retreated 150 meters to the rear and 50 meters to his right over some thirty minutes.[91] The forward movement of the Athenian phalanx would have had no effect on the length of the three thousand–meter allied line. Instead, it would have simply pivoted slightly forward on its far end. The only movement that could have stretched the line to break was its fifty-meter shift to the Athenians' left as it followed Philip backward and to his right. A leftward movement of fifty meters would have forced the entire line to adjust by slightly more than 1 percent of its length. On average, then, to keep the line intact each soldier in the line would have had to move to his left a mere five inches, which is a shorter distance than we would expect to occur randomly in the normal shuffling of soldiers in a packed formation. The distance is simply insufficient to create a large enough gap for Alexander's cavalry squadrons to ride through. Even if one concedes that the allied line stretched and broke, the result would produce a gap of only fifty meters, which would only accommodate the width of a single Macedonian cavalry squadron arranged in Thracian formation. Alexander's successful cavalry attack against the allied infantry line, therefore, must have happened because of other reasons.

Philip's counterattack drove the Athenian phalanx back until it lost its cohesion and broke, trapping three thousand Athenian hoplites in a nearby cul-de-sac. A thousand of them were killed and two thousand taken prisoner.[92] The other men escaped over the Karata Pass, gaining safety in Labadea. The Macedonian infantry in the line's center held the Boeotians in place with a close-order fixing attack while Alexander's cavalry squadrons pushed through the allied line, swung to the right, and drove behind the Boeotian infantry, trapping them against the Macedonian line. With no escape, the Boeotians and Thebans suffered the heaviest casualties of all the allied contingents. Alexander led some cavalry squadrons to the left, trapping the Sacred Band against its own defensive positions. Then his cavalry fell upon it, killing every man. Plutarch tells us, "It is said, moreover, that the band was never beaten until the battle of Chaeronea; and when, after the battle, Philip was surveying the dead, he stopped at the place where the three hundred were lying, all where they had faced and met his *sarissae* with their armor, mingled one with another, he was amazed."[93]

Although to those involved the fight must have seemed to last an eternity, it was probably over within a few hours. If the Athenians, facing only Philip's pikemen and with a clear line of retreat, suffered 30 percent casualties, the other allied contingents must have experienced far greater losses. Deployed next to the destroyed Boeotians, the Achaeans must have also suffered greatly. The Acarnanians in the center of the line broke under the Macedonian infantry's attack and fled the battle. The remaining Boeotians' retreat was clogged by the fleeing Athenians and quickly blocked by Philip's advancing infantry. With no place to go, the Boeotians and Thebans suffered horribly until they surrendered on the field. With Athens defeated, only Thebes and the Boeotian League remained capable of opposing Philip; however, the destruction of their armies, along with many of their leading politicians, at Chaeronea greatly reduced this capability. Philip could have pursued the Athenians, killing many of their leaders, including Demosthenes and the members of the anti-Macedonian faction that had opposed him for so long; but Chaeronea was one of the few battles where Philip did not unleash a lethal pursuit. Philip had other things in mind for the Athenians.

Philip's victory at Chaeronea was a tactical masterpiece of planning, command, and timing. Until Chaeronea, Greek generals had fought in the ranks with their troops and often were in the front rank to set a brave example. Once the generals gave the order to advance, however, they were no longer able to exercise command and control over the battlefield or their troops.[94] Philip was the first Greek general to command his forces from outside the battle space, where he could orchestrate the timing and direction of his forces. For Philip's tactical plan to work at Chaeronea, he had to be in a position to carry out three tasks. First, he had to coordinate the movement of his light infantry. After eliminating the Athenian light infantry holding the acropolis hill on his right, his infantry then had to press forward and to the right to make room for the follow-on deployment of his heavy pike infantry. Next, he had to coordinate the movements of his own phalanx and the brigade on his immediate left to ensure that his retrograde movement did not lose contact with the main line, which would move forward at the oblique. Third, he had to be able to see Alexander's cavalry as it came on line and went into the attack so Philip could halt his retrograde movement and go on the offensive shortly after Alexander made contact with the enemy line.[95]

To accomplish these tasks Philip needed to see the battlefield and to communicate with his troop commanders either by voice or trumpet call.[96] He also had to move freely up and down the line, at least from his far right to his left where his Guard brigades joined the middle brigades. His bodyguards may have been used as messengers to carry instructions to commanders farther down the line. To do it all successfully, Philip had to be on horseback and not, as in some previous battles, on the ground with his elite infantry.[97] Mounted close behind and within earshot of the King's Guard and with his lateral movement preserved, Philip orchestrated the timing and maneuver of his key units. Philip's tactical command performance at Chaeronea was "an illustration of what could be done by the phalanx in the hands of a master."[98]

9 THE END OF PHILIP

With the battle won, Philip made no attempt to withdraw. He assembled his army and attended to the task of performing the rituals of the Greek warrior. The Macedonians collected their dead near the spot where Alexander's cavalry had destroyed the Sacred Band. They cremated the corpses along with their weapons and armor and buried their remains in a mound twenty-three feet high, mute testimony to the scope of Philip's victory. A tumulus of this height could hardly have contained the remains of more than one hundred or two hundred soldiers, a small price indeed for such a great victory. The Macedonian army paraded before the mound to honor their fallen comrades. Philip offered sacrifices to the gods in thanksgiving for his victory and later rewarded those troops who had distinguished themselves in battle. Afterward, Philip and his Macedonians sat on the plain of Chaeronea, an occupying army within a few days' march of Thebes and Athens.

THE AFTERMATH OF VICTORY

All great battles are fought for political goals, the armies being but means to larger ends. It is the degree to which a battle allows the political objectives of the victor to be achieved, more than the successful exercise of military technique, that permits history to define a battle as great. Chaeronea was a great battle precisely because it allowed Philip to finally achieve his most important political and strategic objective of unifying Greece under Macedonian hegemony. It is impossible to imagine Greek history from this time forward without Philip's victory at Chaeronea.

Philip's appreciation of the political context of his victory was evident in the vastly different ways in which he treated Athens and Thebes. To allay Athenian fears regarding his intentions, Philip sent Decades, one of the Athenian prisoners, to Athens to inform its assembly that Philip intended Athens no harm. Out of respect for the Athenian dead, "Philip gave the bodies of the slain for burial," had them cremated, and had an honor guard led by Alexander, Antipater, and Alcimachus carry their ashes to Athens. Philip also freed all Athenian prisoners of war without ransom.[1] Hammond observes that "such a tribute to a country defeated in war was unparalleled then and is unparalleled still."[2] The Athenians were so relieved that they raised a statue to Philip in the Agora.

Philip's treatment of Thebes stands in marked contrast to his treatment of Athens. He allowed the Theban dead to rot in the sun for several days, repeatedly denying Theban requests to recover their slain. When Philip finally allowed them to do so, he charged ransom not only for the Theban prisoners but for the corpses as well.[3] Perhaps because of their bravery or their reputation as the best soldiers in Greece, Philip treated the dead of the Sacred Band with more respect. Their bodies were gathered, laid out, and buried in seven rows.[4] Otherwise, Philip treated Thebes and its soldiers with undisguised contempt as befitted a treacherous ally that had broken the solemn oaths of a treaty.

Macedonia was now the preeminent power in Greece, and Philip intended to use that power to realize two strategic goals. He intended to impose a security regime on Greece that would guarantee Macedonian power for the foreseeable future and for his heirs. Further, he sought to establish the necessary conditions to carry out a successful invasion of Persia, which Isocrates had urged upon him years before as a way of unifying Greece. Isocrates felt the propensity of the Greek states to war with each other would be reduced if they engaged in a common effort to gain access to new lands and resources that would alleviate the chronic poverty that afflicted much of Greece.

No attempt to invade Persia could succeed, however, if the Greek states led a revolt against Macedonian power or formed alliances with each other or with Persia while Philip was away on campaign. Philip not only required the manpower of Greece to succeed against Persia, he also needed to ensure that the states would not attack one another or himself while he was away. Philip understood that many of the conflicts between the Greek states were rooted in genuine security and economic interests, and no institutional arrangement establishing a new security regime for Greece could hold for long unless it was based on a concrete recognition and accommodation of these interests. After Chaeronea, Philip set out to turn Greece into a quiescent ally by imposing Macedonian solutions to the security problems that concerned the major Greek states and by enforcing them with bilateral and common agreements backed by the power of the Macedonian army. In the weeks following Chaeronea, Philip began establishing the new order by concluding bilateral agreements with the major Greek states.

The new arrangements with Athens and Thebes were central to Philip's plan. An alliance with Athens had long been one of Philip's strategic objectives. Initially, Athens was Philip's primary means of balancing Theban power in central Greece. After Chaeronea, Philip wanted Athens in his camp for a more important reason. Philip needed the Athenian navy to control the sea after he landed in Asia to prevent the Persian navy's inevitable counterattack. Philip did not want the disruption of Persia at his back, invading Greece and encouraging the Greek states to revolt. Athens would also serve as the major logistics base for the invasion.[5] Philip's respectful treatment of the Athenian dead at Chaeronea was designed to convince Athens that its future lay in alliance with Macedonia and to abandon its anti-Macedonian sentiment.

Philip proposed a treaty of friendship and alliance in which he promised not to attack Athens or interfere with its domestic constitutional system. There were to be no purges of his political enemies. Indeed, Demosthenes, the leader of the anti-Macedonian faction and Philip's chief political enemy for more than a decade, was permitted to deliver the funeral oration over the Athenian dead. Philip promised Athens its independence and did not impose any Macedonian garrisons on it or its territory. Athens was required, however, to call its settlers home from the Chersonese and Thrace, thus ceding the settlements there to Philip, and to cancel its military alliances with these dependencies. Most importantly, though, Philip permitted Athens to maintain its large navy and retain control of Lemnos, Samos, Delos, and other islands where it had naval bases.[6] The treaty even prohibited any Macedonian trireme from entering the harbor at Piraeus.[7] As a result of these concessions, the Athenian navy continued to be the strongest navy in the Aegean, which, of course, was precisely what Philip needed it to be so it could protect his invasion forces from the Persian fleet.[8] On balance, then,

Athens was treated generously. Later it even entered the League of Corinth and resumed its participation in the religious affairs at Delphi. Even Demosthenes had to admit that Athens was now best served in alliance with Philip.

Closely related to the settlement with Athens was the agreement Philip imposed on Euboea. The island was a key communications route between northern and central Greece and had great strategic value for both Athens and Philip. Philip dissolved the alliance that Athens had forged with the Euboean League in 341 BCE to resist Philip's encroachments there. Under the leadership of Philip's partisans, the league was reconstituted without Athens. The strategic city of Chalcis technically remained independent, but Philip installed a Macedonian garrison in the city to ensure its loyalty. Philip now controlled the closest island to Athens from which, should the need arise, Macedonian troops could quickly intervene in Athenian affairs. It was a development not lost on the Athenians.

Unlike Athens, Philip had no interest in preserving Theban power. Not only had Thebes betrayed its alliance with Philip, but with Athens now firmly in the Macedonian camp, Thebes was also the only major power left in central Greece. Philip set out to reduce its authority and regional influence permanently. Justin tells us that "some of the chief men of their city, too, he put to death; others he banished, seizing upon the property of them all."[9] Pro-Macedonian politicians who had been exiled were recalled and reinstated. From these exiles Philip created a jury of three hundred to hold public trials of Theban officials. He replaced the democratic constitution with an oligarchic arrangement in which key posts were given to Philip's partisans.[10] Philip also forced Thebes to surrender the key frontier town of Oropus to Athens, Nicaea was returned to Locris, and a Macedonian garrison was installed in the Cadmea, the acropolis of Thebes.[11] The Boeotian League continued to exist, but changes in its constitution greatly reduced Theban influence in its affairs. Orchomenus, Plataea, and Thespiae—all formerly destroyed by Thebes—were rebuilt with Boeotian help and financing. They were also made members of the league as Philip's allies so they could act as a check on Thebes. Thebes was also required to relinquish any land that it had seized from Boeotian cities and was forbidden to participate in the Amphictyony.[12]

The remaining issue in Philip's new security arrangements in central Greece was what to do with Phokis. Philip's idea was to rebuild Phokis so it could act as a check on Theban power and serve as a buffer between Boeotia and Thessaly. To this end, he revoked the harsh penalties the Amphictyonic

League imposed after the Sacred War and allowed the reconcentration of its population into cities. The fine was reduced to ten talents a year, and the rebuilding of its towns and cities, an indication of Phokis's sovereignty, began immediately. Philip's political partisans took advantage of Philip's lenient treatment, and many were elected to public office, consolidating their hold on the government.[13] The reduction of Thebes, the weakening of the Boeotian League, the alliance with Athens, the installation of Macedonian garrisons at key points, the rebuilding of Phokis, and Macedonia's preeminent position on the Amphictyonic Council all strengthened Philip's political, diplomatic, and military control of central Greece.

The groundwork for dealing with the other Greek states had been laid by a decade of Macedonian propaganda designed to win the goodwill of the Greeks. The result of this effort, and Philip's adroit handling of the friends he had established over the years, was now put to good use. With the exception of Sparta, almost every state of some importance had within it a group of pro-Macedonian partisans who could be relied on either out of conviction or self-interest to support Philip's ambitions. In state after state, these partisans were either installed by Philip or elected. Once in office, they acted in typically Greek fashion and brought their enemies to book by confiscation, exile, and execution. In this way Philip was able to enforce the new security arrangements with the support of friendly domestic regimes. At the same time, he escaped blame for the revenge that the factions typically took out on one another.

The states of the northern Peloponnese—Megara, Corinth, and the Achaean League—had all been members of the Athenian coalition opposing Philip, but individually they were all too small to mount significant opposition to his plans for the Peloponnesus. Corinth was the most important because of its considerable strategic value as the region's traditional "gatekeeper." When news of Philip's victory at Chaeronea reached Corinth, the city prepared for a siege. But when Philip's army approached, Corinth surrendered without a fight possibly because of a domestic revolution led by Philip's political partisans within the city. With his Macedonian friends already in control, no penalties were imposed on the city except that the Acrocorinth was garrisoned by Macedonian troops.[14] Megara, too, saw a change in government, with pro-Macedonian partisans carrying the day, and the city quickly surrendered to Philip. The Achaean League also surrendered without resistance but was still allowed to exist. The league also formally ceded the city of Naupactus, which Parmenio had captured a few months earlier and turned over to the Aetolians, its new rulers.[15]

Philip now turned his attention to Sparta, the most powerful state in the Peloponnesus. Sparta had not joined the Athenian League or taken any hostile action against Philip. Yet Philip could hardly have permitted Sparta to maintain its position in the region if he were going to impose a common peace on Greece. To do so might invite the Persians to try and entice Sparta against Philip once he had left for Asia and precipitate a revolt at his back. Sparta and its neighbors were constantly in conflict because Sparta needed access to the outside world and the fertile lands on its border to feed its people. Sparta's enemies in the struggle for access to the lands and mountain passes were the border towns of Argos, Arcadia, and Messene. Immediately after the victory at Chaeronea, the three towns approached Philip and sought his support for their claims against Sparta. After settling events in Corinth, Philip marched into Argos, the home of his ancestors and now governed by Philip's partisans. Philip took up the cause of his ancestral home and offered to negotiate a solution with Sparta. When Sparta refused, Philip marched into Laconia with the Macedonian army in autumn of 338 BCE and "laid the region waste." The Spartans were also deprived of their border territories. Philip did not, however, attempt to destroy the Spartan state. His objective was to weaken Sparta relative to its smaller neighbors and prevent its dominance of the region. He succeeded.[16]

To the west, Philip had long had his eyes on Ambracia as the key to controlling Macedonia's southwestern border. Ambracia, a wedge of land between Epirus, Aetolia, and Acarnania, offered Macedonia an outlet to the Ionian Sea. In 342 BCE Philip had moved toward taking the city during his larger campaign against Epirus, but he had to withdraw when the Athenians and Corinthians sent troops to protect the city's liberty. After Chaeronea, Philip's pro-Macedonian partisans either seized the city or were elected to control it, and they surrendered to Philip without resistance. Philip installed a garrison, and his political enemies were driven off to take refuge in Athens. Macedonia's southwestern border was now secure to the Ionian Sea.[17]

Philip used this series of bilateral agreements with the individual city-states to construct a new balance of power and security regime in the different regions of Greece that were important to Macedonian security and Philip's plan to invade Persia. He took great pains to avoid the bloodletting that had often accompanied the victories of Greek states in the past. To be sure, his partisans in various states often resorted to the usual cruelties that accompanied changes of regime in Greek states, but at least the blood was not on Philip's hands. Judged by the standards of city-state warfare in the past, Philip's treatment of his enemies was generous, humane, moderate, and conciliatory. Justin says Philip "managed his conquest that none might think of him as a conqueror."[18] It was strategically brilliant how Philip defined and imposed new security arrangements on the Greek states. By creating new balances of power in the various regions, the major powers in each region—Athens, Sparta, and Thebes—were hemmed in by new coalitions of smaller states that were backed by the power of the Macedonian army. Philip had, in effect, created a new security status quo for the Greek states. The problem he faced now was how to ensure that it endured.

In late 338 BCE Philip issued more an order than an invitation for the city-states to send representatives to a conference at Corinth. The choice of Corinth was highly symbolic, for it had been there in 480 BCE that the Greek states came together to form the common alliance to resist Xerxes' invasion.[19] Philip intended to accomplish something unknown in Greek experience: to convene a meeting of enemies and friends alike to consider the victor's proposals and to plan their own futures. Philip wanted to guarantee the new security regime through a series of institutional arrangements that formalized and regulated the states' behavior in their dealings with one another; he wanted to prevent a return to the frequent civil wars that Plato said "were everyone's lifelong companion" in Greece. Philip aimed to propose a common peace for all Greece.

Justin tells us that Philip was courteous to the delegates and listened intently to their concerns, and there was wide agreement that they should end the revolutionary strife and warfare that plagued Greece. Only Sparta refused to attend, asserting "what was imposed by a conqueror was not peace but servitude."[20] It was agreed that a general framework to protect the peace should be created and that a governing common council should be formed in which each state was represented according to its military and naval power and size (proportional representation). The council was to have wide military, financial, and judicial powers, and its decisions were binding and not subject to veto by the member states. In foreign policy, the council could declare war, conscript forces, and banish or punish offending member states.

Later a permanent administrative structure was inaugurated to call and preside over meetings and to oversee the implementation of the council's decisions on a regular basis. The delegates returned to their states over the winter to consult with their political establishments and consider the outline of Philip's proposal.

In the spring of 337 BCE the delegates returned to Corinth for another meeting and voted to approve Philip's plan. Interestingly, one of the first decisions the council made was to confirm the new status quo arrangements that Philip had already imposed, legitimizing the imposition of the Macedonian garrisons in Ambracia, Thebes, Chalcis, and Acrocorinth and the redrawing of the new frontiers in favor of the smaller states around Sparta.[21] At a later meeting in the summer, the council also established an alliance of itself, its member states, and Macedonia "for all time." The council then authorized the creation of a common armed force drawn from each member's military forces in proportionate numbers to enforce its edicts. Philip was elected its hegemon, and his powers were specified in "the agreements with Philip." In this way, Philip imposed a common peace on Greece, creating a "community of Greeks," or what modern scholars came to call the League of Corinth.[22]

The league was not limited to the former belligerents but was open to all states that agreed to abide by its laws. Thus the specific obligations that the league's members undertook are of interest because they indicate the legal means through which Philip would govern Greece as a single community for the first time in its history. These commitments also prohibited the behavior that commonly caused domestic revolutions and stasis and conflicts between the states. The obligations of the member states were as follows:

- No state was to be compelled to join the common peace against its will.
- All were to abide by the treaties (presumably the ones Philip had already imposed on various states).
- All were to respect each other's liberty, autonomy, and territorial integrity.
- None were to make war against each other unless one of the signatories violated a clause of the agreement.
- None were to interfere with the shipping of another signatory or force their ships into ports other than their destination (piracy).
- All were to abide by the resolutions of the council of plenipotentiary representatives of the signatory states.

- All were to carry out the hegemon's orders.
- None were to give asylum to political exiles or to assist them against the governments of their homelands.
- All were to respect all the constitutions in existence at the time of the pact's signing, with the exception of those of tyrannies.
- None were to redistribute landed property, cancel debts, or free slaves.
- None were to pass laws inflicting punishment by death or exile or confiscation of property for offenses that until then had carried a lighter penalty.
- None were to commit hostile acts against Philip or his heirs.
- All were to cooperate in suppressing any violation of the pact and in punishing the offenders.[23]

The position and powers of the hegemon were central to the success of Philip's new political order. Philip was not a signatory to the pact but the guarantor of the peace itself, of which the council and its obligation were but a part. As hegemon, Philip was also *strategos autokrator*, or "commander in chief" with full powers, who could call up the league's forces to use against any member state that violated its obligations or to meet any foreign threat. If need be, Philip could use the Macedonian army in any manner he chose on his own authority.[24] Philip took great care to always act under the council's authority, but the obligation of the signatories not to "commit hostile acts against Philip or his heirs" essentially made it illegal, or even a cause of war, for a member state to oppose Philip.[25] Paradoxically, Philip had fostered the very union of states that the Athenians had sought and failed to organize against him, and there was little risk now that the new community of Greeks might turn against him. The ultimate guarantee of Philip's control of the new order was, of course, the Macedonian army.

It is reasonable to say that Philip produced a community of Greeks (*to koinon ton Hellenon*) by making the various peoples and polities live within a collective constitutional order with common laws and obligations supported by effective administrative and enforcement mechanisms, including the means to defend itself from internal and external threats. Federal "leagues" of city-states had been attempted before in Greece, but none with the scope of Philip's League of Corinth. Philip as hegemon provided the political leadership of the new order, and his plan to undertake a common effort against Persia provided both a purpose and a future for it. Philip's ambitions had transformed the Macedonian empire and the plethora of warring Greek states into the first national state in the history of Europe.

The new state was organized on a federal model of decentralized authority. Although obligated to observe common federal or national commitments, the individual states were free to organize themselves politically along democratic or oligarchic lines; to maintain their own customs, deities, and language; to write their own local laws; to raise and maintain their own armies; and to impose their own taxes. Each was self-governing and independent, as it had been before, with the exception that it could not make war on another state with impunity.[26] Even the federal obligation to provide military forces for the common defense varied in number and kind—infantry, cavalry, naval vessels—from state to state. The new Greek national state was very similar to the federal nation that emerged in the United States following the Civil War of 1860–65. The experience of that war led the central government to place limits on the power of the individual states to treat their citizens arbitrarily, and the states cannot use force against the central government or other state governments to achieve political ends.

Out of the cauldron of civic violence there began to emerge a new sense of national identity and nationhood. Both American and Greek self-awareness of being a nation, of being one people with a common fate, developed out of the common experience of civil war that produced a new political order. That sense of being one people allowed each Greek state and its citizens to contribute their values, experiences, traditions, resources, and talents to a new national identity and psyche. It was not until Philip's reign that a common sentiment of what it meant to be a Hellene reached all Greeks. Alexander took this culture of Hellenism with him to Asia, but it was Philip, as leader of the Greeks, who created it and in doing so made the Hellenistic Age possible.[27]

In the autumn of 337 BCE the council was again called into session to hear Philip's proposal to invade Persia and punish the Persians for the acts of sacrilege they had committed against Greek sanctuaries.[28] Philip had been technically at war with Persia since the siege of Perinthus in 340 BCE, when Persia had sent supplies to Perinthus and military forces into Thrace.[29] The council authorized Philip to make preparations for the invasion. In the spring of 336 BCE, Philip sent an advanced expeditionary force of ten thousand Macedonian troops under the command of three generals—Parmenio, Attalus, and Amyntas—into Asia Minor.[30] Landing at Ephesus, the Macedonians were welcomed as liberators and marched up country, freeing some Greek cities from Persian subjugation as they went. At Magnesia, the Macedonians were met by the Persians under the command of the Greek mercenary Memnon and suffered some sort of reversal that halted their advance for the time being. Nonetheless, the expedition had established the bridgehead for the follow-on force, which Philip intended to lead in late summer. In the spring of 336 BCE, Philip consulted the Delphic oracle about the Persian campaign. He asked the Pythian priestess whether he would "conquer the king of the Persians." The oracle's response was, "Garlanded is the bull. Fulfillment is here. One there is who will strike the victim."[31] Encouraged, Philip prepared to take his army against the Persians.

A year earlier, in the spring of 337 BCE, Philip acquired another wife, a Macedonian woman named Cleopatra, the ward of a powerful baron named Attalus.[32] While some sources attribute Philip's marriage to so young a woman (she was, perhaps, twenty-two years old) as the folly of a middle-aged man, in fact Philip had sound reasons for marrying Cleopatra. First, she was of child-bearing age. Philip knew that if both he and Alexander were killed during the Persian campaign, Macedonia might well come apart in civil war over the succession unless a legitimate heir, even a child, could claim the assembly's loyalty. Second, Cleopatra was a Macedonian, unlike all but one of Philip's other wives. An heir of Macedonian lineage could more easily lay claim to the assembly's support in the event of Philip's and Alexander's deaths. Philip was hardly the type to lose his head over a woman, and his marriage to Cleopatra made good sense.

After the wedding feast, the males gathered in a typical Macedonian drinking bout. At some point, Attalus, Cleopatra's guardian, raised a toast to the king and his new wife, adding that now Macedonia might have a legitimate heir.[33] Alexander took the comment as a smear on his own legitimacy and hurled a drinking cup at Attalus, calling on Philip to reprimand him. The drunken Philip took Attalus's side in the quarrel and ordered Alexander to apologize. Alexander refused. Philip drew his sword and moved in Alexander's direction, only to stumble and fall to the floor. In a rage, Alexander left the room. The next day he collected his mother and left the court. Olympias went to Epirus and Alexander set off, "going among the Illyrians."

Upon sober reflection, Philip realized the damage he had done and moved to reconcile with Olympias and Alexander who, in due course, returned to Pella. Justin says that Olympias tried to persuade her brother, Alexander, the king of Epirus, to declare war on Philip, and Alexander may have been trying to raise support among the Illyrians for a similar venture. Perhaps to counter any such threat, Philip arranged for his and Olympias's daughter, who was also named Cleopatra, to marry Alexander of Epirus. In July 336 BCE the wedding was held in Aegae.

The day after the marriage ceremony, Philip was to preside over athletic games. A grand procession would take place beforehand in the theater at Aegae. The procession began at sunrise with statues of the twelve Olympian gods carried into the theater. A statue of Philip was carried in close behind. Then, according to Diodorus, came Alexander the heir and Alexander of Epirus walking ahead of Philip.[34] "Philip himself entered, wearing a white cloak. He ordered his bodyguards to follow, removed at some distance from him, as an indication to everyone that he had no need of the protection of guards. Such was the degree of preeminence that he had attained."[35] When Philip reached the center of the theater, he stopped and faced the cheering crowd.

Suddenly, a figure rushed forward and stabbed Philip in the chest, "driving the blow right through the ribs" and "laid him out prostrate and lifeless."[36] Philip's blood stained his white cloak red. The king's bodyguards rushed to his side, but it was too late. Philip died almost immediately. The assassin "sprinted for the gates to the horses he had made ready for his escape" with the bodyguards Leonnatus, Perdiccas, and Attalus in pursuit.[37] The assassin, Diodorus notes,

> had a head start in the pursuit, and would have succeeded in mounting his horse before they could stop him, had he not entangled his sandal in a vine and fallen. As he was getting up from the ground, Perdiccas and those with him seized him, ran him through, and killed him. . . . Such was the end of Philip who, in the course of a reign of twenty four years, had been the greatest of the kings of Europe of his day.[38]

WHO KILLED PHILIP?

Our sources for Philip's assassination are generally poor because none of them could have known whether anyone else was involved in the scheme. All the sources do agree on the assassin's identity: it was Pausanias of Orestes, a canton of Upper Macedonia.[39] Pausanias was able to get close enough to Philip to strike him down because Pausanias had recently been appointed

Map 9. *The Macedonian Empire at the Time of Philip's Death (336 BCE)*

one of Philip's bodyguards.[40] It is unlikely, however, that Pausanias was one of the seven senior trusted somatophylakes who usually protected Philip. More likely Pausanias was one of the *doryphoroi* of the royal hypaspistais,[41] an elite unit of a thousand men called the Royal Hypaspist Guard. Since the entire unit could not have been present that day, it is probable that only a few selected guards were present, one of them Pausanias. Diodorus tells us that Philip himself had "promoted him [Pausanias] to a more honorable position among the bodyguards."[42] Thus Philip had put his own assassin in a position to kill him.

Why did Pausanias kill Philip? According to all three sources, the motive was personal anger and revenge because "Philip allowed him to be outrageously treated by Attalus and company."[43] Diodorus and Justin tell us the "outrage" involved Pausanias's rape by Attalus and his cronies who then turned Pausanias over to the muleteers for further abuse. When Pausanias was a page, Philip had been attracted to him "because of his good looks," and they had engaged in a homosexual affair. After some time, Philip was attracted to another page with the same name and abandoned Pausanias for his new lover. The assassin was angry at being jilted and began to torment the new lover, calling him "an effeminate who was willing to submit to the erotic advances of anyone who desired to initiate them," that is, a male prostitute.[44] The second Pausanias complained to his friend Attalus and threatened to commit suicide. Supposedly, he did so later in a battle against Pleurias of the Illyrians by stepping in front of Philip and "submitting his own body to all the blows aimed at the king."[45] For some reason, Attalus decided to avenge the young man's death.[46] He lured the first Pausanias to his house, where "after filling him with vast quantities of unmixed wine, [he] handed his body over to his stablemen to abuse sexually in drunken rape."[47]

Pausanias was enraged at the assault and appealed to his former lover, Philip, to punish Attalus. While Philip was angry at the enormity of the crime, he refused to punish Attalus "because of his kinship" (Attalus had adopted Cleopatra, Philip's new wife, and was therefore Philip's father-in-law) and "his present need for his services." Philip had already chosen Attalus to command the advanced expedition to Persia. Philip tried to appease Pausanias, however, by "conferring on him valuable gifts and promoted him to a more honorable position among the bodyguards."[48] Aristotle tells us that "the attack on Philip by Pausanias took place because he allowed him to be outraged by Attalus and his henchmen."[49] Seething with anger, Pausanias killed Philip for not punishing Attalus and avenging him.

An important question in determining Pausanias's motives is, when did the abuse at the hands of Attalus take place? Historian E. Badian's view that it took place eight years before the killing cannot be accepted.[50] Badian's dating is based on the time of the Illyrian war (345 BCE) when the insulted Pausanias supposedly committed suicide by exposing himself needlessly in battle. It is difficult to believe that Pausanias's act of vengeful anger occurred some eight years after the event. Diodorus's account of Pausanias's suicide suggests it happened during a war with Pleurias the Illyrian, but there is no evidence of this war. Diodorus may have confused Pleurias with Pleuratos whom Philip had fought in 345 BCE. The most logical interpretation of Diodorus is that Pausanias was raped not long before Philip's murder.[51] Philip married Cleopatra in the spring of 337 BCE, making Attalus his kin, and Attalus left for Asia in the spring of 336 BCE. It was, perhaps, sometime during that year that Pausanias was raped and perhaps only a few months or even weeks before Attalus departed. This timing would account for the rawness of Pausanias's rage.

Immediately following the assassination, the Macedones from Aegae and the surrounding regions were summoned to the assembly under arms to elect a new king. Antipater presented Alexander to the assembly, which then elected Alexander as the new king. A group of leading Macedones donned their armor and escorted Alexander to the palace. Alexander was suspicious of the circumstances surrounding Philip's death. Diodorus tells us that there was more than one horse waiting at the gates for Pausanias. This detail implied that there may have been a second assassin waiting to kill Philip or, more ominously, to kill Alexander as well and exterminate the entire royal house at a single blow. Alexander was supposed to have entered the arena next to Philip, but Philip had changed plans and sent him on ahead. If there was another assassin who did not have opportunity to strike, he was still out there. Alexander ordered an inquiry into the murder.[52]

That Pausanias killed Philip is beyond doubt. Whether the assassination was part of a larger conspiracy has intrigued historians ever since. The usual suspects in any conspiracy to kill Philip are Olympias, Alexander, some or all of the sons of Aeropus of Lyncestis, Amyntas, and the Persian king Darius. By examining the case for and against each alleged conspirator, it is possible to come to some sort of reasonable conclusion as to whom, if anyone, may have been behind Philip's murder.

A few weeks after the murder, the assembly met in its constitutional role as jury in cases of treason. After due deliberation, the jury found all those around Philip that day innocent. Suspicion fell upon the sons of Aeropus, however. The men were either heirs to the Lyncestian royal house or lesser members of the Argead royal house of Philip. Two of the three sons of Aeropus—Heromenes and Arrhabaeus—were accused, found guilty, and executed.[53] The third son, Alexandros Lyncestes, Antipater's son-in-law, was found innocent, swore loyalty to the new king, and was permitted to live. We know nothing about the ambitions of the Lyncestian royal house at the time. Whatever these men's ambitions, they had little to gain by killing Philip when he might more likely die in battle in Asia. If they desired to replace Philip on the throne or to raise a rebellion against him, it would have been easier to accomplish both after Philip had left for Asia.[54]

Another suspect was Amyntas, the son of King Perdiccas III and Philip's nephew, whom Philip had displaced as heir when the assembly elected him king twenty-three years earlier. Amyntas was a respected member of the royal family, married to Philip's daughter Cynane, and demonstrated no discernible political ambitions. If Philip and Alexander were killed in Asia, however, Amyntas would likely have become king as the last surviving son of King Perdiccas. Why, then, not wait to see if both survived the war? Amyntas was surely astute enough to understand that murdering Philip risked destabilizing the Macedonian state and provoking a revolt in Greece as well. Amyntas had nothing to gain by murdering Philip.

Olympias, Philip's wife, became the most frequently mentioned suspect by later Greek and Roman historians. Their belief that she was involved in Philip's murder stemmed from the traditional and terribly warped Greek and Roman views of monarchy, Macedonians as barbarians, the role of women per se, and the misunderstanding of the practice of polygamy in the Macedonian royal house.[55] Olympias could hardly have been motivated by jealously after being married to a man who had six other wives already. Moreover, any new son born of Philip's recent marriage to Cleopatra could not threaten Alexander's claim as heir, and no evidence suggests that Philip ever changed his mind about having Alexander succeed him. There was no apparent challenge to Olympias's position as mother of the next king. Except for her son, she was isolated at court, however, and would have had few allies to protect her if any involvement in Philip's murder became known. Olympias had no significant motive to kill Philip and every reason for him to live.

The same is true for Alexander. Despite his jealousy of his father's achievements and the sometimes violent arguments between the two, Alexander had every reason to believe that he would succeed Philip. Moreover, Alexander was hardly beloved of Philip's barons, particularly Parmenio and Attalus. It might be surmised Attalus also had an interest in Philip's death, for if Cleopatra's son was named an infant king, Attalus would be named regent as the child's blood relative. If Alexander was known to have been involved in the king's murder, some barons would likely have moved quickly against him out of loyalty and vengeance for the killing of their Homeric chief. If Alexander wanted his father dead, he had a better chance of seeing him killed in battle or even killing Philip himself in the midst of a battle.

One historian has suggested that Philip had decided that Alexander would not accompany him to Asia; instead, he was to stay behind as regent of Macedonia and deputy hegemon of the league.[56] If true, Philip's decision, along with appointing Attalus commander of the advance force, may have convinced Alexander that his father intended to deprive him of his chance for military honor and glory. It is certainly plausible that Philip may have reckoned that it was unwise to risk both his life and that of his heir on the grounds that if both were killed the Macedonian empire would disintegrate. While the possibility is plausible, no evidence in the sources supports it. We do not know whether Philip intended to leave Alexander behind. If he did, however, there was still a good chance that Philip might be killed and Alexander made king simply by staying in Macedonia.

In her excellent work on Philip's murder, Elizabeth Carney suggests that "too little attention has been paid to the timing and place of the murder."[57] Regarding its timing, the question is not who benefited from Philip's death so much as who suffered if he lived? Philip was killed in July, just before taking command of the invasion force and leading it into Asia. It is a sound inference, then, that whoever killed Philip either wanted to stop the invasion or, conversely, was completely indifferent to the impact of the king's death on the planned invasion. One important fact is that Philip was killed in a public place. This point suggests that whoever wanted him dead did not have private access to him; otherwise, the murder could have been more easily accomplished and with a greater chance of escaping detection.[58] Olympias, Alexander, and Amyntas, as members of the royal family, all had easy access to Philip in more private and secure settings. Any one of them could have killed him even as he slept. To kill Philip in a public place made no sense for any of these possible conspirators. Finally, Pausanias had horses waiting for him to use in his escape. This planned getaway suggests Pausanias was no martyr to insanity or ideology but someone who wanted to kill Philip and live. But where would he escape? Where in Greece could Pausanias hope to find sanctuary from Macedonian vengeance? These observations raise doubts about a conspiracy carried out by the usual suspects and point instead to an assassination organized or encouraged from outside Macedonia.

The most likely suspect is Darius, the Persian king.[59] The threat of a Macedonian invasion was of great concern to Persia, whose domestic problems had seriously weakened its ability to resist. Two of its satraps in Egypt and Babylon were in open revolt, and the royal house was in shambles. In 338 BCE Bagoas, a court eunuch, killed King Artaxerxes and his two older sons and put the youngest son, Arses, on the throne. Two years later Bagoas killed Arses and all his children. Bagoas next selected Darius Codomannus, a collateral member of the royal family, and installed him on the throne. Darius then killed Bagoas. Darius came to the throne probably in April or May of 336 BCE while Philip's advance expedition was in Asia. The grave concern with which Darius viewed Philip's ambitions can be inferred from one of his first acts after coming to power: he ordered his satraps to make contact with Demosthenes and offer him money to detain "the Macedonian" from invading Persia by causing trouble in Greece.[60] When this plan failed, Darius may have turned to assassination.

From Darius's perspective, murdering Philip had several things to recommend it. First, if Philip's death did not stop the invasion, then it would at least postpone it for a time, as indeed it did. Darius needed time to settle his domestic problems and consolidate his hold on power. Second, Philip's death might touch off a dynastic struggle within Macedonia in which Alexander might lose. Philip's death did in fact result in a purge of powerful Macedonian nobles (Attalus, Parmenio, the Lycestian royal house) and even members of the royal family itself (Amyntas, Cleopatra, and her baby). Unfortunately for Darius, however, Alexander emerged the winner. Third, Philip's death might encourage the revolt of the Greek city-states. Thebes did revolt, causing Alexander to destroy the city and postpone the invasion again. Finally, with Macedonia and Persia already at war, the beauty of a Persian conspiracy to murder Philip was that Persia risked nothing in the attempt.

If Persia had sufficient reason to kill Philip, did it have the means to do so? Here again the answer is yes. The first problem in a successful assassination is gaining general access to the target in order to determine a specific time and place to strike. Persia had open access to Philip's court. Persian influence in the Macedonian court reached back two centuries when Macedonia had been a Persian vassal state. Contacts between Macedonian nobles, the royal family, and intermarriages with Persian princes and nobles were common. A number of Persian nobles with their entourages took up residences in Philip's court for years at a time.⁶¹ Philip's court adopted various features of the Persian court, including a royal chancellery, a court nobility recruited partly from foreigners (including, of course, Persians), an elite corps of battle guards, personal bodyguards, royal pages, and even a royal harem.⁶² The loyalty of the Persians at the Macedonian court should have been suspect from the beginning. These people also served as sources of information about goings-on in Macedonia, including, no doubt, knowledge of Pausanias's rape and anger. No one in Macedonia would have found it strange that Persia might try to assassinate Philip. It was commonly believed throughout Greece that Jason of Pherae had been murdered with Persian complicity in 370 BCE. And just as Philip had, Jason had publicly announced his intention to lead the Greeks against Persia.

A political murder orchestrated from afar requires knowing specifically when and where the target might be accessible to the assassin. Paradoxically, Philip himself provided this critical information to his killers. Philip announced the date and planned the ceremonies that would accompany his daughter's wedding months in advance. In a break with Macedonian tradition, Philip invited envoys from the Greek states, delegates from the Balkan dependencies, friends from abroad, including Persian friends, as well as important Macedonians to the wedding.⁶³ This information provided Persian agents with an opportunity to reach their target, albeit in a public place, under cover of being members of an entourage of some visiting Persian wedding guest. Or the Persians may have already had someone in place in the Macedonian court to recruit Pausanias as the assassin.

Recruiting an assassin is no easy task, but in the case of Pausanias, circumstances may have made it somewhat easier. What happened to Pausanias was no secret and undoubtedly became the subject of court gossip, jokes, and derision. Pausanias was socially isolated and an object of ridicule. It would not have been difficult for a Persian agent to befriend him, offer him sympathy, become his confidant, and feed the outrage with the "legend" that Philip was to blame for what had happened to him. At some point the subject of revenge would have been raised. And here Pausanias's new friend could offer him something no one else could, namely, a sanctuary to which he could flee and live out his life in safety and honor in the Persian court. A Persian agent may even have provided the horses for Pausanias's escape. Pausanias was the perfect tool, already psychologically disposed against the target with the ability to get close enough to strike the lethal blow.

A good argument can be made that the Persians had stronger motives than any of the other suspects for wanting Philip dead. The public place and timing of the murder also point to Persia more than to Alexander, Olympias, or anyone else in Macedonia. Philip's assassination did, in fact, succeed in delaying the invasion, provoking a dynastic struggle, and stimulating a revolt in Greece. In this sense, whoever killed Philip achieved all the goals that Persia would have set for itself if it had indeed intended to murder Philip. Within a year, however, it was clear that Alexander had succeeded his father and planned on carrying out the invasion. Darius reacted to the renewed threat by offering three hundred talents to support a Greek revolt against Macedonia that would keep Alexander in Greece and out of Asia.[64]

Darius may also have attempted to set yet another assassination plot in motion, this time with Alexander as the target. In 335 BCE Amyntas was charged with treason, found guilty, and executed. Plutarch suggests that other discontented Macedonians also plotted against Alexander. One of Amyntas's close friends, also named Amyntas (the son of Antiochos), fled to Persia to escape the same fate as his namesake. According to Arrian, he had established communications between the Persian king and Alexandros Lyncestes, the surviving brother of the two Lyncestian men who had been executed for complicity in Philip's death almost immediately after the murder. In the winter of 334 BCE, Darius sent an agent, Sisines by name, to offer the Macedonian throne to Alexandros if he would kill Alexander. Sisines was captured and the plot revealed. Alexandros was immediately removed from his important post as commander of the Thessalian cavalry, and in 333 BCE he was arrested for treason and executed.[65]

Alexander himself accused the Persians of being involved in his father's murder. Arrian says that in a letter to Darius, Alexander charged the Persian king with Philip's murder, saying, "My father was killed by assassins whom as you openly boasted in your letters, you yourselves hired to commit the crime."[66] Some scholars dismiss Alexander's letter as self-justifying propaganda on the grounds that Alexander himself was involved in the conspiracy. And perhaps so, for the evidence for any conspiracy is largely circumstantial and no suspect can be entirely excluded. There is, however, a much stronger case for the Persians' instigation of Philip's murder than can be assembled for Alexander.

Perhaps it does not matter who killed Philip. What matters is that one of the greatest generals, statesmen, tacticians, and strategists of antiquity was no more.

GREATER THAN ALEXANDER?

This book's claim that Philip of Macedonia was the greatest general in Greece invites the question of whether Philip was greater than Alexander. Alexander's exploits were recorded early on by ancient historians so that even in ancient times he had already become the great romantic warrior hero for kings and generals to emulate.[67] The theme of Alexander's greatness survived the ages almost unchallenged, arriving in modern times largely intact. One consequence was to neglect Philip's contributions to Alexander's accomplishments and to assess Philip's own accomplishments as they compare with Alexander's. It has been commonplace for Alexander's supporters to assert, usually in passing, that Alexander's "inheritance" from Philip was important without, however, examining that inheritance in detail. In fact, Philip's legacy was so significant that without it, there would have been no Alexander the Great.

Alexander's opportunity for greatness began with a single truth: Philip was a great national king who fashioned the first national territorial state in Europe, uniting disparate peoples under Macedonian leadership into a powerful national political entity. Philip enlarged, urbanized, and developed Macedonia's natural and human resources to a degree never seen before in Greece or elsewhere in the West. In doing so, Philip made Macedonia the wealthiest and most resource-rich state in Greece. With Macedonia as his national power base, Philip expanded his sphere of political and military dominance into the first great European land empire in history, uniting all of Greece into a single political entity with common political institutions and a single constitution. It was Philip's wealth and imperial state that provided the material resources—ships, food, troops, reserve manpower, military equipment, money, and animals—that made Alexander's successful assault on the western half of the Persian Empire possible.

The composition of the expeditionary force that Alexander took to Persia amply illustrates the extensive resources Philip's new imperial state had provided. Alexander's army included 12,000 Macedonian infantry (phalanx and Guards brigades); 7,000 Greek hoplites drawn from the League of Corinth's troops; 7,000 troops from the subject tribes, including light cavalry, peltasts, javelin men, 1,000 archers, and Agrianian mounted javelineers; and 5,000 mercenaries (heavy infantry). He had an additional 11,000 or so troops already in Ionia as the advance expeditionary force sent under the joint command of Attalus and Parmenio. Alexander also took with him 1,800

Macedonian cavalry, including the elite Companion cavalry; 1,800 Thessalian heavy cavalry; 900 Thracian and Paeonian scouts; and 600 league cavalry, in addition to the 1,000 cavalry already in country with the advance expedition.[68] Alexander's force amounted to 49,100 men. Usually not mentioned but surely present were Philip's siege engineers and sappers. Philip's establishment of the Macedonian empire made raising such large numbers of troops and equipment possible.

Raising and deploying such a large force were achievements themselves. Sustaining this force's manpower levels in the field was quite another. Alexander's campaigns lasted for a decade and covered ten thousand miles of marching and fighting. His army would have been worn to helplessness without some system of manpower replacement. While it is true that Alexander made some use of Persian and tribal troops, he did so only minimally. Most of Alexander's replacements during a decade of war came from Macedonia, sent by Antipater, who had been left behind as regent. Often these troop replacements exceeded ten thousand men at a time and, in one instance, nineteen thousand. Philip had introduced the system of nationwide recruitment and training of Macedonian militia troops that made it possible to provide large numbers of trained and disciplined soldiers to Alexander on a regular basis. No Greek state other than Macedonia had such a large and comprehensive system of military recruitment and training, and none could have sustained Alexander's army in the field for so long.

It is often overlooked that wars and campaigns take place within a political context; thus, they require more than armies, troops, and equipment. Alexander's campaign against Persia would not have been possible had Philip not first established a civic peace among the warring Greek states. More than anything, Philip's peace and its accompanying guarantee that the Greek states would observe their obligations to the league enabled Alexander to lead an attack on Persia. Without the guarantee of peace among the Greek states, no commander would have dared risk invading Persia while exposing himself to a revolt or an attack in his rear. Without Athenian assurances that its navy would oppose any Persian attempt to attack Greece by sea while Alexander was in the field, Alexander's expedition risked being cut off and destroyed piecemeal. Even the crossing itself depended on Philip's previous successes. Alexander crossed into Asia at the Hellespont. He could only do so because Philip had previously secured Thrace and the Chersonese in a yearlong military campaign and built the strategic platform from which Alexander could launch his invasion.

The strategic vision of taking a Greek army into Asia and conquering the great king of Persia was far more Philip's than Alexander's. The idea had been around for decade long time, espoused by such men as Isocrates as a way of stopping Greek civil strife and bringing the warring states together in the common effort against Persia. At best the idea was less than fully formed, and the political conditions necessary to make an invasion feasible were absent until Philip developed them. It was only after he had done the groundwork that a war against Persia became possible with some expectation of success. Philip made the idea strategically conceivable and planned the invasion in detail. Alexander carried out the invasion, but it was his predecessor, Philip, who transformed thought into action and first gave practical expression to the strategic vision itself.

It is not too strong a statement to say that Philip was a military genius who invented the military instrument that allowed Alexander to carry out his conquest of Asia. Philip's innovations not only revolutionized the Greek way of war but also led to more powerful combat capabilities without which Philip's own conquests and Alexander's in Asia would not have been possible. Philip's new form of infantry warfare—constructed around a new combat formation, the pike phalanx; armed with a new weapon, the sarissa; and capable of greater flexibility, stability, and maneuver than the hoplite phalanx—bequeathed to Alexander his main combat arm for controlling the infantry battlefield. Philip's new phalanx could be employed in numerous ways: in the defense to offset the numerical superiority of the Persian infantry, in the offense to strike at the Persian line with sufficient force to penetrate it, and as a platform of maneuver to anchor the battle line and freeze enemy dispositions while the Macedonian cavalry sought a weak spot through which to penetrate and turn inside the Persian lines. Philip's introduction of the long pike also afforded his infantry a great advantage in close combat over the Persian infantry, which was armed mostly with the short spear, shield, bow, and little armor and was far less formidable than Greek heavy infantry.[69]

Philip also revolutionized the killing capability of Greek cavalry. Until Philip, cavalry in Greece had been only a minor combat element with little killing power, incapable of offensive action, limited in the pursuit, and unable to break infantry formations. Philip enhanced its lethality by replacing the short cavalry javelin with the long xyston lance, which was designed for close combat, and introducing the cavalry wedge to drive through infantry formations. Philip taught the Macedonian cavalry to fight as units instead of individual combatants and trained them in close combat and horsemanship to a level heretofore unseen in Greece. Unlike traditional Greek cavalry, Philip's cavalry was designed to close with the enemy, shatter its formations, and kill it where it stood. If the enemy took flight, Macedonian cavalry was expert in the lethal pursuit, hunting the enemy in small groups and striking it down with the lance and saber.

Philip's cavalry innovations transformed Greek cavalry from an impotent combat arm into the Macedonian army's combat arm of decision. It was the Macedonian cavalry's deadliness in close combat that made Alexander's cavalry so effective against both the Persian infantry and cavalry. The Persians, meanwhile, used their cavalry mostly in the traditional manner, riding close to the enemy and throwing javelins, and lacked any ability for effective close combat. Again and again, Alexander used his cavalry to close the distance with the enemy and bring its destructive power to bear upon his adversaries in close quarters. If Alexander had been equipped with traditional Greek cavalry, Alexander's main combat arm against the Persians would have been practically useless.

Philip's military genius in devising and introducing new infantry and cavalry formations, expanding their tactical roles, and increasing exponentially their combat killing power developed the great military instrument that gave Alexander the advantage in battle and propelled him to victory. Robert Gaebel sums up this dominance in the following terms:

> Except for numbers, Alexander always had superior fighting ability at his disposal, so that a significant military asymmetry existed between his forces and those of his enemies. Most of this superiority resulted from the inherent qualities of the Macedonian army and was based on discipline, training, arms skill, professionalism, and cultural outlook, all of which had been enhanced by experience.[70]

Had Philip not invented a masterful new army, the odds are very good that there would have been no Alexander the Great.

Another innovation that bolstered Alexander's future success was Philip's integration of an engineering and siege capability for the first time in a Greek field army. Philip's siege engineers had almost two decades of field experience before Alexander took them to Asia, and their new Macedonian torsion catapult gave Alexander's army the capability to batter down city walls. Polyeidos, Philip's chief engineer, trained Alexander's chief engineer, Diades. The siege corps itself had been trained to a fine edge by Philip, who employed them in at least eleven sieges in his campaigns. The importance of a siege capability to Alexander's success cannot be overestimated. Before Alexander could invade the interior to meet the Persian army, he first had to secure his hold on the Persian coast and not leave hostile garrisons across his line of communications. Alexander had to quickly reduce the major coastal cities to avoid being caught from behind by the Persian army, which almost happened at the battle of Issus (333 BCE); but Philip's besiegers reduced Miletus, Halicarnassus, Tyre, and Gaza in relatively short order. Had Alexander been forced to rely on the old Greek siege practice of isolation and starvation, it is likely that he would not have gone much beyond the coast, giving the Persian army plenty of time to attack him. The results would have been far different from what history records.

Alexander's far-flung campaigns also depended on another of Philip's major innovations, the commissariat corps. Philip introduced the science of logistics to Greek armies, allowing his armies to march long distances and sustain themselves in the field for months on end. By Alexander's reign, Philip's logisticians had been at their work for two decades. These logistics officers, trained by Philip, supported Alexander's long projection of force and found the means to supply the army over some of the most hostile terrain on the planet. To be sure, the Persians were exemplary logisticians themselves and had an excellent system of interior roads that aided Alexander. But once Alexander moved eastward over deserts and mountains and through jungles, he depended heavily on his own Macedonian logistics officers whom Philip had trained to supply his army.

There is no doubt that Alexander was a brilliant tactician in his own right. Like Napoleon, Alexander was gifted with a coup d'oeil, or intuition, that permitted him to quickly assess the terrain and weakness of the enemy's disposition and to fashion a tactical plan on the spot. His tactics, however, were not radically different from those he had learned from Philip.[71] In Alexander's early battles, the Persian advantage in numbers presented the risk of a single or double envelopment of Alexander's formations. Accordingly, Alexander countered this threat with a swift penetration of the enemy line, turning inward toward the enemy commander's position while assaulting the interior ranks as he advanced. The key to successfully breaking the Persian line was the ability of Alexander's cavalry to close with the enemy at the schwerpunkt, engaging in violent close combat until it drove through the line and exploded behind it. The infantry, always deployed in the center-left of the line across from the enemy commander's location, was used primarily as a platform of maneuver; that is, it held the enemy infantry in check while the Companion cavalry, almost always deployed on the right under Alexander's personal command, maneuvered until it found the weak spot in the enemy line through which to attack. To weaken the enemy cavalry's resistance to his cavalry assault, Alexander employed mounted skirmishers in front of his cavalry to engage the enemy and force it to throw its javelins and to expend its energy in the defense. Alexander then attacked with his fresh Macedonian cavalry.

It was Philip who first used his infantry as a platform of maneuver while unleashing his cavalry to break through the enemy line. As we have seen, Philip originally used this tactic in his battle with Bardylis and then again at Chaeronea. Philip was also adept at reading the terrain and adjusting his forces accordingly as he did at the battles of Livahdi, Illyria, the Crocus Field, and Chaeronea. It is by no means clear that Philip was inferior in this talent to Alexander.

The tale of Alexander's pursuit of Darius, one of the most widely told battle stories of antiquity, demonstrates Alexander's use of strategic pursuit in his campaigns. But here again, Alexander followed Philip's example. Philip first made strategic pursuit possible by introducing a logistics system that sustained his forces in the field over long-distance forced marches. Philip used this offensive operation not only to destroy fleeing enemy armies but also to achieve strategic political ends as well. Philip often conducted lethal pursuits with the political objective of eliminating as much of the enemy's leadership corps and aristocracy as possible to make it easier for the survivors to come to terms with him. Alexander did the same in hunting down Darius, but later he harried and annihilated the leadership of opposing tribal armies almost to the point of genocide. The invention and effective use of the strategic pursuit within the context of Greek warfare must be credited to Philip, and by Alexander's day it was a stock element in the Macedonian commander's tactical repertoire.

Alexander is often given great credit for innovatively assembling units of mixed arms for use on specific missions. Arrian identifies twenty-seven examples of Alexander's combining forces of different arms for specific tactical missions.[72] Later, Alexander redesigned the Macedonian phalanx, mixing Persians with Macedonian pikemen to make it heavier. Just as modern-day planners do, Alexander tailored tactical units to the terrain over which they had to operate, the mission they were to accomplish, and the nature of the force to be engaged. Alexander used a light force of mounted infantry, for example, to close the gap in overtaking Darius.

While Alexander certainly utilized mixed arms units more often and on a greater scale than Philip did, he did so probably because of the varied nature of both Persian and tribal armies that Alexander fought. Many of Arrian's examples apply to the counterinsurgency operations that Alexander mounted in Afghanistan and the Indus Valley, where his opponents were highly mobile units armed with bows and javelins. While traditional Greek armies had utilized specialty units of archers, slingers, peltasts, javelineers, and so on for decades, albeit in minor roles, it was not until Philip's command that such units were regularly incorporated into a standing military force, the Macedonian army. Moreover, Philip's wars in the mountains of western Macedonia and the Balkans forced him to deal with highly mobile tribal forces operating in difficult terrain. During the Thracian campaign, however, Philip seems to have used mixed forces with some regularity and size, so much so that as the campaign went on he found himself short of regular infantry and had to request replacements from Macedonia.

Great generals are not the only causes of their greatness. War is a cooperative enterprise, heavily dependent on the talents and abilities of others and orchestrated by the commander into a coherent whole of activity. The quality of leadership and experience is vitally important at all levels of command to the overall success of any army. Perhaps it is in the qualities of leadership, training, and experience of the Macedonian officer and non-commissioned officer corps that Alexander owes his greatest debt to Philip. Most of the important officers in Alexander's army had served with Philip at various levels of command over the years. They included Parmenio, the old war horse, who was Philip's best field commander; his sons, Philotas and Nicanor, commanding the horse and foot guards, respectively; Hephaestion, Alexander's lover, closest friend, and the commander of half the Companion cavalry; Craterus, commander of the left half of the phalanx; Seleucus, commander of the foot guards; Antigonus the One-Eyed; and Ptolemy, a fellow student with Alexander under Aristotle's tutelage.[73] Even Alexander's peers had seen their first combat under Philip and had risen in rank under Philip's tutelage. Equally important were the unnamed and unremembered battalion commanders, squadron commanders, file commanders, and section leaders—the small-unit officer and noncommissioned officer corps on which the effectiveness of an army depends most—who had served under Philip as well. Perhaps no general in history had ever acquired a better-trained, experienced, and well-led army than Alexander received as his legacy from Philip.

Both Philip and Alexander were heads of state as well as field generals, a fact that radically changes the meaning of their military greatness. In modern times, and even in times later in antiquity, generals are most often not simultaneously heads of government. Accordingly, they are properly judged only by their achievements on the battlefield and not held responsible for larger political concerns. In these circumstances, military performance may be regarded as an end in itself. Alexander and Philip, however, must be judged by a different standard, that is, by the degree to which their military achievements worked to support their objectives as military men and as heads of state. Thus, military competence becomes not an end but a *means* to other ends for which the general is also responsible. The concerns of the general qua general are the tactical and operational elements of war, while the concerns of the general qua statesman are the strategic objectives of the national state.

For the general as strategist, war is but one means to achieve national objectives within the political and cultural context within which wars are fought for specified goals. Philip always properly saw war as a means to his strategic goals, and he much preferred to achieve his objectives by other less kinetic means such as diplomacy. Even to a warrior as Homeric as Philip was, the search for glory and heroism had little place in his strategic thinking. Alexander, by contrast, was the prototypical Homeric warrior fighting for personal glory and reputation, a military adventurer almost entirely lacking in strategic vision. One is hard pressed to discern in accounts of Alexander's adventures any strategic vision that he might have reasonably achieved in his many campaigns. When the Indian philosopher Dandamis met Alexander, he seems to have grasped Alexander's strategic mettle correctly when he asked, "For what reason did Alexander make such a long journey hither?"[74]

Some of Alexander's campaigns, such as crossing the Gedrosian Desert, were undertaken simply to surpass other generals' achievements. Thus,

Alexander chose it, we are told, because with the exception of Semiramis, returning from her conquests of India, no one had ever brought an army successfully through it . . . the Persian king, Cyrus the Great, supposedly had lost all but seven of his men when he crossed it. Alexander knew about these stories, and they had inspired him to emulate and hopefully surpass Cyrus and Semiramis.[75]

With only personal glory and reputation to concern him, Alexander became a fierce and recklessly brave warrior who was wounded seven times.[76] He apparently had little regard for his personal safety and even less for the consequences of his death for either Macedonia or the Argead dynastic line. He "seems to have been possessed of some sort of restless, almost irrational desire for glory unchecked by a larger political sense,"[77] that is, by strategic calculation or vision. For Alexander, war was the crucible of fame, an end in itself, and its exploits the stuff of history and legend.

Philip, by contrast, was the ultimate strategist. He resorted to fighting wars only when other means failed to achieve his objectives, which were rooted in Macedonian national interests more than in enhancing his personal reputation. When at war, Philip showed himself to be an innovative and brave field commander who was wounded no fewer than five times, three of which were life threatening. But Philip was the first Western general to abandon the Homeric practice of fighting in the front ranks of the battle line. He had designed his army to maneuver and strike at his command. To control the flow and tempo of battle, Philip had to command from outside the battle space. He would probably have agreed with Scipio Africanus who, when criticized for moving around the battlefield surrounded by guards with shields to protect him, responded, "My mother bore me a general, not a warrior."[78] Generals were becoming too valuable to be risked in foolish heroics. Philip had already moved beyond the general as warrior hero to the general as battle manager. Alexander, in doing the opposite, was already an anachronism in Greece and would be soon everywhere else as well. Alexander was a magnificent throwback to a simpler age of warfare. The future, however, belonged to men like Philip.

Notes

ORIGINAL SOURCES
In drawing upon the original source materials relevant to Philip II, I have relied on the following works. Whenever the author's name appears in the notes, the reference is to the source for that author as it appears below.

Aeschines: *The Speeches of Aeschines,* trans. Charles Darwin Adams (Whitefish, MT: Kessinger Publishers, 2007).
Arrian (Lucius Flavius Arrianus): *The Anabasis of Alexander,* trans. P. A. Brunt and E. Cliff Robson (Cambridge, MA: Loeb Classical Library, 1983).
Demosthenes: *Demosthenes Orations,* 7 vols., trans. H. Vince (Cambridge, MA: Loeb Classical Library, 1930).
Diodorus: *Diodorus Siculus: The Reign of Philip II: The Greek and Macedonian Narrative from Book XVI,* ed. and trans. E. I. McQueen (London: Bristol Classical Press, 1995).
Justin (Marcus Junianus Justinus): *Epitome of the Philippic History of Pompeius Togus,* trans. John Shelby Watson (London: Henry G. Bohn Press, 1853).
Pausanias: *The Complete Collection of Pausanias in Four Volumes,* trans. W. H. S. Jones (Cambridge, MA: Harvard University Press, 1966).
Polyaenus: *Strategems of War* (Chicago: Ares Publishers, 1994).
Quintus Curtius Rufus: *History of Alexander,* trans. John Yardley (London: Penguin, 1984).
Sextus Julius Frontinus: *Strategemata,* LacusCurtius website, 2007.
Theopompus and Philochorus: F. Jacoby, *Die fragmente der griechischen historiker* (Berlin: Weidmann, 1923).

CHAPTER 1. PHILIPPOS MAKEDONIOS
  1. The incident is reported in various forms by Theopompus, fragment 236, and Diodorus, 16.87.1. Plutarch claims that Philip went on a drunken revel

among the corpses of the slain. For the argument that the incident never happened, see N. G. L. Hammond, *Philip of Macedon* (Baltimore, MD: John Hopkins University Press, 1994), 156.
2. N. G. L. Hammond, *The Macedonian State: Origins, Institutions, and History* (Oxford, UK: Clarendon Press, 1989), 49–50.
3. E. A. Fredericksmeyer, "Alexander and Philip: Emulation and Resentment," *Classical Journal* 85, no. 4 (April–May 1990): 305.
4. Pierre Lévêque, "Philip's Personality," in *Philip of Macedon*, ed. Miltiades B. Hatzopoulos and Louisa D. Loukopoulos (Athens: Ekdotike Athenon, 1980), 187.
5. Richard A. Gabriel, *The Great Captains of Antiquity* (Westport, CT: Greenwood Press, 2001), 81.
6. Elizabeth Carney, "The Politics of Polygamy: Olympias, Alexander, and the Murder of Philip," *Historia* 41, no. 2 (1992): 169–89, for an analysis of polygamy in Macedonia.
7. Hammond, *The Macedonian State*, 74.
8. Diodorus, 16.2.2, says that Philip's father also sent Philip as a hostage to the Illyrians when he was an infant, but the story is not credible. See E. I. McQueen, ed. and trans., *Diodorus Siculus: The Reign of Philip II: The Greek and Macedonian Narrative from Book XVI* (London: Bristol Classical Press, 1995), 63.
9. Hammond, *Philip of Macedon*, 9.
10. Ibid., 18. It is, however, by no means certain that this was the case.
11. Charles Edson, "Early Macedonia," in Hatzopoulos and Loukopoulos, *Philip of Macedon*, 21.
12. A. B. Bosworth, "Philip II and Upper Macedonia," *Classical Quarterly* 21, no. 1 (May 1971): 99.
13. I have accepted Hammond's argument that the most trustworthy accounts of Philip's life are to be found in Diodorus (ca. 30–50 BCE) and Justin (ca. AD 150), whose accounts can be traced to four historians whose lives were contemporary with Philip's. While the interpretations of facts reported by these historians are certainly open to question, the facts themselves can be accepted with some certainty. The source historians are Ephorus, Theopompus, Marsyas Macedon of Pella, and Demophilus, a son of Ephorus. For further analysis of these sources, see Hammond, *Philip of Macedon*, 15. This said, however, I have endeavored to read what few sources of the originals have survived.
14. Justin, 6.1.2. The selection of an infant king was not unknown in Macedonia. In one instance, the infant was brought to the battlefield in his cradle!
15. Justin, 7.5.9.
16. George Cawkwell, *Philip of Macedon* (London: Faber and Faber, 1978), 27.
17. Ian Worthington, *Philip II of Macedonia* (New Haven, CT: Yale University Press, 2008), 27. See also J. R. Ellis, "The Stepbrothers of Philip II," *Historia* 22 (1973): 350–54.
18. J. R. Ellis, "Macedonia Under Philip," in *Philip of Macedon*, ed. Hatzopoulos and Loukopoulos, 146.

19. Quintus Curtius Rufus, 5.2.18–20.
20. Ellis, "Macedonia Under Philip," 146.
21. Hammond, *The Macedonian State*, 69.
22. Polyaenus, 1:4.2.6.
23. Peter Green, *Alexander of Macedon, 356–323 B.C.: A Historical Biography* (Berkeley: University of California Press, 1991), 2. See also A. Aymard, "Le protocole royal grec et son evolution," *Revue des études anciennes* 50 (1948): 232–63.
24. Fredericksmeyer, "Alexander and Philip," 304.
25. Polyaenus, 4.2.9.
26. Green, *Alexander of Macedon*, 6.
27. Cawkwell, *Philip of Macedon*, 51.
28. Curtius, 8.6.2.
29. Cawkwell, *Philip of Macedon*, 51. Mosaics from Macedonian tombs portray these animals as having existed in Macedonia in ancient times, where they were hunted with short spears.
30. Manolis Andronikos, "The Royal Tombs at Aigai (Vergina)," in *Philip of Macedon*, ed. Hatzopoulos and Loukopoulos, 188–231.
31. Hammond, *Philip of Macedon*, 178.
32. Worthington, *Philip II of Macedonia*, 10.
33. Alice Swift Riginos, "The Wounding of Philip II of Macedon: Fact and Fabrication," *Journal of Hellenic Studies* 114 (1994): 104.
34. J. N. Prag, "Reconstructing King Philip: The Nice Version," *American Journal of Archaeology* 94, no. 2 (April 1990): 240. It is unlikely that the arrow was protruding from Philip's eye when he reached the aid station. To do so, an arrow of some twenty-eight inches in length would have had to penetrate Philip's eye socket to a depth of at least four inches to sustain the weight of the arrow's shaft extending outside the eye socket. Such a wound would have penetrated the brain and killed Philip. More likely, the wound may have been caused by a glancing blow that could have sliced the eye and the surrounding skin without striking any of the bone of the eye socket itself. In these circumstances, the skull would have revealed no injury to the surrounding bones upon autopsy.
35. Jonathan H. Musgrave, A. J. Prag, and R. Neave, "The Skull from Tomb II at Vergina: King Philip of Macedon," *Journal of Hellenic Studies* 104 (1984): 75.
36. See McQueen, *Diodorus Siculus*, 102. While all quotations of Diodorus are taken from this source, the commentary of translator E. I. McQueen is attributed directly to him whenever it is cited.
37. Prag, "Reconstructing King Philip," 240.
38. Ibid., 241, for an illustration of the spoon of Diokles.
39. Ibid., 243.
40. Justin, 7.6.15; and Hammond, *Philip of Macedon*, 36.
41. Prag, "Reconstructing King Philip," 239.
42. Riginos, "The Wounding of Philip II of Macedon," 104.

43. Hammond, *Philip of Macedon*, 115.
44. Cawkwell, *Philip of Macedon*, 115, citing Didymus Chalcenterus.
45. Ibid., citing Didymus, 18.67.
46. Riginos, "The Wounding of Philip II of Macedon," 115, citing Didymus as translated by Seneca; and Cawkwell, *Philip of Macedon*, 114, citing Didymus, 18.67, and Didymus, col. 12.63ff.
47. My thanks to Dr. Paul Gagliardi for his help with the medical aspects of the tib-fib fracture. The most effective method for dealing with this type of fracture today uses surgical pins to hold the bones together.
48. Andronikos, "The Royal Tombs," 228. Although the evidence seems rather convincing, there is some debate as to whether the tomb is indeed Philip's. See also Worthington, *Philip II of Macedonia*, 234–41.
49. Justin, 9.3.1–3.
50. Riginos, "The Wounding of Philip II of Macedon," 117.
51. Cawkwell, *Philip of Macedon*, 114–15.
52. Even with modern splints, a tib-fib fracture usually requires surgery and takes at least a year to heal completely.
53. Hammond, *The Macedonian State*, 33.
54. Carney, "The Politics of Polygamy," 170.
55. Hammond, *Philip of Macedon*, 40.
56. Richard A. Gabriel and Karen S. Metz, *The History of Military Medicine, Vol. 1: From Ancient Times to the Middle Ages* (Westport, CT: Greenwood Press, 1992), 28.
57. William S. Arnett, "Only the Bad Died Young in the Ancient Middle East," *International Journal of Aging and Human Development* 21, no. 2 (1985): 155–60.
58. Carney, "The Politics of Polygamy," 171.
59. Justin, 9.8.3.
60. McQueen, *Diodorus Siculus*, 108. See also G. T. Griffith, "Philip as a General and the Macedonian Army," in *Philip of Macedon*, ed. Hatzopoulos and Loukopoulos, 73.
61. Carney, "The Politics of Polygamy," 173.
62. Fredericksmeyer, "Alexander and Philip," 306.
63. Justin, 9.8.3.
64. Carney, "The Politics of Polygamy," 173.
65. Worthington, *Philip II of Macedonia*, 207.
66. Hammond, *Philip of Macedon*, 170–71.
67. Andronikos, "The Royal Tombs," 201.
68. Ibid.
69. Hammond, *Philip of Macedon*, 182.
70. Ibid.
71. Ibid.
72. Cawkwell, *Philip of Macedon*, 50.
73. Hammond, *Philip of Macedon*, 185. It should be noted, however, that both Aeschines and Ctesiphon were both pro-Macedonian, oligarchically minded politicians.
74. Ibid., 175.

75. See Cawkwell, *Philip of Macedon*, 55–56, for Alexander's education.
76. Hammond, *Philip of Macedon*, 187.
77. Justin, 8.4.7.
78. Diodorus, 3.1
79. Justin, book 8.
80. Justin, as quoted in Worthington, *Philip II of Macedonia*, 195.
81. Ibid.
82. Ibid.
83. Ibid.
84. Lévêque, "Philip's Personality," 176–78.
85. Griffith, "Philip as a General," 58.
86. Eugene N. Borza, "Philip II and the Greeks," *Classical Philology* 73, no. 3 (July 1978): 242.
87. Hammond, *Philip of Macedon*, 190.
88. Griffith, "Philip as a General," 72.
89. Diodorus, 16.60.3.
90. Worthington, *Philip II of Macedonia*, 231.
91. It was Alexander, not Philip, who was obsessed with becoming a god while still alive. He broke off his campaign against Persia to travel to Egypt and visit the oracle of Ammon Zeus in the Siwah oasis, where he asked the priests about his true paternity and was told that Zeus himself was his father. After that, he frequently referred to himself as "son of Zeus." While in India, Alexander sought out Indian holy men and philosophers to inquire how a man could become a god.
92. J. F. C. Fuller, *The Generalship of Alexander the Great* (New Brunswick, NJ: Rutgers University Press, 1960), 24.
93. McQueen, *Diodorus Siculus*, 63.
94. Richard A. Gabriel, "Philip of Macedon," in Richard A. Gabriel and Donald Boose, Jr., *Great Captains of Antiquity*, (Westport, CT: Greenwood Press, 1994), 83–110.
95. On the subject of the tactical innovations of Epaminondas, see Richard A. Gabriel and Donald Boose, Jr., "The Greek Way of War: Marathon, Leuctra, and Chaeronea," in *Great Battles of Antiquity*, 121–72.
96. Green, *Alexander of Macedon*, 16.
97. F. E. Adcock, *The Greek and Macedonian Art of War* (Berkeley: University of California Press, 1957), 24–25.
98. Richard A. Gabriel, "The Genius of Philip II," *Military History*, February–March 2009, 41–43.
99. Demosthenes' words appear in *On the Crown*, trans. C. A. Vince and J. H. Vince (1937), as quoted in Fuller, *The Generalship of Alexander the Great*, 24.
100. The debate as to whether the tomb is Philip's continues with most historians concluding that it is indeed Philip in the burial chamber. Worthington, *Philip II of Macedonia*, appendix 6, 234–41, presents the most recent and complete examination of the evidence for both sides in great detail and concludes that the tomb is Philip's.

101. Musgrave, "The Skull from Tomb II at Vergina," 63, 78.
102. Ibid., 64.
103. Richard A. Gabriel, *Scipio Africanus: Rome's Greatest General* (Washington, DC: Potomac Books, 2008), 3.
104. Musgrave, "The Skull from Tomb II at Vergina," 67.
105. Ibid., 76.
106. Worthington, *Philip II of Macedonia*, 205.
107. Alexander may have suffered from a congenital deformity known as torticollis, a condition in which the head and neck are noticeably inclined to one side of the body's midline.
108. Green, *Alexander of Macedon*, 55.
109. Ibid., 66.

CHAPTER 2. THE STRATEGIC ENVIRONMENT

1. The definitive works on the subject of Macedonian history are Hammond, *The Macedonian State*, 4; and N. G. L. Hammond and G. T. Griffith, *A History of Macedonia*, 2 vols. (Oxford, UK: Oxford University Press, 1979). I have relied on them heavily.
2. A. J. Graham, "The Historical Significance of Philip of Macedon," in *The World of Philip and Alexander*, ed. Elin C. Danien (Philadelphia: The University Museum of Archaeology and Anthropology, University of Pennsylvania, 1990), 6.
3. J. R. Ellis, "The Unification of Macedonia," in *Philip of Macedon*, ed. Hatzopoulos and Loukopoulos, 36.
4. Graham, "The Historical Significance," 6.
5. The lower estimate is provided by Worthington, *Philip II of Macedonia*, 7, while the higher estimate is taken from Ellis, "Macedonia Under Philip," 150.
6. Hammond, *The Macedonian State*, 93.
7. Ellis, "The Unification of Macedonia," 36.
8. Arrian, 7.9.2.
9. Graham, "The Historical Significance," 6. There is evidence of some early Neolithic and early Bronze Age settlement in Macedonia as well, but it does not seem directly connected to the later events in Macedonia with which we are concerned.
10. Ibid., 10.
11. Hammond, *The Macedonian State*, 4.
12. J. R. Ellis, "Population Transplants Under Philip II," *Makedonika* 9 (1969): 16; and Ellis, "Macedonia Under Philip," 164–65.
13. Hammond, *Philip of Macedon*, 56.
14. Ibid. Not including, of course, the non-circuit wall leading to Piraeus.
15. Nic Fields, *Ancient Greek Fortifications, 500–300 B.C.*, illustrated by Brian Delf (London: Osprey Publishers, 2006), 10.
16. Worthington, *Philip II of Macedonia*, 226–27.
17. Hammond, *The Macedonian State*, 5–6.

18. Ibid.
19. Curtius, 4.7.31.
20. Hammond, *The Macedonian State*, 49.
21. Worthington, *Philip II of Macedonia*, 34, says that Parmenio was a Paeonian by birth. This assertion is clearly incorrect.
22. Ellis, "Population Transplants Under Philip II," 14–17.
23. Arrian, 7.9.4.
24. Edson, "Early Macedonia," 14.
25. Diodorus, 16.3.2–5.
26. Edson, "Early Macedonia," 14.
27. Hammond, *The Macedonian State*, 79.
28. Ibid., 79–80.
29. Ibid., 77–78.
30. Ibid., 80–81.
31. Ibid., 81–82. See also Edson, "Early Macedonia," 10–16.
32. Alan E. Samuel, "Philip and Alexander as Kings: Macedonian Monarchy and Merovingian Parallels," *American Historical Review* 93, no. 5 (December 1988): 1273.
33. The independent authority of the assembly was evident when Philip was campaigning in Thrace and left Alexander behind and in charge of the country. When a revolt broke out among the Maedi, Alexander secured the assembly's permission to put together a military expedition, lead it into the area, and put down the revolt. Successful, he established a new city in the area and named it after himself.
34. Hammond, *The Macedonian State*, 53–54.
35. Griffith, "Philip as a General," 62.
36. See Michael Flower, *Theopompus of Chios: History and Rhetoric in the Fourth Century B.C.* (Oxford, UK: Clarendon Press, 1994), 110–11.
37. Hammond, *Philip of Macedon*, 7.
38. Hammond, *The Macedonian State*, 56.
39. Ibid.
40. Hammond, *Philip of Macedon*, 41.
41. Robert E. Gaebel, *Cavalry Operations in the Ancient Greek World* (Norman: University of Oklahoma Press, 2002), 158.
42. Ellis, "Population Transplants Under Philip II," 13–14.
43. Diodorus, 16.71.1–2.
44. Justin, 8.5.6–7.
45. Ibid.
46. Ellis, "Population Transplants Under Philip II," 12.
47. Ibid.
48. As in the Roman army, the Macedonian army was trained to undertake construction projects. See Hammond, *Philip of Macedon*, 112.
49. Ibid.
50. Ibid.

51. Hammond, *Philip of Macedon*, 187.
52. Ibid., 111.
53. Lévêque, "Philip's Personality," 180.
54. Ibid.
55. Cawkwell, *Philip of Macedon*, 164.
56. Diodorus, 16.95.1–4.
57. Borza, "Philip II and the Greeks," 242.
58. M. B. Sakellariou, "Panhellenism: From Concept to Policy," in *Philip of Macedon*, ed. Hatzopoulos and Loukopoulos, 122–23.
59. Griffith, "Philip as a General," 73.
60. Ibid.
61. Sakellariou, "Panhellenism," 135.
62. In *Philip II and Macedonian Imperialism* (London: Thames and Hudson, 1976), J. R. Ellis takes the view that it was always Philip's goal to secure an alliance with Athens because he had decided early on that he needed the Athenian navy to support his invasion of Persia. Just when Philip decided to undertake his Persian adventure remains a subject of debate. For the contrary view, see Lévêque, "Philip's Personality," 186.
63. Ibid.
64. Adcock, *The Greek and Macedonian Art of War*, 6–7.
65. Ibid.

CHAPTER 3. THE MACEDONIAN WAR MACHINE
1. Hammond, *The Macedonian State*, 98.
2. Diodorus, 16.3.1.
3. Ibid.
4. Minor M. Markle, "Use of the Sarissa by Philip and Alexander of Macedon," *American Journal of Archaeology* 82, no. 4 (Autumn 1978): 486–87.
5. The ten-man file was later reduced to eight men, although when this change occurred is not known. Perhaps it was when the phalanx acquired more battle experience. Later, Alexander increased the number of men in a file to sixteen. Peter Connolly, *Greece and Rome at War* (Englewood Cliffs, NJ: Prentice-Hall, 1981), 69.
6. Polyaenus, 4.2.10, fails to mention the breastplate in his list of equipment provided to the Macedonian infantryman. None of the other recovered lists of matériel and equipment mention the breastplate. See Minor M. Markle, "The Macedonian Sarissa, Spear, and Related Armor," *American Journal of Archaeology* 81, no. 3 (Summer 1977): 327.
7. Markle, "The Macedonian Sarissa," 326. Asclepiodotus is the only source for the diameter and shape of the phalangite shield. He says it was "eight palms in width and not too hollow." Herodotus tells us that four palms equals a foot.
8. Thomas Day Seymour, *Life in the Homeric Age* (New York: Biblo and Tannen, 1963), 633.

9. Markle, "The Macedonian Sarissa," 328.
10. The weight of the phalangite's weapons and armor is as follows: twenty-four-inch shield, twelve pounds; greaves, two pounds; helmet, twelve pounds; sarissa, twelve pounds; and sword, two pounds. His kit's total weight was forty pounds.
11. See Connolly, *Greece and Rome at War*, 69; and Markle, "The Macedonian Sarissa," 323, for the various ancient sources regarding the length of the sarissa under Philip and Alexander.
12. Markle, "The Macedonian Sarissa," 325.
13. Ibid.
14. Manolis Andronikos, "Sarissa," *Bulletin de correspondance hellénique* 94 (1970) : 98–99.
15. Seymour, *Life in the Homeric Age*, 633.
16. Andronikos, "The Royal Tombs at Aigai," 210.
17. N. G. L. Hammond, "Casualties and Reinforcements of Citizen Soldiers in Greece and Macedonia," *Journal of Hellenic Studies* 109 (1989): 60, citing Aemilius Paulus in *Plutarch's Lives*, XLIV 20.1–2.
18. Fuller, *The Generalship of Alexander the Great*, 48, citing Aemilius Paulus in *Plutarch's Lives* as noted above.
19. Markle, "The Macedonian Sarissa," 331.
20. Cawkwell, *Philip of Macedon*, 33.
21. Markle, "The Macedonian Sarissa," 331, quoting Polybius 18.29-30.
22. Fuller, *The Generalship of Alexander the Great*, 50; and Connolly, *Greece and Rome at War*, 69.
23. Griffith, "Philip as a General," 59.
24. Connolly, *Greece and Rome at War*, 69. When Alexander sailed for Asia, he took twelve *taxeis* (individual regiments) with him and left twelve behind in Macedonia.
25. Ibid., 83, citing Polybius.
26. Adcock, *The Greek and Macedonian Art of War*, 26–27.
27. Hammond, *The Macedonian State*, 101.
28. Ibid., 120.
29. Polyaenus, 46.8.
30. Arrian, 1.6.1–3.
31. A hoplite infantry battle developed in several phases. The hoplites would assemble and advance toward each other's formation in a solid line (*pyknosis*). When the lines faced each other, individuals would sally forth to fight individual contests in true Homeric fashion. This phase was called *en promachois*, or "out in front." Then the two lines of infantry would be given the order to overlap their shields (*synapsismos*) and charge. When the two lines collided, a good deal of shoving (*othismos*) would take place, causing the lines to rotate counterclockwise. Fighting in this fashion suggests the ritualistic, almost ceremonial, origins of Greek combat typical of the Homeric age. Even in the final clash of infantry lines, the crowding made large-scale killing difficult.

32. Polyaenus, 2.38.2.
33. Fuller, *The Generalship of Alexander the Great*, 48, citing Demosthenes in his *Third Philippic*.
34. Hammond, *Philip of Macedon*, 113.
35. Diodorus, 16.8.7.
36. Worthington, *Philip of Macedonia*, 55.
37. Adcock, *The Greek and Macedonian Art of War*, 19.
38. McQueen, *Diodorus Siculus*, 186.
39. Polyaenus, 54.11; and Curtius, 8.1.24.
40. McQueen, *Diodorus Siculus*, 186.
41. Edward M. Anson, "The Hypaspists: Macedonia's Professional Citizen-Soldiers," *Historia* 34, no. 2 (1984): 244–53. Another example was the *eparitoi* of the Arcadian League, created at the insistence of Thebes. This body of citizen-hoplites was maintained year round with federal funds and was quartered at Megalopolis.
42. Griffith, "Philip as a General," 58.
43. Anson, "The Hypaspists," 246.
44. Ibid.
45. Ibid., 248.
46. Ibid., 246.
47. Hammond, *The Macedonian State*, 151.
48. R. D. Milns, "Philip II and the Hypaspists," *Historia* 16, no. 4 (September 1967): 509–12.
49. Cawkwell, *Philip of Macedon*, 33; and see Milns, "Philip II and the Hypaspists," 509–12.
50. Hammond, *The Macedonian State*, 122.
51. Griffith, "Philip as a General," 59.
52. N. G. L. Hammond, "Cavalry Recruited in Macedonia down to 322 B.C.," *Historia* 47, no. 4 (1998): 405.
53. See Ellis, "The Unification of Macedonia," 40, for the number of Alexander's cavalry. Hammond's *The Macedonian State*, 125, puts the number at twenty-eight hundred Companions and fourteen hundred light cavalry.
54. Fuller, *The Generalship of Alexander the Great*, 51; and Hammond, *The Macedonian State*, 125–26. The use of the Greek term *sarissophoroi*, meaning "sarissa-bearing" with regard to cavalry, has led some to believe that some units of Philip's cavalry were armed not with the *xyston* (lance) but with the infantry sarissa. The primary exponent of this view is Markle in "The Macedonian Sarissa" and "Use of the Sarissa."
55. Cawkwell, *Philip of Macedon*, 159.
56. Xenophon makes a point of emphasizing that horses must be well cared for, but often they were not in Greece. Xenophon, *The Cavalry Commander*, trans. G. W. Bowersock (Cambridge, MA: Harvard University Press, 1968), 1.4–8.
57. The most recent works on the cavalry in Greece are Gaebel, *Cavalry Opera-*

tions in the Ancient Greek World; I. G. Spence, *The Cavalry of Classical Greece: A Social and Military History with Particular Reference to Athens* (Oxford, UK: Oxford University Press, 1993); L. J. Worley, *Hippeis: The Cavalry of Ancient Greece* (Boulder, CO: Westview Press, 1994); and G. R. Bugh, *The Horsemen of Athens* (Princeton, NJ: Princeton University Press, 1988). Gaebel's work is the most valuable and readable.

58. Xenophon, *On the Art of Horsemanship*, trans. G. W. Bowersock (Cambridge, MA: Harvard University Press, 1968), 11.6–10.
59. Connolly, *Greece and Rome at War*, 72, says that the Macedonian cavalry was equipped with the Boeotian helmet, which afforded excellent hearing and visibility. It may be that Connolly is following Xenophon here. The only helmet we have from the Macedonian tombs is not Boeotian but the standard iron infantry helmet. We cannot, therefore, be certain that Macedonian cavalry wore the Boeotian helmet.
60. Hammond, "Casualties and Reinforcements," 60. Unlike the cavalry, most infantrymen's wounds were to the thighs.
61. N. G. L. Hammond, *Alexander the Great: King, Commander, and Statesman* (Princeton, NJ: Princeton University Press, 1980), 31, says that Philip may have invented the xyston for the cavalry's use. It is true that Philip standardized the xyston's use in his cavalry, but in all likelihood the spear itself was used for centuries while hunting on horseback, as a number of hunting scenes from tombs suggest.
62. See Markle, "The Macedonian Sarissa" and "Use of the Sarissa," for detailed arguments in support of the position that Macedonian cavalry carried the sarissa as its basic weapon.
63. Hammond, *Alexander the Great*, 31.
64. See Gaebel's account of de Lee's findings. Gaebel, *Cavalry Operations in the Ancient Greek World*, 164. See N. de Lee, *French Lancers* (London: Almark, 1976).
65. Xenophon, *On the Art of Horsemanship*, 12.12.
66. Gaebel, *Cavalry Operations in the Ancient Greek World*, 164.
67. Arian, 1.5.8.
68. Markle, "The Macedonian Sarissa," 339, citing Arrian's *The Tactical Art*, 16.7ff. Two other ancient writers use somewhat different language. Asclepiodotus says the wedge formation "made it easiest for them to ride through" the infantry, while Aelian says, "The narrow front making it serviceable for riding through any gaps that happen to appear." Language not withstanding, these writers seem to agree with Arrian that the wedge was an effective formation for cavalry to penetrate infantry formations. Asclepiodotus's quote is from W. A. Oldfather, *Aeneas Tacticus, Asclepiodotus, and Onasander* (Cambridge, MA: Harvard University Press, Loeb series, 1977), chapter 7; and Aelian's words are taken from *Aelian*, trans. A. M. Devine, *Ancient World* 19, nos. 1 and 2 (1989): 50.
69. Edmund S. Burke, "Philip II and Alexander the Great," *Military Affairs* 47, no. 2 (April 1983): 69.

70. The phrase "intimidating intimacy" is Bob Gaebel's, used in personal correspondence with me. I wish I had thought of it!
71. Gaebel, *Cavalry Operations in the Ancient Greek World*, 165.
72. Xenophon, *The Art of Horsemanship*, 3.4–8.
73. Ibid., 7.1–5.
74. Gaebel, *Cavalry Operations in the Ancient Greek World*, 165.
75. Plutarch, *The Life of Alexander the Great*, ed. Arthur Hugh Clough, trans. John Dryden (New York: Random House, Modern Classics Library, 2004), 9.2.
76. Diodorus, 16.86.3. It must be noted that no ancient source tells us definitively that Alexander was in command of cavalry at Chaeronea. This said, it would have made no sense for Philip to bring two thousand cavalry to the battlefield and not use them. Moreover, without his cavalry, Philip's infantry would have been outnumbered. In addition, Philip posted Parmenio and Antipater with Alexander. Both of these officers were cavalry generals, and it would have made little sense to post them with the infantry. Finally, the speed with which the allied line collapsed after Alexander's troops penetrated their infantry line clearly implies a cavalry attack. Modern scholars have generally concluded that cavalry units fought at Chaeronea and that Alexander was in command of them.
77. Markle, "The Macedonian Sarissa," 339.
78. Ibid. It seems to me that Markle's explanation is wrong on two counts. He asserts that the cavalry used the infantry sarissa and that the cavalry struck the infantry at the charge. The sarissa provides no killing advantage over the xyston in terms of functional length, and the charge is unlikely to work for the usual reasons that a horse will not charge through a line of shields and spears, even as it can be trained to push and press through such a line.
79. One might well ask why hoplites did not attack the horse itself. The answer is that killing a horse with spear or sword was no easy task. The horse's face and chest were likely to be armored, at least to the extent that the armor would limit the penetration of any spear or sword thrust. And if the animal were only wounded, then its pain would cause it to behave erratically and perhaps bolt right through the infantry formation. In addition, the physiology of the horse is such that it limits blood loss when wounded. For the difficulty in killing a horse with ancient weapons, see Deborah Cantrell, "The Horsemen of Israel: Horses and Chariotry in Monarchic Israel" (Ph.D. diss., Department of Religion, Vanderbilt University, 2008), 46–49.
80. Xenophon, *The Cavalry Commander*, 3.14.
81. Gaebel, *Cavalry Operations in the Ancient Greek World*, 166.
82. Ibid.
83. Arrian, 1.15.2–4.
84. Other cavalry formations were the square, the diamond, and the rhomboid formation. The wedge was the most effective for penetrating an infantry line.
85. Hammond, *The Macedonian State*, 130.
86. Ibid., 125.

87. Green, *Alexander of Macedon*, 39.
88. Ibid.
89. Hammond, "Casualties and Reinforcements," 63.
90. Ellis, "The Unification of Macedonia," 40.
91. Ibid., 42.
92. Ibid., 63.
93. Griffith, "Philip as a General," 59.
94. Ibid.
95. Ellis, "The Unification of Macedonia," 41.
96. Fields, *Ancient Greek Fortifications*, 11. The price of a cavalry horse might range from 200 to 1,200 drachmas or about 500 drachmas on average. A drachma represented about a day's wages for a laborer and would purchase a gallon of wine, five pounds of wheat, or one salted fish. A sheep or goat cost 10 to 15 drachmas, and a cow 50. A human slave cost 140 to 360 drachmas, depending on his or her skills. Gaebel, *Cavalry Operations in the Ancient Greek World*, 20.
97. Discipline applied to officers as well. Diodorus, 16.2–3, and Polyaenus, 4.2.1, record that in one instance Philip removed an officer from his command for taking a hot bath in camp, noting that only women used warm water in which to bathe. In another instance, Philip had a young nobleman who had broken ranks to take a drink of water publicly flogged. See Green, *Alexander of Macedon*, 20.
98. Elizabeth Carney, "Macedonians and Mutiny: Discipline and Indiscipline in the Army of Philip and Alexander," *Classical Philology* 91, no. 1 (January 1996): 21–22.
99. Sakellariou, "Philip and the Southern Greeks," 126. See also Griffith, "Philip as a General," 71. Some part of Alexander's success stemmed from his having inherited a corps of first-rate field grade and noncommissioned officers from Philip.
100. Curtius, 3.3.27.
101. Diodorus, 16.3.1.
102. Ibid., 16.3.1–2.
103. Carney, "Macedonians and Mutiny," 25.
104. Although it is thirty years old, the definitive work on the logistics of the Macedonian army remains Donald W. Engels' *Alexander the Great and the Logistics of the Macedonian Army* (Berkeley: University of California Press, 1978).
105. Frontinus, 4.1.6.
106. Richard A. Gabriel, *Soldiers' Lives: The Ancient World* (Westport, CT: Greenwood Press, 2007), 102.
107. See Engels, *Alexander the Great and the Logistics*, 17, for the ancient sources.
108. Frontinus, 4.1.14.
109. Polyaenus, 4.2.10.
110. Curtius, 4.9.19–21.

111. Frontinus, 4.1.6: "and he issued orders that flour for thirty days was to be carried on each man's back."
112. Gabriel, *Soldiers' Lives*, 44.
113. Frontinus, 4.1.6.
114. Based on Engels' figure that a horse could carry a load of 230 pounds.
115. Engels, *Alexander the Great and the Logistics*, 18.
116. Cawkwell, *Philip of Macedon*, 157.
117. Ibid., 162.
118. E. W. Marsden, "Macedonian Military Machinery and Its Designers Under Philip and Alexander," *Thessaloniki* 2 (1977): 212.
119. Ibid.
120. Fields, *Ancient Greek Fortifications*, 16.
121. Ibid., 10–11. Bricks cost thirty-six drachmas per thousand, or almost an average month's pay, making brick walls more expensive than stone.
122. Ibid., 21.
123. Griffith, "Philip as a General," 62.
124. Cawkwell, *Philip of Macedon*, 162.
125. Diodorus, 16.74.2.
126. Marsden, "Macedonian Military Machinery," 220. The prefabricated siege tower was another of Philip's innovations.
127. Duncan B. Campbell and Adam Hook, *Ancient Siege Warfare: Persians, Greeks, Carthaginians, and Romans, 546–146 B.C.* (Oxford, UK: Osprey, 2005), 44. See Griffith, "Philip as a General," 62, for the argument that these primitive catapults were invented for Dionysios I in Sicily some fifty years earlier.
128. Ibid.
129. Griffith, "Philip as a General," 62; and Marsden, "Macedonian Military Machinery," 216–17. Athenaeus Mechanicus (10.5–10) says that Polyeidos "was responsible for all machine construction of this type developed . . . in the reign of Philip son of Amyntus" (Marsden, "Macedonian Military Machinery," 218).
130. Marsden, "Macedonian Military Machinery," 216.
131. Cawkwell, *Philip of Macedon*, 106; and Marsden, "Macedonian Military Machinery," 223.
132. Marsden, "Macdonian Military Machinery," 122.
133. McQueen, *Diodorus Siculus*, 125.
134. Ibid.
135. Cawkwell, *Philip of Macedon*, 122.
136. Worthington, *Philip II of Macedonia*, 69.
137. Ibid., 119.
138. Hammond, *Philip of Macedon*, 186.
139. Hollywood movies have left the impression that oarsmen on ancient ships were slaves when in fact they were almost always skilled and highly paid workers. The cost of outfitting a ship with oarsmen for a campaign sometimes exceeded the cost of constructing the ship.

140. Worthington, *Philip II of Macedonia*, 133.
141. Hammond, *The Macedonian State*, 127–28.

CHAPTER 4. THE UNIFICATION OF MACEDONIA

1. Diodorus, 16.2.6.
2. Ibid.: "The Paeonians began to devastate their land out of contempt for the Macedonians."
3. Ibid., 16.3.1.
4. N. G. L. Hammond, "The Kingdoms in Illyria Circa 400–167 B.C.," *ABSA* 61 (1966): 239–53.
5. *Satyrus*, fragment 5, in McQueen, *Diodorus Siculus*, 65.
6. Ibid., 69.
7. Hammond, *Philip of Macedon*, 24.
8. Diodorus, 16.3.3.
9. Ibid., 16.3.4.
10. Hammond, *Philip of Macedon*, 25.
11. Diodorus, 16.3.5–6.
12. My account of this battle draws upon Hammond, *Philip of Macedon*, 25, for its geography; Diodorus for the general events; and Justin, 7.6.6, for the claim that Argaeus was ambushed by Philip.
13. Diodorus, 16.3.6.
14. Ibid.
15. Ibid., 16.4.1.
16. Hammond, *The Macedonian State*, 137.
17. Cawkwell, *Philip of Macedon*, 74.
18. Diodorus, 16.4.3.
19. Ibid.
20. Cawkwell, *Philip of Macedon*, 30. See also Diodorus, 16.4.1.
21. Diodorus, 16.4.1.
22. Diodorus, 16.2.6.
23. Ibid., 16.4.3.
24. Ibid., 16.4.4.
25. N. G. L. Hammond, "The Battle Between Philip and Bardylis," *Antichthon* 23 (1989): 7. See also Green, *Alexander of Macedon*, 24, who says the battle took place near Monastir close to Lake Okhrida.
26. Diodorus, 16.4.4.
27. Frontinus, 2.3.2.
28. The argument that the Illyrians were armed and fought as the Greeks did is drawn from Diodorus's statement (15.13.2) that Dionysus of Syracuse sent five hundred sets of Greek panoplies to his Illyrian allies in 385 B.C. See Hammond, "The Battle Between Philip and Bardylis," and Hammond, *The Macedonian State*, 100; he argues that most of the armies of the Balkans were equipped and fought similarly to the hoplites.
29. Diodorus, 16.4.6.
30. Hammond, "The Battle Between Philip and Bardylis," 11.

31. Asclepiodotus, *Tactics* 11.6, as cited in ibid., 4.
32. Theopompus, fragment 115, in ibid., 5. See also Frontinus, 2.3.2.
33. Diodorus, 16.4.5.
34. Ibid., 16.4.6.
35. Ibid.
36. Markle, "Use of the Sarissa," 486.
37. Diodorus, 6.4.7.
38. Dell, "Philip and Macedonia's Northern Neighbors," 94.
39. Bosworth, "Philip II and Upper Macedonia," 93–105.
40. Diodorus, 16.8.1.
41. Hammond, "The Battle Between Philip and Bardylis," 8–9, for the geography of the area. See also Cawkwell, *Philip of Macedon*, 21.
42. Dell, "Philip and Macedonia's Northern Neighbors," 94.
43. Ibid., 95.
44. Hammond, *Philip of Macedon*, 40.
45. Bosworth, "Philip II and Upper Macedonia," 102.
46. Polyaenus, 4.2.17.
47. Burke, "Philip II and Alexander the Great," 67.
48. Cawkwell, *Philip of Macedon*, 72–73.
49. Ibid.
50. McQueen, *Diodorus Siculus*, 73, citing Theopompus, fragment 30, and Demosthenes, 7.27 and 23.116.
51. A constant moral theme runs through the work of Theopompus and Demosthenes that asserts Philip captured Greek cities because of the treachery or moral corruption of their inhabitants. In some sense, neither writer could quite comprehend the effectiveness of Philip's siege engineers and the speed with which they were able to reduce cities. Instead, they cast about for other reasons for Philip's success. See Flower, *Theopompus of Chios*, chapters 4 and 7.
52. Diodorus, 16.8.3.
53. Hammond, *Philip of Macedon*, 32.
54. Ibid.
55. Diodorus, 16.8.3.
56. McQueen, *Diodorus Siculus*, 75, citing Demosthenes, 4.35. Demosthenes, 7.10, claims that Philip was allied with the Potideans when he attacked them. For the text of the agreement between Philip and Olynthos, see Marcus N. Tod, ed., *A Selection of Greek Historical Inscriptions*, vol. 2, *From 403 to 323 B.C.* (Oxford, UK: Clarendon Press, 1968), document no. 158.
57. There is no extant account of the siege of Potedia. It is unclear if, as Diodorus says (16.8.5), that Philip took Potedia and then attacked Crenides or, as Hammond and Griffith (*A History of Macedonia*, 246) argue, that the Thracian attack on Crenides occurred while Philip was still besieging Potidea. In this latter view, Philip left the engineers and some troops to continue the siege while he took the remainder of his army to relieve Crenides. See McQueen, *Diodorus Siculus*, 76.

58. Diodorus, 16.8.5.
59. Ibid.
60. Dell, "Philip and Macedonia's Northern Neighbors," 94. See also Tod, *A Selection of Greek Historical Inscriptions*, 2:157.
61. Griffith, "Philip as a General," 71, argues that Philip had long before decided that he would take Crenides and that the Thracian attack provided the opportunity to move up Philip's timetable to do so.
62. McQueen, *Diodorus Siculus*, 84, citing Plutarch, *Life of Alexander*, 3.5.
63. Diodorus, 16.22.3.
64. Ibid., 16.8.6.
65. Ibid.
66. Green, *Alexander of Macedon*, 31.
67. Diodorus, 16.8.7.
68. Hammond, *Philip of Macedon*, 35.

CHAPTER 5. THESSALY AND THE SACRED WAR
1. Griffith, "Philip as a General," 73.
2. Cawkwell, *Philip of Macedon*, 59.
3. Ibid.
4. Justin, 7.6.8, where he says the Thessalian campaign occurred after the Illyrian victory of 358 BCE and before Philip's marriage to Olympias.
5. Cawkwell, *Philip of Macedon*, 60.
6. Ibid., 61. Philip clearly was short of money until he occupied Crenides.
7. Diodorus, 16.14.2.
8. McQueen, *Diodorus Siculus*, 78.
9. Theopompus, fragment 162, as cited in ibid.
10. Theopompus, fragment 81, in ibid., gives the example of Agathocles, a member of the *penestai* (serf) class, who became a drinking companion of Philip's.
11. Contrary to the description found in Justin, 9.8.2, Philinna was not a dancer but a member of the aristocratic class. Satyrus, fragment 5, says Philip married her "in order to conciliate the Thessalians."
12. Polyaenus, 4.2.19.
13. Diodorus, 16.34.4.
14. Worthington, *Philip II of Macedonia*, 48, who cites Justin, 7.6.13–14.
15. McQueen, *Diodorus Siculus*, 95, citing the existence of an Athenian decree dated December 355 BCE honoring one Lachares of Apollonia for sending his son into Methone, thus proving that the city was already under siege by that date.
16. Worthington, *Philip II of Macedonia*, 49, who also cites the decree mentioning Lachares of Apollonia.
17. Diodorus, 16.34.5.
18. Diodorus, 16.31.6, is confused in that he says that Philip sacked Methone, which, as noted in the text, would have made no sense.
19. Justin, 7.6.15.

20. Hammond, *Philip of Macedon*, 38.
21. Ibid.
22. Diodorus, 16.31.6.
23. Ibid. There is reason to doubt Diodorus's claim that Philip took Pagasae right after capturing Methone. Philip had been badly wounded and must have required a month or two to recover before he marched into Thrace. Capturing Pagasae would have likely required a siege, which would also have taken considerable time. It may be that Philip captured Pagasae in the year following his capture of Methone. Lacking any information that would settle the question, however, I have taken Diodorus at his word.
24. Hammond, *Philip of Macedon*, 46.
25. Cawkwell, *Philip of Macedon*, 44.
26. Hammond, *Philip of Macedon*, 46–47.
27. Worthington, *Philip II of Macedonia*, 57, for the Greek cities in Thrace.
28. See Hammond, *Philip of Macedon*, 46, for the date of the official declaration of war.
29. Macedonia was not a member of the council until Philip acquired a seat for it.
30. Cawkwell, *Philip of Macedon*, 63.
31. Justin, 8.1.1–2.
32. Diodorus, 16.30.3.
33. Ibid.
34. Ibid., 16.31.2.
35. Ibid., 16.31.3.
36. McQueen, *Diodorus Siculus*, 95, citing Pausanias, 10.2.4.
37. Diodorus, 16.31.4.
38. Hammond, *Philip of Macedon*, 46, citing Pausanias, 10.2.5.
39. The Phokians usually governed their armies by a board of three generals, but in emergencies they granted one of them supreme power. See McQueen, *Diodorus Siculus*, 95.
40. Diodorus, 16.35.1, provided the size of Phayllos's relief force but offers no details on the battle in which Philip defeated him.
41. Ibid., 16.35.2.
42. Polyaenus, 36.3.2–5.
43. The armies did carry their catapult bolts with them, however, and it is curious that no mention is made of them in light of the fact that the traction-powered, stone-throwing catapults could also fire bolts. See Marsden, "Macedonian Military Machinery," 211–23. See also Campbell and Hook, *Ancient Siege Warfare*.
44. Griffith, "Philip as a General," 66.
45. Polyaenus, 18.4.
46. The figure for the cavalry is an estimate based on Hammond's calculations that Alexander's two thousand cavalry at Chaeronea took up more than a half kilometer of frontage. N. G. L. Hammond, "The Two Battles of Chaeronea," *Klio* 31 (1938): 211.

47. Sir Ralph Payne-Gallway, "The Catapult," in *A Summary of the History, Construction, and Effects in Warfare of the Projectile-Throwing Engines of the Ancients* (London: Longmans, Green, 1907), 20.
48. Diodorus, 16.35.2.
49. Cawkwell, *Philip of Macedon*, 61.
50. Diodorus, 16.34.5.
51. Diodorus, 16.35.1–5, in *Diodorus Siculus*, trans. C. Bradford Welles (Cambridge, MA: Harvard University Press, 1963), 335. McQueen's translation has transposed the numbers for the respective armies, saying Onomarchus had three thousand cavalry and Philip three hundred. The reverse was the case.
52. Diodorus, 16.35.5.
53. The number of Athenian ships usually stationed at Neapolis is taken from Luke Ueda-Sarson's "Crocus Field: 353 BC," an online site for historical battle scenarios for DBM, July 8, 2002, 1, at http://www.ne.jp/asahi/luke/ueda-sarson/CrocusField.html.
54. A trireme of this period had a crew of about a hundred men and could transport about a hundred infantry. There were no horse transports with Chares' fleet, suggesting that only infantry, and no cavalry, were aboard.
55. My thanks to my friend, Matthew Gonzales, an associate professor of classics at Saint Anselm College, for sharing his knowledge of the Macedonian coast with me. One can get a good idea of its difficult coastline from Google Earth.
56. Hammond, *Philip of Macedon*, 47.
57. Justin, 8.2.3.
58. Diodorus, 16.35.6.
59. Pausanias, 10.2.5, as cited by McQueen, *Diodorus Siculus*, 105.
60. Eusebius, *Praeparatio Evangelica*, 8.14.33, as cited by McQueen, *Diodorus Siculus*, 105.
61. Hammond, *Philip of Macedon*, 48.
62. Minor M. Markle, "The Strategy of Philip in 346 B.C.," *Classical Quarterly* 24, no. 2 (December 1974): 267.
63. Diodorus, 16.38.1.
64. Satyrus, fragment 5, as cited in McQueen, *Diodorus Siculus*, 108.
65. Justin, 8.3.1, says that Pagasae and its revenues became Philip's personal possession.
66. McQueen, *Diodorus Siculus*, 108, citing Demosthenes, 1.12.
67. Hammond, *Philip of Macedon*, 48.
68. Justin, 11.3.2.
69. G. T. Griffith, "Philip of Macedon's Early Intervention in Thessaly (358–352 B.C.)," *Classical Quarterly* 20, no. 1 (May 1970): 78.
70. Hammond, *Philip of Macedon*, 49.
71. Cawkwell, *Philip of Macedon*, 62.
72. Diodorus, 16.38.1.

73. Cawkwell, *Philip of Macedon*, 66, citing Justin, 8.2.8.
74. Ibid., 67.

CHAPTER 6. THE ROAD TO EMPIRE
1. Diodorus, 16.34.3.
2. Worthington, *Philip II of Macedonia*, 68.
3. Diodorus, 16.34.3.
4. J. R. Ellis, "Philip's Thracian Campaign of 352–351," *Classical Philology* 72, no. 1 (January 1977): 35.
5. Ibid.
6. Justin, 8.3.6. See also McQueen, *Diodorus Siculus*, 120, citing Demosthenes, *Olynthiac*, 1.13, and Isocrates, 5.21. 7. McQueen, *Diodorus Siculus*, 120, citing Demosthenes, 3.3–4.
8. Cawkwell, *Philip of Macedon*, 81.
9. Ellis, "Philip's Thracian Campaign," 38–39.
10. McQueen, *Diodorus Siculus*, 120, citing Demosthenes, 1.13, and Isocrates, 5.21.
11. Ibid.; and Hammond, *Philip of Macedon*, 51, citing Demosthenes' *The First Philippic*.
12. McQueen, *Diodorus Siculus*, 120.
13. Dell, "Philip and Macedonia's Northern Neighbors," 95. See also Justin, 8.6.5.
14. Hammond, *Philip of Macedon*, 120.
15. Ibid., 50.
16. Justin, 8.3.10.
17. Cawkwell, *Philip of Macedon*, 85.
18. Hammond, *Philip of Macedon*, 50, citing Demosthenes, 1.12.13.
19. Worthington, *Philip II of Macedonia*, 69, citing Theopompus, fragment 127.
20. The fact that Apollonides went to Athens, where he was awarded Athenian citizenship, could hardly have calmed Philip's concerns.
21. Worthington, *Philip II of Macedonia*, 69.
22. Diodorus, 16.52.9. See also E. Badian, "Philip II and the Last of the Thessalians," *Ancient Macedonia* 6 (1999): 117–20.
23. To avoid being vulnerable against Athenian naval attacks, the Euboeans in 410 BCE narrowed the channel between Euboea and Boeotia at Chalcis to a width sufficient only for a single trireme to pass at a time. They then bridged and fortified the gap. By Philip's day, the bridge and its fortifications were part of Chalcis. See Cawkwell, *Philip of Macedon*, 88.
24. Worthington, *Philip II of Macedonia*, 82, citing Aeschines, 3.87.
25. Cawkwell, *Philip of Macedon*, 89.
26. Ibid., 87.
27. Hammond, *Philip of Macedon*, 50, citing Aeschines, 2.72.
28. Worthington, *Philip II of Macedonia*, 78, citing Diodorus, 16.52.9.
29. Hammond, *Philip of Macedon*, 52. See also McQueen, who attributes the

quote to Demosthenes, 9.11, in *Diodorus Siculus*.
30. Diodorus, 16.53.2.
31. Ibid.
32. McQueen, *Diodorus Siculus*, 123, citing Demosthenes, 9.11.
33. It was standard Athenian propaganda to attribute the defeat of any of its allies' cities to treachery and betrayal from within in an effort to belittle Philip's military accomplishments. In the case of Olynthos, however, the claim of treachery might well be true. Philip spent two months hammering at the city's walls with apparently little effect until, suddenly, the city surrendered. The account makes little sense unless Olynthos was betrayed in some manner from within, say, by someone opening the gates at night or reducing the forces in one sector of the wall and rendering them vulnerable to a concerted attack.
34. McQueen, *Diodorus Siculus*, 120, citing Demosthenes, 19.194–98.
35. Ibid.
36. Diodorus, 16.53.3.
37. Ibid.
38. Worthington, *Philip II of Macedonia*, 79, citing Demosthenes, 9.26. See also Diodorus, 16.53.3.
39. The description of the ruins is from Cawkwell, *Philip of Macedon*, 82.
40. Diodorus, 16.53.3.
41. Ibid., 16.38.6.
42. Ibid., 16.56.2.
43. Ibid., 16.58.2.
44. Ibid., 16.58.3.
45. Cawkwell, *Philip of Macedon*, 95.
46. Worthington, *Philip II of Macedonia*, 87.
47. Ibid., 88.
48. Diodorus, 16.59.2.
49. Cawkwell, *Philip of Macedon*, 95.
50. Worthington, *Philip II of Macedonia*, 92.
51. Cawkwell, *Philip of Macedon*, 98.
52. Dell, "Philip and Macedonia's Northern Neighbors," 97.
53. Ellis, *Philip II and Macedonian Imperialism*, 110–11. I am following Ellis's chronology here.
54. Dell, "Philip and Macedonia's Northern Neighbors," 97.
55. Ibid., 98.
56. Worthington, *Philip II of Macedonia*, 93, citing Theopompus, fragment 164.
57. The degree to which Thrace was isolated can be discerned from the fact that while Athens was debating the truce, Cersobleptes made a formal request to join the Athenian Confederacy and thus be eligible to request help from Athens. The assembly ignored his request.
58. George Cawkwell, "Philip and the Amphictyonic League," in *Philip of Macedon*, ed. Hatzopoulos and Loukopoulos, 88–89.

59. Worthington, *Philip II of Macedonia*, 96, citing Aeschines.
60. George Cawkwell, "Philip and Athens," in Hatzopoulos and Loukopoulos, *Philip of Macedon*, 103.
61. Diodorus, 16.59.2.
62. Ibid.
63. Ibid., 16.59.3.
64. Ibid., 16.59.2.
65. Ibid., 16.59.3.

CHAPTER 7. WARRIOR DIPLOMAT
1. Isocrates, *First Epistle*, 9.8.
2. Diodorus, 16.59.3.
3. Ibid., 16.59.4.
4. Aeschines, 2.142, cited in McQueen, *Diodorus Siculus*, 136.
5. Hammond, *Philip of Macedon*, 94.
6. Diodorus, 16.60.2.
7. Pausanias, 10.3.1–2.
8. Hammond, *Philip of Macedon*, 94.
9. Demosthenes, 19.39.
10. Diodorus, 16.60.2.
11. Ibid.
12. Ibid.
13. Hammond, *Philip of Macedon*, 94.
14. Worthington, *Philip II of Macedonia*, 103.
15. Cawkwell, *Philip of Macedon*, 111.
16. Diodorus, 16.60.1.
17. Worthington, *Philip II of Macedonia*, 103. Hammond questions whether the votes were awarded to Philip himself, as Worthington says, or if they were awarded to the Macedonoi, that is, to the tribe. Given that all other votes in the league are attributed to tribes, Hammond may be correct.
18. Diodorus, 16.60.1.
19. Ibid., 16.60.4.
20. Demosthenes, 6.22.
21. Diodorus, 16.60.4.
22. Sakellariou, "Philip and the Southern Greeks," 121.
23. Demosthenes, 6.9.
24. Ibid., 19.261.
25. Ibid., 16.16.
26. Cawkwell, *Philip of Macedon*, 104.
27. Diodorus, 16.60.5.
28. Cawkwell, *Philip of Macedon*, 112.
29. Markle, "The Strategy of Philip in 346 B.C.," 255.
30. See Hammond, *Philip of Macedon*, 111; and McQueen, *Diodorus Siculus*, 137, for this argument.
31. Hammond, *Philip of Macedon*, 101.

32. Borza, "Philip II and the Greeks," 240.
33. Ellis, *Philip II and Macedonian Imperialism*, 124.
34. Markle, "The Strategy of Philip in 346 B.C.," 268.
35. Borza, "Philip II and the Greeks," 241.
36. Worthington, *Philip II of Macedonia*, 108.
37. Diodorus, 16.69.7.
38. Dell, "Philip and Macedonia's Northern Neighbors," 95.
39. Justin, 8.6.3.
40. McQueen, *Diodorus Siculus*, 145.
41. See chapter 1 of this volume for details on Philip's lower leg fracture and a medical estimate of the time needed to recover from his wound.
42. Diodorus, 16.66.7.
43. Justin, 8.5.7.
44. Ibid.
45. Ibid., 9.2.15.
46. Ibid.
47. Dell, "Philip and Macedonia's Northern Neighbors," 95. In fact, there is no evidence of war at this time. The claim that there a war did take place is probably a result of Diodorus's confusion about when Pausanias, Philip's alleged former lover, was killed in battle if, indeed, he really was.
48. One of these rulers, Aristomedes, fled to Persia, where he served in the Persian forces against Alexander.
49. Worthington, *Philip II of Macedonia*, 111.
50. Hammond, *Philip of Macedon*, 118, citing Demosthenes, 7.32, says that Philip was in personal command of the forces in Thessaly at this time. Cawkwell, *Philip of Macedon*, 115, citing the severity of Philip's leg fracture, argues that Philip did not take the field in person. I am inclined toward Cawkwell's view.
51. Hammond, *Philip of Macedon*, 119.
52. Theopompus, fragment 115.
53. Hammond, *Philip of Macedon*, 119.
54. Worthington, *Philip II of Macedonia*, 116.
55. Diodorus, 16.72.1.
56. Hammond, *Philip of Macedon*, 121.
57. Worthington, *Philip II of Macedonia*, 117.
58. Demosthenes, 7.32.
59. Demosthenes, 9.34.
60. Demosthenes, 18.244.
61. Worthington, *Philip II of Macedonia*, 119.
62. Diodorus, 16.71.1–2.
63. Cawkwell, *Philip of Macedon*, 63.
64. Herodotus, 5.3.1, as cited by Hammond, *Philip of Macedon*, 123.
65. I have accepted Hammond's geography here. He was an intelligence officer in the area during World War II and has authored an atlas on the area's geography.

66. Demosthenes, 9.49.
67. Demosthenes, 8.14.
68. Hammond, *Philip of Macedon*, 125.
69. Ibid.; and Demosthenes, 8.44.
70. Diodorus, 16.71.1–2.
71. Ibid.
72. Theopompus, fragment 217, cited by Hammond, *Philip of Macedon*, 124.
73. Athenaeus, 13.557. See also Elizabeth Carney, *Women and Monarchy in Macedonia* (Norman: University of Oklahoma Press, 2000), 67–68, for Meda.
74. Dell, "Philip and Macedonia's Northern Neighbors," 98.
75. Ibid. The first to hold the office was Alexander of Lyncestis, Antipater's son-in-law. Later, he was implicated in a Persian plot to kill Alexander and executed at the order of the assembly.
76. Ibid.
77. Worthington, *Philip II of Macedonia*, 127.
78. Hammond, *Philip of Macedon*, 125.
79. Demosthenes, 12.2.
80. Hammond, *Philip of Macedon*, 130.
81. Demosthenes, 12.7.

CHAPTER 8. THE WAR WITH ATHENS

1. Worthington, *Philip II of Macedonia*, 129. See also Demosthenes' letter, 12.23.
2. Hammond, *Philip of Macedon*, 131.
3. Demosthenes, 12.18–19.
4. McQueen, *Diodorus Siculus*, 150–51; and Aeschines, 2.81.
5. Diodorus, 16.74.2.
6. Cawkwell, *Philip of Macedon*, 117, citing Demosthenes, 18.89.
7. Cawkwell, *Philip of Macedon*, 127.
8. Diodorus, 16.74.4.
9. Ibid.
10. Ibid., 16.76.1.
11. Ibid.
12. Worthington, *Philip II of Macedonia*, 131.
13. Diodorus, 16.76.1–2.
14. Ibid., 16.74.3–4.
15. Ibid.
16. Ibid., 16.75.2.
17. The satraps that came to the aid of Byzantium were probably Arsites of Hellespontine Phrygia and Rhosaces of Lydia. McQueen, *Diodorus Siculus*, 151, and Worthington, *Philip II of Macedonia*, 131, suggest that it was Arsites who sent the Persian mercenary force to Thrace.
18. Diodorus, 16.75.2.
19. Demosthenes, 12.3; and McQueen, *Diodorus Siculus*, 152.

20. Diodorus, 16.76.3.
21. Ibid.
22. Theopompus, fragment 217.
23. See Worthington, *Philip II of Macedonia*, 132, for the argument that Philip's attack on Byzantium was ill conceived.
24. Justin, 8.6.4–7; and Demosthenes, 7.32.
25. Cawkwell, *Philip of Macedon*, 139–40.
26. Diodorus, 16.76.4.
27. The evidence for Philip having besieged Selymbria is poor according to McQueen, *Diodorus Siculus*, 152.
28. Polyaenus, 4.2.20.
29. Worthington, *Philip II of Macedonia*, 133; Hammond, *Philip of Macedon*, 134; and Cawkwell, *Philip of Macedon*, 141, all assert that Philip made a night attack on Byzantium that failed, but they cite no ancient sources in support. There is tentative evidence in fragment 390 of F. Jacoby's opus, *Die fragmente der griechischen historiker*. The issue is not so much whether the attack occurred but when it occurred, either immediately on Philip's arrival outside Byzantium or some weeks later.
30. Theopompus, fragment 192; and Demosthenes, 50.18.
31. Diodorus and Philochorus agree that it was Athens that declared war on Philip. Cawkwell and Worthington, citing Demosthenes' account of Philip's letter of September 340 BCE, argue that a state of war existed between Athens and Philip. In his efforts to convince the assembly to declare war on Philip, Demosthenes had continually argued that Athens was already at war; however, the claim was only part of Demosthenes' political effort to persuade the assembly to officially declare war. It was not a declaration of war per se.
32. Frontinus, 1.4.13, as cited by Hammond, *Philip of Macedon*, 134.
33. Theopompus, fragment 217; and Worthington, *Philip II of Macedonia*, 134.
34. Diodorus says that the attack on Byzantium was the reason Athens declared war on Philip. If so, it was only the technical casus belli since both sides had been eager for a war for two years.
35. Diodorus, 16.77.3; and Frontinus, 1.4.13.
36. McQueen, *Diodorus Siculus*, 155.
37. Justin, 9.2.
38. Ibid.
39. The Greeks and Romans distinguished Scythia Minor from the larger Scythia Major that ran from the Danube to the Sea of Azov, a twenty-day ride across the steppe.
40. Justin, 9.2.
41. Ibid.
42. Ibid.
43. Ibid.
44. Ibid.

45. Ibid.
46. Curiously, Scythian graves commonly reveal saddles buried with the deceased. Perhaps, just as the Plains Indians of North America, the Scythians used saddles when traveling but preferred to ride bareback in battle.
47. Justin, 9.2.
48. Ibid.
49. See chapter 1 of this volume for a detailed analysis of Philip's wound suffered at the hands of the Triballi.
50. Dell, "Philip and Macedonia's Northern Neighbors," 98.
51. Hammond, *Philip of Macedon*, 137.
52. The garrison at Nicaea comprised Thessalian troops probably under Macedonian command. Demosthenes, 6.22, tells us they were Thessalians but has nothing to say about their commanders. Whoever manned the garrison, however, it is clear that Philip considered it his own.
53. Hammond, *Philip of Macedon*, 141–42; and Cawkwell, *Philip of Macedon*, 141.
54. Hammond, *Philip of Macedon*, 140.
55. Ibid., 144.
56. Theopompus, fragment 328; and Demosthenes, 18.152–58.
57. Sakellariou, "Philip and the Southern Greeks," 122.
58. Demosthenes, 18.214.
59. I have accepted Hammond, *Philip of Macedon*, 147, and Worthington, *Philip II of Macedonia*, 145, for the area's geography, though neither author cites original sources for it. This said, the geography squares nicely with what can be discerned on Google Earth.
60. Green, *Alexander of Macedon*, 71.
61. Ibid.
62. Pausanias, 8.6.2; and Demosthenes, 18.3.
63. Philochorus, fragment 56.
64. Polyaenus, 4.2.8.
65. Ibid. From Philip's position at Cytinium, Macedonia was to the north and where, ostensibly, Antipater was. It was a curious messenger indeed who was captured while moving south through the Gravia Pass but on his way north!
66. Ibid.
67. The distances were obtained by utilizing the path measurement function on Google Earth.
68. See Worthington, *Philip II of Macedonia*, 148, for Parmenio as the commander at Gravia. Polyaenus has Philip in command, but this description is surely incorrect since we find Parmenio in command of the forces that took Naupactus a few weeks later.
69. Green, *Alexander of Macedon*, 71–72.
70. Worthington, *Philip II of Macedonia*, 146; and Hammond, *Philip of Macedon*, 148, citing Aeschines, 3.146–47, for the time required for Parmenio to finish off Chares' troops.

71. Diodorus, 16.86.1.
72. See Hammond, "The Two Battles of Chaeronea," 206; and Hammond, *Philip of Macedon*, 148, for the Greek deployment.
73. Diodorus, 16.85.5.
74. Ibid.
75. Justin, 9.3.
76. Hammond, *Philip of Macedon*, 150–53.
77. Diodorus, 16.86.1.
78. Ibid.
79. Polyaenus, 4.2.2.
80. Ibid.
81. Ibid., 4.1.2.
82. Hammond, *Philip of Macedon*, 154.
83. Johannes Kromayer and Georg Veith, *Schlachten-Atlas zur antiken Kriegsgeschichte* (Leipzig, Germany: Wagner and Debes, 1922–28), text 37. Hammond, "Two Battles of Chaeronea," adopts the figure of thirty minutes for Philip's withdrawal based on Kromayer and Veith's analysis.
84. Diodorus, 16.86.4.
85. Ibid., 16.86.3.
86. Markle, "The Macedonian Sarissa," 339, citing Arrian, *Tactica*, 16.6.
87. Ibid.
88. Connolly, *Greece and Rome at War*, 71.
89. Hammond, Cawkwell, and Worthington espouse this view.
90. The earliest example of an academic publication expounding this view, Hammond's "The Two Battles of Chaeronea," appeared in 1938.
91. Kromayer and Veith, *Schlachten-Atlas*, text 37.
92. Diodorus, 16.86.4–5.
93. Markle, "Use of the Sarissa," 82, citing *Plutarch's Lives*, 18.5. The presence of the sarissa among the dead of the Sacred Band could well imply that they were killed by infantry or a combination of infantry and cavalry. It is conceivable that Alexander had stationed some infantry units directly across from the Sacred Band to fix them in place so they could not hinder his cavalry penetration on his flank. Once he had penetrated the allied line and encircled the Sacred Band, the infantry might have joined the cavalry in the attack against it.
94. Adcock, *The Greek and Macedonian Art of War*, 89.
95. Diodorus, 16.86.4, maintains that Philip began his infantry attack after Alexander had attacked the allied infantry line.
96. The texts are silent on the use of trumpets, but their use may reasonably be presumed since Philip had used them before to control his troops.
97. Philip was lame by this time. His condition almost necessitated being mounted while in command of troops.
98. Adcock, *The Greek and Macedonian Art of War*, 27.

CHAPTER 9. THE END OF PHILIP

1. Justin, 9.4.1–5.
2. Hammond, *Philip of Macedon*, 157.
3. Justin, 9.4.
4. It has been believed since Roman times that the monument of the Lion of Chaeronea marks the spot where Philip arranged and buried the corpses of the Theban band. It is believed the Thebans later erected the monument itself, but no inscription tells us who erected it. Plutarch, a native of Chaeronea, tells us nothing about it. See Hammond, *Philip of Macedon*, 156; and Cawkwell, *Philip of Macedon*, 148–49.
5. Griffith, "Philip as a General," 62–63.
6. Carl Roebuck, "The Settlements of Philip II with the Greek States in 338 B.C.," *Classical Philology* 43, no. 2 (April 1948): 81.
7. Diodorus, 16.87.3.
8. Ibid.; and Hammond, *Philip of Macedon*, 157.
9. Justin, 9.4.
10. Ibid.
11. Diodorus, 16.87.3.
12. Sakellariou, "Panhellenism," 141.
13. Roebuck, "The Settlements of Philip II," 78.
14. Ibid., 83.
15. Ibid., 84.
16. Ibid., 87.
17. Ibid., 76.
18. Justin, 9.4.
19. Sakellariou, "Panhellenism," 142.
20. Justin, 9.5.
21. Demosthenes, 17.2.
22. Sakellariou, "Panhellenism," 141.
23. Ibid., 142–43.
24. Ibid.
25. Ibid., 144.
26. A common critique of Philip's success is that it came at the price of the liberty of Greek states. See Cawkwell, *Philip of Macedon*, 176. Given the horrors that these "free" states perpetrated against each other and their own citizens, and that many of them were oligarchies to begin with, it is difficult to see how Philip's putting an end to these practices amounted to depriving them of their liberty. It is similar to arguing that the American Civil War, in depriving the Southern states of the practice of slavery and open rebellion, somehow made them less free.
27. Hammond, *Philip of Macedon*, 164.
28. Diodorus, 16.89.1.
29. Alexander says as much in his letter to Darius: "For you gave help to the people of Perinthus, who wronged my father, and Ochus sent troops into Thrace, which we controlled." Arrian 2.14.5.

30. Justin, 9.5.
31. Cawkwell, *Philip of Macedon*, 178.
32. E. Badian, "The Death of Philip," *Phoenix* 17, no. 4 (Winter 1963): 244.
33. Plutarch, *Life of Alexander*, 9.6–11.
34. The version presented here is taken from Diodorus. Justin, however, says that Philip was "walking between the two Alexanders," not in front of them.
35. Diodorus, 16.93.1–2.
36. Ibid., 16.95.3.
37. Ibid.
38. Ibid. 39. The original sources for the assassination are Aristotle, Diodorus, and Justin. For a list of the academic commentaries on Philip's murder, see Carney, "The Politics of Polygamy," 169.
40. Diodorus, 16.93.3.
41. McQueen, *Didorus Siculus*, 176.
42. Diodorus, 16.93.8.
43. Aristotle, *Politics*, 1311b2–4.
44. For the manner in which Macedonians viewed sexual contact between males, see Flower, *Theopompus of Chios*, 108–9.
45. Diodorus, 16.93.3–6. The whole story of Pausanias's suicide is suspect.
46. Why Attalus wanted to avenge Pausanias is unknown.
47. Diodorus, 16.93.7. Justin says that Pausanias was raped by Attalus and his cronies before being turned over to the stablemen.
48. Ibid., 16.93.8.
49. Aristotle, 1311b3.
50. Badian, "The Death of Philip," 247.
51. McQueen, *Diodorus Siculus*, 178.
52. N. G. L. Hammond, "The End of Philip," in *Philip of Macedon*, ed. Hatzopoulos and Loukopoulos, 170, presents the widely accepted version of the murder. Justin 9.6, however, says that Philip was not out front and struck down in full view of the assembled crowd; instead, he was walking between the two Alexanders in a "narrow passage" where Pausanias "killed him as he was going through it." If Justin is correct, it is unlikely that there was a second assassin since a second assassin would have probably been close enough to slay Philip's son Alexander at the same time.
53. Ibid., 170.
54. Carney, "The Politics of Polygamy," 184.
55. See chapter 1 of this volume on these subjects.
56. Worthington, *Philip of Macedonia*, 185.
57. Carney, "The Politics of Polygamy," 183.
58. Ibid.
59. Carney excepted, scholars have not taken seriously the idea that Persia was involved in Philip's murder. For the case against Persian involvement, see R. Develin, "The Murder of Philip II," *Antichthon* 15 (1981): 86–99; and J. R. Ellis, "The Assassination of Philip II," in *Ancient Macedonian Studies in Honor*

of Charles F. Edson (Thessaloniki, Greece: Institute for Balkan Studies, 1981), 99–137.
60. Hammond, *Philip of Macedon*, 169, citing Diodorus, 17.7.1, and Plutarch's *Demosthenes*, 20-3.4, as original sources.
61. E. A. Fredericksmeyer, "Persian Influence at Philip's Court," *American Journal of Archaeology* 85, no. 3 (July 1981): 333.
62. Ibid.
63. Hammond, "The End of Philip," 168.
64. Worthington, *Philip of Macedonia*, 168.
65. Curtius, 3.7.11–15; Arrian, 1.25; and Hammond, "The End of Philip," 171–72.
66. Arrian, 2.24.5.
67. The basic original sources for Alexander are Diodorus, Plutarch, Justin, and Arrian, with Arrian's records being the most valuable and complete. In my opinion the most valuable modern works are Peter Green's *Alexander of Macedon* and the classic work by J. F. C. Fuller, *The Generalship of Alexander the Great*.
68. See Green, *Alexander of Macedon*, 158, for the composition of Alexander's invasion army.
69. Except for the famous Immortals, who were heavily armored and fought with long spears.
70. Gaebel, *Cavalry Operations in the Ancient World*, 191.
71. For Alexander's tactics, see A. R. Burn, "The Generalship of Alexander the Great," *Greece and Rome* 12, no. 2 (October 1965): 146–54. See also Gaebel, *Cavalry Operations in the Ancient World*, 183–93. For greater detail, see Fuller, *The Generalship of Alexander the Great*.
72. Arrian, 1.5.10. See also Gaebel, *Cavalry Operations in the Ancient World*, 194, for other citations in Arrian on the same subject.
73. See Burn, "The Generalship of Alexander the Great," 142–43, for Alexander's debt to Philip's officers.
74. Guy MacLean Rogers, *Alexander: The Ambiguity of Greatness* (New York: Random House, 2004), 222.
75. Ibid., 229.
76. Alexander was wounded in the thigh at Issus, in the shoulder by an arrow at the siege of Gaza, in the leg by an arrow on the march to Maracanda, in the face and neck by a thrown stone at Cyropolis, in the shoulder by an arrow while en route to India, in the ankle at Massaga, and in the right breast by an arrow that drew blood but did not puncture the lung at the citadel in the territory of the Malli. He suffered seven wounds in all, with two being life threatening.
77. Cawkwell, *Philip of Macedon*, 164.
78. Gabriel, *Scipio Africanus*, 10. The anecdote is provided by Frontinus, 4.7.4.

Selected Bibliography

Adams, A. "Macedonian Kingship and the Right of Petition." *Ancient Macedonia* 4 (1986): 43–52.
Adcock, F. E. *The Greek and Macedonian Art of War*. Berkeley: University of California Press, 1957.
Aeschines. *The Speeches of Aeschines*. Translated by Charles Darwin Adams. Whitefish, MT: Kessinger Publishers, 2007.
Anderson, J. K. *Ancient Greek Horsemanship*. Berkeley: University of California Press, 1961.
Andronikos, Manolis. "The Royal Tombs at Aigai (Vergina)." In *Philip of Macedon*, edited by Miltiades Hatzopoulos and Louisa Loukopoulos, 188–231. Athens: Ekdotike Athenon, 1980.
———. "Sarissa." *Bulletin de correspondence hellénique* 94 (1970): 98–99.
Anson, Edward M. "The Hypaspists: Macedonia's Professional Citizen-Soldiers." *Historia* 34, no. 2 (1984): 146–48.
———. "The Meaning of the Term *Makedones*." *Ancient World* 10 (1984): 67–68.
Arnett, William S. "Only the Bad Died Young in the Ancient Middle East." *International Journal of Aging and Human Development* 21, no. 2 (1985): 155–60.
Arrianus, Lucius Flavius. *Anabasis of Alexander*. Translated by P. A. Brunt and E. Cliff Robson. Cambridge, MA: Loeb Classical Library, 1983.
Aymard, A. "Le protocole royal grec et son evolution." *Revue des études anciennes* 50 (1948): 232–63.
Badian, E. "The Death of Philip." *Phoenix* 17, no. 4 (Winter 1963): 244–50.
———. "Greeks and Macedonians." In *Macedonia and Greece in Late Classical and Early Hellenistic Times*, edited by Beryl Barr-Sharrar and Eugene N. Borza, 33–51. Washington, DC: National Gallery of Art, 1982.
———. "Philip II and the Last of the Thessalians." *Ancient Macedonia* 6 (1999): 117–20.
Bartsiokas, A. "The Eye Injury of King Philip II and the Skeletal Evidence from the Royal Tomb at Vergina." *Science* 288, no. 5465 (April 2000): 511–14.

Borza, Eugene N. *In the Shadow of Olympus: The Emergence of Macedon.* Princeton, NJ: Princeton University Press, 1990.
———. "Philip II and the Greeks." *Classical Philology* 73, no. 3 (July 1978): 236–43.
———. "Timber and Politics in the Ancient World: Greeks and Macedonians." *Proceedings of the American Philosophical Society* 131 (1987): 32–52.
Bosworth, A. B. "Philip II and Upper Macedonia." *Classical Quarterly* 21, no. 1 (May 1971): 93–105.
Bradford, Arthur S., ed. *Philip II of Macedon: A Life from the Ancient Sources.* Westport, CT: Greenwood Press, 1992.
Buckler, J. *Philip and the Sacred War.* Leiden, the Netherlands: Brill, 1989.
Bugh, G. R. *The Horsemen of Athens.* Princeton, NJ: Princeton University Press, 1988.
Burke, Edmund M. "Philip II and Alexander the Great." *Military Affairs* 47, no. 2 (April 1983): 67–70.
Burn, A. R. "The Generalship of Alexander." *Greece and Rome* 12, no. 2 (October 1965): 140–54.
Campbell, Duncan B., and Adam Hook. *Ancient Siege Warfare: Persians, Greeks, Carthaginians and Romans, 546–146 B.C.* Oxford, UK: Osprey, 2005.
Cantrell, Deborah. "*The Horsemen of Israel: Horses and Chariotry in Monarchic Israel.*" Ph.D. diss., Department of Religion, Vanderbilt University, 2008.
Carney, Elizabeth. "The Female Burial in the Antechamber of Tomb II at Vergina." *Ancient World* 22 (1991): 17–26.
———. "Macedonians and Mutiny: Discipline and Indiscipline in the Army of Philip and Alexander." *Classical Philology* 91, no. 1 (January 1996): 19–44.
———. "The Politics of Polygamy: Olympias, Alexander, and the Murder of Philip." *Historia* 41, no. 2 (1992): 169–89.
———. *Women and Monarchy in Macedonia.* Norman: Oklahoma University Press, 2000.
Carter, J. M. "Athens, Euboea, and Olynthos." *Historia* 20 (1971): 418–29.
Cawkwell, George. "The Defence of Olynthos." *Classical Quarterly* 12 (1962): 122–40.
———. "Demosthenes' Policy After the Peace of Philocrates." *Classical Quarterly* 13 (1963): 120–38, 200–231.
———. "Philip and Athens." In *Philip of Macedon,* edited by Hatzopoulos and Loukopoulos, 100–111.
———. "Philip and the Amphictyonic League." In *Philip of Macedon,* edited by Hatzopoulos and Loukopoulos, 78–89.
———. *Philip of Macedon.* London: Faber and Faber, 1978.
Connolly, Peter. *Greece and Rome at War.* Englewood Cliffs, NJ: Prentice-Hall, 1981.
Curtius Rufus, Quintius. *History of Alexander.* Translated by John Yardley. London: Penguin, 1984.
de Lee, N. *French Lancers.* London: Almark, 1976.
Dell, Harry J. "Philip and Macedonia's Northern Neighbors." In *Philip of Macedon,* edited by Hatzopoulos and Loukopoulos, 90–99.

———. "The Western Frontier of the Macedonian Monarchy." *Ancient Macedonia* 1 (1970): 115–26.
Demosthenes. *Demosthenes Orations,* 7 vols. Translated by H. Vince. Cambridge, MA: Loeb Classical Library, 1930.
Develin, R. "The Murder of Philip II." *Antichthon* 15 (1981): 86–99.
Devine, A. M. "Macedonia from Philip II to the Roman Conquests." *Classical Review* 45, no. 2 (1995): 325–26.
Diodorus Siculus. *The Reign of Philip II: The Greek and Macedonian Narrative from Book XVI.* Translated by E. I. McQueen. London: Bristol Classical Press, 1995.
Edson, Charles. "Early Macedonia." In *Philip of Macedon,* edited by Hatzopoulos and Loukopoulos, 10–35.
Ellis, John R. "Amyntas Perdikka, Philip II and Alexander the Great: A Study in Conspiracy." *Journal of Hellenic Studies* 91 (1971): 15–24.
———. "The Assassination of Philip II." In *Ancient Macedonian Studies in Honor of Charles E. Edson, 99–137.* Thessaloniki, Greece: Institute for Balkan Studies, 1981.
———. "Macedonia Under Philip." In *Philip of Macedon,* edited by Hatzopoulos and Loukopoulos, 146–65.
———. *Philip II and Macedonian Imperialism.* London: Thames and Hudson, 1976.
———. "Philip's Thracian Campaign of 352–351." *Classical Philology* 71, no. 1 (January 1977): 32–39.
———. "Population Transplants Under Philip II." *Makedonika* 9 (1969): 9–16.
———. "The Security of the Macedonian Throne Under Philip II." *Ancient Macedonia* 1 (1970): 68–75.
———. "The Stepbrothers of Philip II." *Historia* 22 (1973): 350–54.
———. "The Unification of Macedonia." In *Philip of Macedon,* edited by Hatzopoulos and Loukopoulos, 36–47.
Engels, Donald W. *Alexander the Great and the Logistics of the Macedonian Army.* Berkeley: University of California Press, 1978.
Erdkamp, P. *Hunger and the Sword: Warfare and Food Supply in Roman Republican Wars.* Amsterdam: J. C. Gieben, 1998.
Erskine, Andrew. "The Pezetairoi of Philip II and Alexander III." *Historia* 38, no. 4 (1989): 385–94.
Fears, J. R. "Pausanias: The Assassin of Philip." *Atheneum* 53 (1975): 111–35.
Fields, Nic. *Ancient Greek Fortifications, 500–300 B.C.* Illustrated by Brian Delf. London: Osprey Publishers, 2006.
Flower, Michael. *Theopompus of Chios: History and Rhetoric in the Fourth Century B.C.* Oxford, UK: Clarendon Press, 1994.
Fredricksmeyer, E. A. "Again the So-Called Tomb of Philip II." *American Journal of Archaeology* 85, no. 3 (July 1981): 330–34.
———. "Alexander and Philip: Emulation and Resentment." *Classical Journal* 85, no. 4 (April–May 1990): 300–315.
———. "Persian Influence at Philip's Court." *American Journal of Archaeology* 85, no. 3 (July 1981): 328–37.

Frontinus, Sextus Julius. *Strategemata*. LacusCurtius website, 2007.
Fuller, J. F. C. *The Generalship of Alexander the Great*. New Brunswick, NJ: Rutgers University Press, 1960.
Gabriel, Richard A. "The Genius of Philip II." *Military History*, February–March 2009, 41–43.
———. *Great Captains of Antiquity*. Westport, CT: Greenwood Press, 2001.
———. "Philip of Macedon." In Gabriel, *Great Captains of Antiquity*.
———. *Scipio Africanus: Rome's Greatest General*. Washington, DC: Potomac Books, 2008.
———. *Soldier's Lives: The Ancient World*. Westport, CT: Greenwood Press, 2007.
Gabriel, Richard A., and Donald Boose, Jr. "The Greek Way of War: Marathon, Leuctra, and Chaeronea." In *Great Battles of Antiquity*, edited by Richard A. Gabriel and Donald Boose, Jr. Westport, CT: Greenwood Press, 1994.
Gabriel, Richard A., and Karen S. Metz. *The History of Military Medicine, Vol. 1: From Ancient Times to the Middle Ages*. Westport, CT: Greenwood Press, 1992.
Gaebel, Robert E. *Cavalry Operations in the Ancient Greek World*. Norman: University of Oklahoma Press, 2002.
Ginouves, R. *Macedonia: From Philip II to the Roman Conquest*. Princeton, NJ: Princeton University Press, 1994.
Graham, A. J. "The Historical Significance of Philip of Macedon." In *The World of Philip and Alexander: A Symposium on Greek Life and Times*, edited by Elin C. Danien, 1–14. Philadelphia: The University Museum of Archaeology and Anthropology, University of Pennsylvania, 1990.
Green, Peter. *Alexander of Macedon, 356–323 B.C.: A Historical Biography*. Berkeley: University of California Press, 1991.
Greenwald, W. S. "Polygamy and Succession in Argead Macedonia." *Arethusa* 22 (1989): 19–45.
Griffith, G. T. "Philip as a General and the Macedonian Army." In *Philip of Macedon*, edited by Hatzopoulos and Loukopoulos, 58–77.
———. "Philip of Macedon's Early Intervention in Thessaly (358–352 BC)." *Classical Quarterly* 20, no.1 (May 1970): 67–80.
Hammond, N. G. L. *Alexander the Great: King, Commander, and Statesman*. Princeton, NJ: Princeton University Press, 1980.
———. "Alexander's Campaign in Illyria." *Journal of Hellenic Studies* 94 (1974): 66–87.
———. "The Battle Between Philip and Bardylis." *Antichthon* 23 (1989): 1–9.
———. "Casualties and Reinforcements of Citizen Soldiers in Greece and Macedonia." *Journal of Hellenic Studies* 109 (1989): 56–68.
———. "Cavalry Recruited in Macedonia down to 322 B.C." *Historia* 47, no. 4 (1998): 404–25.
———. "The End of Philip." In *Philip of Macedon*, edited by Hatzopoulos and Loukopoulos, 166–75.
———. "The King and the Land in the Macedonian Kingdom." *Classical Quarterly* 38 (1988): 382–91.

———. "The Kingdoms in Illyria Circa 400–167 B.C." *ABSA* 61 (1966): 239–53.
———. *The Macedonian State: Origins, Institutions, and History.* Oxford, UK: Clarendon Press, 1989.
———. *Philip of Macedon.* Baltimore, MD: Johns Hopkins University Press, 1994.
———. "Royal Pages, Personal Pages, and Boys Trained in the Macedonian Manner During the Period of the Temenid Monarchy." *Historia* 39 (1990): 261–90.
———. "Training in the Use of the Sarissa and Its Effects in Battle, 359–333 B.C." *Antichthon* 14 (1980): 53–63.
———. "The Two Battles of Chaeronea." *Klio* 31 (1938): 186–218.
———. "The Various Guards of Philip II and Alexander III." *Historia* 40 (1991): 396–417.
Hammond, N. G. L., and G. T. Griffith. *A History of Macedonia.* 2 vols. Oxford, UK: Oxford University Press, 1979.
Hanson, Victor D., ed. *Hoplites: The Classical Greek Battle Experience.* London: Routledge, 1991.
———. *The Western Way of War: Infantry Battle in Classical Greece.* New York: Alfred Knopf, 1989.
Hatzopoulos, Miltiades B. "Succession and Regency in Classical Macedonia." *Ancient Macedonia* 4 (1986): 279–92.
Hatzopoulos, Miltiades B., and Louisa D. Loukopoulos, eds. *Philip of Macedon.* Athens: Ekdotike Athenon, 1980.
Hogarth, D. G. *Philip and Alexander of Macedon: Two Essays in Biography.* New York: Scribner's Sons, 1897.
Jacoby, F. *Die fragmente der griechischen historiker.* Berlin: Weidmann, 1923.
Justin, Marcus Junianus. *Epitome of the Philippic History of Pompeius Trogus.* Translated by John Shelby Watson. London: Henry G. Bohn Press, 1853.
Keyser, P. T. "The Use of Artillery by Philip II and Alexander the Great." *Ancient World* 15 (1994): 27–49.
Kromayer, Johannes, and Georg Veith. *Schlachten-Atlas zur antiken Kriegsgeschichte.* Leipzig, Germany: Wagner and Debes, 1922–28.
Lendon, J. E. *Soldiers and Ghosts: A History of Battle in Classical Antiquity.* New Haven, CT: Yale University Press, 2005.
Lévêque, Pierre. "Philip's Personality." In *Philip of Macedon,* edited by Hatzopoulos and Loukopoulos, 176–87.
Lloyd, A. "Philip II and Alexander the Great: The Moulding of Macedon's Army." In *Battle in Antiquity,* 169–98. London: The Classical Press of Wales, 1997.
Manti, P. A. "The Cavalry Sarissa." *Ancient World* 8, no.1 (1983): 73–80.
———. "The Macedonian Sarissa, Again." *Ancient World* 24, no. 1 (1994): 77–91.
Markle, Minor M. "The Macedonian Sarissa, Spear, and Related Armor." *American Journal of Archaeology* 81, no. 3 (Summer 1977): 323–39.
———. "The Strategy of Philip in 346 B.C." *Classical Quarterly* 24, no. 2 (December 1974): 253–68.
———. "Use of the Sarissa by Philip and Alexander of Macedon." *American Journal of Archaeology* 82, no. 4 (Autumn 1978): 483–97.

Marsden, E. W. "Macedonian Military Machinery and Its Designers Under Philip and Alexander." *Thessaloniki* 2 (1977): 211–23.

Milns, R. D. "Philip II and the Hypaspists." *Historia* 16, no. 4 (September 1967): 509–12.

Musgrave, Jonathan H., A. J. Prag, and R. Neave. "The Skull from Tomb II at Vergina: King Philip II of Macedon." *Journal of Hellenic Studies* 104 (1984): 60–78.

Pausanias. *The Complete Collection of Pausanias in Four Volumes.* Translated by W. H. S. Jones. Cambridge, MA: Harvard University Press, 1966.

Payne-Gallway, Sir Ralph. *A Summary of the History, Construction, and Effects in Warfare of the Projectile-Throwing Engines of the Ancients.* London: Longmans, Green, 1907.

Perlman, S. "Greek Diplomatic Tradition and the Corinthian League of Philip of Macedon." *Historia* 34, no. 2 (1985): 153–74.

Plutarch. *The Life of Alexander the Great.* Edited by Arthur Hugh Clough. Translated by John Dryden. New York: Random House, Modern Classics Library, 2004.

Polyaenus. *Stratagems of War, Vols. 1 and 2.* Chicago: Ares Publishers, 1994.

Prag, J. N. "Reconstructing King Philip: The Nice Version." *American Journal of Archaeology* 94, no. 2 (April 1990): 237–47.

Pritchett, W. K. "Observations on Chaeronea." *American Journal of Archaeology* 62 (1958): 307–11.

Raaflaub, Kurt A., ed. *War and Peace in the Ancient World.* Malden, MA: Blackwell, 2007.

Rahe, P. A. "The Annihilation of the Sacred Band at Chaeronea." *American Journal of Archaeology* 85 (1981): 84–87.

Rawlings, Louis. *Ancient Greeks at War.* Manchester, UK: Manchester University Press, 2007.

Rice, T. T. *The Scythians.* New York: Praeger, 1957.

Riginos, Alice Swift. "The Wounding of Philip II of Macedon: Fact and Fabrication." *Journal of Hellenic Studies* 114 (1994): 103–19.

Roebuck, Carl. "The Settlements of Philip II with the Greek States in 338 B.C." *Classical Philology* 43, no. 2 (April 1948): 73–92.

Rogers, Guy MacLean. *Alexander: The Ambiguity of Greatness.* New York: Random House, 2004.

Ryder, T. T. B. "The Diplomatic Skills of Philip II." In *Ventures into Greek History*, edited by Ian Worthington, 228–57. New York: Oxford University Press, 1994.

Sabin, Philip, Hans van Wees, and Michael Whitby. *The Cambridge History of Greek and Roman Warfare.* Cambridge, UK: Cambridge University Press, 2007.

Sakellariou, M. B. "Panhellenism: From Concept to Policy." In *Philip of Macedon*, edited by Hatzopoulos and Loukopoulos, 128–45.

———. "Philip and the Southern Greeks: Strengths and Weaknesses." In *Philip of Macedon*, edited by Hatzopoulos and Loukopoulos, 112–27.

Samuel, Alan E. "Philip and Alexander as Kings: Macedonian Monarchy and Merovingian Parallels." *The American Historical Review* 93, no. 5 (December 1988): 1270–86.

Sealey, Raphael. *A History of the Greek City States, ca. 700–338 B.C.* Berkeley: University of California Press, 1976.
Seymour, Thomas Day. *Life in the Homeric Age.* New York: Biblo and Tannen, 1963.
Spence, I. G. *The Cavalry of Classical Greece: A Social and Military History with Particular Reference to Athens.* Oxford, UK: Oxford University Press, 1993.
Sprawski, S. "Philip II and the Freedom of the Thessalians." *Electrum* 9 (2003): 61–64.
Strauss, Barry S. "Philip II of Macedon: Athens and Silver Mining." *Hermes* 112, no. 4 (1984): 418–27.
Tod, Marcus N., ed. *A Selection of Greek Historical Inscriptions.* 2 vols. Oxford, UK: Clarendon Press, 1968.
Tomlinson, R. A. "Ancient Macedonian Symposia." *Ancient Macedonia* 1 (1970): 308–15.
Worley, L. J. *Hippeis: The Cavalry of Ancient Greece.* Boulder, CO: Westview Press, 1994.
Worthington, Ian. *Philip II of Macedonia.* New Haven, CT: Yale University Press, 2008.
van Wees, Hans., ed. *War and Violence in Ancient Greece.* London: Duckworth, 2000.
Xenophon. *The Cavalry Commander.* Translated by G. W. Bowersock. Cambridge, MA: Harvard University Press, 1968.
———. *On the Art of Horsemanship.* Translated by G. W. Bowersock. Cambridge, MA: Harvard University Press, 1968.
Yalichev, S. *Mercenaries in the Ancient World.* London: Constable Press, 1997.

Index

Abae, 158, 169
Abdera, xii, 125
Acanthus, 150
Acarnania, 205, 215, 228
Acarnanians, 221
Achaea, 173, 181, 213, 221; Achaean League, 227
Achilles, 6, 7, 32, 47
Acrocorinth, 230
acropolis of Chaeronea, 214, 216
Adcock, F. E., 59, 67
Adriatic Sea, 88, 98, 293
Aecides, 180
Aegae, 36
Aegean, xiii, 160, 172, 180, 181, 182, 183, 189, 190
Aeropus of Lyncestis, 237
Aeschines, 18
Aetolia, 205, 213, 228
Afghanistan, 249
agema, 23, 71
Agis, 105, 113
Agora, 224
Agrianian archers, 243; javelineers, 70
Akrotiri frescoe, 65
Albania, 88, 177
Alcimachus, 224
Aleuadae family, 118, 179
Alexander the Great, xii, xiii, 1, 2, 3, 5, 8, 10, 16, 17, 19, 25, 29, 34, 37, 39, 49, 55, 56, 61, 62, 67, 69, 71, 73, 78, 115, 118, 196, 202, 214, 217, 218, 224, 232, 233, 237, 238, 240, 242, 246, 249, 250; army, 83; cavalry, 219–223; Companions, 47; engineers, 92; Persian expeditionary force, 243–244; physical description of, 30
Alexander II, 7, 61, 71, 118
Alexander of Pherae, 73, 109, 125, 139
Alexander Romance, 30
Alexandros, xiii, 180, 234
Alexandros I, 41
Alexandros II, 40, 147
Alexandros Lyncestes, 237, 242
Alexandros the Molossian, xii
Algae, 101, 234, 237
all-weather roads, 51
Alpinus, 158, 160
Amadocus, 124, 127, 144, 145, 146, 161, 174
Ambracia, 181, 182, 228, 230
Ambraciote Gulf, 181
American Plains Indians, 78
Amphaxitis, 4, 104
Amphictyonic Council, 20, 22, 125, 135, 136, 140, 158, 171, 204, 206, 227
Amphictyonic League, xiii, 168–174, 206, 207, 213, 226
Amphictyonic peace, 174
Amphictyonies, 125, 171, 211
Amphilochus, 187
Amphipolis, 203
Amphipolis, xi, 43, 44, 62, 88, 91, 94, 97–100, 103, 113, 115, 117, 133, 144, 148, 160, 162, 167;

291

Amphipolis, siege of, 110–112
Amphissa, xiii, 204, 206, 209, 210, 211, 212, 213
Amyntas, xiv, 232, 237, 238, 239, 242
Amyntas III, xi, 3, 14
Amyntas IV, xi, 5, 15, 17, 103
Anabasis, 25
Andronikos, Manilos, 12, 28, 29
Anticyra, 214
Antigonus the One-Eyed, 249
Antipater, 17, 56, 94, 159, 161, 179, 187, 189, 190, 194, 198, 200, 211, 214, 217, 224, 237, 244
Aphesis, xiv
Apollo, 135
Apollo's Saviors, 22
Apollo's shrine, 171
Apollo's treasure, 22
Apollonia, xii, 151, 152, 199, 200
Apollonides, 149
Apsus River, 88
Araxerxes, 188
Arcadia, 173, 228
Archelaus, 4, 5, 36, 48, 98, 118, 119
archers, 70, 195, 215
Archidamus III, 158
archon, xii, 20, 140, 141, 151, 179
Ardiaei, 11, 176, 177
arete, 7
Arethusa, 151
Argaeus, 98, 100, 101, 102, 111, 117
Argaeus II, 62, 98, 99
Argead kings, 2
Argead royal house, 29, 237, 251
Argives, 173
Argos, 2, 36, 173, 181, 228
Aristodemus, 159, 160
Aristotle, xiii, 19, 46, 49, 56, 150, 236, 249
Arrhabaeus, 9, 237
Arrhabaeus of Lyncestis, 5
Arrhidaeus, 16, 17, 99, 120, 149
Arrian, 69, 76, 78, 219, 242, 248, 249
Art of Horsemanship, 78
Artabazus, 30, 127
Artaxerxes, 240
artillery, 195
Arybbas, xii, xiii, 109, 147, 180, 181
Asclepiodotus, 106

Asia, 187, 188, 190, 228, 237, 238, 240, 242, 244, 245
Asia Minor, 42, 232
assault troops, 91
asthetairoi, 11, 73, 217
Atheas, xiii, 16, 17, 18, 199–203
Athenaeus, 18
Athenian Assembly, 181, 187, 188
Athenian grain fleet, xiii, 95, 132, 146, 172, 182, 191, 197
Athenian fleet, 4, 100, 134, 136, 197
Athenian Sacred Trireme, 153
Athenian mercenaries, 154
Athenian navy, 95, 175, 225
Athens, xiii, 3, 19, 34, 36, 38, 42, 43, 57, 58, 62, 63, 87, 93–98, 100, 103, 110, 113, 118, 117, 124, 125, 132, 133, 139–146, 148–159, 161, 162, 165–171, 174, 175, 176, 180, 182, 187, 188, 189, 190, 196, 197, 204–211, 223, 224, 225, 227, 229
Attalus, xiv, 16, 17, 232–249, 243
Attica, 38, 152, 162, 165, 172, 204
Audata, xi, 15, 98, 109
Axius River, 4, 33, 36, 41, 43, 50, 62, 88, 97

Babylon, 240
Badian, E., 236
Bagoas, 240
Balkans, 2, 5, 17, 42, 53, 57, 88, 249; Alexander's campaign of 335 BCE, 69–70
Balkan Range, 88
Bardylis, xi, 5, 15, 41, 73, 98, 109, 177, 248
Barsine, 30
battering rams, 91, 112
battle of annihilation, 215
battle guard, 104
battle manager, 251
bear pelts, 6
belly-shooters, 91
Berisades, 113
Beroe, xiii, 186
Black Sea, 42, 124, 132, 143, 146, 172, 183, 185, 186, 190, 191, 197, 199, 203
blasphemy, 23
blocking force, 69
Boeotia, 126, 127, 132, 133, 134, 140,

152, 157, 168, 169, 170, 171, 173, 174, 175, 188, 204, 206
Boeotian League, 168, 207, 221, 226, 227
Boeotian plain, 214
bolt-shooting artillery, 91
Bonaparte, Napoleon, 39, 63, 69, 91, 247
Bosporus, xiii, 91, 195, 196, 197, 198
Boucheta, 181
breast band, 85
British Boat Service, 72
Bronze Age, 36
Bucephalus, 118
buckler, 64, 82
Bulgaria, 88, 183
Bulgaria, 88
Bunker Hill, battle of, 86
butt spike, 75
Byzantium, xiii, 16, 57, 87, 91, 92, 98, 110, 144, 145, 146, 174, 182, 185, 186, 190–195, 200, 201, 205, 211; siege of, 194–198

Cabyle, 185, 186, 187, 198
Caesar, 5
Callias, 152, 187, 188
Callixeina, 30
Cambunian Mountains, 117
caracole, 73
Cardia, xiii, 47, 132, 143, 187–190, 194
Carney, Elizabeth, 239
Carystus, 152
Cassopia, 181
catapults, 129
cavalry scouts, 73
Cawkwell, George, 71, 73, 179
Celsus, 10
Central Thrace, 127, 144, 161, 182, 184, 186
Cephissus River, 206, 209, 210, 212, 214, 216, 220
Cersobleptes, xiii, 124, 127, 132, 143, 145, 146, 156, 158, 159, 161, 162, 175, 182, 183, 185, 186
Chaeronea, 1, 17, 20, 57, 66, 71, 73, 82, 93, 127, 128, 209, 214, 215, 222, 225, 228, 227, 248; battle of, xiii, 16, 69, 70, 78, 83, 214–222; plain of, 216
Chalcidian League, xii, 43, 99, 111, 112, 114, 155

Chalcidian Peninsula, 95, 101, 111, 112, 154
Chalcidice, xii, 143, 149, 150–156, 172, 177, 210
Chalcis, 152, 187, 226, 230
Chares, 134, 143, 151, 153, 189, 190, 197, 198, 211, 212, 213
Chares, 134
Charias, 92
Charidemos, 145, 146
Chersonese, 132, 143, 144, 157, 158, 159, 160, 162, 172, 174, 175, 182, 187, 193, 196, 198, 244; Philip's campaign in, 189–194
chief shepherd, 37, 45
chief wife, 15
Chios, 196, 197, 198
Chridemos, 153
Cicero, Marcus Tullius, 92
Cineas, 118, 120
Cirphis, 214
citizen states, 2, 6, 19, 34, 38, 39, 42, 228, 229, 241; weaknesses of, 27–28
Civil War, 232
Clausewitz, Carl von, 7, 55
Cleitus, 76, 177
Cleopatra, xiv, 16, 17, 233–238, 240
cleruchs, 187
clientele system, 92
collection, 80
combat arm of decision, 72, 76, 108, 130, 246
commissariat corps, 247
Companions, 11, 45, 47, 48, 49, 54, 62, 73, 81, 82, 83, 109, 155; Companion cavalry, 47, 133, 244, 248; Companion infantry, 217
composite bow, 201
congenital hypoplasia, 29
Constantine, 194
continuous arms drill, 84
Corcyra, 215
Coriae, 157
Corinth, xiv, 173, 181, 215, 227–230; Gulf of, 213
cornel wood, 64, 75
Coronea, 132, 157, 169
Corsiae, 169

corvee labor, 51
Cos, 196, 197
Cothelas, xiii, 16, 186
Cottyphus, 204
Cotys, 99, 100, 124
coup d'oeil, 247
Craterus, 249
Crenides, xii, 51, 113, 114, 115, 124
Cretan archers, 184
Critobulus of Cos, 10, 11, 47
Crocus Field, 133, 134, 143, 157, 158, 180, 248; battle of, xii, 22, 16, 69, 73, 81, 132–138
Crooksville, 51
Ctesiphon, 18, 159
cuirass, 64
curtain walls, 90
Curtius (Quintius Curtius Rufus), 38, 46, 70, 84, 86
Cynane, 15, 238
Cynoscephalae, battle of, 73, 109
Cyprus, 188
Cyrus the Great, 251
Cytinium, 206, 208

Dalmatian coast, 177
Dandamis, 250
Danube River, 12, 42, 69, 74, 88, 183, 185, 199, 204; delta, 191, 199; plain, 185
Dardanelles, 44
Dardanians, 11, 40, 41, 98, 176, 177
Darius, 56, 67, 237, 240, 242, 248, 249
de Lee, N., 75
decadarchy, 179
Decades, 224
degas, 86
dekadarch, 63, 67
Delos, 225
Delphi, xii, 22, 121, 122, 125, 133, 135, 136, 138, 148, 158, 169, 170, 226; oracle of, 125, 233
Demaratus of Corinth, 47
Demetrius, 11, 197
Demosthenes, 7, 13, 14, 18, 28, 56, 70, 82, 93, 112, 113, 146–149, 154, 155, 159, 173, 175, 179, 181, 184, 197, 210, 221, 225, 226, 240

Diades, 92, 247
Didymus Chalcenterus, 11, 13, 177
Diodorus Siculus, 5, 18, 23, 24, 55, 64, 70, 78, 84, 91, 97, 100, 102, 103, 104, 105, 106, 108, 112, 113, 120–124, 126, 127, 128, 129, 131, 133, 134, 138, 139, 140, 154, 155, 157, 164, 165, 174, 176, 180, 182, 185, 191, 192, 194, 195, 215–220, 234–237
Diopeithes of Supnium, 187, 188, 193, 194
Dium, 122, 159
Dobric, 201
Dobruja, 191, 199, 200, 202
Doris, 206
dory, 75
doryphoroi, 235
double-raters, 83
Drin River, 177
Drongylos, 185, 186
dwellers around, 125
dynastic quarrels, 9

Eastern Thrace, 124, 127, 132, 143, 144, 145, 158, 172, 175, 182, 186, 202
economy of force, 26
Edirne, 185
Egypt, 30, 188, 240
eikon, 23
Eion, 98
Elatea, xii, 167, 170, 173, 206, 208, 210, 214
Eleans, 173
elected generals, 84
Elimea, 40
Elimiotis, 4, 14, 104, 109
Elis, 181
engineers, 88, 89, 90, 111, 135, 150, 154, 163, 193, 195, 144, 146
Epaminondas, xi, 4, 24, 25, 26, 63, 108; tactics of, 25–27
Ephesus, 232
Ephorus, 21
epikouros, 70
Epirote, 181
Epirus, xii, xiii, 40, 109, 138, 147, 148, 180, 181, 228, 233
Eregli, 16
Erigyius, 47
Erymanthian boar, 8

Etesian winds, 103, 111, 113, 122, 151, 153, 154
Euboea, 151, 152, 153, 160, 172, 187, 205, 215; Confederacy of, 187; League, 116
Eumenes of Cardia, 94
Eurydice, 3, 4, 5, 109
Eusebius, 138
Euthrycrates, 93, 149, 154

First Epistle to Philip, 174
Foot Companions, 54, 61
forage, 86, 87
forced march, 87
forensic archaeologists, 29
fortified camp, 86
Fourth Sacred War, 58
Frontinus, Sextus Julius, 85, 86, 106, 108, 198
Fuller, J. F. C., 23

Gaebel, Robert, 77
Galepsos, xii
Gallipoli, 124, 189
Gaugamela, battle of, 67, 71
Gaza, 247
Gedrosian Desert, 250
General of Thrace, 186
Getae, xiii, 16, 17, 18, 87, 185, 186, 191, 203
Getic priests, 186
Goat Town, 36
gold staters, 114
Golden Horn, 195
Gomphi, 139
gorytos, 18
Grabus, 113, 114
Granicus, battle of, 68, 76
grastraphetes, 91
Gravia Pass, 206, 209, 211, 212
Great Balkan Mountains, 183, 185, 186, 191, 203
greaves, 12, 64, 75
Greek imperial age, 2
Green, Peter, 30
Griffith, G. T., 71
Gulf of Pagasae, 42, 94, 136, 187
Gygaea, 3

Haemon brook, 216
Haemus Mountains, 183
Hagia Sophia, 195
Haliacmon River, 33, 88, 105
Halicarnassus, 92, 247
Halus, xii, 57, 160, 162, 163, 164, 169
Hammond, N. G. L., 179, 224
Hannibal, 29
Hebrus River, 183, 185; valley of, 186
Hector, 65
hegemon, xiv, 20, 231, 239; hegemones, 47
hegemonoi, 203
Hellenes, 24, 232
Hellenism, 232
Hellenistic Age, 232
Hellespont, 44, 94, 132, 156, 162, 175, 190, 191, 205, 244
Hephaestion, 249
Herakles, 2, 8, 21, 31, 36, 200
Heraion Orus, 161
Heraion Teichos, 144, 145
Herion, 197
Herodotus, 25, 183, 201
Heromenes, 9, 237
Hestiaeotis, 179
hetairoi, 47
Histories (of Herodotus), 25
History of the Peloponnesian War, 25
Histriani, 199, 203
hollow wedge formation, 67
Holonnesus, 180
Homer, 6, 8
Homeric ideal, 45–46
Homeric Greece, 32
Homeric rituals, 8–9
Homeric warrior, 21, 250
hoplite, 63, 78, 79, 158, 210, 213, 214, 243, 245; equipment, 64; infantry, 58, 78, 130, 183, 184
hoplite phalanx, 58, 61–63, 68, 69, 78, 107
hoplon, 64, 202
horse collar, 85
horseshoe, 77
Hydaspes River, 88
Hypaspist Guard, 71
hypaspistai, 71, 83

ilai, 73
Iliad, 6, 9, 21, 32, 64, 65

Index

Illyria, xi, 3, 4, 9, 14, 40, 57, 85, 97, 100, 103, 104, 109, 114, 138, 139, 143, 146, 147, 148, 149, 177, 184, 248; Illyrians, xi, xii, xiii, 13, 14, 19, 34, 40, 41, 44, 49, 50, 61, 62, 63, 67, 69, 71, 81, 98, 100, 233; army of, 97; cavalry, 106–107; wars, 56; war with Bardylis, 105–109
Imbros, 153
incest, 6, 14
India, 251
Indo-Aryans, 41
Indus Valley, 249
infantry phalanx, 25, 84
intimidating intimacy, 77, 107
Ionia, 58, 175, 182, 243
Ionian Sea, 228
Iphicrates, 4
iron breastplate, 74
Iron Gates, 5, 40
iron helmet, 64, 74
Isocrates, 245
Issus, battle of, 30, 69, 247
Ister River, 200
Istrus River, 12

Jambol, 185
Jason of Pherae, 16, 42, 119, 124, 139, 241
javelin, 70, 72, 73, 75, 77, 78, 82, 184, 248, 249; javelineers, 70, 215, 243, 249
jus sanguinis, 38
jus territoriale, 38
Justin (Marcus Junianus Justinus), 5, 12, 16, 18, 19, 20, 49, 50, 51, 123, 126, 145, 149, 155, 177, 178, 194, 201, 202, 203, 215, 226, 229, 233, 236

Karaevlialti, 144
Karata Pass, 216, 221
katapeltai Makedonikoi, 92
Ketriporis, 113, 114, 124, 146
King's Field Army, 53, 54, 83, 109, 110, 196, 215
King's Guard, 107, 108, 216, 217, 222
Kirli Dirven Pass, 106
kleroukhoi, 38
kopis, 76
Kosovo, 11, 98

krater, 10
Kromayer, Johannes, 220
Kul-Oba tombs, 201
kurgan, 201; cup, 201
kydos, 7

Labadea, 214
Laconia, 27, 228
Laemedon, 47
Lake Bole, 150
Lake Loudias, 36
Lake Lychnitis, 109
Lake Ohrid, 109
Lake Prepsa, 88
Lamia, 164, 205, 206
Larissa, 16, 118, 120, 164, 179
larnax, 9, 17
Lasthenes, 93, 149, 154
Latria, 181
leader of ten, 63
League of Corinth, xiv, 20, 226, 230, 231, 243
Lebadea, 221
Lemons, 153, 225
Leonidas, 8, 30
Leonnaus, 234
lethal pursuit, 81, 109
Leucas, 181, 215
Leuctra, battle of, 27, 102, 108, 158
Livahdi pass, 101, 102
Livahdi Ridge, battle of, 100–104, 113, 248
locked shields formation, 66
Locris, 163, 204, 205, 207, 226
logistics, 58, 85, 88, 247
Loris, 122, 126
Lower Macedonia, 3, 33, 34, 40, 41, 53
Ludias River, 101
Lycophron, 124, 127, 133, 138
Lykuressi stream, 216, 219
Lyncestian royal house, 3, 237, 240
Lyncestis, 5, 14
Lyncus, 40; plain of, 106, 109, 110
Lyppeios, xi, 113, 117
Lysis of Tarentum, 24

Macedones, 38, 46, 109, 123, 147, 237
Macedonia, 33; external treats, 39–44;

geography, 40–43; people, 33–39; state structure, 44–47
Macedonian army, 163, 167, 168, 170, 175, 177, 179, 186, 197, 204, 205, 214, 223, 225, 228, 229, 231
Macedonian army, phalanx, 62–72; cavalry, 72–82; intelligence service, 92–94; manpower and training, 82–85; logistics, 85–88; noncommissioned officer corps, 250; officer corps, 249–250; siege craft, 88–92
Macedonian Assembly, 4, 44–46, 103, 237
Macedonian boar hunt, 65
Macedonian cantons, 4
Macedonian cavalry, 34, 61, 72, 73, 136, 210, 215, 216, 219, 244, 246, 248; dynamics of the attack, 79–81; mounts, 74; tactics, 77–78; training, 76–77
Macedonian catapults, 92
Macedonian dialect, 6
Macedonian infantry, 54, 164, 221, 243
Macedonian navy, 94, 95, 115, 124, 144, 153, 157, 189, 192, 197
Macedonian phalangite, 63, 130, equipment of, 64–65
Macedonian phalanx, xi, 62, 63, 66, 69, 72, 102, 131, 215, 249; ability to maneuver, 25–26, 63–64, 65, 66
Macedonian pikemen, 68, 192
Macedonian West Point, 48
Macedonic tribes, 36
machaira, 75, 76, 137, 202
Maedi, 185, 196
Maeotian marshes, 199
Magnesia, 94, 139, 151, 178, 233
Mantias, 100, 103
Mantinea, 181
Mantinea, battle of, 125, 168
mare-milkers, 202
Maritza River, 183
Marius, Gaius, 86
Maronea, 125
Masteira, 185, 186
Mecyberna, 151, 152
Meda, xiii, 16, 17, 186
Medians, 16
Megalopolis, 181

Megara, 173, 215, 227
Meluna pass, 118
Memnon, 233
Menelaus, 99, 149
mercenaries, 70, 71, 134, 154, 157, 160, 165, 210, 211, 213, 215
Messene, 228
Messenia, 27, 173, 181
Methone, xii, 14, 44, 47, 91, 101, 111, 112, 126, 127; siege of, 121–125
Metohija, 11
Miletus, 247
militia 53, 58, 84, 85, 109, 110, 147, 196, 244
miners, 91
misthophoros, 70
Mnesimachus, 82
Molossia, 16, 40, 109, 146, 180; tribal state, 147–148
Monastir, 50
Morone, xii
Mount Callidromos, 206
Mount Hellicon, 209
Mount Oeta, 206
Mount Pangaeus, xii, 114
Mount Parnassus, 209
Mount Pieria, 122
mud brick, 90
muddy boots general, 21
Mycenaean age, 6, 25; weapons of, 65
Mytilene, 47

Napoleonic lance, 75
nation building, 50–51
national territorial state, 232, 243, 250
Naupactus, 205, 213, 228
Neaolis, 125
Neapolis, xii, 134
Neon, 126
Neoptolemus, 147
Nestus River, 42, 87, 88, 114, 115, 124, 160, 161, 186
Nicaea, 158, 160, 165, 170, 178, 204, 206, 207, 226
Nicanor, 249
Nicesipolis, xii, 7, 16, 139
Nisean horses, 74
Normandy, battle of, 86

Numidian cavalry, 78
Nymphaea, 147

Octavia, 5
Odessus, 185, 186, 201
Odrysae, 99, 185
Oetaeans, 168
Oisyme, xii
Olympias, xi, 7, 14, 16, 30, 109, 115, 147, 180, 233, 237, 238, 239, 242
Olympic Games, 22, 171
Olympic Truce, 159
Olynthian cavalry, 149
Olynthos, xii, 22, 43, 52, 91, 93, 100, 112, 113, 114, 133, 141, 143, 145, 152, 153, 154, 156, 159, 160, 162, 170, 208
On Horsemanship, 25
Onomarchus, xii, 19, 81, 127, 128–132, 143, 146, 157; Onomarchus' defeat, 133–138
Orchomenus, 157, 169, 226
Orestes, 40
Orion River, 88
Orobus, 226
oxcart, 85
oxen, 85

pack animals, 86, 87
Paeonia, xi, 41, 73, 85, 104, 105, 110, 143, 146, 147, 148, 149
Paeonians, xii, 40, 41, 50, 62, 63, 97, 100, 114, 115, 117
Paeonian javelineers, 53
Paeonian scouts, 244
Pagasae, xii, 91, 118, 120, 124, 139, 151, 163, 174, 178; Gulf of, xiii
page schools, 53
palisade, 86
Pallone, 111
palton, 75
Pammenes, 24, 25, 127
Pan-Euboean League, 152
Pandosia, 181
Panegyricus, 31
panniers, 85
Parapotamii, 209, 214
Parauaea, 147
Parmenio, xii, xiv, 17, 27, 30, 39, 47, 56, 114, 158, 164, 179, 189, 194, 196, 198, 200, 212, 213, 214, 217, 218, 228, 232, 238, 240, 243, 249
Patroclus, 9
patronymic, 6
Paulus, Aemilius, 66
Pausanias, 4, 43, 99, 100, 126, 137, 169
Pausanias of Orestes, 234, 235, 236, 237, 239, 240
Peace of Philocrates, 162, 163, 180, 181, 187, 190
Peitholaus, 124, 138, 151
Pelagonia, 39, 40, 47
Pelasgiotis, 179
Pella, 4, 18, 19, 36, 37, 39, 41, 43, 48, 87, 88, 91, 97, 101, 105, 111, 112, 114, 143, 144, 145, 146, 147, 156, 159, 163, 174, 176, 178, 180, 185, 188, 233
Pelopidas, 3, 4, 24, 73, 109
Peloponnese, xiii, 27, 36, 87, 140, 157, 163, 165, 173, 180, 188, 205, 214, 227, 228
Peloponnesian wars, 25, 49, 56, 70, 72, 90
pelta, 183
peltasts, 53, 71, 151, 183, 187, 195, 202, 215, 243, 249
Peneus River, 88
pentakosiarchoi, 66
penteconter, 94, 95
Perdiccas I, 4, 5, 36, 104, 105, 234
Perdiccas III, xi, 15, 19, 44, 61, 97, 98, 234, 238
Perinthus, xiii, 16, 41, 57, 91, 92, 144, 145, 146, 174, 186, 190–196
Perrhaebia, 119, 120
Persia, 2, 23, 31, 32, 41, 52, 91, 174, 176, 182, 191, 193, 196, 205, 209, 224, 228, 231, 232, 241, 242, 244, 245; Persian army, 86, 205; Persian Empire, 243; Persian navy, 225; Persian wars, 25
pezetairoi, 54, 61, 107, 217
Phaedriadae Cliffs, 22, 138, 169
Phakos, 36
Phalaecus, 157–162, 164, 165, 168
Pharcedon, 70
Pharsalus, 157, 174
Phayllos, xii, 127, 138, 140, 157

Pherae, xii, 16, 87, 122, 125–129, 132, 133, 134, 135, 138, 139, 140, 151, 163, 164, 174, 179,
Phila of Larissa, xi, 4, 16, 105, 120
Philip of Macedonia (382–336 BCE), hostage, 3, 4; in Thebes, 23–28; homeric world of, 5–9; education, 8, 9; wounds and injuries, 10–14; personality, 18–23; religion, 21–23; wives, 14–18; physical appearance, 28–32; grand strategy of, 54–59; rise to power, 98–100; sieges, 91–92; ambush by Onomarchus, 127–132; Epirus campaign, 146–148; Thracian campaign, 143–146; war with Olynthos, 148–156; end of the Sacred War, 157–166; Amphictyonic Peace, 168–171; second Illyrian campaign, 176–179; intervention in Epirus, 180–181; Thessaly rebellion, 178–179; Scythian campaign, 199–204; battle of Chaeronea, 214–222; assassination of, 234–243; greater than Alexander, 243–251
Philippeioi, 114
Philippeion, 22
Philippi, xii, 52, 87, 115, 144, 146, 182
Philippopolis, xiii, 50, 139, 183, 185, 186
Philippos Makedonios, 6
Philocrates, 161
philoi, 47
Philomelos, 125, 126
Philotas, 249
Phoenica, 175, 188
Phokis, xiii, 14, 58, 121, 122, 124, 125, 127, 129, 138, 141, 151, 158, 159, 160, 161, 162, 163, 168, 169, 170, 171, 174, 175, 205, 206, 208, 214, 226; army, 158–160; cavalry, 136, 137; hoplites, 136–137
Phrynon, 159
Phthiotis, 179
pike infantry, 81, 202
pike phalanx, 72, 73
piracy, 160, 180, 187
Piraeus dockyards, 94, 225
Plataea, 226; battle of (449 BCE), 41, 61
platform of maneuver, 81, 245, 248

Plato, 19, 229
Pleuratos, xiii, 11, 176, 177
Pleurias, 177
Pleurias of the Illyrians, 236
plinthion, 106, 107
Pliny, 11
Plovdiv, 50
Plutarch, 13, 30, 65, 78, 221, 242
Polyaenus, 7, 67, 70, 86, 121, 128, 129, 130, 131, 211, 212, 218, 220
Polybius, 66
Polyeidos of Thessaly, 47, 66, 92, 196, 247
polygamy, 14, 15, 238
Poneropolis, 51
Potidaea, xii, 44, 91, 101, 103, 111–115, 122, 148
prodromoi, 73
promanteia, 171
Propontus, 41
prostitutes, 14
proxenoi, 94
Proxenus, 158, 209, 211
Ptolemy, 3, 4, 49, 249
pursuit, 245, 246, 248
Pydna, xii, 44, 49, 65, 66, 91, 94, 111, 112, 115; battle of, 65–66
pyknosis, 66
Pyrrhus, 180
Pythagoreans, 24
Pythian Games, 20, 171, 233

rafts, 88
realpolitik, 24
Rhizon Gulf, 177
Rhodes, 196, 197, 198
Rhodope Mountains, 183
Rogues Town, 51
Roman centurions, 83
Rome, 52
Roxanne of Bactria, 17
Royal Hypaspist Guard, 217, 235
Royal Page School, 19, 48, 49, 53, 109

Sacred Band, 24, 25, 26, 71, 78, 215–221, 223, 224,
Sacred War, origins of, xii, xiii, 20, 78, 124, 125, 127, 138, 141, 151, 161, 162, 164, 167, 168, 172, 178, 227

saddle, 76, 77, 201
Samos, 225
sappers, 91
sarissa, 13, 64, 65, 75, 102, 130, 147, 217, 245
sarissa-bearing cavalry, 73
sarissophori, 73
Sarnousii, 51, 71, 177
satraps, 193, 197, 240
saviors of Apollo, 135
scaling ladders, 70, 91, 195
schwerpunkt, 26, 248
Scipio Africanus, 29, 78, 251
scythed chariots, 67
Scythia, xiii, 10, 12, 18, 57, 74, 87, 191, 200, 201; archers, 70, 202; Philip's campaign in, 51; cavalry, 13, 201; horse archers, 53, 201; Scythian point, 10; straight sword, 202
Sea of Marmara, 41, 42, 95, 132, 143, 144, 159, 186, 190, 191, 193, 197, 199
Second Athenian Confederacy, 152
Second Epistle to Philip, 174
Seleucus, 249
Selymbria, 191, 194, 195, 196, 200
Semiramis, 251
Serbia, 98
Sestus, 143, 189
shield bearers, 71
Shipka Pass, 183, 185, 186
shoulder barging, 80
Sicily, 91
siege craft, 90
siege equipment, 144
siege machinery, 90, 189, 192
siege towers, 91, 195
siege train, 91, 111
sieges, 246
Silivri, 191
Simus, 179
Sisines, 242
Siwan, 30
skolotoi, 201
slat and bandage splint, 11–12
slaves, 37, 38, 52, 85, 169, 202
slingers, 70, 195
Socrates, 31, 167, 174, 224
Sofia, 88

somatophylakes, 217, 235
Sparta, 27, 43, 58, 125, 140, 151, 157, 158, 159, 162, 163, 165, 168, 172–175, 227–230
Spartans, 25, 26, 40, 160
spear-won lands, 45, 52, 82, 203
Special Forces, 72
Sperchius River, 141
Speusippus, 19
spoon of Diokles, 10
stabbing spear, 73, 107
Stageira, xii, 150, 155
Stara Zagora, 186
stirrup, 76, 77, 78, 201
stone-shooting catapults, 92, 128
Strabo, 135, 203
strategic forced march, 27
strategic platform, 191
strategic pursuit, 248
strategic range, 87
strategic vision, 250
strategos autokrator, 20, 231
strategy of overthrow, 59
Stratocles, 218
Stratonica, 150, 155
straw-filled tents, 88
Strymon River, xi, 16, 36, 41, 43, 44, 88, 94, 97, 98, 110, 185, 196, 203
stud farms, 74
Successors, 69; armies of, 67
Susa, 188, 205
symposia, 9
synapsismos, 66

Tarn, W. W., 71
Taulanti, 113
taxeis, 66
Tekirdag, 144
Temenids, 2, 37
Temenid dynasty, 13, 17, 21, 45, 73
Temenid kings, 36
ten-stater men, 83
Terachoritae, 194
Teres, xii, 182, 185, 186
Teres II, 161
territorial state, 38, 39, 50
tetrades, 179
tetrarch, 179

The Cavalry Commander, 25, 89
Theagenes, 214, 215, 216
Thebes, xi, xiii, 3, 4, 24, 25, 27, 40, 41, 42, 43, 58, 62, 71, 88, 118, 121, 122, 125, 126, 127, 157, 158, 162, 163, 168, 169, 170, 171, 174, 175, 204, 205, 206, 207, 208, 210, 211, 223–227, 229, 230, 240
Theophrastus, 30, 65
Theopompus, 5, 11, 47, 71, 112, 149, 177, 186, 194, 215
Thermaic Gulf, 4, 33, 36, 40, 43, 44, 94, 97, 101, 103, 110, 112, 113, 115, 122, 123, 133, 148, 156, 159, 172, 210
Thermopylae, xii, xiii, 56, 140, 141, 143, 152, 156, 157, 163, 164, 165, 174; pass of, 134, 159, 160, 161, 167, 168, 171–175, 204
Thespian, 226
Thessalian cavalry, 53, 118, 164, 179, 184, 189, 215, 242
Thessalian League, 16, 120, 122, 124, 127, 128, 132, 133, 157, 179
Thessalian infantry, 135
Thessaliotis, 179
Thessalonice, 16, 139
Thessaly, xii, xiii, xi, 16, 33, 42, 56, 63, 72, 88, 122, 135, 138, 141, 140, 143, 147, 151, 157, 167–171, 172, 174, 176, 184, 226; geography, 117; military power, 118; politics, 118–120
Third Sacred War, xii
Thrace, xi, xii, xiii, 10, 29, 33, 34, 40, 41, 42, 44, 50, 51, 52, 58, 69, 73, 76, 87, 94, 100, 110, 112, 113, 115, 124, 133, 138, 139, 141, 148, 157, 159, 161, 167, 172, 174, 177, 189, 191, 194, 198, 199, 201, 205, 225, 232, 244; cavalry wedge, 42, 78, 79, 219; peltasts, 70; Philip's Thracian campaign of 340 BCE, 83
Thronium, 158, 160
Thucyidides, 25
tib-fib fracture, 11–12
tibia, 12
time, 7
Timotheus, 111

Tiristasis, 187
Tithorea, 126
To Philip, 174
Topkapi, 195
Torone, 152
torsion catapults, 47, 196, 247
traction catapults, 92, 128
transhuman pastoralism, 34, 37
triaconter, 94, 95
Triballi, xiii, 12, 34, 40, 74, 87, 203
trireme, 4, 94, 95, 134, 144, 158, 210, 225
Troy, 32, 62
trumpet call, 222
tshelniku, 37, 38, 45, 46
tumulus, 223
Twelve Labors, 8
tyrant of Pherae, 119, 120, 127
Tyre, 92, 247

United States, 232
University of Manchester, 29
Upper Cantons, 40, 41, 47, 53, 71, 82, 85, 97, 98, 106, 109, 110, 114, 115, 117, 184, 217
Upper Macedonia, xi, 3, 34, 36, 50, 51, 110, 147

Vale of Tempe, 117, 122
Varna, 185
Vegetius, 86
Veith, Georges, 220
Vergina, 17, 36
Volustana pass, 118

wagons, 85
wanax, 6
wasting diseases, 157
Waterloo, battle of, 86
wedge formation, 42, 73, 76, 77, 81, 82, 86, 246, 216
Western Thrace, 97, 98, 124, 127, 146, 161
wild boar, 8
witches, 7

Xandika, 3
xenia, 92
xenia kai pilia, 92
Xenophon, 25, 74, 75, 76, 78, 81
xenos misthophoros, 70

Xerxes, 135, 193, 229
xiphos, 64
xyston, 4, 75, 107, 245

Zama, battle of, 78
Zeus, 21, 159, 171
Zeus Ammon shrine, 30

About the Author

Richard A. Gabriel is a distinguished adjunct professor in the Department of History and War Studies at the Royal Military College of Canada in Kingston, Ontario, and the Department of Security Studies at the Canadian Forces College in Toronto. He was a professor of history and politics at the U.S. Army War College and held the Visiting Chair in Ethics at the Marine Corps University. He is a retired U.S. Army officer and the author of forty-four books and eighty published articles on military history and other subjects. His books have been the subject of a number of television programs on the History Channel, most recently the eight-part series *Battles B.C.* and *The Art of War*, a study of Sun Tzu's principles applied to modern war. Dr. Gabriel's most recent books are *Subotai the Valiant: Genghis Khan's Greatest General* (2006), *Muhammad: Islam's First Great General* (2007), *Scipio Africanus: Rome's Greatest General* (2008), and *Thutmose III: The Military Biography of Egypt's Greatest Warrior King* (2009). He lives in New Hampshire, where he flies his antique open-cockpit airplane.